HALLIWELL'S GUIDE TO THE BEST CHILDREN'S FILMS

By the same author

Halliwell's Filmgoer's Companion
Halliwell's Film Guide
Halliwell's Guide to the Best Comedies

HALLIWELL'S GUIDE TO
THE BEST CHILDREN'S FILMS

▪▫▫▪▫▫▫▪▫▫▫▫▫

Edited by
John Walker

HarperCollins*Publishers*

HarperCollins*Publishers*
77–85 Fulham Palace Road,
Hammersmith, London W6 8JB

A Paperback Original 1994
1 3 5 7 9 8 6 4 2

Copyright © Ruth Halliwell and John Walker 1994

The Author asserts the moral right to
be identified as the author of this work

A catalogue record for this book
is available from the British Library

ISBN 0 00 638117 0

Set in Meridien by
Rowland Phototypesetting Ltd, Bury St Edmunds, Suffolk

Printed in Great Britain by
HarperCollinsManufacturing, Glasgow

All rights reserved. No part of this publication may be
reproduced, stored in a retrieval system, or transmitted,
in any form or by any means, electronic, mechanical,
photocopying, recording or otherwise, without the prior
permission of the publishers.

This book is sold subject to the condition that it shall not,
by way of trade or otherwise, be lent, re-sold, hired out or
otherwise circulated without the publisher's prior consent
in any form of binding or cover other than that in which it
is published and without a similar condition including this
condition being imposed on the subsequent purchaser.

CONTENTS

Introduction vii

Explanatory Notes xi

Guide to Children's Films 1

INTRODUCTION

Film producers and directors have recently rediscovered the appeal of children, and of movies intended for a family audience. Not since the heyday of the dimpling Shirley Temple have child stars commanded such a world-wide following, or been able to dictate terms to studios as some can do now. Never before have animated films drawn such crowds, or made as much money, or been nominated for so many Oscars as the latest creations from Walt Disney. The most commercially successful director in the world is that Peter Pan among film-makers, Steven Spielberg, who appeals to the child in most of us.

This sudden conversion of studios to a wholesale, wholesome approach is partly a response to complaints that movies were becoming too violent. But it owes more to the example of *Home Alone*, which became the most successful comedy yet made and catapulted Macauley Culkin to a position where he can command $5 million or more for a role. (Not bad for someone who has still to reach his teens.)

Yet even now you can search long to find films that children will like – or that adults will enjoy watching with them. And it's often difficult to know how suitable for family viewing are video releases and films on television. This guide aims to make those choices easier in the future. It lists more than 1,200 movies that should satisfy the young and provide pleasing entertainment that can cross several generation gaps.

That doesn't mean that everything here will please everyone, for children's tastes change vastly between the ages of four and fourteen, which is the range this guide covers.

A liking for the balletic comedy of Charlie Chaplin or the carefully honed slapstick of Laurel and Hardy is a sophisticated taste that few under the age of eleven will appreciate. The ability to sit through, or even enjoy, a Care Bears movie will rarely last beyond the age of six.

But all tastes are catered for: from cartoon and animated films to comedy, science-fiction, adventure, ballet, monsters of an unthreatening kind, James Bond and filmed classics from *Little Women* to *Lord of the Flies*. It includes not only films that you can buy or rent but those that are likely to turn up on television in these days of saturation coverage of old movies. It takes in many years of film making, from silent comedies to the noisier modern day varieties and indicates which films should currently be available on VHS video-cassette or laser disk. (A word of warning here: these days video releases quickly become unobtainable and it is impossible to be entirely up-to-date on what is still available and what has been deleted.)

The movies listed here have been carefully selected from the standard reference book *Halliwell's Film Guide*, now in its 9th edition, which contains details of nearly 20,000 films of all kinds. Biographical information on many of the stars and directors mentioned here can be found in the 10th edition of *Halliwell's Filmgoer's Companion*.

Most of the films in this guide have either a 'U' or a 'PG' certificate. A very few have a '15' rating. These include the two Gremlins films, *The Karate Kid* (though its sequels were rated 'PG'), *The Beastmaster* (though *Beastmaster 2* has a 'PG' rating), *The Lord of The Rings*, the most recent version of *The Lord of The Flies* and the comedies *Nuns on the Run*, *The Naked Gun* and *The Naked Gun 2½*. But any child who sat happily through *Jurassic Park* will certainly find them less frightening, although the same rule applies: sensitive children may find them upsetting. They are included because they seem to me, if not to the British Board of Film Classification that found man-eating dinosaurs to be acceptable viewing by small children, to be innocuous and likely to be enjoyed by thirteen- or fourteen-year-olds.

A 'PG' rating indicates, of course, Parental Guidance and this guide should help parents in the essential task of checking the suitability of many films for their children. The movies listed are not so much children's films as family ones and they are most likely to be enjoyed when watched by the family. Film is essentially a communal experience, at its best in the cinema but still entertaining in the home, particularly when the pleasure can be shared with others.

John Walker
January, 1994

EXPLANATORY NOTES

Alphabetical Order

Unlike some books which take the complete title into account, as though there were no gaps between words, we have always persevered with the old-fashioned word-at-a-time arrangement. Thus, all titles starting with *In* are used up before one goes on to titles beginning *Incredible*. Hyphenated or apostrophized words are counted as one word. Compressions such as *Dr* and *St* are treated as though they had been spelled out, as *Doctor* and *Saint*. *Mac* and *Mc* are regarded as interchangeable under *Mac*. Titles consisting of initials, such as *C. C. and Company* or *D.O.A.* are dealt with at the beginning of each alphabetical section, except where they have become acronyms (i.e. pronounceable as one word, e.g. AWOL). In all cases the complete title is given as billed, though the definite and indefinite articles are not counted in the alphabetical arrangement where they occur as the first word of a title. The spelling of the country of origin is used, e.g. *My Favorite Blonde* and not *My Favourite Blonde*.

Individual Entries

All entries follow the same format and the notes are set out below in the order in which they will be encountered.

Publicity tags
These were used in the promotion of the film and, in the manner of trailers, precede the entry.

Ratings
These range from none to four stars. Four stars indicate a film outstanding in many ways, a milestone in cinema history, remarkable for acting, direction, writing, photography or some other aspect of technique. Three stars indicate a very high standard of professional excellence or great historical interest. Or, if you like, three strong reasons for admiring it. Two stars indicate a good level of competence and a generally entertaining film. One star indicates a film not very satisfactory as a whole; it could be a failed giant or a second feature with a few interesting ideas among the dross. No stars at all indicates a totally routine production or worse; such films may be watchable but are at least equally missable.

Country of origin
This is the first item on the second line.

Year of release
This comes after the country of origin and is intended to indicate the year when the film was first shown, which is not necessarily the year that it was made. Dating is sometimes an onerous task, and the result debatable.

Running time
This is given in minutes, signified by 'm'. So far as possible, this is the original release time. Very many films are cut as they appear in different countries, sometimes by twenty minutes or more. An engineering function of British television results in an imperceptible speeding-up of projection and a consequent loss of one minute in every twenty-five. A hundred-minute film, therefore, will run only ninety-six minutes on the box.

Colour
This is indicated by 'bw' for black and white films and 'colour' for the others. The colour process used, such as Technicolor, is given when known.

Other notable points
These are given at the end of the second line, indicating the use of a special process, such as Panavision.

Production credit
This is the central credit on the third line. To the left comes the name of the distributor, which is followed by the production company if different. To the right comes the name or names of the actual producer – in brackets, unless he has a stake in the production, in which case he follows an oblique. These days, many films tend to have more producers of one kind or another than actors. The credit here refers to the person bearing the title of producer rather than to the executive producer, associate producer, production executive and so on.

Video
'V' indicates that the film is available on VHS video-cassette.
'V(W)' indicates that the film is available on VHS video-cassette in wide-screen format.
'V(C)' indicates that the film is available on VHS video-cassette in a computer-colourized version.
'L' indicates that the film is available on laser disc in either American NTSC format or British PAL format.

Alternative title
This is given on a separate line, usually with a note of the country in which it was used. If no such distinction exists, the formula aka (also known as) is used. Alternative titles are also listed individually, cross-referenced to the main entry for the film to which they belong.

Synopsis
This is a brief description of the film's plot.

Assessment
Again, this is brief and to the point.

Writer credit
(w) This appears first since the script precedes direction and is therefore, at least sometimes, more important than the director credit. The author of the screenplay is given; if this derives from a novel, play, musical, or story, this is given next, together with the original author.

Director credit
(d) This follows next. If the director is also the writer, then there will be a combined *'wd'* credit.

Photography credit
(ph) This indicates the cinematographer or lighting cameraman, otherwise known as the director of photography, rather than the actual camera operator.

Music credit
(m) This means the composer of the background music score. Sometimes there is only a music director *(md)* who orchestrates library or classical music. When noteworthy songs are performed in a film, or are specially written for it, those responsible are indicated by a credit for music and lyrics *(m/ly)* or simply *songs*.

Other credits
These include art director *(ad)*, choreographer *(ch)*, costume designer *(costume)*, film editor *(ed)*, production designer *(pd)* and special effects *(sp)*. They are given when they seem important and when they can be found. In some cases it has not been possible to track down all the credits one would wish.

Cast
A list of the principal actors is given, roughly in order of importance.

Italics
These denote a contribution of a particularly high standard.

Critical comments
Brief quotes from well-known professional critics are appended to many entries, sometimes because they wittily confirm the assessments and sometimes because they provide alternative opinions. The absence of a quote casts no reflection whatever on the film, only on the difficulty of finding an opinion worth quoting.

Additional notes
Any points of interest about the film are given after the symbol †.

Academy Awards
Awards (AA) and nominations (AAN) are listed for all principal categories, including best picture, acting, direction, photography, music score and songs, and some minor ones, such as sound and make-up, when they seem of interest.

'They're too wild for one world!'
Abbott and Costello Go to Mars
US 1953 76m bw
U-I (Howard Christie)

Two incompetents accidentally launch a space ship and land first in Louisiana, then on Venus.

Dismal knockabout, badly made.

w John Grant, D. D. Beauchamp d Charles Lamont ph Clifford Stine m Joseph Gershenson

Bud Abbott, Lou Costello, Mari Blanchard, Robert Paige, Martha Hyer

Abbott and Costello in Hollywood*
US 1945 85m bw
MGM (Martin Gosch)

Two agents have hectic adventures in a film studio.

Tolerable star romp on one of their biggest budgets, climaxing in a roller coaster ride.

w Nat Perrin, Lou Breslow d S. Sylvan Simon ph Charles Schoenbaum m George Bassman

Bud Abbott, Lou Costello, Frances Rafferty, Warner Anderson, Robert Z. Leonard

Abbott and Costello in the Foreign Legion
US 1950 80m bw
U-I (Robert Arthur)

Incompetent legionnaires become heroes to the fury of their sergeant.

Dull star vehicle on ramshackle sets, with no memorable routines.

w John Grant, Leonard Stern, Martin Ragaway d Charles Lamont ph George Robinson m Joseph Gershenson

Bud Abbott, Lou Costello, Patricia Medina, Walter Slezak, Douglass Dumbrille

Abbott and Costello Lost in Alaska
US 1952 76m bw
U-I (Howard Christie)

Two San Francisco firemen take a melancholy prospector back to Alaska to find a gold mine.

Sub-standard comedy vehicle with poor production.

w Martin Ragaway, Leonard Stern d Jean Yarbrough ph George Robinson m Joseph Gershenson

Bud Abbott, Lou Costello, *Tom Ewell*, Mitzi Green, Bruce Cabot

Abbott and Costello Meet Captain Kidd*
US 1952 70m Supercinecolor
Warner/Woodley (Alex Gottlieb)

Two servants have a treasure map, and a fearsome pirate wants it.

Crude knockabout: the stars are way

HALLIWELL'S GUIDE TO THE BEST CHILDREN'S FILMS

below their best, and a famous actor is embarrassed.

w Howard Dimsdale, John Grant d Charles Lamont ph Stanley Cortez m Raoul Kraushaar

Bud Abbott, Lou Costello, Charles Laughton, Hillary Brooke, Leif Erickson

Abbott and Costello Meet the Invisible Man*
US 1951 82m bw
U-I (Howard Christie)

A boxer accused of murder makes himself invisible while two detectives clear him.

Quite a bright comedy with good trick effects.

w Robert Lees, Frederic I. Rinaldo, John Grant d Charles Lamont ph George Robinson m Hans Salter

Bud Abbott, Lou Costello, Arthur Franz, Nancy Guild, Adele Jergens, Sheldon Leonard

'When every face wore a custard pie, and vamps broke hearts with a winking eye!'
Abbott and Costello Meet the Keystone Kops*
US 1954 79m bw
U-I (Howard Christie)

In pioneer film days, two incompetents are sold a dud studio by a con man, but succeed as stunt men.

Flabby comedy which never seems to get going until the chase finale; notable chiefly for a guest appearance by Mack Sennett.

w John Grant d Charles Lamont ph Reggie Lanning m Joseph Gershenson

Bud Abbott, Lou Costello, Lynn Bari, Fred Clark, Frank Wilcox, Maxie Rosenbloom

'It's all about a wacky prof who invents an anti-gravity goo that flew!'
The Absent-Minded Professor*
US 1961 97m bw
Walt Disney (Bill Walsh)

A lighter-than-air substance called flubber enables its inventor to drive his Model-T through the sky and catch some spies.

Foolishly engaging fantasy comedy with goodish trick effects.

w Bill Walsh d Robert Stevenson ph Edward Colman m George Bruns sp Robert A. Mattey, Peter Ellenshaw, Eustace Lycett

Fred MacMurray, Tommy Kirk, Keenan Wynn, Nancy Olson, Leon Ames, Ed Wynn, Edward Andrews

† Sequel: *Son of Flubber* (1963).
AAN: Edward Colman

'Creepy. Kooky. Spooky. Ooky.'
The Addams Family*
US 1991 99m DeLuxe
Columbia TriStar/Paramount/Orion (Scott Rudin)
V, L

An imposter turns up at the Addams family mansion, claiming to be a long-lost elder brother.

Owing more to the TV series of the 1960s than to the macabre wit of the original *New Yorker* cartoons, an ill-conceived, coarse-grained comedy that nevertheless was a success at the box-office.

w Caroline Thompson, Larry Wilson *cartoons* based on characters created by Charles Addams d Barry Sonnenfeld ph Owen Roizman m Marc

Shaiman   pd Richard
MacDonald   sp visual effects
supervisor Alan Munro, Chuck
Comisky   ed Dede Allen, Jim Miller

Anjelica Huston, Raul Julia,
Christopher Lloyd, Dan Hedaya,
Elizabeth Wilson, Judith Malina,
Carel Struycken, Dana Ivey, Paul
Benedict, Christopher Hart (whose
hand appears as The Thing)

'Plays like a collection of sitcom one-
liners augmented by feature-film
special effects — a combination that is
stretched well beyond its limits.' –
Variety

'Misguided graveyard slapstick.' – *New Yorker*

'Motherhood just got a little stranger.'
Addams Family Values
US   1993   94m   colour
UIP/Paramount (Scott Rudin)

The older Addams children try to kill
the new baby, but he is damage-proof.

An elongated sit-com with a few good
gags in a muddled narrative.

w Paul Rudnik   cartoons based on
characters created by Charles
Addams   d Barry Sonnenfeld
ph Donald Peterman   m Marc
Shaiman   pd Ken Adam

Angelica Huston, Raul Julia,
Christopher Lloyd, Joan Cusack,
Christina Ricci, Carol Kane, Jimmy
Workman

'The cast simply earn their bread and
butter doing revue turns.' – *Derek
Malcolm, Guardian*

The Adventures of Hajji Baba*
US   1954   93m   DeLuxe
  Cinemascope
Allied Artists/Walter Wanger

In ancient Arabia, a barber helps and
falls in love with an escaping princess.

A reasonably dashing sword and sandal
romp which no one takes very seriously.

w Richard Collins   d Don Weis
ph Harold Lipstein   m Dimitri
Tiomkin   pd Gene Allen

John Derek, Elaine Stewart, Thomas
Gomez, Amanda Blake, Paul Picerni,
Rosemarie Bowe

Adventures of Milo and Otis (dubbed)*
Japan   1986   75m
  Eastmancolor   Panavision
Virgin/Fuji (Hisashi Hieda)
V
original title: *Koneko Monogatari*

A puppy leaves a farm to search for
his friend, a kitten, who has floated
downriver in a box.

Innocuous adventure, using real animals,
that may appeal to the very young.

w Mark Saltzman   story Masanori
Hata   d Masanori Hata
ph Hideo Fuji, Shinji Tomita
m Michael Boddicker   ad Takeharu
Sakahuchi   ed Chizuko Osada

Dudley Moore (narrator)

'Youngsters and pet lovers will adore
this film. Grown-ups with a less
positive attitude to the animal
kingdom are well advised to stay
away.' – *Empire*

† The film was the second most
popular ever made in Japan.

'Only the rainbow can duplicate its
brilliance!'
The Adventures of Robin Hood****
US   1938   102m   Technicolor
Warner (Hal B. Wallis)
V, L

Rebel outlaw Robin Hood outwits

Guy of Gisbourne and the Sheriff of Nottingham, and saves the throne for the absent King Richard.

A splendid adventure story, rousingly operatic in treatment, with dashing action highlights, fine comedy balance, and incisive acting all round. Historically notable for its use of early three-colour Technicolor; also for convincingly recreating Britain in California.

w Seton I. Miller, Norman Reilly Raine d William Keighley, Michael Curtiz ph Tony Gaudio, Sol Polito, W. Howard Greene m Erich Wolfgang Korngold ad Carl Jules Weyl ed Ralph Dawson

Errol Flynn (Sir Robin of Locksley), Basil Rathbone (Sir Guy of Gisbourne), Claude Rains (Prince John), Olivia de Havilland (Maid Marian), Alan Hale (Little John), Patric Knowles (Will Scarlet), Eugene Pallette (Friar Tuck), Ian Hunter (King Richard), Melville Cooper (Sheriff of Nottingham), Una O'Connor (Bess), Herbert Mundin (Much the Miller's Son), Montagu Love (Bishop of Black Canons), Howard Hill (Captain of Archers)

PRINCE JOHN: 'Any objections to the new tax, from our Saxon friends?'
ROBIN to Gisbourne during duel: 'Did I upset your plans?'
GISBOURNE: 'You've come to Nottingham once too often!'
ROBIN: 'When this is over, my friend, there'll be no need for me to come again!'
PRINCE JOHN: 'Ho, varlets, bring Sir Robin food! Such insolence must support a healthy appetite!'
ROBIN: 'It's injustice I hate, not the Normans!'

'Magnificent, unsurpassable . . . the film is lavish, brilliantly photographed, and has a great Korngold score.' – NFT, 1974

'Mostly the picture is full of movement, some of it dashing in fine romantic costume style, some of it just sprightly. The excitement comes from fast action – galloping steeds, men swinging Tarzan-like from the trees, hurling tables and chairs, rapid running swordplay, the sudden whiz of Robin's arrows coming from nowhere to startle his enemies – more than from any fear that Robin might be worsted. Somehow the whole thing has the air of being a costume party, a jolly and rather athletic one, with a lot of well-bred Englishmen playing at being in the greenwood.' – James Shelley Hamilton, National Board of Review

† At the time of its release this was Warners' most expensive film, costing more than two million dollars. Chico, California, stood in for Sherwood Forest; the archery contest was shot at Busch Gardens, Pasadena. Curtiz took over direction when it was felt that the action lacked impact.

AA: Erich Wolfgang Korngold; Carl Jules Weyl; Ralph Dawson
AAN: best picture

Adventures of the Wilderness Family

US 1975 101m colour
Pacific International

An urban family runs into trouble when it takes to the wilds.

Naïve little four-wall family movie in which the pretty scenery (Utah and the Canadian Rockies) and the animals compensate for the dramatic inadequacies.

wd Stewart Raffil

Robert Logan, Susan Damante Shaw

† Further Adventures of the Wilderness Family appeared in 1977.

The Adventures of Tom Sawyer***
US 1938 91m Technicolor
David O. Selznick (William H. Wright)
L

Small-town Mississippi boy tracks down a murderer, Injun Joe.

Set-bound but excellent version of the children's classic by Mark Twain.

w John Weaver d Norman Taurog ph James Wong Howe, Wilfrid Cline m Max Steiner ad Lyle Wheeler

Tommy Kelly (Tom), May Robson (Aunt Polly), Walter Brennan (Muff Potter), Victor Jory (Injun Joe), Victor Kilian (Sheriff), Jackie Moran (Huckleberry Finn), Ann Gillis (Becky Thatcher), Donald Meek (Sunday School Superintendent), Margaret Hamilton (Mrs Sawyer), Marcia Mae Jones (Mary Sawyer)

'The familiar characters emerge in all their old amiability, the atmosphere is there and so is the excitement.' – MFB
'Should make Mark Twain circulate in his grave like a trout in a creel.' – Otis Ferguson
'Another Selznick International box office clean-up . . . that there exists a broad audience for films whose essential appeal is to the family trade has always been true. Snow White touched a source of almost unlimited audience draw: Tom Sawyer follows to the same customers.' – Variety
AAN: Lyle Wheeler

Africa Texas Style*
GB 1967 109m Eastmancolor
Paramount/Vantors (Andrew Marton)

A Kenyan settler hires two Texas cowboys to help in his scheme of wild game ranching.

Excellent location sequences are dragged down by a very boring script, but it's a good family film nevertheless.

w Andy White d Andrew Marton ph Paul Beeson m Malcolm Arnold

John Mills, Hugh O'Brian, Nigel Green, Tom Nardini, Adrienne Corri, Ronald Howard

† Forerunner of TV series, Cowboy in Africa.

Air Raid Wardens
US 1943 67m bw
MGM (B. F. Zeidman)
V

Rejected by the armed services, two incompetent air raid wardens accidentally round up Nazi spies.

Well below par star comedy: their incomparable dignity has disappeared.

w Jack Jevne, Martin Rackin, Charles Rogers, Harry Crane d Edward Sedgwick ph Walter Lundin m Nathaniel Shilkret

Stan Laurel, Oliver Hardy, Edgar Kennedy, Jacqueline White, Stephen McNally, Nella Walker, Donald Meek

'Imagine if you had three wishes, three hopes, three dreams and they all could come true.'
Aladdin****
US 1992 90m Technicolor
Buena Vista/Walt Disney (John Musker, Ron Clements)

An urchin with a magic lamp falls in love with a runaway princess.

Another brilliant return to classic form from Disney, notable for its quick-change genie to match the exuberance of Robin Williams' characterisation, and some innovative computer animation.

wd John Musker, Ron Clements, Ted Elliott, Terry Rossio *m* Alan Menken *pd* R. S. Vander Wende *m/ly* Alan Menken, Howard Ashman, Tim Rice *ed* H. Lee Peterson

voices of Scott Weinger, Brad Kane (Aladdin's singing), Robin Williams, Linda Larkin, Lea Salonga (Jasmine's singing), Jonathan Freeman, Frank Welker, Gilbert Gottfried, Douglas Seale

'Floridly beautiful, shamelessly derivative and infused with an irreverent, sophisticated comic flair.' – *Variety*
'A rollicking, bodaciously choreographed fantasy right out of Busby Berkeley.' – *Washington Post*

AA: Alan Menken (score); song: 'Whole New World' (*m* Alan Menken, *l* Tim Rice)
AAN: song: 'Friends like Me' (*m* Alan Menken, *l* Howard Ashman); sound; sound effects editing

Alakazam the Great*

Japan 1960 88m Eastmancolor
Toei (Hiroshi Okawa)
original title: *Saiyu-ki*

The arrogant monkey king of the animals is sent by his human master on a pilgrimage; he defeats evil King Gruesome and returns a hero.

Smartly animated, Disney-inspired cartoon based on the same legend as *Monkey*, translated by Arthur Waley.

w Osamu Tezuka, Keinosuke Uekusa *d* Taiji Yabushita

'Wild nights of sheer delights! Burning days of bold adventure! When beauty was the booty and the prize of all was love!'

Ali Baba and the Forty Thieves*

US 1943 87m Technicolor
Universal (Paul Malvern)

A deposed prince pretending to be a bandit regains his rightful throne.

Absurd but likeable wartime pantomime without much humour: a typical big-budget production of its studio and period.

w Edmund L. Hartmann *d* Arthur Lubin *ph* George Robinson *m* Edward Ward

Jon Hall, Maria Montez, Scotty Beckett, Turhan Bey, Frank Puglia, Andy Devine, Kurt Katch

† Remake: *Sword of Ali Baba*, which over twenty years later used much of the same footage.

Ali Baba and the Forty Thieves*

France 1954 90m Eastmancolor
Films du Cyclope

Ali Baba is sent to buy a new wife for his master, and accidentally finds a thieves' treasure cave...

Sporadically amusing but finally disappointing version of the Arabian Nights story; it looks hasty.

w Jacques Becker, Marc Maurette, Maurice Griffe *d* Jacques Becker *ph* Robert Le Fèbvre *m* Paul Misraki

Fernandel, Samia Gamal, Dieter Borsche, Henri Vilbert

Alice***

GB/Switzerland/West Germany 1988 85m Eastmancolor
Condor-Hessisches/SRG/Film Four (Peter-Christian Fueter)
V, L
original title: *Neco z Alenky*

A young girl follows a rabbit through a broken glass case into Wonderland.

A free, sometimes disturbing interpretation with surrealist overtones, of Lewis Carroll's masterpiece by a great animator that, with its mix of live actors and animation, comes closer than any other to conjuring the curious atmosphere of the original.

wd Jan Svankmajer *novel* Alice in Wonderland by Lewis Carroll
ph Svatoluk Maly *ad* Eva Svankmerova, Jiri Blaha *ed* Marie Drvotova

Kristyna Kohoutova

Alice in Wonderland**
US 1933 75m bw
Paramount (Louis D. Lighton)

Intriguing but disappointing version of the nonsense classic, keeping to the Tenniel drawings by dressing an all-star cast in masks, thereby rendering them ineffective.

w Joseph L. Mankiewicz, William Cameron Menzies *novel* Lewis Carroll *d* Norman Z. McLeod
ph Henry Sharp, Bert Glennon
m Dimitri Tiomkin

Charlotte Henry, W. C. Fields (Humpty Dumpty), Cary Grant (Mock Turtle), Gary Cooper (White Knight), Edward Everett Horton (Mad Hatter), Edna May Oliver (Red Queen), Jack Oakie (Tweedledum), Leon Errol (Uncle), Charles Ruggles (March Hare), May Robson (Queen of Hearts), Louise Fazenda (White Queen), Ned Sparks (Caterpillar), Alison Skipworth (Duchess)

'Nothing grows out of anything else in this phantasmagoria. It's like reading a whole volume of separate four-line gags.' – *Variety*
'Lavishly produced, with great care given to costumes and settings and make-up, but the spirit is missing.' – *New Yorker*, 1977

† Ida Lupino was brought from the UK for the title role, but not used.

Alice in Wonderland*
US 1951 75m Technicolor
Walt Disney
V, L

Fully animated cartoon version which has good moments but modernizes and Americanizes the familiar characters.

w various *d* Clyde Geronimi, Hamilton Luske, Wilfred Jackson
supervisor Ben Sharpsteen
m Oliver Wallace

voices of Kathryn Beaumont, Ed Wynn, Richard Haydn, Sterling Holloway, Jerry Colonna, Verna Felton, Bill Thompson
AAN: Oliver Wallace

Alice's Adventures in Wonderland*
GB 1972 101m Eastmancolor Todd-AO
TCF/Josef Shaftel (Derek Horne)

Live-action version which starts amiably enough but soon becomes flat and uninventive, with a star cast all at sea and tedium replacing the wit of the original.

wd William Sterling *ph* Geoffrey Unsworth *m* John Barry
pd Michael Stringer

Fiona Fullerton, Michael Crawford (White Rabbit), Robert Helpmann (Mad Hatter), Dudley Moore (Dormouse), Spike Milligan (Gryphon), Peter Sellers (March Hare), Dennis Price (King of Hearts), Flora Robson (Queen of Hearts), Rodney Bewes (Knave of Hearts), Peter Bull (Duchess), Michael Hordern (Mock Turtle), Ralph Richardson (Caterpillar), etc

All Creatures Great and Small*
GB 1974 92m Eastmancolor
EMI/Venedon (David Susskind, Duane Bogie)

The pre-war Yorkshire life of a country vet.

Simple-minded popular entertainment of a long-forgotten kind, oddly sponsored by American TV in the shape of Readers' Digest and the Hallmark Hall of Fame.

w Hugh Whitemore   novel James Herriot   d Claude Whatham
ph Peter Suschitzky   m Wilfred Josephs

Anthony Hopkins, Simon Ward, Lisa Harrow, Freddie Jones, Brian Stirner, T. P. McKenna, Brenda Bruce, John Collin

† 1976 sequel: *It Shouldn't Happen to a Vet*.

All Dogs Go To Heaven
Eire 1989 85m Technicolor
Rank/Sullivan Bluth/Goldcrest/Don Bluth, Gary Goldman, John Pomeroy
V, L

A dead dog returns to Earth to seek revenge on the vicious gangster dog who had him killed.

Skilful animation goes to waste in a confused and confusing narrative.

w David N. Weiss   d Dan Kuenster, Gary Goldman   m Ralph Burns
pd Don Bluth, Larry Leker   m/ly Charles Strouse, T. J. Kuenster, Al Kasha/Joel Hirschhorn/Michael Lloyd

voices of Burt Reynolds, Vic Tayback, Judith Barsi, Dom DeLuise, Loni Anderson, Melba Moore, Charles Nelson Reilly

Allegro Non Troppo*
Italy 1977 74m colour/bw
Essential/Bruno Bozzetto

A mix of live action and animation to create a modernistic version of *Fantasia*, e.g. Ravel's 'Bolero' is danced by a Coca-Cola bottle.

w Bruno Bozzetto, Guido Manuli, Maurizio Nichetti   d Bruno Bozzetto   ph Mario Masini
md Herbert von Karajan, Hans Stadlmair, Lorin Maazel
m Debussy, Dvorak, Ravel, Sibelius, Vivaldi, Stravinsky

Maurizio Nichetti, Nestor Garay, Maurizio Micheli, Maria Luisa Giovanni

An Alligator Named Daisy
GB 1955 88m Technicolor Vistavision
Rank (Raymond Stross)

A young songwriter finds himself saddled with a pet alligator.

The ultimate in silly animal comedies, this does score a few laughs.

w Jack Davies   novel Charles Terrot   d J. Lee-Thompson
ph Reg Wyer   m Stanley Black

Donald Sinden, Diana Dors, Jean Carson, James Robertson Justice, Stanley Holloway, Roland Culver, Margaret Rutherford, Avice Landone, Richard Wattis, Frankie Howerd, Jimmy Edwards, Gilbert Harding

'Apart from a fairly Kafkaesque scene in which Daisy is discovered in an upright piano, the situation is treated with little wit or comic invention.' – *MFB*

The Amazing Dobermans
US 1976 99m colour
Doberman Associates

Most ambitious of three low-budget independent movies (others, *The Daring Dobermans* and *The Doberman Gang*) about a group of trained dogs;

this one concerns an ex-con who hires them out for guard duty.

A fair low-budget production for family audiences.

w Richard Chapman   d Byron Chudnow

Fred Astaire, James Franciscus, Parley Baer, Billy Barty

The Amazing Mr Blunden**
GB 1972 99m Eastmancolor
Hemdale/Hemisphere (Barry Levinson)

In 1918, a widow and her two children meet a kindly gentleman who offers them work in his old mansion. Here they meet two ghost children, discover that he is a ghost too, and travel a hundred years back in time to right a wicked wrong.

Involved ghost story for intellectual children, made generally palatable by oodles of period charm and good acting.

wd Lionel Jeffries   story The Ghosts by Antonia Baker   ph Gerry Fisher   m Elmer Bernstein   pd Wilfrid Shingleton

Laurence Naismith, Diana Dors, James Villiers, David Lodge, Lynne Frederick, Dorothy Alison, Rosalyn Lander, Marc Granger

'Easy period charm . . . fills every crevice.' – Clyde Jeavons

An American Tail*
US 1986 80m DeLuxe
Universal/Steven Spielberg (Don Bluth, John Pomeroy, Gary Goldman)
V, L

Russian mice encounter all kinds of trouble when in the 1880s they emigrate to the United States.

Expensive cartoon feature with old-fashioned full animation but not much in the way of narrative interest or indeed humour.

w Judy Freudberg, Tony Geiss
d Don Bluth (also designer)

voices: Cathianne Blore, Christopher Plummer, Dom De Luise, Madeline Kahn

'Every character and every situation have been presented a thousand times before . . . anyone over the age of 12 will likely experience more boredom than pleasure.' – Variety
AAN: song, 'Somewhere Out There' (James Horner, Barry Mann, Cynthia Weil)

'Look Out Pardeners, There's A New Mouse In Town!'
An American Tail: Fievel Goes West**
US 1991 75m colour
UIP/Universal/Amblin (Steven Spielberg, Robert Watts)
V, L

A confidence trickster of a cat persuades a family of mice to move to the West.

Enjoyable and high-spirited animated film that borrows plot and attitudes from classic Westerns.

w Flint Dille   story Charles Swenson   d Phil Nibbelink, Simon Wells   m James Horner

voices of Phillip Glasser, James Stewart, Erica Yohn, Cathy Cavadini, Nehemiah Persoff, Dom De Luise, Amy Irving, John Cleese, Jon Lovitz

Amy
US 1981 100m Technicolor
Walt Disney

A spinster is taught a little about life and love.

Unmemorable family comedy drama.

w Noreen Stone   d Vincent McEveety

Jenny Agutter, Barry Newman, Kathleen Nolan, Chris Robinson, Margaret O'Brien, Nanette Fabray

And Now for Something Completely Different**
GB 1971 88m colour
Columbia/Kettledrum/Python (Patricia Casey)
L

Monty Python's Flying Circus perform again a selection of sketches from the BBC television series.

The first Monty Python film, intended to introduce the team's humour to an American audience. It lacks any overall coherence, but many of the individual sketches are a joy.

w Graham Chapman, John Cleese, Terry Gilliam, Eric Idle, Terry Jones, Michael Palin   d Ian Macnaughton   ph David Muir   ad Colin Grimes   ed Thom Noble

Graham Chapman, John Cleese, Terry Gilliam, Eric Idle, Terry Jones, Michael Palin, Carol Cleveland

'Very funny.' – MFB

Andy Hardy Comes Home*
US 1958 81m bw
MGM (Red Doff)

Fortyish Andy returns to Carvel, his home town, to negotiate a land deal.

Rather dismal sequel to the celebrated series of Hardy family comedies which were enormously popular in the early forties: a thirteen-year gap is too long, and although most of the family is reunited the old Judge is sadly missed.

w Edward Everett Hutshing, Robert Morris Donley   d Howard W. Koch   ph William W. Spencer, Harold E. Wellman   m Van Alexander

Mickey Rooney, Fay Holden, Cecilia Parker, Patricia Breslin, Sara Haden, Jerry Colonna

† See also under *Hardy Family*.

Angora Love**
US 1929 20m bw silent
Hal Roach
V

Laurel and Hardy keep a goat in their lodgings.

Lively comedy, even funnier when remade two years later as *Laughing Gravy*.

w Leo McCarey and H. M. Walker   d Lewis R. Foster

Laurel and Hardy, Edgar Kennedy, Charlie Hall

Animal Crackers***
US 1930 98m bw
Paramount
V, L

Thieves covet a valuable oil painting unveiled at a swank party.

An excuse for the Marx Brothers, and a lively one in patches, though sedate and stage bound in treatment. The boys are all in top form, and many of the dialogue exchanges are classics.

w *Morrie Ryskind*   musical play Morrie Ryskind, George F. Kaufman   d Victor Heerman   ph George Folsey   m/ly Bert Kalmar, Harry Ruby

Groucho, Chico, Harpo, Zeppo, Margaret Dumont, Lillian Roth, Louis Sorin, Robert Greig, Hal Thompson
  GROUCHO: 'You're the most beautiful woman I've ever seen, which doesn't say much for you.'

GROUCHO: 'One morning I shot an elephant in my pajamas. How he got into my pajamas I'll never know.'

GUESTS: 'Hooray for Captain Spaulding, the African explorer!'

GROUCHO: 'Did someone call me schnorrer?'

GUESTS: 'Hooray, hooray, hooray!'

ZEPPO: 'He went into the jungle, where all the monkeys *throw* nuts.'

GROUCHO: 'If I stay here, I'll *go* nuts.'

GUESTS:
'Hooray, hooray, hooray!
He put all his reliance
In courage and defiance
And risked his life for science.'

GROUCHO: 'Hey, hey!'

MRS RITTENHOUSE: 'He is the only white man who covered every acre . . .'

GROUCHO: 'I think I'll try and make her . . .'

GUESTS: 'Hooray, hooray, hooray!'

'A hit on the screen before it opened, and in the money plenty.' – *Variety*

Animal Farm**

GB 1955 75m Technicolor
Louis de Rochemont/Halas and Batchelor
L

Oppressed by the cruelty and inefficiency of their master, the animals take over a farm but find fresh tyrants among themselves.

George Orwell's political fable – 'all animals are equal but some animals are more equal than others' – is faithfully followed in this ambitious but rather disappointingly flat cartoon version. *w/p/d* John Halas, Joy Batchelor *m* Matyas Seiber

voices: Maurice Denham

'A melodramatic fantasy that is mordant, tender and quixotic, shot with ironic humour.' – *New York Times*

Anne of Green Gables*

US 1934 79m bw
RKO (Kenneth MacGowan)

An orphan girl goes to the country to live with her aunt.

Standard version of the classic for young girls.

w Sam Mintz *novel* L. M. Montgomery *d* George Nicholls Jnr *ph* Lucien Andriot *m* Max Steiner

Anne Shirley (who had been known as Dawn O'Day and legally adopted the name of her character in this, her first starring role), Tom Brown, O. P. Heggie, Helen Westley, Sara Haden, Charley Grapewin

'Made up and monotonous – tragedy having its breakfast in bed.' – *Otis Ferguson*

† *Anne of Windy Willows*, with the same stars and production team, followed in 1940.

Annie

US 1982 128m Metrocolor
 Panavision
Columbia/Ray Stark (Joe Layton)
V

In 1933 an orphan waif charms a munitions millionaire and is adopted by him.

Misguided opening-out of a charming stage musical based on the comic strip which is basically a reversal of *Oliver Twist*. Some of the best numbers have been discarded, the dancing is ponderous, the acting distinctly uneasy, and the choice of director stupefying. None of it works at all.

w Carol Sobieski, from the stage play *book* Thomas Meehan *ly* Martin Charnin *m* Charles Strouse *comic strip* Harold Gray *d* John Huston *ph* Richard Moore *m* Ralph Burns *pd* Dale Hennesy

Albert Finney, Carol Burnett, Aileen Quinn, Ann Reinking, Bernadette Peters, Tim Curry, Geoffrey Holder, Edward Herrmann (as Franklin D. Roosevelt)

'Whatever indefinable charm the stage show had is completely lost in this lumbering and largely uninteresting and uninvolving exercise, where the obvious waste reaches almost Pentagonian proportions.' – *Variety*
'The whole thing has the air of a vast, hollow Christmas tree bauble intended not so much for children as for the infantile-minded middle-aged.' – *Sunday Times*
'This is the film I want on my tombstone.' – *Ray Stark*
'Funeral services may be held starting this week at a theatre near you.' – *Time*

† The cost of *Annie*, starting with $9,000,000 for the rights, rose to $42,000,000. It was not recovered.
AAN: art direction; original song score

Any Old Port*
US 1932 20m bw
Hal Roach
V

Stan and Ollie are sailors on leave, and Ollie enters Stan for a boxing match.

Minor star comedy with good moments but a weak finish.

w H. M. Walker *d* James W. Horne

Laurel and Hardy, Walter Long

The Apple Dumpling Gang
US 1974 100m Technicolor
Walt Disney (Bill Anderson)
L

Three orphan children strike gold in 1878 California.

Better-than-average Disney romp.

w Don Tait *novel* Jack M. Bickham *d* Norman Tokar *ph* Frank Phillips *m* Buddy Baker

Bill Bixby, Susan Clark, David Wayne, Don Knotts, Tim Conway, Slim Pickens, Harry Morgan, John McGiver, Marie Windsor, Iris Adrian

† *The Apple Dumpling Gang Rides Again*, a shoddy sequel under the direction of Vincent McEveety, appeared in 1979 with fragments of the old cast but no panache.

The Apple Dumpling Gang Rides Again
US 1979 88m Technicolor
Walt Disney (Ron Miller)

Two incompetent bank robbers trying to go straight find themselves in trouble with a sheriff, the cavalry, Indians and a rival gang.

Limp, slow-paced comedy Western that is a dull sequel to an ordinary original.

w Don Tait *d* Vincent McEveety *ph* Frank Phillips *m* Buddy Baker *ad* John B. Mansbridge, Frank T. Smith *ed* Gordon D. Brenner

Tim Conway, Don Knotts, Tim Matheson, Kenneth Mars, Elyssa Davalos, Jack Elam, Robert Pine, Harry Morgan, Ruth Buzzi

'They came home with the milk!'
Appointment with Venus**
GB 1951 89m bw
GFD/British Film Makers (Betty E. Box)
US title: *Island Rescue*

During World War II, a pedigree cow

is rescued from the German-occupied Channel Islands.

Curious but generally agreeable mixture of comedy and war adventure, pleasantly shot on Sark.

w Nicholas Phipps novel Jerrard Tickell d Ralph Thomas ph Ernest Steward m Benjamin Frankel

David Niven, Glynis Johns, George Coulouris, Barry Jones, Kenneth More, Noel Purcell, Bernard Lee, Jeremy Spenser

Arabian Adventure
GB 1979 98m colour
Badger Films/John Dark

The dictator of Jadur promises his daughter's hand in marriage if a young prince will seek and find a magic rose.

Artless juggling of elements from *The Thief of Baghdad*, including magic carpets, monsters and a bottle djinn.

w Brian Hayles d Kevin Connor ph Alan Hume m Ken Thorne pd Elliot Scott

Christopher Lee, Oliver Tobias, Mickey Rooney, Milo O'Shea, Elizabeth Welch, Peter Cushing, Capucine

'Resolutely well mounted, but somehow lacking that necessary fillip of Hollywood vulgarity or exuberance.' – John Pym, MFB

Arabian Nights*
US 1942 86m Technicolor
Universal (Walter Wanger)

The Caliph of Baghdad is deposed by his half-brother but wins back his throne with the help of a dancer and an acrobat.

Well presented oriental adventure which has nothing to do with its source material but entertained multitudes in search of relief from total war and was followed by several vaguely similar slices of hokum with the same stars.

w Michael Hogan d John Rawlins ph Milton Krasner, William V. Skall, W. Howard Greene m Frank Skinner ad Alexander Golitzen, Jack Otterson

Jon Hall, Maria Montez, Sabu, Leif Erickson, Thomas Gomez, Turhan Bey, John Qualen, Billy Gilbert, Shemp Howard
AAN: Milton Krasner, William V. Skall, W. Howard Greene; Frank Skinner; art direction

The Aristocats**
US 1970 78m Technicolor
Walt Disney (Wolfgang Reiterman, Winston Hibler)

Two cats are deliberately lost by a butler who fears they will inherit his mistress's wealth; but a variety of animal friends restore them to their rightful place.

Cartoon feature, a moderate example of the studio's work after Disney's death, with rather too few felicitous moments.

w Larry Clemmons and others d Wolfgang Reitherman

voices of Phil Harris, Eva Gabor, Sterling Holloway, Scatman Crothers, Paul Winchell, Hermione Baddeley, Roddy Maude-Roxby

'It's a wonderful world, if you'll only take the time to go around it!'
Around the World in Eighty Days***
US 1956 178m Technicolor Todd-AO
UA/Michael Todd
V, L

A Victorian gentleman and his valet

win a bet that they can go round the world in eighty days.

Amiable large-scale pageant resolving itself into a number of sketches, which could have been much sharper, separated by wide screen spectacle. What was breathtaking at the time seems generally slow and blunted in retrospect, but the fascination of recognizing 44 cameo stars remains. The film is less an exercise in traditional skills than a tribute to its producer's energy.

w James Poe, John Farrow, S. J. Perelman   novel Jules Verne
d Michael Anderson, Kevin McClory   ph Lionel Lindon
m Victor Young   titles Saul Bass
ad James W. Sullivan, Ken Adams
ed Gene Ruggiero, Paul Weatherwax

David Niven, Cantinflas, Robert Newton, Shirley Maclaine, Charles Boyer, Joe E. Brown, Martine Carol, John Carradine, Charles Coburn, *Ronald Colman*, Melville Cooper, *Noel Coward*, Finlay Currie, Reginald Denny, Andy Devine, Marlene Dietrich, Luis Dominguin, Fernandel, *John Gielgud*, Hermione Gingold, Jose Greco, Cedric Hardwicke, Trevor Howard, Glynis Johns, *Buster Keaton*, Evelyn Keyes, Beatrice Lillie, Peter Lorre, Edmund Lowe, A. E. Matthews, Mike Mazurki, Tim McCoy, Victor McLaglen, John Mills, Alan Mowbray, Robert Morley, Jack Oakie, George Raft, Gilbert Roland, Cesar Romero, Frank Sinatra, *Red Skelton*, Ronald Squire, Basil Sidney, *Harcourt Williams*, Ed Murrow

'Michael Todd's "show", shorn of the ballyhoo and to critics not mollified by parties and sweetmeats, is a film like any other, only twice as long as most ... the shots of trains and boats seem endless.' – David Robinson

AA: best picture; James Poe, John Farrow, S. J. Perelman; Lionel Lindon; Victor Young
AAN: Michael Anderson; art direction; editing

Asterix and the Big Fight

France/West Germany   1989
81m   Eastmancolor
Palace/Gaumont/Extrafilm (Nicolas Pesques)
V
original title: *Le Coup De Menhir*

Asterix attempts to restore the village soothsayer's memory in order to make a potion to defeat the invading Romans.

Dull adaptation of a far wittier comic-book original.

w George Roubicek   novel *Asterix and the Big Fight* and *Asterix and the Soothsayer* by Rene Goscinny and Alberto Uderzo   d Philippe Grimond   ph Craig Simpson
m Michel Colombier   pd Nicolas Pesques   ed Jean Goudier

voices of Bill Oddie, Bernard Bresslaw, Ron Moody, Sheila Hancock, Peter Hawkins, Brian Blessed, Michael Elphick, Andrew Sachs, Tim Brooke-Taylor, Douglas Blackwell

Asterix in Britain

Denmark/France   1986   74m
Eastmancolor
Gaumont Dargaud (Yannik Piel)
V

Asterix and friends go to Britain to help the locals repel the Roman invasion.

Amiable animated version of the comic-book characters, poking good-natured fun at national stereotypes.

w Pierre Tchernia   comic Goscinny

and Uderzo   d Pino Van Lamsweerde   m Vladimir Cosma

voices of Jack Beaver, Bill Kearns, Graham Bushnell, Herbert Baskind, Ed Marcus

At the Earth's Core
GB 1976 90m Technicolor
Amicus (John Dark)

Scientists testing a geological excavator are carried by it to the centre of the Earth, and find a prehistoric land inhabited by feuding tribes.

Mainly feeble science fiction for kids, with occasional amusing moments.

w Milton Subotsky   novel Edgar Rice Burroughs   d Kevin Connor   ph Alan Hume   m Mike Vickers   pd Maurice Carter   sp Ian Wingrove

Doug McClure, Peter Cushing, Caroline Munro, Cy Grant, Godfrey James, Keith Barron

'Papier mâché people-eaters, idiotic situations, and a frequent sense of confusion as to what is going on.' – *David Stewart, Christian Science Monitor*

Atlantis, the Lost Continent
US 1961 91m Metrocolor
MGM/Galaxy/George Pal

A Greek fisherman is imprisoned when he returns a maiden he has rescued to her island home of Atlantis, but escapes just before volcanic eruption overtakes the decadent nation.

Penny-pinching fantasy spectacle with very little entertainment value.

w Daniel Mainwaring   play Sir Gerald Hargreaves   d George Pal   ph Harold E. Wellman   m Russell Garcia

Anthony Hall, Joyce Taylor, John Dall, Edward Platt, Frank de Kova, Jay Novello

Babar: The Movie
Canada/France 1989 76m colour
Winstone/Nelvana/Ellipse (Patrick Loubert, Michael Hirsch, Clive A. Smith)
V, L

King Babar tells his children of his adventures as a young elephant.

Lacklustre story, with simple animation.

w Peter Sauder, J. D. Smith, John de Klein, Raymond Jaffelice, Alan Bunce story Peter Sauder, Patrick Loubert, Michael Hirsch, based on characters created by Jean de Brunhoff, Laurent de Brunhoff d Alan Bunce m Milan Kymlicka pd Ted Bastien m/ly Maribeth Solomon ad Clive Powsey, Carol Bradbury ed Evan Landis

voices of Gordon Pinsent, Elizabeth Hanna, Lisa Yamanaka, Marsha Moreau, Bobby Beckon, Amos Crawley, Gavin Magrath, Sarah Polley

Babes in Arms**
US 1939 96m bw
MGM (Arthur Freed)

The teenage sons and daughters of retired vaudevillians put on a big show.

Simple-minded backstage musical which marked the first enormously successful teaming of its two young stars.

w Jack McGowan, Kay Van Riper Broadway show Rodgers and Hart d/ch Busby Berkeley ph Ray June m Roger Edens, George Stoll m/ly Rodgers and Hart and others

Judy Garland, Mickey Rooney, Charles Winninger, Douglas Macphail, Leni Lynn, June Preisser songs: 'Where or When'; 'Babes in Arms'; 'I Cried for You'; 'God's Country'; 'Good Morning'; 'You Are My Lucky Star'

'A topflight filmusical entertainment. It will click mightily in the key deluxers, and roll up hefty profits for exhibits in the subsequent runs and smaller situations.' – *Variety*
AAN: Roger Edens, George Stoll; Mickey Rooney

Babes in Toyland**
US 1934 77m bw
Hal Roach
V, L
aka: *Wooden Soldiers; March of the Wooden Soldiers; Laurel and Hardy in Toyland*

Santa Claus's incompetent assistants accidentally make some giant wooden soldiers, which come in useful when a villain tries to take over Toyland.

Comedy operetta in which the stars have pleasant but not outstanding material; the style and decor are however sufficient to preserve the film as an eccentric minor classic.

w Nick Grinde, Frank Butler

original book Glen MacDonough
d Gus Meins, Charles Rogers
ph Art Lloyd, Francis Corby
m Victor Herbert

Stan Laurel, Oliver Hardy, Charlotte Henry, Henry Brandon, Felix Knight, Florence Roberts, Johnny Downs, Marie Wilson

'It is amusing enough to entertain older persons who remember when they were young.' – *Variety*

Babes in Toyland
US 1961 105m Technicolor
Walt Disney
L

A misfiring remake, all charm and no talent apart from some excellent special effects at the climax.

w Ward Kimball, Joe Rinaldi, Lowell S. Hawley *d* Jack Donohue
ph Edward Colman *md* George Bruns *sp* Eustace Lycett, Robert A. Mattey, Bill Justice, Xavier Atencio, Yale Gracey

Ray Bolger (miscast as the villain), Tommy Sands, Annette Funicello, Tommy Kirk, Gene Sheldon (imitating Stan Laurel), Henry Calvin (imitating Oliver Hardy), Ed Wynn, Kevin Corcoran
AAN: George Bruns

Baby – Secret of the Lost Legend
US 1985 95m Technicolor
Supertechnirama
Touchstone (Jonathan T. Taplin)
L

Palaeontologists in the African jungle discover a family of living dinosaurs.

Technically and dramatically less than effective, this latter-day *King Kong* demonstrates yet again the Disney company's difficulties in hitting the right note for the modern family audience.

w Clifford and Ellen Green *d* B. W. L. Norton *ph* John Alcott
m Jerry Goldsmith *sp* Philip Meador, Peter Anderson

William Katt, Sean Young, Patrick McGoohan, Julian Fellowes

Back to the Future***
US 1985 116m Technicolor
Universal/Steven Spielberg (Bob Gale, Neil Canton)
V(W), L

With the help of a not-so-crazy scientist, a teenager goes back thirty years to make a man out of his dimwit father.

Lighthearted Twilight Zone fantasy which certainly pleased the international multitudes.

w Robert Zemeckis, Bob Gale
d Robert Zemeckis *ph* Dean Cundey *m* Alan Silvestri
pd Lawrence G. Paull *ed* Arthur Schmidt, Harry Keramidas

Michael J. Fox, Christopher Lloyd, Crispin Glover, Lea Thompson, Claudia Wells

'Accelerates with wit, ideas, and infectious, wide-eyed wonder.' – *Variety*
AAN: original screenplay

Back to the Future II
US 1989 108m DeLuxe
UIP/Amblin Entertainment (Bob Gale, Neil Canton)
V, V(W), L

A scientist and his young friend discover, on their return from a trip to the future, that the present has been altered for the worse.

Extraordinarily raucous, confusingly

plotted, poorly performed (rarely have actors aged so unconvincingly) sequel that amounts to little more than a trailer for the third part of the series.

w Bob Gale story Bob Gale, Robert Zemeckis d Robert Zemeckis ph Dean Cundey m Alan Silvestri pd Rick Carter ad Margie Stone McShirley ed Arthur Schimdt, Harry Keramidas

Michael J. Fox, Christopher Lloyd, Lea Thompson, Thomas F. Wilson, Harry Waters Jr, Charles Fleischer, Joe Flaherty

'They've saved the best trip to the last. But this time they may have gone too far.'
Back to the Future III**
US 1990 118m DeLuxe
UIP/Amblin (Bob Gale, Neil Canton)
V, V(W), L

A teenager travels back in time to rescue his friend, a scientist stranded in the Wild West.

Good-natured fun at the expense of classic Western movies.

w Bob Gale story Robert Zemeckis d Robert Zemeckis ph Dean Cundey m Alan Silvestri pd Rick Carter ed Arthur Schmidt, Harry Keramidas

Michael J. Fox, Christopher Lloyd, Mary Steenburgen, Thomas F. Wilson, Lea Thompson, Elisabeth Shue, Matt Clark, Richard Dysart, James Tolkan

'Has a joyousness seldom seen on the screen these days, a sense of exuberance in the breaking of boundaries of time, space and genre.' – Variety

Bambi****
US 1942 72m Technicolor
Walt Disney

The story of a forest deer, from the book by Felix Salten.

Anthropomorphic cartoon feature, one of Disney's most memorable and brilliant achievements, with a great comic character in Thumper the rabbit and a climactic forest fire sequence which is genuinely thrilling. A triumph of the animator's art.
supervisor David Hand m Frank Churchill, Edward Plumb

voices of Peter Behn, Paula Winslowe

'The ultimate stag movie.' – anon
AAN: Frank Churchill, Edward Plumb; song 'Love Is a Song' (m Frank Churchill, ly Larry Morey)

The Bandit of Sherwood Forest*
US 1946 87m Technicolor
Columbia (Leonard S. Picker, Clifford Sanforth)

Robin Hood frustrates the Regent who plans to usurp the throne from the boy king.

A lively romp through Sherwood Forest with a capable cast.

w Wilfrid H. Pettit, Melvin Levy novel Son of Robin Hood by Paul A. Castleton d George Sherman, Henry Levin ph Tony Gaudio, William Snyder, George Meehan m Hugo Friedhofer

Cornel Wilde, Anita Louise, Edgar Buchanan, Jill Esmond, Henry Daniell, George Macready, Russell Hicks, John Abbott, Lloyd Corrigan

The Barefoot Executive*
US 1970 96m Technicolor
Walt Disney (Bill Anderson)

A TV network discovers that its most infallible average viewer is a chimpanzee.

Quite a beguiling little farcical comedy with mild doses of satire.

w Joseph L. McEveety d Robert Butler ph Charles F. Wheeler m Robert F. Brunner

Kurt Russell, Harry Morgan, Joe Flynn, Wally Cox, Heather North, Alan Hewitt, Hayden Rorke

Batman*
US 1966 105m DeLuxe
TCF/Greenlawn/National Periodical Publications (William Dozier)
L

The cloaked avenger saves an important executive from the clutches of four of the world's most notorious criminals.

Glossy feature version of the old and new serials about the comic strip hero who scurries around in his Batmobile making sure that justice is done. The scriptwriter's invention unfortunately flags halfway, so that despite a fairly sharp production the result is more childish than camp.

w Lorenzo Semple Jnr d Leslie Martinson ph Howard Schwartz m Nelson Riddle

Adam West, Burt Ward, Cesar Romero, Frank Gorshin, Burgess Meredith, Lee Meriwether, Alan Napier, Neil Hamilton

Batman**
US 1989 126m Technicolor
Warner (Jon Peters, Peter Guber)
V, V(W), L

A young boy who witnesses his parents' murder grows up to become Batman, a masked and emotionally disturbed vigilante who battles against an arch-criminal known as The Joker.

The campness of earlier versions of the comic-book hero gives way to a gloomier psychological interpretation that loses much of the fun of the original, while the brilliant production design, of a grim, grey metropolis, overshadows all. Narrative is reduced to a succession of set-pieces.

w Sam Hamm, Warren Skaaren d Tim Burton ph Roger Pratt m Danny Elfman pd Anton Furst m/ly Prince, John L. Nelson sp John Evans ed Ray Lovejoy

Michael Keaton, Jack Nicholson, Kim Basinger, Robert Wuhl, Pat Hingle, Billy Dee Williams, Michael Gough, Jack Palance, Jerry Hall

'A moderately entertaining fantasy, with good design, some strong performances and a desperate need of a script doctor.' – *Adam Mars-Jones, Independent*

AA: best art direction

Batman Returns**
US 1992 126m Technicolor
Warner (Denise Di Novi, Tim Burton)
V

Batman does battle with Catwoman and The Penguin.

More comic-strip story-telling, done as a succession of set pieces, with the towering design of the city and its sewers overshadowing the performances.

w Daniel Waters story Daniel Waters, Sam Hamm d Tim Burton ph Stefan Czapsky m Danny Elfman pd Bo Welch ed Chris Lebenzon, Bob Badami

Michael Keaton, Danny DeVito, Michelle Pfeiffer, Christopher Walken, Michael Gough, Michael Murphy, Cristi Conaway, Pat Hingle

HALLIWELL'S GUIDE TO THE BEST CHILDREN'S FILMS

'Resembles nothing so much as a blacker, spikier but less focused version of a Disney animation feature made flesh.' – *Derek Malcolm, Guardian*

'A blend of playful novelty and reassuring familiarity – a difficult mixture to get right.' – *New Yorker*

AAN: Visual effects; make-up

Batteries Not Included

US 1987 106m DeLuxe
UIP/Universal (Ronald L. Schwarz)
V, L

A Manhattan neighbourhood where everyone has problems is helped out by miniature flying saucers with angelic intentions.

Frank Capra would have done it much better.

w Matthew Robbins, Brad Bird, Brent Maddock, S. S. Wilson   story Mick Garris   d Matthew Robbins
ph John McPherson   m James Horner   pd Ted Haworth
ed Cynthia Scheider

Hume Cronyn, Jessica Tandy, Frank McRae, Elizabeth Pena, Michael Carmine

Battle Beneath the Earth*

GB 1967 92m Technicolor
MGM/Reynolds/Vetter (Charles Reynolds)
US title: *Battle Beneath the Sea*

Enemy agents burrow under the US by means of a giant laser.

Agreeable schoolboy science fiction with fair special effects.

w L. Z. Hargreaves   d Montgomery Tully   ph Kenneth Talbot
m Ken Jones   sp Tom Howard

Kerwin Mathews, Vivienne Ventura, Robert Ayres, Peter Arne, Martin Benson

Battle Beyond the Stars*

US 1980 104m Metrocolor
New World/Roger Corman (Ed Carlin)
L

A small planet hires help to repel invaders.

Impertinent and sometimes amusing space fiction rip-off of *Seven Samurai*, with plenty of in-jokes and quite pleasant special effects.

w John Sayles   d Jimmy T. Murakami   ph Daniel Lacambre
m James Horner   ad Jim Cameron, Charles Breen

Richard Thomas, Robert Vaughn, John Saxon, George Peppard, Sam Jaffe, Morgan Woodward, Darlanne Fluegel, Sybil Danning

Battlestar Galactica

US 1979 125m colour
Universal (John Dykstra)

A spaceship crew battles its way back towards Earth.

Cobbled together from episodes of an unsuccessful TV series, the movie resembles a space version of another TV series, *Bonanza*, and borrows heavily from *Star Wars* to little effect.

w Glen A. Larson   d Richard A. Colla   ph Ben Coleman   m Stu Phillips   ad John E. Chilberg II
sp Apogee   ed Robert L. Kimble, Leon Ortiz-Gil, Larry Strong

Richard Hatch, Dirk Benedict, Lorne Greene, Ray Milland, Lew Ayres, Jane Seymour, Wilfred Hyde-White, John Colicos, Patrick Macnee

Be Big*

US 1931 20m bw
Hal Roach
V

Ollie feigns illness to avoid a trip with

his wife, but Stan's help proves disastrous.

Comedy warm-up for *Sons of the Desert;* Ollie spends most of the second reel trying to rid himself of a tight boot.

w H. M. Walker   d James Parrott

Laurel and Hardy, Anita Garvin, Isabelle Keith

The Bear**
France   1989   98m   Eastmancolor   Panavision
Tri-Star/Renn/Price Entertainment (Claude Berri)
V, L

An orphaned bear cub tries to cope with life in the wild.

Charming film, told from the bear's point of view, with natural sounds substituting for dialogue.

w Gérard Brach   novel *The Grizzly King* by James Oliver Curwood
d Jean-Jacques Annaud
ph Philippe Rousselot   m Philippe Sarde   pd Toni Ludi   ed Noelle Boisson

Bart, Youk, Jack Wallace, Tcheky Karyo, André Lacombe
AAN: best film editing

The Bears and I
US   1974   89m   Technicolor
Walt Disney (Winston Hibler)

An army veteran goes to live near an Indian settlement and adopts three bear cubs, later becoming a Park Ranger.

Simple, pleasing outdoor family film.

w John Whedon   novel Robert Franklin Leslie   d Bernard McEveety   ph Ted D. Landon   m Buddy Baker

Patrick Wayne, Chief Dan George, Andrew Duggan, Michael Ansara

The Beastmaster
US   1982   118m   colour
EMI/Ecta/Leisure Investments (Paul Pepperman, Sylvio Tabet)
V

A royal child, stolen at birth by a witch, is rescued by a peasant who brings him up skilled in the martial arts.

Comic strip sword and sorcery: fairly high budget but very low intelligence.

w Don Coscarelli, Paul Pepperman
d Don Coscarelli   ph John Alcott   m Lee Holdridge
pd Conrad E. Angone   ed Roy Watts

Marc Singer, Tanya Roberts, Rip Torn, John Amos, Rod Loomis

Beastmaster 2: Through the Portals of Time
US   1991   107m   CFI colour
Republic/Films 21 (Sylvio Tabet)
V

A mythical warrior and his animal friends are transported through time to present-day Los Angeles to battle against his evil brother.

More comic-strip sword and sorcery: very low budget, even lower intelligence.

w R. J. Robertson, Jim Wynorski, Sylvio Tabet, Ken Hauser, Doug Miles   novel *The Beastmaster* by André Norton   d Sylvio Tabet
ph Ronn Schmid   m Robert Folk   pd Allen Jones   ed Adam Bernardi

Marc Singer, Kari Wuhrer, Wings Hauser, Sarah Douglas, Charles Young

'Despite this low-budget sequel's silly dialogue and cheesy special effects . . . a mildly engaging tongue-in-cheek fantasy.' – *Variety*

'The most beautiful love story ever told.'
Beauty and the Beast***
US 1991 85m Technicolor
Buena Vista/Walt Disney/Silver Screen Partners IV (Don Hahn)

A prince, turned into a beast by enchantment, is rescued by the love of a beautiful girl.

A return to top form by Disney, with excellent animation and a singable score. The picture has been credited with starting a new Hollywood fashion for animated musicals.

w Linda Woolverton   d Gary Trousdale, Kirk Wise   m/ly Alan Menken, Howard Ashman
ad Brian McEntee   ed John Carnochan

voices of Paige O'Hara, Robby Benson, Jerry Orbach, Angela Lansbury, Richard White, David Ogden Stiers, Jesse Corti, Rex Everhart, Bradley Michael Pierce, Jo Anne Worley, Kimmy Robertson

'A lovely film that ranks with the best of Disney's animated classics.' – *Variety*
'It's got storytelling vigour and clarity, bright eclectic animation, and a frisky musical wit.' – *New Yorker*

AA: Alan Menken; song 'Beauty and the Beast' (m Alan Menken, ly Howard Ashman)
AAN: film; song 'Belle'; song 'Be Our Guest'; sound

Bedknobs and Broomsticks
US 1971 117m Technicolor
Walt Disney (Bill Walsh)
V, L

In 1940 three evacuee children and a kindly witch ride on a magic bedstead and defeat the invasion of England.

Extraordinarily dishevelled and incompetent Disney follow-up to *Mary Poppins*, a very muddled narrative with few high points and evidence of much cutting. Redeemed occasionally by camera trickery.

w Bill Walsh, Don DaGradi
d Robert Stevenson   ph Frank Phillips   m/ly Richard M. Sherman, Robert B. Sherman   sp Eustace Lycett, Alan Maley, Danny Lee

Angela Lansbury, David Tomlinson, Roy Smart, Cindy O'Callaghan, Sam Jaffe, Roddy McDowall, Bruce Forsyth, Tessie O'Shea, Reginald Owen

AA: special visual effects (Alan Maley, Eustace Lycett, Danny Lee)
AAN: Richard M. Sherman, Robert B. Sherman; song 'The Age of Not Believing' by the Shermans

'The head of the family is the one with the tail.'
Beethoven
US 1992 87m DeLuxe
UIP/Universal (Joe Medjuck, Michael C. Gross)
V

A St Bernard dog causes havoc in a family household to the delight of the children and the annoyance of their father.

Predictable comedy of the dreariest kind.

w Edmond Dantes, Amy Holden Jones   d Brian Levant   ph Victor J. Kemper   m Randy Edelman
pd Alex Tavoularis   ed Sheldon Kahn, William D. Gordean

Charles Grodin, Bonnie Hunt, Dean Jones, Oliver Platt, Stanley Tucci,

David Duchovny, Patricia Heaton, Laurel Cronin, O-Lan Jones

'Could be called harmless if it wasn't so badly made and blandly characterised.' – *Derek Malcolm, Guardian*

'Laugh? We wait like locked-in dogs whose noses are pressed to the window for the first sign of life or human interest coming up the driveway. Wit we have already despaired of in reel one.' – *Nigel Andrews, Financial Times*

† Inevitably, a sequel is on its way.

The Belles of St Trinian's*
GB 1954 91m bw
BL/London Films/Launder and Gilliat
V

At an unruly and bankrupt school for girls, more time is spent backing horses than studying subjects, and the headmistress's bookmaker brother has a scheme or two of his own.

Fairly successful film version of Ronald Searle's awful schoolgirl cartoons, the emphasis shifted to a grotesque older generation with the star in drag. An enormous commercial success, but the three sequels *Blue Murder at St Trinian's*, *The Pure Hell of St Trinian's*, *The Great St Trinian's Train Robbery* went from bad to awful.

w Frank Launder, Sidney Gilliat, Val Valentine   d Frank Launder
ph Stan Pavey   m Malcolm Arnold

Alastair Sim, George Cole, Joyce Grenfell, Hermione Baddeley, Betty Ann Davies, Renée Houston, Beryl Reid, Irene Handl, Mary Merrall

'Not so much a film as an entertainment on celluloid, a huge charade, a rich pile of idiotic and splendidly senseless images.' – *David Robinson*

Below Zero**
US 1930 20m bw
Hal Roach

Street musicians treat a policeman to lunch on the contents of a found wallet which turns out to be his.

Slow-paced but likeable star comedy from their best period.

w H. M. Walker   d James Parrott

Laurel and Hardy, Frank Holliday, Tiny Sandford

The Belstone Fox*
GB 1973 103m Eastmancolor Todd-AO 35
Rank/Independent Artists (Sally Shuter)
V

A fox and a hound grow up together but the fox leads to tragedy for its masters.

Good animal and countryside photography barely compensate for a fragmentary story with unpleasant moments or for a muddled attitude towards humans and animals; one is not clear what audience the result is supposed to appeal to.

wd James Hill   novel *The Ballad of The Belstone Fox* by David Rook
ph John Wilcox, James Allen
m Laurie Johnson

Eric Porter, Rachel Roberts, Jeremy Kemp, Bill Travers, Dennis Waterman

Benji*
US 1974 86m CFI color
Mulberry Square (Joe Camp)

A stray mongrel dog saves two kidnapped children.

Family film par excellence which rang the box-office bell in a big way in the US. Its modest merits are rather beside the point.

wd Joe Camp   *ph* Don Reddy
m Euel Box

Peter Breck, Edgar Buchanan, Terry Carter, Christopher Connelly

† A sequel, *For the Love of Benji*, followed in 1977. In 1980 came the curious *Oh Heavenly Dog* (qv). Then in 1987 the same team presented a quirky movie of a different kind: *Benji the Hunted* (qv).
AAN: song 'I Feel Love' (*m* Euel Box, *ly* Betty Box)

Benji the Hunted
US   1987   88m   CFI Color
Mulberry Square/Embark/Buena Vista (Ben Vaughn)

A mongrel dog is shipwrecked and fosters a pack of cougar cubs.

Freaky fable about a dog with a high IQ; but the training is remarkable.

wd Joe Camp   *ph* Don Reddy
m Euel Box, Betty Box   *sp* Bryan L. Renfro, Frank and Juanita Inn (Benji's trainers)

Benji, Frank Inn (trainer), Red Steagall

Berth Marks
US   1929   20m   bw   silent
Hal Roach
V, V(C)

Stan and Ollie, on a train, have to share an upper berth.

Overstretched single-situation comedy, one of the team's poorest.

w Leo McCarey, H. M. Walker
d Lewis R. Foster

Laurel and Hardy

Big**
US   1988   102m   DuArt/DeLuxe
TCF (James L. Brooks, Robert Greenhut, Anne Spielberg, Gary Ross)
V

A 13-year-old boy has his wish to grow 'big' granted by a carnival wishing machine.

Magic fun, better done than it has been since *Turnabout* in 1940.

w Gary Ross, Anne Spielberg
d Penny Marshall   *ph* Barry Sonnenfeld   *m* Howard Shore
pd Santo Loquasto

Tom Hanks, Elizabeth Perkins, John Heard, Jared Rushton, Robert Loggia, David Moscow
AAN: Tom Hanks; best original screenplay

Big Business****
US   1929   20m   bw   silent
Hal Roach
V

Stan and Ollie fail to sell a Christmas tree to a belligerent householder.

Classic silent comedy consisting largely of a brilliant tit-for-tat routine of reciprocal destruction, to which scripting, acting and editing equally combine.

w Leo McCarey, H. M. Walker
d James W. Horne   *ed* Richard Currier

Laurel and Hardy, James Finlayson

Big Foot and the Hendersons: see *Harry and the Hendersons*

Big Red
US   1962   89m   Technicolor
Walt Disney (Winston Hibler)

An orphan boy protects a dog which later saves him from a mountain lion.

Simple boy-and-dog yarn with impressive Canadian settings.

w Louis Pelletier   *d* Norman Tokar   *ph* Edward Colman
m Oliver Wallace

Walter Pidgeon, Gilles Payant, Emile Genest

Black Beauty
US 1946 74m bw
TCF (Edward L. Alperson)

In Victorian England, a girl searches for her lost colt.

Stilted children's film with little relation to the book.

w Lillie Hayward, Agnes Christie Johnston   novel Anna Sewell   d Max Nosseck   ph J. Roy Hunt   m Dimitri Tiomkin

Mona Freeman, Richard Denning, Evelyn Ankers, J. M. Kerrigan, Terry Kilburn

Black Beauty*
GB 1971 106m colour
Tigon/Chilton (Tony Tenser)
L

A luckless horse passes from hand to hand but is finally restored to its original young master and has a happy retirement.

Pleasant, episodic animal story which stays pretty close to the book. A shade yawn-inducing for adults, but fine for children.

w Wolf Mankowitz   novel Anna Sewell   d James Hill   ph Chris Menges   m Lionel Bart, John Cameron

Mark Lester, Walter Slezak, Peter Lee Lawrence, Patrick Mower, John Nettleton, Maria Rohm

The Black Cauldron*
US 1985 80m Technicolor
Walt Disney Productions (Joe Hale)

A medieval hero combats magic swords, wicked witches and skeletal tyrants.

Assured but somehow quite forgettable Disney cartoon feature.

w David Jonas, Vance Gerry, Ted Berman, Richard Rich, Al Wilson, Roy Morita, Peter Young, Art Stevens, Joe Hale, from *The Chronicles of Prydain* by Lloyd Alexander   d Ted Berman, Richard Rich   key animator Walt Stanchfield   m Elmer Bernstein

voices of Freddie Jones, Nigel Hawthorne, John Hurt, John Huston, John Byner, Arthur Malet

† Production allegedly took ten years and cost 25 million dollars.

'A journey that begins where everything ends!'
The Black Hole*
US 1979 98m Technicolor Technovision
Walt Disney (Ron Miller)
V

A research team in space is welcomed aboard a mysterious survey ship poised on the edge of a black hole.

The special effects are superb, though achieved through a general gloom which is barely acceptable. But the story is an ill-worked-out remake of *Twenty Thousand Leagues Under the Sea*, the characterization is ridiculously inept, and the final disclosure that black holes are doorways to hell sends one home rather bemused.

w Jeb Rosebrook, Gerry Day   d Gary Nelson   ph Frank Phillips   m John Barry   pd Peter Ellenshaw

Maximilian Schell, Robert Forster, Anthony Perkins, Joseph Bottoms, Yvette Mimieux, Ernest Borgnine

'As pastiche, it sounds promising; as drama, encumbered with references to Cicero and Goethe, it is merely tedious.' – *John Halford, MFB*
'Rated PG, but the only danger to children is that it may make them think that outer space is not much fun any more.' – *New Yorker*
AAN: Frank Phillips

Black Jack
GB 1979 110m colour
Enterprise/Kestrel (Tony Garnett)

In 1750 Yorkshire, a rascally French sailor recovers from a hanging and has adventures on the road with a young apprentice.

The purpose of this costume adventure, from these creators, is obscure, but the execution of it is muddled and amateurish.

w none credited   *novel* Leon Garfield   *d* Kenneth Loach
ph Chris Menges   *m* Bob Pegg
ad Martin Johnson   *ed* Bill Shapter

Jean Franval, Stephen Hirst, Louise Cooper

'Ploddingly unpersuasive. Not only narrative clarity but simple credibility is lacking.' – *Tim Pulleine, MFB*

The Black Stallion*
US 1980 117m Technicolor
UA/Omni Zoetrope (Francis Coppola)
L

After a 1946 shipwreck, a boy and a stallion are cast up on the African shore; many years later, he rides the horse to victory at Santa Anita.

1980 seems a bit late for boy-and-horse pictures, but this one is so beautifully directed and photographed, if drastically overlong, that most adults thought their children should see it.

w Melissa Mathison, Jeanne Rosenberg, William D. Witliff
novel Walter Farley   *d* Carroll Ballard   *ph* Caleb Deschanel
m Carmine Coppola

Kelly Reno, Mickey Rooney, Teri Garr, Clarence Muse, Hoyt Axton

'A perfect gem – the beautiful craftsmanship alone makes it a joy to behold.' – *Variety*
AAN: Mickey Rooney

The Black Stallion Returns
US 1983 93m Technicolor
MGM-UA/Coppola/Zoetrope (Tom Sternberg)
L

Rather desperate sequel in which a teenager loses his horse in Morocco and gets him back after various daredevil adventures.

Tame, predictable and boring.

w Richard Kletter, Jerome Kass
novel Walter Farley   *d* Robert Dalva   *ph* Carlo DiPalma
m Georges Delerue   *ad* Aurelio Crugnolo   *ed* Paul Hirsch

Kelly Reno, Ferdy Mayne, Woody Strode, Vincent Spano, Allen Goorwitz

'Well-intentioned, but overall it doesn't look like a winner.' – *Variety*

Blackbeard's Ghost
US 1967 107m Technicolor
Walt Disney (Bill Walsh)
V, L

The famous pirate returns as a ghost to help the old ladies who own a hotel he loved.

Ponderous and lengthy comedy, partially salvaged by performances.

w Bill Walsh, Don Da Gradi
d Robert Stevenson   *ph* Edward Colman   *m* Robert F. Brunner

Peter Ustinov, Dean Jones, Suzanne Pleshette, Elsa Lanchester, Richard Deacon

Blockheads***
US 1938 60m bw
Hal Roach/Stan Laurel
V, V(C)

Twenty years after World War I, Stan is still guarding a trench because nobody told him to stop. Olly takes him home to meet the wife, with disastrous consequences.

The last first-class Laurel and Hardy comedy is shapeless but hilarious, a fragmented reworking of earlier ideas, all of which work beautifully. Gags include encounters with a tip-up truck and an automatic garage, and a brilliantly worked out sequence up and down several flights of stairs.

w James Parrott, Harry Langdon, Felix Adler, Charles Rogers, Arnold Belgard   d John G. Blystone
ph Art Lloyd   m Marvin Hatley

Stan Laurel, Oliver Hardy, Billy Gilbert, Patricia Ellis, Minna Gombell, James Finlayson

'Hodge-podge of old-fashioned slapstick and hoke.' – Variety
AAN: Marvin Hatley

Bloomfield
GB 1969 95m Technicolor
World Film Services/Limbridge (John Heyman, Wolf Mankowitz)
US title: *The Hero*

A 10-year-old Israeli boy hitchhikes to Jaffa to see his football idol play his last game.

Sentimental whimsy, unattractively interpreted.

w Wolf Mankowitz   d Richard Harris   ph Otto Heller   m Johnny Harris

Richard Harris, Romy Schneider, Kim Burfield, Maurice Kaufmann, Yossi Yadin

Blotto*
US 1930 20m bw
Hal Roach
V, V(C)

Ollie helps Stan escape his wife for a night on the town, but the lady takes revenge.

Palatable star comedy with a strained second half following a splendidly typical opening.

w Leo McCarey, H. M. Walker
d James Parrott

Laurel and Hardy, Anita Garvin

The Blue Bird***
US 1940 98m Technicolor (bw prologue)
TCF (Gene Markey)

In a Grimm's Fairy Tale setting, the two children of a poor woodcutter seek the bluebird of happiness in the past, the future and the Land of Luxury, but eventually discover it in their own back yard.

An imaginative and often chilling script clarifies Maurice Maeterlinck's fairy play, and the art direction is outstanding, but the children are necessarily unsympathetic and the expensive production paled beside the success of the more upbeat *Wizard of Oz*, which was released almost simultaneously. Slashed for re-release, the only existing prints now open with confusing abruptness and no scene-setting before the adventures begin.

w Ernest Pascal   d Walter Lang
ph Arthur Miller, Ray Rennahan
m Alfred Newman   ad Richard Day, Wiard B. Ihnen

Shirley Temple, Johnny Russell, *Gale Sondergaard* (as the cat), *Eddie Collins* (as the dog), Nigel Bruce, Jessie Ralph, Spring Byington, Sybil Jason, Helen Ericson, Russell Hicks, Al Shean, Cecilia Loftus

'One of the most deliciously lovely productions to be brought to the screen.' – *MFB*

AAN: Arthur Miller, Ray Rennahan

The Blue Bird

US/USSR 1976 83m
    Technicolor Panavision
TCF/Edward Lewis/Lenfilm

Abortive remake of the above, widely touted as the first Russian–American co-production, but sabotaged by a flabby script, unsuitable casting and unresolved production problems.

w Hugh Whitemore, Alfred Hayes
d George Cukor   ph Freddie Young, Ionas Gritzus   m Irwin Kostal, Andrei Petrov

Elizabeth Taylor (as Mother, Maternal Love, Light and the Witch), Ava Gardner, Cicely Tyson, Jane Fonda, Harry Andrews, Will Geer, Mona Washbourne, George Cole

'It works so hard at making history that it forgets to make sense.' – *David Sterritt, Christian Science Monitor*
'If you have any naughty children you want to punish, take them to *The Blue Bird* and make them sit all the way through it.' – *William Wolf, Cue*
'It turns a work for adults that children can enjoy into a charade for children that must sicken adults.' – *John Simon, New Yorker*
'Senile and interminable.' – *Stephen Farber, New West*
'Lavishly done; limited box office.' – *Variety*

Blue Murder at St Trinians*

GB 1957 86m bw
British Lion/John Marvel (Launder and Gilliat)
V

The awful schoolgirls win a UNESCO prize trip which takes them to Rome where they become involved with a jewel thief.

Possibly the best of this series, which isn't saying much. See *The Belles of St Trinians*.

w Frank Launder, Val Valentine, Sidney Gilliat   d Frank Launder
ph Gerald Gibbs   m Malcolm Arnold

Terry-Thomas, George Cole, Joyce Grenfell, Alastair Sim, Judith Furse, Sabrina, Lionel Jeffries, Lloyd Lamble, Thorley Walters, Kenneth Griffith, Eric Barker, Richard Wattis

The Blue Peter

GB 1955 93m Eastmancolor
British Lion/Beaconsfield (Herbert Mason)
US title: *Navy Heroes*

A confused war hero becomes a trainer at an Outward Bound school for boys.

Pleasant but uninspired open air adventure for young people.

w Don Sharp, John Pudney
d Wolf Rilla   ph Arthur Grant
m Antony Hopkins

Kieron Moore, Greta Gynt, Sarah Lawson, Mervyn Johns, Ram Gopal, Edwin Richfield, Harry Fowler, John Charlesworth

BMX Bandits

Australia 1984 90m colour
    Panavision
Rank/BMX/Nilsen (Tom Broadbridge, Paul Davies)

Bike enthusiasts become unpopular when they cause havoc in the streets, but become heroes when they capture bank robbers.

Lively action piece with unacceptable behaviour followed by reformation and an old-fashioned moral for early teenagers.

w Patrick Edgeworth   story Russell Hagg   d Brian Trenchard-Smith   ph John Seale   m Colin Stead, Frank Strangio   pd Ross Major   ed Alan Lake

David Argue, John Ley, Nicole Kidman, Bryan Marshall, Angelo d'Angelo

The Boatniks*
US   1970   100m   Technicolor
Walt Disney (Ron Miller)

An accident-prone coastguard officer creates havoc at a yachting marina but is acclaimed a hero after catching three jewel thieves.

Simple fresh-air farce for the family, pleasantly set but flatly directed.

w Arthur Julian   d Norman Tokar   ph William Snyder   m Robert F. Brunner

Phil Silvers, Robert Morse, Stefanie Powers, Norman Fell, Mickey Shaughnessy, Wally Cox, Don Ameche, Joey Forman

The Bohemian Girl*
US   1936   74m   bw
Hal Roach
V, V(C), L

Gypsies kidnap a nobleman's daughter and bring her up as their own.

One of several operettas reworked for Laurel and Hardy, this is an inoffensive entertainment which devotes too little care to their need for slowly built-up gag structure; their sequences tend to fizzle out and the singing is a bore.
operetta Michael W. Balfe   d James Horne, Charles Rogers   ph Art Lloyd, Francis Corby   md Nathaniel Shilkret   ed Bert Jordan, Louis McManus

Stan Laurel, Oliver Hardy, Mae Busch, Antonio Moreno, Jacqueline Wells, Darla Hood, Zeffie Tilbury, James Finlayson, Thelma Todd (for one song, apparently dubbed: presumably before her sudden death she had been cast as the heroine)

'A comedy with little or no comedy'.
– Variety

† There was in 1922 a British silent version with a splendid cast including Ivor Novello, Gladys Cooper, C. Aubrey Smith, Ellen Terry and Constance Collier.

Bomba the Jungle Boy
US   1949   71m   bw or sepia
Monogram (Walter Mirisch)

Photographers in Africa meet a junior Tarzan who rescues their girl friend.

Cut-rate hokum starring the lad who had played Johnny Weissmuller's 'son' in earlier Tarzan movies; it led to several tedious sequels.

w Jack de Witt, from the comic strip by Roy Rockwell   d Ford Beebe   ph William Sickner   m Edward Kay

Johnny Sheffield, Peggy Ann Garner, Onslow Stevens, Charles Irwin

† Sequels were as follows:

1948: BOMBA ON PANTHER ISLAND (76m) with Allene Roberts
1949: BOMBA AND THE LOST VOLCANO (76m) with Donald Woods; BOMBA AND

THE HIDDEN CITY (71m) with Paul Guilfoyle
1950: BOMBA AND THE ELEPHANT STAMPEDE (71m) with Myron Sealey
1951: BOMBA AND THE AFRICAN TREASURE (70m) with Lyle Talbot; BOMBA AND THE JUNGLE GIRL (70m) with Karen Sharpe; BOMBA AND THE LION HUNTERS (75m) with Morris Ankrum
1953: SAFARI DRUMS (71m) with Douglas Kennedy
1954: THE GOLDEN IDOL (71m) with Paul Guilfoyle; KILLER LEOPARD (70m) with Beverly Garland
1955: LORD OF THE JUNGLE (69m) with Wayne Morris

Bonnie Prince Charlie
GB 1948 140m approx (later cut to 118m) Technicolor
British Lion/London Films (Edward Black)
V

The hope of the Stuarts returns from exile but is eventually forced to flee again.

Good highland photography combines with appalling studio sets, an initially confused narrative, a draggy script and uneasy performances to produce an ill-fated attempt at a British historical epic. Alexander Korda, who masterminded it, sulked in public at the critical roasting, but on this occasion the critics were right.

w Clemence Dane   d Anthony Kimmins   ph Robert Krasker   m Ian Whyte

David Niven, Margaret Leighton, Jack Hawkins, Judy Campbell, Morland Graham, Finlay Currie, John Laurie

'I have a sense of wonder about this film, beside which *The Swordsman* seems like a dazzling work of veracity and art. It is that London Films, having surveyed the finished thing, should not have quietly scrapped it.' – *Richard Winnington*

'The picture is not lacking in moments of unconscious levity, what with David Niven rallying his hardy Highlanders to his standard in a voice hardly large enough to summon a waiter.' – *New Yorker*

'Time has made it the film industry's biggest joke. But the joke turns a little sour when one reflects how extravagance, recklessness and sheer bungling administration during the fat and prosperous years left the British film industry so poor and vulnerable when the hard times came along.' – *Gerald Garret, 1975*

Bonnie Scotland*
US 1935 80m bw
MGM/Hal Roach
V

Two Americans journey to Scotland to collect a non-existent inheritance, then follow their friend in the army and wind up in India.

Generally disappointing star comedy which still contains excellent sequences when it is not vainly trying to preserve interest in a boring plot. An obvious parody on *Lives of a Bengal Lancer*, released earlier that year; Scotland has almost nothing to do with it.

w Frank Butler, Jeff Moffitt   d James Horne   ph Art Lloyd, Walter Lundin   ed Bert Jordan

Stan Laurel, Oliver Hardy, James Finlayson, Daphne Pollard, William Janney, June Lang

'Packed with Laurel and Hardy hokum and good for plenty of laughs' – *Boxoffice*

Born Free**

GB 1966 95m Technicolor
Panavision
Columbia/Open Road (Carl Foreman)/High Road/Atlas (Sam Jaffe, Paul Radin)
V, L

A Kenyan game warden and his wife rear three lion cubs, one of which eventually presents them with a family.

Irresistible animal shots salvage this rather flabbily put together version of a bestselling book. An enormous commercial success, it was followed by the even thinner *Living Free*, by a TV series, and by several semi-professional documentaries.

w Gerald L. C. Copley book Joy Adamson d James Hill
ph Kenneth Talbot m John Barry

Virginia McKenna, Bill Travers, Geoffrey Keen

AA: John Barry; title song (*m* John Barry, *ly* Don Black)

The Boy and the Pirates

US 1960 84m Eastmancolor
Perceptovision
United Artists

A small boy finds an old bottle on the seashore, wishes he could live in pirate days, and hey presto.

Modest juvenile fantasy on the lines of *The Wizard of Oz* but without the talent.

w Lillie Hayward, Jerry Sackheim
d Bert I. Gordon

Charles Herbert, Susan Gordon, Murvyn Vye, Paul Guilfoyle

Boys Will Be Boys**

GB 1935 75m bw
Gaumont/Gainsborough (Michael Balcon)
V

An incompetent headmaster thwarts a jewel robber.

The first recognizable Will Hay vehicle, based in part on J. B. Morton's Narkover sketches.

w Will Hay, Robert Edmunds
d William Beaudine ph Charles Van Enger m Louis Levy

Will Hay, Gordon Harker, Jimmy Hanley, Davy Burnaby, Norma Varden, Claude Dampier, Charles Farrell, Percy Walsh

'It is hard to see how his distinctive sketch writing could have found a satisfactory screen equivalent. Nevertheless, a good augury of the films to come.' – *Ray Seaton and Roy Martin, 1978*

The Brass Bottle

US 1964 89m Eastmancolor
U-I/Scarus (Robert Arthur)

A young architect finds an old brass bottle which contains a troublesome genie.

Simple-minded farce with little invention and poor trickwork.

w Oscar Brodney novel F. Anstey d Harry Keller
ph Clifford Stine m Bernard Green sp Roswell Hoffman

Tony Randall, Burl Ives, Barbara Eden, Edward Andrews, Ann Doran

Brats*

US 1930 20m bw
Hal Roach

Stan and Ollie have trouble baby-sitting their own mischievous kids.

Fairly ambitious star comedy with trick sets and photography enabling Laurel and Hardy to play their own sons. About half the gags come off.

w Leo McCarey, H. M. Walker, Hal Roach d James Parrott
ph George Stevens ed Richard Currier

Stan Laurel, Oliver Hardy

The Brave Little Toaster

US 1987 90m DeLuxe
Castle Premier/Hyperion/Kushner-Locke/
  Wang Film/Global Communications
  (Donald Kushner, Thomas L. Wilhite)
L

Domestic appliances go in search of their owner.

Odd fantasy of pots and pans with no more than adequate animation.

w Jerry Rees, Joe Ranft
novel Thomas M. Disch d Jerry Rees m David Newman

voices of Jon Levitz, Tim Stack, Timothy E. Day, Thurl Ravenscroft, Deanna Oliver, Phil Hartman, Joe Ranft

The Brave One*

US 1956 100m Technicolor
  Cinemascope
King Brothers

A small boy saves the life of his pet bull when it is sent into the ring.

Mildly beguiling minor drama for those who adore small boys and bulls.

w Harry Franklin, Merrill G. White story Robert Rich
d Irving Rapper ph Jack Cardiff
m Victor Young ed Merrill G. White

Michel Ray, Rodolfo Hoyos, Elsa Cardenas, Joi Lansing, Carlos Navarro

AA: Robert Rich. (There was much confusion when the mysterious Rich turned out to be Dalton Trumbo, who was blacklisted at the time.)
AAN: editing

Brewster's Millions

US 1985 97m Technicolor
Universal (Lawrence Gordon, Joel Silver)

A baseball player learns that in order to inherit 30 million dollars he must spend one million a day for 30 days.

Frantically noisy remake of an old chestnut.

w Herschel Weingrod, Timothy Harris d Walter Hill ph Ric Waite m Ry Cooder pd John Vallone ed Freeman Davis, Michel Ripps

Richard Pryor, John Candy, Lonette McKee, Stephen Collins, Jerry Orbach, Pat Hingle, Tovah Feldshuh

Bright Eyes*

US 1934 84m bw
Fox (Sol M. Wurtzell)

An orphan finds herself torn between foster-parents.

The first of Shirley Temple's genuine star vehicles has a liveliness and cheerfulness hard to find today. As a production, however, it is decidedly economical.

w William Conselman d David Butler ph Arthur Miller
m Samuel Kaylin

Shirley Temple, James Dunn, Lois Wilson, Jane Withers, Judith Allen

'It seems a cinch to please generally, the family and sentimental strata particularly.' – Variety

Buck Privates*
US 1941 84m bw
Universal (Alex Gottlieb)
GB title: *Rookies*

Two incompetents accidentally enlist in the army.

Abbott and Costello's first starring vehicle is a tired bundle of army jokes and old routines separated by plot and romance, but it sent the comedians right to the top, where they stayed for ten years.

w Arthur T. Horman *d* Arthur Lubin *ph* Milton Krasner *md* Charles Previn

Bud Abbott, Lou Costello, Lee Bowman, Alan Curtis, Jane Frazee, *The Andrews Sisters, Nat Pendleton*, Samuel S. Hinds, Shemp Howard

AAN: Charles Previn; song 'The Boogie Woogie Bugle Boy of Company B' (*m* Hugh Prince, *ly* Don Raye)

Buck Privates Come Home
US 1946 77m bw
U-I (Robert Arthur)
GB title: *Rookies Come Home*

Incompetent war veterans are demobilized and find civilian life tough.

Thin star comedy with a good final chase.

w John Grant, Frederic I. Rinaldo, Robert Lees *d* Charles T. Barton *ph* Charles Van Enger

Bud Abbott, Lou Costello, Beverly Simmons, Tom Brown, Nat Pendleton

Buck Rogers in the 25th Century
US 1979 89m colour
Universal (Richard Coffey)

Launched 500 years into the future, an astronaut helps save civilization.

Dull and bland version of comic strip heroics, originally made for television, which lacks even the low-budget charm of the 30s serial.

w Glen A. Larson, Leslie Stevens *d* Daniel Haller *ph* Frank Beascoechea *m* Stu Phillips *ad* Paul Peters *ed* John J. Dumas

Gil Gerard, Pamela Hensley, Erin Gray, Henry Silva, Tim O'Connor, Joseph Wiseman, Duke Butler, Felix Silla, Mel Blanc (voice)

The Buddy Holly Story
US 1978 113m colour
Columbia/Innavisions/ECA (Fred Bauer)
L

The life of a fifties rock-and-roller who died young in an accident.

Solidly carpentered showbiz biopic for the youth market.

w Robert Gitler *d* Steve Rash *ph* Stevan Larner *md* Joe Renzetti

Gary Busey, Dan Stroud, Charles Martin Smith, Bill Jordan, Maria Richwine

'A B movie leavened by grade-A talent.' – Les Keyser, *Hollywood in the Seventies*

AA: Joe Renzetti
AAN: Gary Busey

Buddy's Song
GB 1990 106m Eastmancolor
Castle Premier/Buddy/Bill Curbishley, Roy Baird, Roger Daltrey
V, L

A rock 'n' roll father becomes manager of his son's more modern band, with mixed results.

Dreary attempt at a generation gap musical, unlikely to appeal to any age-group.

w Nigel Hinton novel Nigel Hinton d Claude Whatham ph John Hooper m Roger Daltrey pd Grant Hicks ed John Grover

Roger Daltrey, Chesney Hawkes, Sharon Duce, Michael Elphick, Douglas Hodge, Paul McKenzie

'Breezy, anodyne fare better suited to the tube.' – *Variety*

Bugsy Malone**
GB 1976 93m Eastmancolor
Rank/Bugsy Malone Productions (David Puttnam, Allan Marshall)
V, L

New York 1929: gangster Fat Sam fights it out with Dandy Dan, and the best man wins the girl.

Extremely curious musical gangster spoof with all the parts played by children and the guns shooting ice cream. Very professionally done, but one wonders to whom it is supposed to appeal.

wd *Alan Parker* ph Michael Seresin, Peter Biziou m/songs Paul Williams pd Geoffrey Kirkland

Scott Baio, Jodie Foster, Florrie Dugger, John Cassisi

'If for nothing else, you would have to admire it for the sheer doggedness of its eccentricity.' – *David Robinson, The Times*
'All the pizazz in the world couldn't lift it above the level of empty camp.' – *Frank Rich, New York Post*
'I only wish the British could make adult movies as intelligent as this one.' – *Michael Billington, Illustrated London News*
'In an uncanny way the movie works as a gangster movie and we remember that the old Bogart and Cagney classics had a childlike innocence too. The world was simpler then. Now it's so complicated maybe only a kid can understand the Bogart role.' – *Roger Ebert*
AAN: Paul Williams

The Bulldog Breed
GB 1960 97m bw
Rank (Hugh Stewart)
V

A grocer joins the navy.

Elementary raw recruit comedy with many familiar ruses.

w Jack Davies, Henry Blyth, Norman Wisdom d Robert Asher

Norman Wisdom, Edward Chapman, Ian Hunter, David Lodge, Robert Urquhart, Eddie Byrne, Peter Jones

'A farce which ought never to have put to sea.' – *MFB*

Bush Christmas
GB 1947 77m bw
ABFD/Children's Entertainment Films (Ralph Smart)

Australian children on holiday help catch horse thieves.

Rather stolid family feature which got a reputation it hardly deserved.

wd Ralph Smart

Chips Rafferty, John Fernside, Stan Tolshurst, Pat Penny, Thelma Grigg, John McCallum

Busy Bodies**
US 1933 20m bw
MGM/Hal Roach
V

Stan and Ollie are involved in various disasters in a sawmill.

Though not among their most sympathetic comedies, this is a

sustained and brilliantly contrived slapstick sequence.

w Anon (and Stan Laurel) d Lloyd French ph Art Lloyd ed Bert Jordan

Laurel and Hardy, Tiny Sandford, Charlie Hall

C

Calamity Jane**
US 1953 101m Technicolor
Warner (William Jacobs)
V, L

Calamity helps a saloon owner friend find a star attraction, and wins the heart of Wild Bill Hickok.

Agreeable, cleaned-up, studio-set Western musical patterned after *Annie Get Your Gun*, but a much friendlier film, helped by an excellent score.

w James O'Hanlon d David Butler ph Wilfrid Cline md Ray Heindorf ch Jack Donohue m/ly Sammy Fain, Paul Francis Webster

Doris Day, Howard Keel, Allyn McLerie, Phil Carey, Dick Wesson, Paul Harvey

AA: song 'Secret Love'
AAN: Ray Heindorf

Call of the Wild*
US 1935 81m bw
Twentieth Century (Darryl F. Zanuck)

A young widow falls in love with a wild Yukon prospector.

Inaccurate but pleasing adaptation of an adventure novel with dog interest.

w Gene Fowler, Leonard Praskins novel Jack London d William Wellman ph Charles Rosher m Alfred Newman

Clark Gable, Loretta Young, Jack Oakie, Reginald Owen, Frank Conroy

'The lion-hearted dog emerges as a stooge for a rather conventional pair of human lovebirds . . . looks like box office.' – *Variety*

Call of the Wild
GB/W. Germany/Spain/Italy/France 1972 105m Eastmancolor
Massfilms/CCC/Izaro/Oceania/UPF (Harry Alan Towers)

During the Klondike gold rush, a stolen dog becomes a miner's best friend before joining the wolf-pack.

Closer to the book than the previous version, but curiously scrappy and unsatisfactory.

w Harry Alan Towers, Wyn Wells, Peter Yeldman d Ken Annakin ph John Vabrera, Dudley Lovell m Carlo Rustichelli

Charlton Heston, Michèle Mercier, Raimund Harmstorf, George Eastman

Camelot**
US 1967 181m Technicolor Panavision 70
Warner (Jack L. Warner)
V, L

King Arthur marries Guinevere, loses her to Lancelot, and is forced into war.

A film version of a long-running Broadway show with many excellent moments. Unfortunately the director cannot make up his mind whether to go for style or realism, and has chosen actors who cannot sing. The result is cluttered and overlong, with no real sense of period or sustained imagination, but the photography and the music linger in the mind.

w Alan Jay Lerner, novel *The Once And Future King* by T. H. White d Joshua Logan ph Richard H. Kline pd/costumes John Truscott md Ken Darby, Alfred Newman m/ly Frederick Loewe, Alan Jay Lerner ad Edward Carere

Richard Harris, Vanessa Redgrave, David Hemmings, Lionel Jeffries, Laurence Naismith, Franco Nero

'One wonders whether the fashion for musicals in which only the chorus can actually sing may be reaching its final stage.' — *MFB*
'Three hours of unrelieved glossiness, meticulous inanity, desperate and charmless striving for charm.' — *John Simon*
'The sets and costumes and people seem to be sitting there on the screen, waiting for the unifying magic that never happens.' — *New Yorker, 1977*
songs: 'The Merry Month of May'; 'Camelot'; 'If Ever I Would Leave You'; 'Take Me to the Fair'; 'C'est Moi'

AA: art direction; costumes; music direction
AAN: cinematography

Candleshoe
GB 1977 101m Technicolor
Walt Disney Productions (Hugh Attwooll)
L

An attempt to pass off a fake heiress to an English stately home is prevented by the resourceful butler.

Slackly handled comedy adventure full of easy targets and predictable incidents.

w David Swift, Rosemary Anne Sisson novel *Christmas at Candleshoe* by Michael Innes d Norman Tokar ph Paul Beeson m Ron Goodwin

David Niven, Helen Hayes, Jodie Foster, Leo McKern, Veronica Quilligan, Ian Sharrock, Vivian Pickles

'It might have been conceived by a computer called upon to produce the definitive pastiche of a Disney film of the 1970s.' — *Financial Times*

The Cannonball Run
US 1980 95m Technicolor
Golden Harvest (Albert S. Ruddy)
V, L

The adventures of ill-assorted contestants in the illegal Cannonball coast-to-coast race.

Well-known stars are all at sea in this comedy/disaster extravaganza, which seems to have begun as a joke rather than a script.

w Brock Yates d Hal Needham ph Michael Butler md Al Capps

Burt Reynolds, Roger Moore, Farrah Fawcett, Dom DeLuise, Dean Martin, Sammy Davis Jnr, Adrienne Barbeau, Jack Elam, Bert Convy, Jamie Farr, Peter Fonda, Molly Picon, Bianca Jagger

'Lacking any recognizable plot or characterization, or indeed incidental invention, it merely offers a parade of inept whimsy and lame intra-mural reference.' — *Tim Pulleine, MFB*
'Moviegoers who relish the screech of tyres taking a fast turn on a narrow bend should have a whale of a time.' — *Daily Mail*

Cannonball Run II
US 1983 108m Technicolor
Golden Harvest/Warner (Albert S. Ruddy)

An Arab sheik puts up a million-dollar prize for the Cannonball Run.

Dispirited rehash of number one, with poor technique and non-performances by stars who should have known better than to get involved.

w Hal Needham, Albert S. Ruddy, Harvey Miller   d Hal Needham
ph Nick McLean   m Al Capps
ad Thomas E. Azzari   ed William Gordean, Carl Kress

Burt Reynolds, Dom DeLuise, Sammy Davis Jnr, Dean Martin, Jamie Farr, Telly Savalas, Shirley Maclaine, Frank Sinatra, Susan Anton, Catherine Bach, Richard Kiel, Tim Conway, Sid Caesar, Don Knotts, Ricardo Montalban, Jim Nabors, Henry Silva

Can't Stop the Music
US 1980 124m Metrocolor Panavision
EMI/Allan Carr

A Greenwich Village pop group hits the bigtime.

Curiously old-fashioned youth musical, unwisely touted as something special, which it isn't.

w Bronte Woodward, Allan Carr
d Nancy Walker   ph Bill Butler
m Jacques Morali

The Village People, Valerie Perrine, Paul Sand, Bruce Jenner, Tammy Grimes, June Havoc, Barbara Rush, Jack Weston

'The hype disaster of the 80s, a grisly rehash of the let's-start-a-group-of-our-own plot, peopled with butch gay stereotypes of both sexes pretending to be straight. The pervasive tackiness is unrelieved.' – Time Out
'Desperately knowing about the eighties but fixed remorselessly in a time warp of fifties hokum.' – Guardian
'All noise, lights, slogans, movement and dazzle, like a 124m commercial devoted to selling you a product you can't use.' – Sunday Times
'One doesn't watch it, one is attacked by it.' – New England Entertainment Digest
'Considering the low level of wit, perhaps the Village People should consider renaming themselves the Village Idiots.' – Los Angeles Magazine
'This shamefully tacky musical extravaganza fails on every aesthetic level.' – Los Angeles Herald Examiner
'A forced marriage between the worst of sitcom plotting and the highest of high camp production numbers.' – New West

The Canterville Ghost*
US 1944 95m bw
MGM (Arthur Field)
V

The young girl heiress of an English castle introduces GIs to the resident ghost.

Leaden comedy a long way after Oscar Wilde, sunk by slow script and direction, but partly salvaged by the respective roguishness and infant charm of its stars.

w Edwin Blum   d Jules Dassin
ph Robert Planck   m George Bassman

Charles Laughton, Margaret O'Brien, Robert Young, William Gargan, Rags Ragland, Peter Lawford, Una O'Connor, Mike Mazurki

† In the mid 1970s, a television version starring David Niven was made by HTV.

'A million dollars worth of adventure! To do justice in words to its fascination is impossible!'

'His sword carved his name across the continents – and his glory across the seas!'
Captain Blood**
US 1935 119m bw
Warner (Harry Joe Brown)
V, L

A young British surgeon, wrongly condemned by Judge Jeffreys for helping rebels, escapes and becomes a Caribbean pirate.

Modestly produced but quite exhilarating pirate adventure notable for making a star of Errol Flynn. Direction makes the most of very limited production values.

w Casey Robinson   novel Rafael Sabatini   d Michael Curtiz   ph Hal Mohr   m Erich Wolfgang Korngold   ad Anton Grot

Errol Flynn, Olivia de Havilland, Basil Rathbone, Lionel Atwill, Guy Kibbee, Ross Alexander, Henry Stephenson, Forrester Harvey, Hobart Cavanaugh, Donald Meek

'A lavish, swashbuckling saga of the Spanish Main . . . it can't fail at the wickets.' – *Variety*
'Here is a fine spirited mix-up with clothes and wigs which sometimes hark back to the sixteenth century and sometimes forward to the period of Wolfe . . . one is quite prepared for the culminating moment when the Union Jack breaks proudly, anachronistically forth at Peter Blood's masthead.' – *Graham Greene*
'Magnificently photographed, lavishly produced, and directed with consummate skill.' – *Picturegoer*
AAN: best picture

Captain January*
US 1936 74m bw
TCF (Darryl F. Zanuck)

A little girl is rescued from a shipwreck by a lighthouse keeper.

Standard Shirley Temple vehicle with pleasing dialogue and numbers.

w Sam Hellman, Gladys Lehman, Harry Tugend   novel Laura E. Richards   d David Butler   ph John F. Seitz   m Louis Silvers   m/ly Lew Pollack, Sidney Mitchell, Jack Yellen

Shirley Temple, Guy Kibbee, Buddy Ebsen, Slim Summerville, June Lang, Sara Haden, Jane Darwell

Captain Nemo and the Underwater City
GB 1969 106m Metrocolor Panavision
MGM/Omnia (Steven Pallos, Bertram Ostrer)

Six survivors from an Atlantic shipwreck are picked up by a mysterious submarine and have adventures in a spectacular underwater city.

Further adventures of Jules Verne's engaging Victorian character from *Twenty Thousand Leagues under the Sea*. Here however the general production values are stolid rather than solid, and the script makes heavy weather.

w Pip Baker, Jane Baker, R. Wright Campbell   d James Hill   ph Alan Hume, Egil Woxholt   m Walter Stott   ad Bill Andrews

Robert Ryan, Chuck Connors, Bill Fraser, Kenneth Connor, Nanette Newman, John Turner, Luciana Paluzzi, Allan Cuthbertson

Captain Sinbad*
US/Germany 1963 88m Eastmancolor Wonderscope
King Brothers

Sinbad returns to Baristan and by means of magic deposes a sultan.

Rather splendid adventure fantasy

with a European flavour, good trick effects and full-blooded performances.

w Samuel B. West, Harry Relis d Byron Haskin ph Gunther Senftleben, Eugen Shuftan m Michel Michelet ad Werner and Isabell Schlicting sp Tom Howard

Guy Williams, Pedro Armendariz, Heidi Bruhl, Abraham Sofaer

Captains Courageous**
US 1937 116m bw
MGM (Louis D. Lighton)
V, L

A spoiled rich boy falls off a cruise liner and lives for a while among fisherfolk who teach him how to live.

Semi-classic Hollywood family film which is not all that enjoyable while it's on but is certainly a good example of the prestige picture of the thirties. (It also happened to be good box-office.)

w John Lee Mahin, Marc Connelly, Dale Van Every novel Rudyard Kipling d Victor Fleming ph Harold Rosson m Franz Waxman ed Elmo Vernon

Spencer Tracy, Lionel Barrymore, Freddie Bartholomew, Mickey Rooney, Melvyn Douglas, Charley Grapewin, Christian Rub, John Carradine, Walter Kingsford, Leo G. Carroll, Charles Trowbridge

'Will not have to go begging for patronage . . . one of the best pictures of the sea ever made.' – *Variety*
'Another of those grand jobs of movie-making we have come to expect from Hollywood's most profligate studio.' – *Frank S. Nugent, New York Times*

† 1977 brought a TV movie remake.

AA: Spencer Tracy
AAN: best picture; script; editing

Car Wash
US 1976 96m Technicolor
Universal
V

Various eccentrics congregate around the Dee Luxe Car Wash.

Zany ethnic (black) comedy with little rhyme or reason in its development but a certain vigour in some of its sketches. A subsequent TV series didn't last.

w Joel Schumacher d Michael Schultz

Franklyn Ajaye, Sully Boyar, Richard Pryor, Ivan Dixon, Antonio Fargas, Tracy Reed

'Its specialty is yanking laughs by having blacks do dirtier versions of the standard pranks that naughty kids used to do in comedies.' – *Pauline Kael*

The Care Bears' Adventure in Wonderland!
Canada 1987 75m colour
Fox/Nelvana Productions (Michael Hirsch, Patrick Loubert, Clive A. Smith)
V

The Care Bears go through the looking glass with Alice.

Undemanding and uninteresting whimsy for the under-sixes.

w Susi Snooks, John DeKlein story Peter Sauder d Raymond Jafelice m Trish Cullen, John Sebastian

voices of Colin Fox, Bob Dermer, Eva Almos, Dan Hennessy, Jim Henshaw

The Care Bears Movie

US 1985 75m colour
Nelvana (Michael Hirsch, Patrick Loubert, Clive Smith)
V

Magical bears combat an evil spirit who aims to make everybody miserable.

Cartoon feature, sluggishly animated and narrated, with appeal to nobody over five years old. Produced as a back-up to a range of toys.

w Peter Sauder d Arna Selznick m John Sebastian

voices of Mickey Rooney, Georgia Engel, Harry Dean Stanton

Carry On Abroad*

GB 1972 88m Eastmancolor
Fox-Rank/Peter Rogers
V

A couple who go on a package holiday to Spain find that their hotel is still being built and there is a staff of no more than three.

Every opportunity for bathroom jokes is relished in what is otherwise an average effort.

w Talbot Rothwell d Gerald Thomas ph Alan Hume m Eric Rogers ad Lionel Couch ed Alfred Roome

Sidney James, Kenneth Williams, Charles Hawtrey, Joan Sims, Bernard Bresslaw, Barbara Windsor, Kenneth Connor, Peter Butterworth, Jimmy Logan, June Whitfield, Hattie Jacques

'Travelling well-trodden paths of slapstick, *double entendre* and nudging innuendo.' – *Nigel Andrews*

Carry On Again Doctor

GB 1969 89m Eastmancolor
Rank/Adder (Peter Rogers)
V

A doctor, exiled to a tropical island, returns to Britain with a special slimming cure.

A slight air of desperation hangs over the often-used setting of a hospital, and most of the jokes remain in intensive care.

w Talbot Rothwell d Gerald Thomas ph Ernest Steward m Eric Rogers pd Jack Blezard ed Alfred Roome

Sidney James, Kenneth Williams, Jim Dale, Charles Hawtrey, Joan Sims, Barbara Windsor, Hattie Jacques, Patsy Rowlands, Peter Butterworth, Pat Coombs

'Perhaps the team go that much further than ever before. Their fans will be delighted; those who aren't won't care.' – *Richard Davis, Films and Filming*

Carry On at Your Convenience

GB 1971 90m Eastmancolor
Rank/Peter Rogers
V

A union leader at the firm of W. C. Boggs, makers of fine toiletware, keeps ordering the workers to come out on strike.

No toilet joke is left unplumbed here, and the result is dire.

w Talbot Rothwell d Gerald Thomas ph Ernest Steward m Eric Rogers ed Alfred Roome

Sidney James, Kenneth Williams, Charles Hawtrey, Joan Sims, Bernard Bresslaw, Hattie Jacques, Kenneth Cope, Patsy Rowlands, Jacki Piper, Richard O'Callaghan

'One of the least funny of this staggeringly successful series.' – *Eric Braun*
'Even more scrappily assembled than

usual and, with the exception of a fairly amusing parody of sex education films, the level of humour, though noticeably cleaner than of late, is still rock bottom.' – *David McGillivray*

Carry On Behind**
GB 1975 90m Eastmancolor
Fox-Rank/Peter Rogers
V

Archaeologists arrive to search for Roman remains at a caravan site full of holiday-makers.

One of the best of the series and certainly the last watchable film the team produced.

w Dave Freeman   *d* Gerald Thomas   *ph* Ernest Steward   *m* Eric Rogers   *ed* Alfred Roome

Elke Sommer, Kenneth Williams, Joan Sims, Bernard Bresslaw, Kenneth Connor, Peter Butterworth, Jack Douglas, Windsor Davies, Liz Fraser, Patsy Rowlands

'Emerges as the most consistently funny *Carry On* in many years ... a strong vein of comedy is mined from the simple situation of campsite overcrowding, with some of the best sight gags involving a lugubrious Irish wolf-hound and a foul-mouthed mynah bird.' – *Verina Glaessner, MFB*

Carry On Cabby*
GB 1963 91m bw
Anglo Amalgamated/Peter Rogers
V

The neglected wife of the owner of a taxi firm sets up a rival firm with women drivers.

A deft farcical battle of the sexes.

w Talbot Rothwell   *d* Gerald Thomas   *ph* Alan Hume   *m* Eric Rogers   *ed* Archie Ludski

Sidney James, Charles Hawtrey, Kenneth Connor, Hattie Jacques, Esma Cannon, Liz Fraser, Bill Owen, Milo O'Shea, Jim Dale

'The golden formula of the *Carry On* series is back with a bang.' – *Variety*

Carry On Cleo*
GB 1964 92m Eastmancolor
Anglo Amalgamated/Peter Rogers
V

Ancient Britons are captured by the Romans while Mark Antony carries on with Cleopatra.

Sporadically amusing parody of the Elizabeth Taylor epic, though it should have been much funnier.

w Talbot Rothwell   *d* Gerald Thomas   *ph* Alan Hume   *m* Eric Rogers   *ad* Bert Davey   *ed* Archie Ludski

Sidney James, Kenneth Williams, Charles Hawtrey, Joan Sims, Kenneth Connor, Jim Dale, Amanda Barrie, E. V. H. Emmett, Sheila Hancock, Jon Pertwee

'Gags, both verbal and visual, suffer from repetition.' – *Variety*

† As a result of a court case for breach of copyright brought by Twentieth Century-Fox, the film's poster, which parodied the advertising for *Cleopatra*, had to be withdrawn.

'Up your anchor for a well crewed voyage!!'
Carry On Columbus
GB 1992 91m colour
Island World/Comedy House/Peter Rogers
(John Goldstone)
V

Columbus's voyage to find a route to the East is sabotaged by spies in the pay of the Sultan of Turkey.

Ill-starred attempt, with a succession of single entendres and some inept performances, to revive a tired old formula.

w Dave Freeman d Gerald Thomas ph Alan Hume m John Du Prez pd Harry Pottle ed Chris Blunden

Jim Dale, Bernard Cribbins, Maureen Lipman, Peter Richardson, Rik Mayall, Alexei Sayle, Charles Fleischer, Larry Miller, Leslie Phillips, Julian Clary, Sara Crowe, Rebecca Lacey, Nigel Planer, June Whitfield, Richard Wilson

'Painfully unfunny, lacking imagination and energy.' – *Philip French, Observer*

Carry On Constable*
GB 1960 86m bw
Anglo Amalgamated/Peter Rogers
V

Four new and inept constables report for duty at their local police station.

In part a parody of the popular TV series *Dixon of Dock Green* and moderately amusing despite the absence of a plot.

w Norman Hudis story Brock Williams d Gerald Thomas ph Ted Scaife m Bruce Montgomery ad Carmen Dillon ed John Shirley

Sidney James, Kenneth Williams, Charles Hawtrey, Joan Sims, Kenneth Connor, Eric Barker, Leslie Phillips, Hattie Jacques, Shirley Eaton, Cyril Chamberlain, Irene Handl, Esma Cannon, Freddie Mills

'Simply an anthology of police gags and situations.' – *Variety*

Carry On Cowboy**
GB 1965 95m Eastmancolor
Anglo Amalgamated/Peter Rogers
V

A sanitary engineer is given the task of cleaning up a town being terrorized by outlaws.

Amusing parody of *High Noon* and other classic Westerns.

w Talbot Rothwell d Gerald Thomas ph Alan Hume m Eric Rogers ad Bert Davey ed Rod Keys

Sidney James, Kenneth Williams, Charles Hawtrey, Joan Sims, Jim Dale, Percy Herbert, Angela Douglas, Bernard Bresslaw, Peter Butterworth, Jon Pertwee

'Less a string of irrelevant situations than usual, giving the team more opportunity for comedy thesping.' – *Variety*

Carry On Cruising
GB 1962 89m Eastmancolor
Anglo Amalgamated/Peter Rogers
V

The captain of a cruise liner finds his peace of mind threatened by new crew members and tourists.

Weak comedy that doesn't seem to know where it's going.

w Norman Hudis story Eric Barker d Gerald Thomas ph Alan Hume m Bruce Montgomery, Douglas Gamley ad Carmen Dillon ed John Shirley

Sidney James, Kenneth Williams, Kenneth Connor, Liz Fraser, Dilys Laye, Esma Cannon, Lance Perceval, Ronnie Stevens, Cyril Chamberlain, Anton Rodgers

'Direction by Gerald Thomas is boisterously effective.' – *Variety*

Carry On Dick

GB 1974 91m Eastmancolor
Rank/Peter Rogers
V

Bow Street Runners ask a village clergyman to help them catch the highwayman Dick Turpin, better known as Big Dick.

Inspiration flags in a comedy where both cast and director seem hardly interested in what they were doing, probably because they had been doing it for too long.

w Talbot Rothwell story Lawrie Wyman, George Evans d Gerald Thomas ph Ernest Steward m Eric Rogers ed Alfred Roome

Sidney James, Kenneth Williams, Kenneth Connor, Barbara Windsor, Hattie Jacques, Bernard Bresslaw, Joan Sims, Peter Butterworth, Jack Douglas, Patsy Rowlands, Bill Maynard

'These tireless upholders of the "saucy" postcard tradition soldier on with their perennial rib-poking, elbow-nudging, albeit scarcely jaw-breaking esprit ... Maybe their continuing appeal is beyond criticism – or according to taste, beneath it.' – *Nigel Gearing, MFB*

Carry On Doctor*

GB 1968 94m Eastmancolor
Rank/Peter Rogers
V

Hospital patients revolt against a tyrannical matron when their favourite doctor is sacked.

Occasionally amusing farce.

w Talbot Rothwell d Gerald Thomas ph Alan Hume m Eric Rogers ed Alfred Roome

Frankie Howerd, Sidney James, Kenneth Williams, Jim Dale, Charles Hawtrey, Joan Sims, Barbara Windsor, Hattie Jacques, Anita Harris, Bernard Bresslaw, Peter Butterworth

'Usual unabashed mixture of double-meanings, down-to-earth vulgarity, blue jokes.' – *Variety*

Carry On – Don't Lose Your Head

GB 1966 90m Eastmancolor
Rank/Peter Rogers
V
aka: *Don't Lose Your Head*

A foppish Briton, the Black Fingernail, rescues French aristocrats from the guillotine during the French Revolution.

A limp parody of *The Scarlet Pimpernel* causes no more than a few chuckles.

w Talbot Rothwell d Gerald Thomas ph Alan Hume m Eric Rogers ed Rod Keys

Sidney James, Kenneth Williams, Jim Dale, Charles Hawtrey, Joan Sims, Peter Butterworth, Dany Robin, Peter Gilmore

'A crazy debauch of duelling, doublecrossing and disaster. The troupers jump through their well-known hoops with agility.' – *Variety*

Carry On – Follow That Camel

GB 1966 90m Eastmancolor
Rank/Peter Rogers
V
aka: *Follow That Camel*

An English gentleman, accused of behaving badly at cricket, joins the Foreign Legion to regain his honour.

An ill-match between American and English styles of vaudeville and music-hall humour results in a direly unamusing movie.

w Talbot Rothwell   d Gerald Thomas   ph Alan Hume   m Eric Rogers   ed Alfred Roome

Phil Silvers, Kenneth Williams, Jim Dale, Charles Hawtrey, Joan Sims, Peter Butterworth, Anita Harris, Bernard Bresslaw, Angela Douglas, Peter Gilmore

'It all works with considerable bounce, with elements of parody of Beau Geste-style movies for those alert to them. All the regular comics are on first-rate form.' – *Variety*

'A Great Guy With His Chopper!'
Carry On Henry**
GB 1971 89m Eastmancolor
Rank/Adder (Peter Rogers)
V

King Henry tries to get rid of his wife when he discovers she smells of garlic.

A coarsely successful parody of *Anne of the Thousand Days* and other period films.

w Talbot Rothwell   d Gerald Thomas   ph Alan Hume   m Eric Rogers   ed Alfred Roome

Sidney James, Kenneth Williams, Charles Hawtrey, Joan Sims, Terry Scott, Barbara Windsor, Kenneth Connor, Peter Butterworth, Peter Gilmore, Patsy Rowlands

'They have managed to come up with a bit of a winner . . . there is a delicious send up of that most boring and perennial line of cinematic yawns, the historical romance.' – *Peter Buckley*
'The cast is the familiar stock company at full force; the script is from Talbot Rothwell at his most characteristic; and the film is at any rate better looking than most of its shoe-string predecessors.' – *John Pidgeon, MFB*

Carry On Jack
GB 1964 91m Eastmancolor
Anglo Amalgamated/Peter Rogers
V
US title: *Carry On Venus*

A midshipman finds himself at the mercy of a bullying captain and they are both put overboard after a mutiny.

Salty but unamusing parody of *Mutiny on The Bounty* and other sea-faring sagas.

w Talbot Rothwell   d Gerald Thomas   ph Alan Hume   m Eric Rogers   ad Jack Shampan   ed Archie Ludski

Bernard Cribbins, Kenneth Williams, Charles Hawtrey, Juliet Mills, Donald Houston, Percy Herbert, Peter Gilmore, Jim Dale, Anton Rogers, Cecil Parker, Patrick Cargill

'Gerald Thomas steers his cast through a maze of mixups and misadventures.' – *Variety*

Carry On Matron*
GB 1972 87m Eastmancolor
Rank/Peter Rogers
V

A con-man persuades his son to dress as a nurse in order to infiltrate a maternity hospital to steal contraceptive pills.

Intermittently amusing comedy.

w Talbot Rothwell   d Gerald Thomas   ph Ernest Steward   m Eric Rogers   ad Lionel Couch   ed Alfred Roome

Sidney James, Kenneth Williams, Charles Hawtrey, Joan Sims, Hattie Jacques, Bernard Bresslaw, Terry Scott, Kenneth Cope, Barbara Windsor, Kenneth Connor, Jacki Piper, Patsy Rowlands, Jack Douglas

'A largely successful if slightly patchy addition to the series; its comic highlight involves Sid James, required to assume a medical alias, introducing himself as "Dr Zhivago".' – *Kenneth Thompson, MFB*

Carry On Nurse**
GB 1959 86m bw
Anglo Amalgamated/Peter Rogers
V

Male patients in a hospital rebel against the dictatorial matron.

The first true *Carry On*, done when the whole notion was still fresh and the cast responded with glee to its crudities.

w Norman Hudis   *story* Patrick Cargill, Jack Searle   *d* Gerald Thomas   *ph* Reg Wyer   *m* Bruce Montgomery   *ad* Alex Vetchinsky   *ed* John Shirley

Shirley Eaton, Kenneth Williams, Charles Hawtrey, Hattie Jacques, Joan Sims, Kenneth Connor, Terence Longden, Bill Owen, Leslie Phillips, Wilfrid Hyde-White, Irene Handl

'The yocks come thick and fast.' – *Variety*

'A seaside postcard come to life, a shameless procession of vulgarities. Utterly irresistible.' – *Andy Medhurst, Sight and Sound*

† The film topped the box-office in Britain and was surprisingly successful in the US where it ran for two-and-a-half years.

Carry On Regardless
GB 1960 90m bw
Anglo Amalgamated/Peter Rogers
V

A group of incompetent unemployed join an odd-job agency.

Less a film than a series of sketches, which are very variable in quality.

w Norman Hudis   *d* Ralph Thomas   *ph* Alan Hume   *m* Bruce Montgomery   *ed* John Shirley

Sidney James, Kenneth Williams, Charles Hawtrey, Joan Sims, Kenneth Connor, Bill Owen, Liz Fraser, Terence Longden, Esma Cannon, Hattie Jacques, Fenella Fielding

'Ingenuity of scriptwriter Norman Hudis is sometimes a bit strained, but he has come up with some sound comedy situations.' – *Variety*

Carry On Screaming*
GB 1966 97m Eastmancolor
Anglo Amalgamated/Peter Rogers
V

Police investigate a mad doctor and his sister, who are turning young women into mannequins.

A send-up of Hammer horrors that manages to emulate the garishness of the originals.

w Talbot Rothwell   *d* Gerald Thomas   *ph* Alan Hume   *m* Eric Rogers   *ed* Rod Keys

Harry H. Corbett, Kenneth Williams, Jim Dale, Charles Hawtrey, Fenella Fielding, Joan Sims, Angela Douglas, Bernard Bresslaw, Peter Butterworth, Jon Pertwee

'Puts the skids under horror pix. Snag is that most horror films themselves teeter on the edge of parody and it is rather tough trying to burlesque a parody.' – *Variety*

Carry On Sergeant
GB 1958 83m bw
Anglo Amalgamated/Insignia (Peter Rogers)

An army training sergeant accepts a bet that his last platoon of raw recruits will win the Star Squad award.

Shabby farce with humdrum script and slack direction, saved by energetic performances.

w Norman Hudis   play The Bull Boys by R. F. Delderfield   d Gerald Thomas   ph Peter Hennessy   m Bruce Montgomery

Bob Monkhouse, William Hartnell, Kenneth Williams, Charles Hawtrey, Shirley Eaton, Eric Barker, Dora Bryan, Bill Owen, Kenneth Connor

'They're At It Again – O.O.O.H!'

Carry On Spying
GB 1964 87m bw
Anglo Amalgamated/Peter Rogers
V

British spies are sent to recapture a secret formula stolen by the Society for Total Extinction of Non-Conforming Humans, otherwise known as Stench.

A feeble parody of the Bond films.

w Talbot Rothwell, Sid Colin   d Gerald Thomas   ph Alan Hume   m Eric Rogers   ed Archie Ludski

Kenneth Williams, Bernard Cribbins, Charles Hawtrey, Barbara Windsor, Eric Pohlmann, Eric Barker, Dilys Laye, Jim Dale, Richard Wattis

'A dazzling return to form, milking every last drop from the ripe targets of espionage in general and Bond in particular.' – Andy Medhurst, Sight and Sound

Carry On Teacher*
GB 1959 86m bw
Anglo Amalgamated/Peter Rogers
V

Pupils at a school sabotage the headmaster's attempts to get another job because they don't want to lose him.

Amiable comedy that is less frenetic than many in the series, and all the better for it.

w Norman Hudis   d Gerald Thomas   ph Reginald Wyer   m Bruce Montgomery   ed John Shirley

Ted Ray, Kenneth Williams, Charles Hawtrey, Leslie Phillips, Joan Sims, Kenneth Connor, Hattie Jacques, Rosalind Knight, Cyril Chamberlain

'The laughs come readily.' – Variety

Carry On up the Jungle
GB 1970 89m Eastmancolor
Rank/Peter Rogers
V

An ornithologist journeys to Africa in search of the rare Oozulum bird.

A tired parody of Tarzan and jungle films; the jokes get lost in the undergrowth.

w Talbot Rothwell   d Gerald Thomas   ph Ernest Steward   m Eric Rogers   ad Alex Vetchinsky   ed Alfred Roome

Frankie Howerd, Sidney James, Charles Hawtrey, Joan Sims, Terry Scott, Kenneth Connor, Bernard Bresslaw, Jacki Piper

'The film is an assured success.' – Films and Filming

Carry On up the Khyber***
GB 1968 88m Eastmancolor
Rank/Adder (Peter Rogers)
V

A Scots regiment, the Third Foot and Mouth, fails to defend British interests in India.

The best of the series, a wonderfully vulgar and ripe low comedy on an imperial theme.

w Talbot Rothwell   *d* Gerald Thomas   *ph* Alan Hume   *m* Eric Rogers   *ed* Alfred Roome

Sidney James, Kenneth Williams, Charles Hawtrey, Joan Sims, Roy Castle, Bernard Bresslaw, Peter Butterworth, Terry Scott, Angela Douglas, Cardew Robinson, Julian Holloway, Peter Gilmore

'Continues to rely primarily on low-comedy visual and verbal gag situations for its yocks.' – *Variety*

† The movie was filmed in Wales.

The Cat from Outer Space
US   1978   103m   Technicolor
Walt Disney Productions (Ron Miller)

A superintelligent extraterrestrial cat is forced to land on Earth for running repairs.

Fairly modest studio offering which pleased its intended market but could have been sharper.

w Ted Key   *d* Norman Tokar   *ph* Charles F. Wheeler   *m* Lalo Schifrin   *sp* Eustace Lycett, Art Cruickshank, Danny Dee

Ken Berry, Roddy McDowall, Sandy Duncan, Harry Morgan, McLean Stevenson, Jesse White, Alan Young, Hans Conried

Cattle Annie and Little Britches
US   1980   98m   CFI colour
Hemdale/UATC (David Korda)

In 1893, two girls head west in search of adventure.

Rather winsome family Western, with too little real action and too much romping about.

w Robert Ward   *novel* Robert Ward   *d* Lamont Johnson   *ph* Larry Pizer   *m* Sanh Berti, Tom Slocum

Burt Lancaster, John Savage, Rod Steiger, Diane Lane, Amanda Plummer, Scott Glenn, Steven Ford

Centennial Summer**
US   1946   102m   Technicolor
TCF (Otto Preminger)

A Philadelphia family responds to the Great Exposition of 1876.

Pleasing family comedy with music, the kind of harmless competence Hollywood used to throw off with ease but can no longer manage.

w Michael Kanin   *novel* Albert E. Idell   *d* Otto Preminger   *ph* Ernest Palmer   *m* Alfred Newman   *m/ly* Jerome Kern, Oscar Hammerstein II, E. Y. Harburg, Leo Robin

Jeanne Crain, Cornel Wilde, Linda Darnell, William Eythe, Walter Brennan, *Constance Bennett*, Dorothy Gish

AAN: Alfred Newman; song 'All Through the Day' (*m* Jerome Kern, *ly* Oscar Hammerstein II)

A Challenge for Robin Hood*
GB   1967   96m   Technicolor
Hammer (Clifford Parkes)

A retelling of the original Robin Hood legend.

Unassuming, lively, predictable adventure hokum.

w Peter Bryan   *d* C. Pennington-Richards   *ph* Arthur Grant   *m* Gary Hughes

Barrie Ingham, James Hayter, Leon Greene, John Arnatt, Peter Blythe, Gay Hamilton, William Squire

'Two men chasing dreams of glory!'
Chariots of Fire***
GB   1981   121m   colour
TCF/Allied Stars/Enigma (David Puttnam)
V, L

In the 1924 Paris Olympics, a Jew and a Scotsman run for Britain.

A film of subtle qualities, rather like those of a BBC classic serial. Probably not quite worth the adulation it received, but full of pleasant romantic touches and sharp glimpses of the wider issues involved.

w Colin Welland d Hugh Hudson ph David Watkin m Vangelis

Ben Cross, Ian Charleson, Nigel Havers, Nicholas Farrell, Daniel Gerroll, Cheryl Campbell, Alice Krige, John Gielgud, Lindsay Anderson, Nigel Davenport, Ian Holm, Patrick Magee

'The whole contradictory bundle is unexpectedly watchable.' – *Jo Imeson, MFB*
'A piece of technological lyricism held together by the glue of simple-minded heroic sentiment.' – *Pauline Kael*
'A hymn to the human spirit as if scored by Barry Manilow.' – *Richard Corliss, Film Comment*

AA: best picture; Colin Welland; Vangelis; costume design (Milera Canonero)
AAN: Hugh Hudson; editing (Terry Rawlings); Ian Holm (supporting actor)

BFA: best picture; costume design; Ian Holm

Charley and the Angel*
US 1974 93m Technicolor
Walt Disney (Bill Anderson)

A small-town sporting goods storekeeper in the thirties escapes death three times and finds an impatient angel waiting for him.

Mild sentimental whimsy on the lines of *On Borrowed Time*, but with a happy ending and attractive period trappings.

w Roswell Rogers novel *The Golden Evenings of Summer* by Will Stanton d Vincent McEveety ph Charles F. Wheeler m Buddy Baker

Fred MacMurray, Cloris Leachman, Harry Morgan, Kurt Russell, Kathleen Cody, Edward Andrews, Barbara Nichols

Charlie the Lonesome Cougar*
US 1967 75m colour
Disney

The growing-up of a cougar.

Amiable true-life adventure.

w Jack Speirs d Winston Hibler

Charlotte's Web
US 1972 96m Technicolor
Sagittarius/Hanna-Barbera
V, L

Farmyard animals who sense their fate are stimulated and encouraged by a resourceful spider.

Interesting but overlong and rather plodding version of a stylish book for children; the animation has no style at all.

w Earl Hanmer Jnr novel E. B. White d Charles A. Nichols, Iwao Takamoto md Irwin Kostal m/ly Richard and Robert Sherman

voices of Debbie Reynolds, Henry Gibson, Paul Lynde, Martha Scott, Agnes Moorehead

Cheaper by the Dozen**
US 1950 86m Technicolor
TCF (Lamar Trotti)

Efficiency expert Frank Gilbreth and his wife Lillian have twelve children, a fact which requires mathematical conduct of all their lives.

Amusing family comedy set in the twenties, unconvincing in detail though based on a book by two of the children. A great commercial success and a Hollywood myth-maker. Sequel: *Belles on their Toes* (qv).

w Lamar Trotti   book Frank B. Gilbreth Jnr, Ernestine Gilbreth Carey   d Walter Lang   ph Leon Shamroy   md Lionel Newman   m Cyril Mockridge   ad Lyle Wheeler, Leland Fuller

Clifton Webb, Myrna Loy, Jeanne Crain, Edgar Buchanan, Barbara Bates, Betty Lynn, Mildred Natwick, Sara Allgood

Checkers
US   1937   79m   bw
TCF

The niece of a ne'er-do-well horse owner brings him success.

One of the most successful vehicles of Shirley Temple's arch rival.

w Lynn Root, Frank Fenton, Karen de Wolf   play Rida Johnson Young   d H. Bruce Humberstone

Jane Withers, Stuart Erwin, Una Merkel, Marvin Stephens, Andrew Tombes, Minor Watson

'Will delight the moppet's following ... due for heavy dual booking.' – *Variety*

Chickens Come Home*
US   1931   30m   bw
Hal Roach
V(C)

Stan helps his boss Ollie to evade the attentions of an old flame.

Rather heavy and untypical, but mainly very enjoyable star comedy, a remake of *Love 'Em and Weep* in which all three leading players had appeared four years earlier in different roles.

w H. M. Walker   story Hal Roach   d James W. Horne   ph Art Lloyd, Jack Stevens   ed Richard Currier

Laurel and Hardy, James Finlayson, Mae Busch, Thelma Todd

Child in the House
GB   1956   88m   bw
Eros/Golden Era (Ben Fisz)

When her mother is ill and her father in hiding from the police, a 12-year-old girl goes to stay with her fussy uncle and aunt.

Modest family drama of the novelette type in which adult problems are put right by the wisdom of a child.

wd C. Raker Endfield   novel Janet McNeill   ph Otto Heller   m Mario Nascimbene   ad Ken Adam

Eric Portman, Phyllis Calvert, Stanley Baker, Mandy Miller, Dora Bryan, Joan Hickson, Victor Maddern, Percy Herbert

The Chimp*
US   1932   30m   bw
Hal Roach
V

Stan and Ollie try to get lodgings without revealing that their friend is a chimp, their share of a bankrupt circus.

The circus scenes are better than the rather tired farce which follows, especially as it is so similar to *Laughing Gravy*.

w H. M. Walker   d James Parrott   ph Walter Lundin   ed Richard Currier

Laurel and Hardy, James Finlayson, Billy Gilbert, Tiny Sandford

Chitty Chitty Bang Bang
GB 1968 145m Technicolor Super Panavision 70
UA/Warfield/DFI (Albert R. Broccoli)
V, L

An unsuccessful inventor rescues a derelict car and gives it magical properties, then helps the children who own it to overthrow the government of a country which hates children.

A bumpy ride. Sentiment, slapstick, whimsy and mild scares do not combine but are given equal shares of the limelight, while poor trickwork prevents the audience from being transported.

w Roald Dahl, Ken Hughes d Ken Hughes ph Christopher Challis m Irwin Kostal ad Ken Adam m/ly The Sherman Brothers ad Rowland Emmett

Dick Van Dyke, Sally Ann Howes (as Truly Scrumptious), Lionel Jeffries, Robert Helpmann, Gert Frobe, Benny Hill, James Robertson Justice
AAN: title song

Chomps
US 1979 89m Movielab
American International (Joseph Barbera)

A young inventor is successful with a robot dog (Canine Home Protection System).

Rather feeble family-oriented comedy.

w Dick Robbins, Duane Poole story Joseph Barbera d Don Chaffey ph Charles F. Wheeler m Hoyt Curtin pd Ted Shell ed Warner Leighton, Dick Darling

Wesley Eure, Jim Backus, Valerie Bertinelli, Chuck McCann, Regis Toomey, Red Buttons, Hermione Baddeley

A Christmas Story*
US 1983 93m colour
MGM/UA (René Dupont, Bob Clark)
V

In an Indiana suburb during the 1940s, a schoolboy hopes to get a rifle for Christmas.

Curious, almost plotless family comedy of the old school, with the difference that some grotesquerie and tastelessness is added. On the whole, however, an amusing entertainment for adults who don't mind their mood of sentimental nostalgia being tilted at by the director of Porky's.

w Jean Shepherd, Leigh Brown, Bob Clark novel In God We Trust, All Others Pay Cash by Jean Shepherd d Bob Clark ph Reginald H. Morris m Carl Zittrer, Paul Zaza pd Gavin Mitchell ed Stan Cole

Peter Billingsley, Melinda Dillon, Darren McGavin, Ian Petrella

A Chump at Oxford**
US 1940 63m bw
Hal Roach
V

Two street cleaners foil a bank hold-up and are presented with an Oxford education.

Patchy but endearing Laurel and Hardy romp, starting with an irrelevant two reels about their playing butler and maid, but later including Stan's burlesque impersonation of Lord Paddington.

w Charles Rogers, Harry Langdon, Felix Adler d Alfred Goulding ph Art Lloyd m Marvin Hatley ed Bert Jordan

Stan Laurel, Oliver Hardy, James Finlayson, Forrester Harvey, Wilfrid Lucas, Peter Cushing

'Ranks with their best pictures – which, to one heretic, are more agreeable than Chaplin's. Their clowning is purer; they aren't out to better an unbetterable world; they've never wanted to play Hamlet.' – *Graham Greene*

Cinderella**
US 1950 75m Technicolor
Walt Disney
V

The Perrault fairy tale embroidered with animal characters.

A feature cartoon rather short on inspiration, though with all Disney's solid virtues. The mice are lively and the villainous cat the best character.

supervisor Ben Sharpsteen
d Wilfred Jackson, Hamilton Luske, Clyde Geronimi   *m* Oliver Wallace, Paul J. Smith

voices of Ilene Woods, William Phipps, Eleanor Audley, Rhoda Williams, Lucille Bliss, Verna Felton
AAN: Oliver Wallace, Paul J. Smith; song 'Bibbidy Bobbidy Boo' (*m/ly* Mack David, Al Hoffman, Jerry Livingston)

Cinderfella
US 1960 91m Technicolor
Paramount/Jerry Lewis
V

Luxury pantomime featuring a male Cinderella.

Annoyingly lavish and empty star vehicle with precious little to laugh at: Lewis' own jokes are strung out to snapping point and no one else gets a look in.

wd Frank Tashlin   *ph* Haskell Boggs   *m* Walter Scharf

Jerry Lewis, Ed Wynn, Judith Anderson, Anna Maria Alberghetti, Henry Silva, Robert Hutton, Count Basie

'A drought of comic inspiration, followed by a flood of mawkish whimsy, gradually increases one's early misgivings to a degree which finally verges on revulsion.' – *Peter John Dyer*

The Circus*
US 1928 72m (24 fps) bw silent
(UA) Charles Chaplin
V

A tramp on the run from the police takes refuge in a circus and falls for an equestrienne.

Pathos often descends to bathos in this self-constructed star vehicle which has far too few laughs.

wd Charles Chaplin   *ph* Rollie Totheroh, Jack Wilson, Mark Marlott

Charles Chaplin, Merna Kennedy, Allan Garcia, Harry Crocker

AA: Special Award to Chaplin for acting, writing, directing and producing the film

City beneath the Sea
US 1970 98m DeLuxe
Warner/Kent/Motion Pictures International (Irwin Allen)
GB theatrical release title: *One Hour to Doomsday*

An undersea city is threatened by an errant planetoid.

Futuristic adventure from a familiar stable; it will satisfy followers of *Voyage to the Bottom of the Sea*. Originally made for TV.

w John Meredyth Lucas d Irwin Allen ph Kenneth Peach m Richard La Salle ad Roger E. Maus, Stan Jolley

Stuart Whitman, Robert Wagner, Rosemary Forsyth, Robert Colbert, Burr de Benning, Richard Basehart, Joseph Cotten, James Darren, Sugar Ray Robinson, Paul Stewart

City Lights***
US 1931 87m bw silent (with music and effects)
UA/Charles Chaplin
V, L

A tramp befriends a millionaire and falls in love with a blind girl.

Sentimental comedy with several delightful sequences in Chaplin's best manner.

wd/m Charles Chaplin ph Rollie Totheroh md Alfred Newman

Charles Chaplin, Virginia Cherrill, Florence Lee, Harry Myers

'Chaplin has another good picture, but it gives indications of being short-winded, and may tire fast after a bombastic initial seven days ... he has sacrificed speed to pathos, and plenty of it.' – *Variety*
'Even while laughing, one is aware of a faint and uneasy feeling that Chaplin has been pondering with more than a bit of solemnity on conventional story values, and it has led him further than ever into the realms of what is often called pathetic.' – *National Board of Review*

'They dared the most romantic journey that has ever challenged the imagination!'

City under the Sea
GB 1965 84m Eastmancolor Colorscope
Bruton/AIP (Daniel Haller)
V
US title: *War Gods of the Deep*

An American heiress in Cornwall meets Victorian smugglers who have lived a hundred years under the sea in Lyonesse.

Childlike, unpersuasive nonsense which wastes some good talent.

w Charles Bennett, Louis M. Heyward d Jacques Tourneur ph Stephen Dade m Stanley Black

Vincent Price, David Tomlinson, Susan Hart, Tab Hunter, Henry Oscar, John Le Mesurier

Clarence the Cross-Eyed Lion
US 1965 98m Metrocolor
MGM (Leonard Kaufman)

Adventures of animal farmers in Africa.

Amiable theatrical 'pilot' for the *Daktari* TV series.

w Alan Caillou, Marshall Thompson, Art Arthur d Andrew Marton ph Lamar Boren

Marshall Thompson, Betsy Drake, Richard Haydn, Cheryl Miller

Clash of the Titans
GB 1981 118m Metrocolor Dynarama
MGM/Charles H. Schneer, Ray Harryhausen
L

Perseus sets out to win Andromeda despite the impossible obstacles set for him by Thetis, which include a number of mythical monsters.

Star-packed but feebly imagined mythological spectacular, further hampered by gloomy photography which is presumably required to offset the jerkiness of the monsters. A very few moments provide the right kind of elation.

w Beverley Cross d Desmond Davis ph Ted Moore m Laurence Rosenthal pd Frank White sp Ray Harryhausen

Laurence Olivier, Claire Bloom, Maggie Smith, Ursula Andress, Jack Gwillim, Harry Hamlin, Judi Bowker, Burgess Meredith, Siân Phillips, Flora Robson, Freda Jackson, Donald Houston

'There's a real possibility some audiences will be turned to stone before Medusa even appears.' – *Geoff Brown, MFB*
'Unspeakable dialogue, muddy photography and a motley, lacklustre cast.' – *Sight and Sound*

'You'll graduate with a perpetual smile!'
College*
US 1927 65m (24 fps) bw silent
Buster Keaton Productions (Joseph M. Schenck)
L

A brainy high school student becomes a college football star.

Disappointing comedy from this great stone-faced clown: the plums are there, but few and far between.

w Carl Harbaugh, Bryan Foy d James W. Horne ph J. Devereux Jennings, Bert Haines

Buster Keaton, Ann Cornwall, Harold Goodwin, Snitz Edwards, Florence Turner

Come Clean**
US 1931 20m bw
Hal Roach

Two much-married men go out for ice-cream and bring back a woman of the streets they have saved from suicide.

Splendid star comedy with the famous characterizations fully rounded.

w H. M. Walker d James W. Horne ph Art Lloyd ed Richard Currier

Laurel and Hardy, Mae Busch, Charlie Hall, Gertrude Astor, Linda Loredo

† Remade in 1942 as *Brooklyn Orchid*, with William Bendix and Joe Sawyer.

The Computer Wore Tennis Shoes
US 1970 90m Technicolor
Disney

While mending a computer a college student gets an electric shock and becomes omniscient.

Ho-hum Disney comedy, eager to please but instantly forgotten.

w Joseph L. McEveety d Robert Butler

Kurt Russell, Cesar Romero, Joe Flynn, William Schallert, Alan Hewitt

Condorman
US 1981 90m Technicolor Panavision
Walt Disney (Jan Williams)

The author of a 'superman' comic tries to act like his hero in real life.

Very mildly amusing spy spoof with inadequate special effects.

w Marc Sturdivant, Glen Caron, Mickey Rose novel *The Game of X* by Robert Sheckley d Charles Jarrott ph Charles F. Wheeler m Henry Mancini pd Albert Witherick sp Art Cruickshank

Michael Crawford, Oliver Reed, Barbara Carrera, James Hampton, Jean-Pierre Kalfon

'Its laughter will ring through the centuries!'

A Connecticut Yankee in King Arthur's Court*

US 1949 106m Technicolor
Paramount (Robert Fellows)
L
GB title: *A Yankee in King Arthur's Court*

Gossamer musical version of the above with the emphasis on song and knockabout.

Palatable, with the 'Busy Doin' Nothin'' sequence the most memorable.

w Edmund Beloin   d Tay Garnett   ph Ray Rennahan   md Victor Young   m/ly Johnny Burke, Jimmy Van Heusen

Bing Crosby, Rhonda Fleming, William Bendix, *Cedric Hardwicke*, Murvyn Vye

'The tacky pageantry is more suited to the opening of a West Coast supermarket than to an English court in the 6th century.' – *Pauline Kael, 70s*

The Count of Monte Cristo**

US 1934 114m bw
Reliance (Edward Small)

After spending years in prison, Edmond Dantes escapes and avenges himself on those who framed him.

Classic swashbuckler, extremely well done with due attention to dialogue as well as action; a model of its kind and period.

w Philip Dunne, Dan Totheroh, Rowland V. Lee   novel Alexandre Dumas   d Rowland V. Lee   ph Peverell Marley   m Alfred Newman

Robert Donat, Elissa Landi, Louis Calhern, Sidney Blackmer, Raymond Walburn, O. P. Heggie, William Farnum

'A near-perfect blend of thrilling action and grand dialogue.' – *Variety*

County Hospital**

US 1932 20m bw
Hal Roach
V, V(C)

Ollie is in hospital; Stan brings him some hardboiled eggs and some nuts, and nearly wrecks the place.

Archetypal star comedy with brilliant character and slapstick sequences, let down by a badly processed car ride home.

w H. M. Walker   d James Parrott   ph Art Lloyd   ed Bert Jordan, Richard Currier

Laurel and Hardy, Billy Gilbert, William Austin, May Wallace

Courage Mountain

US 1989 98m CFI colour
Entertainment/Epic/Stone Group (Stephen Ujlaki)
V, L

A Swiss schoolgirl, stranded in Italy with some friends, makes her way back home.

A new adventure, told in an old-fashioned way, of that one-time children's favourite Heidi.

w Weaver Webb   story Fred Brogger, Mark Brogger   d Christopher Leitch   ph Jacques Steyn   m Sylvester Levay   pd Robb Wilson King   ed Martin Walsh

Juliette Caton, Charlie Sheen, Leslie Caron, Yorgo Voyagis, Laura Betti, Jan Rubes, Joanna Clarke

The Court Jester***
US 1955 101m Technicolor Vistavision
Paramount/Dena (Melvin Frank, Norman Panama)
V, L

Opposition to a tyrannical king is provided by the Fox, but it is one of the rebel's meekest men who, posing as a jester, defeats the usurper.

One of the star's most delightful vehicles, this medieval romp has good tunes and lively action, not to mention an exceptional cast and the memorable 'chalice from the palace' routine.

wd Norman Panama, Melvin Frank *ph* Ray June *m/ly* Sylvia Fine, Sammy Cahn *ad* Hal Pereira, Roland Anderson

Danny Kaye, Glynis Johns, *Basil Rathbone*, Cecil Parker, *Mildred Natwick*, Angela Lansbury, Edward Ashley, Robert Middleton, Michael Pate, Alan Napier

The Crazy World of Laurel and Hardy**
US 1964 83m bw
Hal Roach/Jay Ward

A compilation of Laurel and Hardy extracts from their classic period.

Although the material is in itself excellent and some of the build-up sequences well done, the clips are all too short to achieve maximum impact, and virtually none is identified.

w Bill Scott *m* Jerry Fielding *narrator* Garry Moore

Creatures the World Forgot
GB 1971 95m Technicolor
Columbia/Hammer (Michael Carreras)

Quarrels break out between rival tribes of Stone Age men.

Feeble follow-up to *One Million Years BC* and *When Dinosaurs Ruled the Earth*: someone forgot to order any monsters.

w Michael Carreras *d* Don Chaffey *ph* Vincent Cox *m* Mario Nascimbene *pd* John Stoll *ed* Chris Barnes

Julie Ege, Brian O'Shaughnessy, Robert John, Marcia Fox, Rosalie Crutchley

'Ask me no questions: believe only what you see!'

The Crimson Pirate*
GB 1952 104m Technicolor
Warner/Norma (Harold Hecht)
L

An 18th-century pirate and an eccentric inventor lead an island's people in rebellion against a tyrant.

One suspects that this started off as a straight adventure and was turned halfway through production into a spoof; at any rate, the effect is patchy but with spirited highlights, and the star's acrobatic training is put to good use.

w Roland Kibbee *d* Robert Siodmak *ph* Otto Heller *m* William Alwyn

Burt Lancaster, Nick Cravat, Eva Bartok, Torin Thatcher, James Hayter, Margot Grahame, Noel Purcell, Frank Pettingell

Crin Blanc**
France 1953 47m bw
Albert Lamorisse
aka: *Wild Stallion*

A small boy befriends and rides a wild horse in the Camargue.

A favourite short film of great beauty, but a shade overlong for its content.

wd *Albert Lamorisse* ph Edmond Séchan m Maurice Le Roux

Alain Emery, Pascal Lamorisse

Crooks in Cloisters
GB 1963 97m Technicolor Scope
ABPC

Forgers pose as monks but are reformed by the country life.

Busy comedy full of familiar faces; perhaps a small cut above the *Carry Ons*.

w Mike Watts d Jeremy Summers

Ronald Fraser, Barbara Windsor, Grégoire Aslan, Bernard Cribbins, Davy Kaye, Wilfred Brambell

The Cure****
US 1917 20m approx bw silent
Mutual/Charles Chaplin

A dipsomaniac sent to a spa gets his booze mixed up with the spa water.

One of the funniest of the Chaplin shorts, with no pathos intervening (nor come to that much plot); it is simply a succession of balletic slapstick scenes of the highest order.

wd *Charles Chaplin* ph William C. Foster, Rollie Totheroh

Charles Chaplin, Edna Purviance, Eric Campbell, Henry Bergman

'Big laughs come in small packages.'
Curly Sue
US 1991 101m Technicolor
Warner (John Hughes)
V, L

A con-man and a nine-year-old orphan win the heart of a successful woman lawyer.

Gruesomely sentimental and manipulative comedy.

wd John Hughes ph Jeffrey Kimball m Georges Delerue
pd Doug Kraner ed Peck Prior, Harvey Rosenstock

James Belushi, Kelly Lynch, Alisan Porter, John Getz

'With its mix of childish gags and shameless melodrama, *Curly Sue* could make off with a tidy box-office take.' – *Variety*
'John Hughes here graduates from the most successful comedy in film history to scripting and directing a large piece of non-biodegradable tosh.' – *Nigel Andrews, Financial Times*
'Lacks the charm, good jokes or vigour to hide its contrivances.' – *Geoff Brown, The Times*

Curly Top*
US 1935 78m bw
Fox (Darryl F. Zanuck, Winfield Sheehan)

An orphan waif is adopted by a playboy, and not only sets his business right but fixes his romantic interest in her sister.

Archetypal Temple vehicle, a loose remake of *Daddy Longlegs*.

w Patterson McNutt, Arthur Beckhard d Irving Cummings
ph John Seitz m/ly Ray Henderson, Ted Koehler, Edward Heyman, Irving Caesar

Shirley Temple, John Boles, Rochelle Hudson, Jane Darwell, Rafaela Ottiano, Esther Dale, Arthur Treacher, Etienne Girardot

'Cinch b.o. for almost any house.' – *Variety*

Curucu, Beast of the Amazon
US 1956 76m colour
Universal

Amazon explorers set out to find a man masquerading as a monster.

Rubbishy hokum, for tolerant kids.

wd Curt Siodmak

John Bromfield, Beverly Garland, Tom Payne

D

Dad's Army**
GB 1971 95m Technicolor
Columbia/Norcon (John R. Sloan)
V

Misadventures of a number of elderly gents in Britain's wartime Home Guard.

Expanded big-screen version of the long-running TV series, a pleasant souvenir but rather less effective than was expected because everything is shown – the town, the Nazis, the wives – and thus the air of gentle fantasy disappears, especially in the face of much coarsened humour.

w Jimmy Perry, David Croft
d Norman Cohen   ph Terry Maher   m Wilfred Burns

Arthur Lowe, John Le Mesurier, John Laurie, James Beck, Ian Lavender, Arnold Ridley, Liz Fraser, Clive Dunn, Bill Pertwee, Frank Williams, Edward Sinclair

The Dancing Masters
US 1943 63m bw
TCF (Lee Marcus)
V

Laurel and Hardy run a ballet school, and get involved with gangsters and inventors.

Insubstantial star comedy featuring reworkings of old routines, and a back-projected runaway bus climax.

w Scott Darling, George Bricker
d Mal St Clair   ph Norbert Brodine   m Arthur Lange
ad James Basevi, Chester Gore
ed Norman Colbert

Stan Laurel, Oliver Hardy, Trudy Marshall, Bob Bailey, Margaret Dumont, Matt Briggs, Robert Mitchum

Dangerous When Wet**
US 1953 95m Technicolor
MGM (George Wells)

An entire Arkansas family is sponsored to swim the English Channel.

A bright and lively vehicle for an aquatic star, who in one sequence swims with Tom and Jerry. Amusing sequences give opportunities to a strong cast.

w Dorothy Kingsley   d Charles Walters   ph Harold Rosson
md George Stoll   m/ly Johnny Mercer, Arthur Schwartz

Esther Williams, Charlotte Greenwood, William Demarest, Fernando Lamas, Jack Carson, Denise Darcel, Barbara Whiting

Danny the Champion of the World*
GB 1989 99m colour
Portobello Productions (Eric Abraham)
V

A poacher's son devises a plan to discomfort the obnoxious squire.

Pleasant film aimed at a family audience, if it still exists.

w John Goldsmith novel Roald Dahl d Gavin Millar ph Oliver Stapleton m Stanley Myers pd Don Homfray ed Peter Tanner, Angus Newton

Jeremy Irons, Robbie Coltrane, Samuel Irons, Cyril Cusack, Michael Hordern, Lionel Jeffries, Ronald Pickup, Jean Marsh, Jimmy Nail, William Armstrong, John Woodvine

Darby O'Gill and the Little People*
US 1959 90m Technicolor
Walt Disney

An Irish caretaker falls down a well and is captured by leprechauns, who allow him three wishes to rearrange his life.

Pleasantly barmy Irish fantasy with brilliant trick work but some tedium in between.

w Lawrence Edward Watkin stories H. T. Kavanagh d Robert Stevenson ph Winton C. Hoch m Oliver Wallace sp Peter Ellenshaw, Eustace Lycett, Joshua Meador

Albert Sharpe, Jimmy O'Dea, Sean Connery, Janet Munro, Kieron Moore, Estelle Winwood, Walter Fitzgerald, Denis O'Dea, J. G. Devlin, Jack MacGowran

'One of the best fantasies ever put on film.' – Leonard Maltin

The Dark Avenger*
GB 1955 85m Eastmancolor
  Cinemascope
Allied Artists (Vaughan N. Dean)
US title: The Warriors

The Black Prince quells some French rebels.

Good-humoured historical romp with the ageing star in his last swashbuckling role, helped by a good cast and brisk pace.

w Daniel B. Ullman d Henry Levin ph Guy Green m Cedric Thorpe Davie

Errol Flynn, Peter Finch, Joanne Dru, Yvonne Furneaux, Patrick Holt, Michael Hordern, Moultrie Kelsall, Robert Urquhart, Noel Willman

The Dark Crystal**
GB 1982 94m Technicolor
  Panavision
Universal/AFD/ITC (David Lazer)
V

Two young people defeat the evil creatures who have taken over the world by replacing a shard which has been taken from the Dark Crystal.

Surprisingly effective piece of mysticism performed entirely by puppets from the Muppet stable.

w David Odell d Jim Henson, Frank Oz conceptual designer Brian Froud ph Oswald Morris pd Harry Lange ed Ralph Kemplen

'A dazzling technological and artistic achievement . . . could teach a lesson in morality to youngsters at the same time as it is entertaining their parents.' – Variety

D.A.R.Y.L.
US 1985 99m TVC colour
  Panavision
Columbia (Burt Harris, Gabrielle Kelly)
V, L

A mysterious young man is really a robot, 'data analysing robot youth lifeform'; but he begins to have feelings . . .

Muddled sentimental fantasy which

doesn't seem to know where it's going.

w David Ambrose, Allan Scott, Jeffrey Ellis d Simon Wincer ph Frank Watts m Marvin Hamlisch pd Alan Cassie ed Adrian Carr

Mary Beth Hurt, Michael McKean, Kathryn Walker, Colleen Camp

'The kind of project that must have looked great on paper.' – *Variety*

'One of the greatest stories of love and adventure ever told is brought to the screen as Dickens himself would wish it!'

David Copperfield**
US 1934 132m bw
MGM (David O. Selznick)
V, L

Disliked by his cruel stepfather and helped by his eccentric aunt, orphan David grows up to become an author and eventually to marry his childhood sweetheart.

Only slightly faded after sixty years, this small miracle of compression not only conveys the spirit of Dickens better than the screen has normally managed but is a particularly pleasing example of Hollywood's handling of literature and of the deployment of a great studio's resources. It also overflows with memorable character cameos, and it was a box-office giant.

w Hugh Walpole, Howard Estabrook novel Charles Dickens d George Cukor ph Oliver T. Marsh montage Slavko Vorkapich m Herbert Stothart ad Cedric Gibbons ed Robert J. Kern

Freddie Bartholomew (young David), *Frank Lawton* (David as a man), *W. C. Fields* (Micawber), *Roland Young* (Uriah Heep), *Edna May Oliver* (Aunt Betsy), *Lennox Pawle* (Mr Dick), *Basil Rathbone* (Mr Murdstone), Violet Kemble Cooper (Miss Murdstone), Maureen O'Sullivan (Dora), Madge Evans (Agnes), Elizabeth Allan (Mrs Copperfield), *Jessie Ralph* (Peggotty), Lionel Barrymore (Dan Peggotty), Hugh Williams (Steerforth), Lewis Stone (Mr Wickfield), *Herbert Mundin* (Barkis), Elsa Lanchester (Clickett), Jean Cadell (Mrs Micawber), Una O'Connor (Mrs Gummidge), John Buckler (Ham), Hugh Walpole (the Vicar), Arthur Treacher (donkey man)

'One of the best ensembles ever ... unusually good production which will win general approval.' – *Variety*
'Though half the characters are absent, the whole spectacle of the book, Micawber always excepted, is conveyed.' – *James Agee*
'The most profoundly satisfying screen manipulation of a great novel that the camera has ever given us.' – *André Sennwald*
'Perhaps the finest casting of all time.' – *Basil Wright, 1972*

† Charles Laughton was originally cast as Micawber, but resigned from the role after two days of shooting. It was said at the time that 'he looked as though he were about to molest the child'.
AAN: best picture; editing

Davy Crockett*
US 1955 93m Technicolor
Walt Disney

Episodes in the career of the famous Tennessee hunter and Indian scout who died at the Alamo.

Disjointed and naive but somehow very fresh and appealing adventures; made for American television (as 3 × 50m episodes) but elsewhere an enormous hit in cinemas.

w Tom Blackburn *d* Norman Foster *ph* Charles Boyle *m* George Bruns

Fess Parker, Buddy Ebsen, Basil Ruysdael, William Bakewell, Hans Conried, Kenneth Tobey, Nick Cravat

† 1956 sequel on similar lines: *Davy Crockett and the River Pirates*.

A Day at the Races****
US 1937 109m bw/blue-tinted ballet sequence
MGM (Lawrence Weingarten)
V, L

The Marxes help a girl who owns a sanatorium and a racehorse.

Fashions in Marxism change, but this top quality production, though lacking their zaniest inspirations, does contain several of their funniest routines and a spectacularly well integrated racecourse climax. The musical and romantic asides are a matter of taste but delightfully typical of their time.

w Robert Pirosh, George Seaton, George Oppenheimer *d* Sam Wood *ph* Joseph Ruttenberg *m* Franz Waxman *ch* Dave Gould

Groucho, Chico, Harpo, Margaret Dumont, Maureen O'Sullivan, Allan Jones, Douglass Dumbrille, Esther Muir, Sig Rumann

'The money is fairly splashed about; the capitalists have recognized the Marx Brothers; ballet sequences, sentimental songs, amber fountains, young lovers. Easily the best film to be seen in London, but all the same I feel a nostalgia for the old cheap rickety sets.' – *Graham Greene*
AAN: Dave Gould

The Day of the Dolphin*
US 1973 104m Technicolor Panavision
Avco-Embassy/Icarus (Robert E. Relyea)
V, L

A marine biologist researching dolphins off the Florida coast discovers they are being used in a plot to blow up the President's yacht.

A strangely unexpected and unsuccessful offering from the talent involved: thin and repetitive as scientific instruction (the dolphins' language in any case topples it into fantasy), and oddly childlike as spy adventure.

w Buck Henry *novel* Robert Merle *d* Mike Nichols *ph* William A. Fraker *m* Georges Delerue *pd* Richard Sylbert

George C. Scott, Trish Van Devere, Paul Sorvino, Fritz Weaver

'The whole thing seems to have been shoved through the cameras as glibly as possible, so that everyone concerned could grab the money and run.' – *Stanley Kauffmann*
'An eight and a half million dollar Saturday afternoon special for sheltered nine-year-olds.' – *Judith Crist*
'Dolphins may live in a state of ecstasy, but the cast of this film seems lost in a state of confusion, wondering whether they are in an enlightened documentary, juvenile fantasy, or lurid soap opera.' – *Les Keyser, Hollywood in the Seventies*
'The most expensive Rin Tin Tin movie ever made.' – *Judith Crist*
AAN: Georges Delerue

Days of Thrills and Laughter***
US 1961 93m bw
TCF (Robert Youngson)

Appealing if rather miscellaneous silent film compilation with the accent on action and thrills as well as comedy.

Like the other Youngson histories, a boon to film archivists despite a facetious commentary. *m* Jack Shaindlin *narrator* Jay Jackson

Stan Laurel, Oliver Hardy, Snub Pollard, Douglas Fairbanks, Charles Chaplin, Pearl White, Houdini, Harry Langdon, Ben Turpin, Charlie Chase, Boris Karloff, Warner Oland, Fatty Arbuckle, Keystone Kops

A Day's Pleasure*

US 1919 20m bw silent
First National/Charles Chaplin
V

Mishaps of a family picnic.

Very mild Chaplin, reaching for but not achieving a kind of lyric quality. Amusing bits rather than scenes.

wd Charles Chaplin *ph* Rollie Totheroh

Charles Chaplin, Edna Purviance, Jackie Coogan, Henry Bergman, Babe London

'You may not like these people, nor pity them, but you'll never forget this picture!'

Dead End***

US 1937 92m bw
Samuel Goldwyn

A slice of life in New York's east side, where slum kids and gangsters live in a river street next to a luxury apartment block.

Highly theatrical film of a highly theatrical play, more or less preserving the single set and overcoming the limitations of the script and setting by sheer cinematic expertise. It is chiefly remembered, however, for introducing the Dead End Kids to a delighted world.

w Lillian Hellman *play* Sidney Kingsley *d* William Wyler *ph* Gregg Toland *m* Alfred Newman *ad* Richard Day

Joel McCrea, Sylvia Sidney, *Humphrey Bogart*, Wendy Barrie, Claire Trevor, Allen Jenkins, *Marjorie Main*, James Burke, Ward Bond, *The Dead End Kids* (Billy Halop, Leo Gorcey, Bernard Punsley, Huntz Hall, Bobby Jordan, Gabriel Dell)

'Tense and accurate transcription, but sordid and depressing . . . in for a disappointing career.' – *Variety*
AAN: best picture; Gregg Toland; Claire Trevor; Richard Day

Deep Waters

US 1948 85m bw
TCF

A problem orphan boy is content when adopted by a lobster fisherman.

Forgettable family film, smoothly directed and photographed.

w Richard Murphy *d* Henry King *ph* Joseph LaShelle *m* Cyril Mockridge

Jean Peters, Dana Andrews, Dean Stockwell, Cesar Romero, Anne Revere

The Delicate Delinquent

US 1956 101m bw Vistavision
Paramount/Jerry Lewis

A New York policeman tries to make friends with an eccentric youth who mixes with thugs; the boy decides to train as a policeman.

Jerry Lewis' first film without Dean Martin: a sobering experience combining zany comedy, sentiment, pathos and social comment. The mixture fails to rise.

wd Don McGuire   *ph* Haskell Boggs   *m* Buddy Bregman

Jerry Lewis, Darren McGavin, Martha Hyer, Robert Ivers, Horace McMahon

Demetrius and the Gladiators**
US 1954 101m Technicolor Cinemascope
TCF (Frank Ross)
V, V(W), L

A Greek slave who keeps Christ's robe after the crucifixion is sentenced to be one of Caligula's gladiators and becomes involved in Messalina's wiles.

Lively, efficient sequel to *The Robe*, with emphasis less on religiosity than on the brutality of the arena and our hero's sexual temptations and near-escapes. Good Hollywood hokum.

w Philip Dunne   *d* Delmer Daves   *ph* Milton Krasner   *m* Franz Waxman

Victor Mature, Susan Hayward, Michael Rennie (as Peter), Debra Paget, Anne Bancroft, Jay Robinson, Barry Jones, William Marshall, Richard Egan, Ernest Borgnine

'An energetic attempt to fling the mantle of sanctity over several more millions of the entertainment dollar.'
– *The Times*

The Desert Hawk
US 1950 77m Technicolor
Universal-International

Against an Arabian Nights background, a cheerful outlaw abducts a princess.

Tolerable cloak-and-sandal action comedy.

w Aubrey Wisberg, Jack Pollexfen, Gerald Drayson Adams   *d* Frederick de Cordova

Richard Greene, Yvonne de Carlo, Jackie Gleason, George Macready, Rock Hudson, Carl Esmond

Desert Law
Italy 1990 155m Eastmancolor
Titanus/Reteitalia/International Dean Film (Rossella Angeletti, David Pash)
V

A New York businesswoman hires an ex-CIA agent to rescue her son, who has been kidnapped by his Arab grandfather to become the future leader of a tribe of desert warriors.

Glossy and competent thriller, most likely to appeal to 10-year-olds who can identify with the central character of a young boy.

w Adriano Bolzoni, Sergio Donati, Luigi Montefiori   *d* Duccio Tessari   *ph* Giorgio Di Battista   *m* Ennio Morricone   *pd* Luciano Sagoni   *ed* Maria Morra

Rutger Hauer, Carol Alt, Omar Sharif, Elliott Gould, Kabir Bedi, Brett Halsey, Peter Sands

'What nation will survive?'
Destroy all Monsters
Japan 1969 89m colour
Toho/AIP

Moon invaders gain control of Godzilla and his friends.

Typically inept Japanese monster rally full of men in rubber suits.

w Kaoru Mabuchi   *d* Ishiro Honda

Akira Kubo, Jun Tazaki, Kyoko Ai

The Devil and Max Devlin
US 1981 95m Technicolor
Walt Disney (Jerome Courtland)

An unscrupulous apartment manager is knocked down by a bus. Finding himself in hell, he is offered freedom if he can buy three young souls within two months.

Frowsty Freudian comedy, a very unhappy indication of the depths to which Disney productions have sunk since Walt's death. To carry this kind of thing off requires a hundred times more style than is evidenced here.

w Mary Rodgers d Steven Hilliard Stern ph Howard Schwartz m Buddy Baker

Elliott Gould, Bill Cosby, Susan Anspach, Adam Rich, Charles Shamata, Ronnie Schell

Diamonds Are Forever*
GB 1971 120m Technicolor Panavision
UA/Eon/Danjaq (Harry Saltzman, Albert R. Broccoli)
V, V(W), L

Seeking a diamond smuggler, James Bond has adventures in Amsterdam, a Los Angeles crematorium, various Las Vegas gambling parlours, and a secret installation in the desert.

Campy, rather vicious addition to a well-worn cycle, with an element of nastiness which big-budget stunts cannot conceal. Panavision does not help, and Connery's return to the role for a final throw is disappointing.

w Richard Maibaum, Tom Mankiewicz novel Ian Fleming d Guy Hamilton ph Ted Moore m John Barry pd Ken Adam

Sean Connery, Jill St John, Charles Gray, Lana Wood, Jimmy Dean, Bruce Cabot, Bernard Lee, Lois Maxwell

'It has been claimed that the plot is impossible to describe, but I think I could if I wanted to. I can't think why anyone would want to, though.' – Roger Ebert

Digby: the Biggest Dog in the World
GB 1973 88m Technicolor
TCF/Walter Shenson

An old English sheepdog accidentally eats a chemical intended to increase the size of vegetables . . .

Nice to see this kind of gimmick used for comedy instead of horror, but the result is rather tame and old-fashioned, though for several years it made a pleasant television offering for Christmas.

w Michael Pertwee d Joseph McGrath ph Harry Waxman m Edwin T. Astley sp Tom Howard

Jim Dale, Spike Milligan, Angela Douglas, Milo O'Shea, Dinsdale Landen, Garfield Morgan, Victor Spinetti, Bob Todd

Dimples**
US 1936 82m bw
TCF (Darryl F. Zanuck, Nunnally Johnson)

In the New York Bowery in pre-Civil War days, a child and her reprobate grandfather win the hearts of high society.

Excellent Temple vehicle with good period flavour.

w Arthur Sheekman, Nat Perrin d William A. Seiter ph Bert Glennon m Louis Silvers m/ly Jimmy McHugh, Ted Koehler

Shirley Temple, Frank Morgan, Helen Westley, Berton Churchill, Robert Kent, Delma Byron, Astrid Allwyn

Dirty Work***
US 1933 20m bw
Hal Roach

Chimney sweeps cause havoc in the house of an eccentric scientist.

Hilarious star comedy with splendid timing and comedy touches.

w H. M. Walker   d Lloyd French   ph Kenneth Peach   ed Bert Jordan

Laurel and Hardy, Lucien Littlefield, Sam Adams

'Have no fear, Doc Savage is here!'
Doc Savage, Man of Bronze
US 1975 100m Technicolor
Warner (George Pal)

A thirties superman and his assistants the Amazing Five fly to South America to avenge the death of Doc's father.

Stolid, humourless adaptation from a comic strip, totally lacking in the necessary panache.

w George Pal, Joe Morhaim   *stories* Kenneth Robeson   d Michael Anderson   ph Fred Koenekamp   m John Philip Sousa

Ron Ely, Paul Gleason, Bill Lucking, Michael Miller, Eldon Quick

'A slick, ultra-self-conscious camp that denies the material its self-respect.' – *Colin Pahlow*
'Nothing in this unfortunate enterprise is likely to please anyone: former Savage fans will be enraged, newcomers bored, and children will probably feel superior to the whole mess . . .' – *New Yorker*

Doctor at Large
GB 1957 104m Eastmancolor
Rank (Betty E. Box)

Simon Sparrow tries two country practices, but returns at last to St Swithin's.

Hit-or-miss medical comedy with honours about even.

w Nicholas Phipps   *novel* Richard Gordon   d Ralph Thomas   ph Ernest Steward   m Bruce Montgomery

Dirk Bogarde, Muriel Pavlow, James Robertson Justice, Donald Sinden, Shirley Eaton, Derek Farr, Michael Medwin, Edward Chapman, Barbara Murray, Gladys Henson, Lionel Jeffries, A. E. Matthews, Athene Seyler, George Coulouris

Doctor at Sea*
GB 1955 93m Technicolor VistaVision
Rank/Group Films (Betty E. Box)

Simon Sparrow becomes medical officer on a cargo steamer.

Reasonably lively comedy of errors with nice seascapes and predictable jokes.

w Nicholas Phipps, Jack Davies   d Ralph Thomas   ph Ernest Steward   m Bruce Montgomery

Dirk Bogarde, Brigitte Bardot, Brenda de Banzie, James Robertson Justice, Maurice Denham, Michael Medwin, Hubert Gregg, Raymond Huntley, Geoffrey Keen, George Coulouris, Jill Adams, James Kenney

'Brisk professional humour has given way to the more elementary business of traditional British farce.' – *Penelope Houston, MFB*

Dr Dolittle
US 1967 152m DeLuxe Todd-AO
TCF/APJAC (Arthur P. Jacobs)
V

In a Victorian English village, Dr Dolittle is a veterinary surgeon who talks to his patients; escaping from a lunatic asylum, he travels with friends to the South Seas in search of the Great Pink Sea Snail.

Lumpish family spectacular with no

imagination whatever, further handicapped by charmless performances and unsingable songs.

w/songs Leslie Bricusse   novels Hugh Lofting   d Richard Fleischer   ph Robert Surtees   md Lionel Newman, Alex Courage   pd Mario Chiari

Rex Harrison, Anthony Newley, Samantha Eggar, *Richard Attenborough*, William Dix, Peter Bull

AA: song 'Talk to the Animals'; special effects (L. B. Abbott)
AAN: best picture; Robert Surtees; Lionel Newman, Alex Courage; Leslie Bricusse (*m*)

Doctor in Clover

GB 1966 101m Eastmancolor
Rank/Betty E. Box-Ralph Thomas

Grimsdyke goes back to his old hospital for a refresher course and finds a rejuvenating drug useful in his philandering.

Depressing mixture of smut and slapstick.

w Jack Davies   novel Richard Gordon   d Ralph Thomas   ph Ernest Steward   m John Scott

Leslie Phillips, James Robertson Justice, Shirley Anne Field, Joan Sims, John Fraser, Arthur Haynes, Fenella Fielding, Noel Purcell, Jeremy Lloyd, Eric Barker, Terry Scott, Alfie Bass

Doctor in Distress

GB 1963 102m Eastmancolor
Rank/Betty E. Box-Ralph Thomas

Simon Sparrow goes back to work for Sir Lancelot Spratt and finds his old mentor in love.

Tedious flummery whose characters fail to perform with the old pizazz.

w Nicholas Phipps, Ronald Scott Thorn   d Ralph Thomas   ph Ernest Steward   m Norrie Paramour

Dirk Bogarde, James Robertson Justice, Mylene Demongeot, Samantha Eggar, Barbara Murray, Donald Houston, Jessie Evans, Ann Lynn, Leo McKern, Dennis Price

Doctor in the House**

GB 1954 91m Eastmancolor
Rank (Betty E. Box)
V

Amorous and other misadventures of medical students at St Swithin's Hospital.

A comedy with much to answer for: several sequels and an apparently endless TV series. The original is not bad, as the students, though plainly over age, constitute a formidable mass of British talent at its peak.

w Nicholas Phipps   novel Richard Gordon   d Ralph Thomas   ph Ernest Steward   m Bruce Montgomery

Dirk Bogarde, Kenneth More, Donald Sinden, Donald Houston, Kay Kendall, Muriel Pavlow, *James Robertson Justice*, Geoffrey Keen

'Works its way with determined high spirits through the repertoire of medical student jokes.' – *MFB*
'An uproarious, devil-may-care, almost wholly ruthless picture.' – *Dilys Powell*

† Sequels, of increasing inanity and decreasing connection with the original characters, were: *Doctor at Sea, Doctor at Large, Doctor in Love, Doctor in Distress, Doctor in Clover* and *Doctor in Trouble*. *Carry on Doctor* and *Carry on Again Doctor* were horses of a different colour.

Doctor in Trouble

GB 1970 90m Technicolor
Rank/Betty E. Box

Dr Burke inadvertently becomes a stowaway on an Atlantic cruise.

Witless tailpiece to the Doctor saga, like a half-hearted wrapping-up of discarded jokes from the other episodes.

w Jack Davies   novel Doctor on Toast by Richard Gordon   d Ralph Thomas   ph Ernest Steward   m Eric Rogers

Leslie Phillips, Harry Secombe, Angela Scoular, Irene Handl, Robert Morley, Simon Dee, Freddie Jones, James Robertson Justice, Joan Sims, John Le Mesurier, Fred Emney

'The cinematic equivalent of an end-of-the-pier summer show.' – *Films and Filming*

Doctor No***

GB 1962 111m Technicolor
UA/Eon (Harry Saltzman, Albert R. Broccoli)
V, L

A British secret service agent foils a master criminal operating in the West Indies.

First of the phenomenally successful James Bond movies, mixing sex, violence and campy humour against expensive sets and exotic locales. Toned down from the original novels, they expressed a number of sixties attitudes, and proved unstoppable box-office attractions for twenty-five years. The first was, if not quite the best, reasonably representative of the series.

w *Richard Maibaum*, Johanna Harwood, Berkely Mather   novel Ian Fleming   d Terence Young   ph Ted Moore   m Monty Norman

Sean Connery, Ursula Andress, Jack Lord, Joseph Wiseman, John Kitzmiller, Bernard Lee, Lois Maxwell, Zena Marshall, Eunice Gayson, Anthony Dawson

† The subsequent titles, all qv, were *From Russia with Love* (1963), *Goldfinger* (1964), *Thunderball* (1965), *You Only Live Twice* (1967), *On Her Majesty's Secret Service* (1969), *Diamonds Are Forever* (1971), *Live and Let Die* (1973), *The Man with the Golden Gun* (1974), *The Spy Who Loved Me* (1977), *Moonraker* (1979), *For Your Eyes Only* (1981), *Octopussy* (1983), *A View To A Kill* (1985), *The Living Daylights* (1987), *Licence To Kill* (1989). *Never Say Never Again* (1984) was not part of the series, though it brought back Sean Connery as Bond.

Dr Who and the Daleks

GB 1965 83m Techniscope
British Lion/Regal/Aaru (Milton Subotsky, Max J. Rosenberg)

Three children and their grandfather accidentally start his time machine and are whisked away to a planet where villainous robots rule.

Junior science fiction from the BBC series. Limply put together, and only for indulgent children.

w Milton Subotsky   d Gordon Flemyng   ph John Wilcox   m Malcolm Lockyer

Peter Cushing, Roy Castle, Jennie Linden, Roberta Tovey, Barrie Ingham

† A sequel, no better, emerged in 1966: *Daleks: Invasion Earth 2150 AD*, with similar credits except that

Bernard Cribbins instead of Roy Castle provided comic relief.

A Dog of Flanders
US   1959   97m   DeLuxe
   Cinemascope
TCF/Associated Producers (Robert B. Radnitz)

A small boy wants to be an artist; when he runs away in frustration, his shaggy dog, formerly a stray, leads his family to him.

Old-fashioned tear-jerker for well-brought-up children, previously filmed as a silent; quite accomplished in presentation.

w Ted Sherdeman   novel Ouida
d James B. Clark   ph Otto Heller   m Paul Sawtell, Bert Shefter

David Ladd, Donald Crisp, Theodore Bikel, Max Croiset, Monique Ahrens

Dogpound Shuffle
Canada   1974   97m   Eastmancolor
Elliott Kastner/Bulldog
aka: *Spot*

An old Irish hobo lives on the earnings of his dancing dog.

Dog-eared 'family film' which didn't seem to entertain many families.

wd Jeffrey Bloom

Ron Moody, David Soul, Ray Stricklyn

A Dog's Life*
US   1918   30m approx   bw
   silent
First National/Charles Chaplin

A tramp and a stray mongrel help each other towards a happy ending.

Threatening sentiment is kept at bay by amusing sight gags in this pleasing star featurette.

wd Charles Chaplin   ph Rollie Totheroh

Charles Chaplin, Edna Purviance, Chuck Riesner, Henry Bergman, Albert Austin, Scraps

'The fun never sets on the British Empire!'
Don't Raise the Bridge, Lower the River
GB   1967   100m   Technicolor
Columbia/Walter Shenson

An American turns his English wife's home into a discotheque.

Dreary comedy apparently intent on proving that its star can be just as unfunny abroad as at home.

w Max Wilk   d Jerry Paris
ph Otto Heller   m David Whitaker

Jerry Lewis, Terry-Thomas, Jacqueline Pearce, Bernard Cribbins, Patricia Routledge, Nicholas Parsons, Michael Bates

The Double McGuffin
US   1979   100m   colour
Mulberry Square/Joe Camp

Kids turn into amateur detectives when they find that a visiting foreign leader is to be assassinated.

Barely tolerable lightweight mystery for an audience which probably doesn't exist.

wd Joe Camp   ph Don Reddy
m Euel Box   pd Harland Wright

Ernest Borgnine, George Kennedy, Elke Sommer, Rod Browning

Doughboys*
US   1930   80m approx   bw
MGM/Buster Keaton (Lawrence Weingarten)
GB title: *Forward March*

A young eccentric joins the army.

Simple-minded farce with a few good routines for the star.

w Richard Schayer d Edward Sedgwick ph Leonard Smith

Buster Keaton, Sally Eilers, Cliff Edwards, Edward Brophy

'Keaton's first talker is comedy with a kick.' – *Variety*

The Dove*
US 1974 104m Technicolor Panavision
St George Productions (Gregory Peck)

Yachtsman Robin Lee Graham makes a five-year voyage around the world.

Bland, rather stolid adventure story for boat-niks, based on real incidents; good to look at.

w Peter Beagle, Adam Kennedy book Robin Lee Graham, Derek Gill d Charles Jarrott ph Sven Nykvist m John Barry

Joseph Bottoms, Deborah Raffin, John McLiam, Dabney Coleman

'Postcard views flick by to the strains of a saccharine score.' – *David McGillivray*

Down Memory Lane*
US 1949 70m bw
Aubrey Schenck

A kaleidoscope of Mack Sennett comedy shorts, linked by Steve Allen as a disc jockey. Much Bing Crosby; Fields in *The Dentist*; an appearance by Sennett himself.

d Phil Karlson

'Only sorcery can destroy it!'
Dragonslayer
US 1981 110m Metrocolor Panavision
Walt Disney/Paramount (Howard W. Koch, Hal Barwood)

A sorcerer's apprentice uses his master's magic amulet to ward off various dangers.

Heavy-going sword-and-sorcery fable, not helped at all by slow plotting and dark photography. The dragons, however, are genuinely fierce.

w Hal Barwood, Matthew Robbins d Matthew Robbins ph Derek Vanlint m Alex North pd Elliot Scott sp Thomas Smith

Peter MacNichol, Caitlin Clarke, Ralph Richardson, John Hallam, Peter Eyre, Albert Salmi

'Verges on the nasty for the nippers; sails too close to *déjà vu* for fantasy fans.' – *Time Out*
AAN: Alex North; visual effects (Dennis Muren and others)

Driftwood
US 1947 90m bw
Republic

An orphan is adopted by a kindly doctor.

Lavender-scented family yarn with pleasant backgrounds and expert performances.

w Mary Loos, Richard Sale d Allan Dwan

Natalie Wood, Ruth Warrick, Walter Brennan, Dean Jagger, Charlotte Greenwood

Duck Soup**
US 1933 68m bw
Paramount
L

An incompetent becomes President of Fredonia and wages war on its scheming neighbour.

The satirical aspects of this film are fascinating but appear to have been unintentional. Never mind, it's also the most satisfying and undiluted Marx Brothers romp, albeit the one without instrumental interludes. It does include the lemonade stall, the mirror sequence, and an endless array of one-liners and comedy choruses.

w Bert Kalmar, Harry Ruby, Arthur Sheekman, Nat Perrin d Leo McCarey ph Henry Sharp m/ly Bert Kalmar, Harry Ruby ad Hans Dreier, Wiard Ihnen

The Four Marx Brothers, Margaret Dumont, Louis Calhern, Edgar Kennedy, Raquel Torres

'Practically everybody wants a good laugh right now, and this should make practically everybody laugh.' – *Variety*
'So much preliminary dialogue is necessary that it seems years before Groucho comes on at all; and waiting for Groucho is agony.' – *E. V. Lucas, Punch*
'The most perfect of all Marxist masterpieces.' – *Time Out, 1984*

The Duke Wore Jeans
GB 1958 89m bw
Insignia (Peter Rogers)

An aristocrat persuades his cockney double to woo a princess on his behalf.

Moderately lively comedy with songs, tailored for Britain's new musical star.

w Norman Hudis d Gerald Thomas

Tommy Steele, June Laverick, Michael Medwin, Alan Wheatley, Eric Pohlmann

Dumbo****
US 1941 64m Technicolor
Walt Disney
V, L

A baby circus elephant finds that his big ears have a use after all.

Delightful cartoon feature notable for set-pieces such as the drunken nightmare and the crows' song.

w various d Ben Sharpsteen m Frank Churchill, Oliver Wallace

voices of Sterling Holloway, Edward Brophy, Verna Felton, Herman Bing, Cliff Edwards

AA: music
AAN: song, 'Baby Mine' (m Frank Churchill, ly Ned Washington)

Dusty
Australia 1982 85m colour Panavision
Kestrel Films/Dusty Productions (Gil Brealey)

An old shepherd takes to the bush to save his half-wild dog from being shot by sheep farmers.

Sentimental tale with pleasant landscape photography.

w Sonia Berg novel Frank Dalby Davison d John Richardson ph Alex McPhee m Frank Strangio pd Robbie Perkins ad Ivana Perkins ed David Greig

Bill Kerr, Noel Trevarthen, Carol Burns, John Stanton, Nicholas Holland

Dutch
US 1991 107m DeLuxe
TCF (John Hughes, Richard Vane)
V, L
GB title: *Driving Me Crazy*

An arrogant and snobbish twelve-year-old boy is reformed by his divorced mother's working-class boyfriend.

Inert comedy of class warfare, part of the cycle of buddy-buddy movies in which antagonists at the beginning become friends by the end.

w John Hughes *d* Peter Faiman *ph* Charles Minsky *m* Alan Silvestri *pd* Stan Jolley *ed* Paul Hirsch, Adam Bernardi

Ed O'Neill, Ethan Randall, Christopher McDonald, Ari Meyers, E. G. Daily, L. Scott Caldwell, Kathleen Freeman

E

E.T. ****
US 1982 115m DeLuxe
Universal (Steven Spielberg, Kathleen Kennedy)
V, V(W), L

When an alien spacecraft is disturbed in a Los Angeles suburb, one of its crew members is left behind and befriended by a small boy.

Stupefyingly successful box-office fairy tale by the current wonder kid Spielberg, taken to the world's heart because he dares to make films without sex, violence or bad language. This one could hardly be simpler, but it works; and the ailing cinema would love to know how to repeat the trick several times a year.

w Melissa Mathison   *d* Steven Spielberg   *ph* Allen Daviau   *m* John Williams   *pd* James D. Bissell,   *sp* Creator of E.T.: Carlo Rimbaldi

Dee Wallace, Henry Thomas, Peter Coyote, Robert MacNaughton, Drew Barrymore, K. C. Martel

'The most moving science-fiction movie ever made on earth.' – *Pauline Kael, New Yorker*
'E.T. is the closest film to my own sensibilities, my own fantasies, my own heart.' – *Steven Spielberg*

† E.T. = extra-terrestrial.

AA: visual effects; music; sound

AAN: best picture; direction; original screenplay; cinematography; editing

BFA: best score

The Early Bird
GB 1965 98m Eastmancolor
Rank/Hugh Stewart
V

A milkman gets involved in an intercompany war.

Star farcical comedy; not the worst of Wisdom, but overlong and mainly uninventive.

w Jack Davies, Norman Wisdom, Eddie Leslie, Henry Blyth   *d* Robert Asher   *ph* Jack Asher   *m* Ron Goodwin

Norman Wisdom, Edward Chapman, Jerry Desmonde, Paddie O'Neil, Bryan Pringle, Richard Vernon, John Le Mesurier, Peter Jeffrey

Early to Bed
US 1928 20m bw silent
Hal Roach

Stan becomes Ollie's butler but rebels when his friend's fortune goes to his head.

One of the most untypical and seldom seen of the stars' comedies, with both prankishly out of character. On its own account however it is mainly very funny.

w H. M. Walker   *d* Emmett

Flynn *ph* George Stevens
ed Richard Currier

Laurel and Hardy

Earth Girls Are Easy
US 1988 100m colour
Panavision
Fox/De Laurentiis/Kestrel Films (Tony Garnett)
V, L

Three aliens crashland on Earth and learn to enjoy disco dancing.

Ineffectual teenage musical.

w Julie Brown, Charlie Coffey, Terrence E. McNally *d* Julien Temple *ph* Oliver Stapleton *md* Nile Rodgers *pd* Dennis Gassner *ed* Richard Halsey

Geena Davis, Jeff Goldblum, Jim Carrey, Damon Wayans, Julie Brown, Michael McKean, Charles Rocket, Larry Linville, Rick Overton

Earth Versus the Flying Saucers
US 1956 83m bw
Columbia (Charles H. Schneer)
I

Saucermen from another planet try to disintegrate the Earth.

Elementary science fiction with special effects in a similar if enthusiastic vein.

w George Worthing Yates, Raymond T. Marcus *story* Curt Siodmak
d Fred F. Sears *sp* Ray Harryhausen

Hugh Marlowe, Joan Taylor, Donald Curtis, Morris Ankrum

Easter Parade**
US 1948 109m Technicolor
MGM (Arthur Freed)
V, L

A song and dance man quarrels with one partner but finds another.

A musical which exists only in its numbers, which are many but variable. All in all, an agreeable lightweight entertainment without the style to put it in the top class.

w Sidney Sheldon, Frances Goodrich, Albert Hackett *d* Charles Walters *ph* Harry Stradling
md Roger Edens, Johnny Green
m/ly Irving Berlin

Fred Astaire, Judy Garland, Ann Miller, Peter Lawford, Clinton Sundberg, Jules Munshin

'The important thing is that Fred Astaire is back, with Irving Berlin calling the tunes.' – *Newsweek*

† Fred Astaire was actually second choice, replacing Gene Kelly who damaged an ankle.

AA: Roger Edens, Johnny Green

Easy Street****
US 1917 22m approx bw
silent
Mutual/Charles Chaplin

In a slum street, a tramp is reformed by a dewy-eyed missionary, becomes a policeman, and tames the local bully.

Quintessential Chaplin, combining sentimentality and social comment with hilarious slapstick.

wd Charles Chaplin *ph* William C. Foster, Rollie Totheroh

Charles Chaplin, Edna Purviance, Albert Austin, Eric Campbell

Ebirah, Horror of the Deep
Japan 1966 85m
Eastmancolor Tohoscope
Toho (Tomoyuki Tanaka)

Scientists creating nuclear weapons on an island guarded by a giant lobster are foiled with the aid of Godzilla.

The usual hokum, enlivened by fight sequences that have Godzilla heading rocks with the aplomb of a football striker, and a giant moth that looks as if it has been made from an old carpet.

w Shinichi Sekizawa   d Jun Fukuda   ph Kazuo Yamada   ad Takeo Kita   sp Eiji Tsuburaya

Akira Takarada, Kuni Mizuno, Akihiko Hirata, Jun Tazaki, Hideo Sunazuka, Chotaro Togin, Toru Watanabe

Edward Scissorhands**
US 1990 98m colour
Fox (Denise De Novi)
V

A boy with artificial hands upsets the community in which he lives.

Bizarre fairy-tale with a good deal of charm.

w Caroline Thompson   story Tim Burton   d Tim Burton   ph Stefan Czapsky   m Danny Elfman   pd Bo Welsh   ad Tom Duffield   ed Richard Halsey

Johnny Depp, Winona Ryder, Dianne Wiest, Anthony Michael Hall, Alan Arkin, Kathy Baker, Robert Oliver, Conchata Ferrell, Vincent Price

'A delightful and delicate comic fable.' – *Variety*
AAN: best makeup

El Cid*
US/Spain 1961 184m Super Technirama
Samuel Bronston
V

A legendary 11th-century hero drives the Moors from Spain.

Endless glum epic with splendid action sequences as befits the high budget.

w Frederic M. Frank, Philip Yordan   d Anthony Mann   ph Robert Krasker   m Miklos Rozsa

Charlton Heston, Sophia Loren, Raf Vallone, Genevieve Page, John Fraser, Gary Raymond, Herbert Lom, Hurd Hatfield, Massimo Serato, Andrew Cruickshank, Michael Hordern, Douglas Wilmer, Frank Thring

'A Lone Ranger liberation tale.' – *Judith Crist*
AAN: Miklos Rozsa; song 'The Falcon and the Dove' (m Miklos Rozsa, ly Paul Francis Webster)

Electric Dreams
GB 1984 112m Metrocolor
Virgin/MGM-UA (Rusty Lemorande, Larry de Waay)
V

A computer becomes jealous of its owner's love affair.

Gruesomely extended revue sketch which totally fails to develop its characters and offers instead a very sparing amount of cleverness.

w Rusty Lemorande   d Steve Barron   ph Alex Thomson   m Giorgio Moroder   pd Richard MacDonald

Lenny Von Dohlen, Virginia Madsen, Maxwell Caulfield, Bud Cort, Don Fellows

Elephant Boy**
GB 1937 91m bw
London Films (Alexander Korda)

In India, a boy elephant keeper helps government conservationists.

Documentary drama which seemed fresh and extraordinary at the time, has dated badly since, but did make an international star of Sabu.

w John Collier, Akos Tolnay, Marcia de Sylva *novel* Toomai of the Elephants *by* Rudyard Kipling d Robert Flaherty, Zoltan Korda ph Osmond Borradaile m John Greenwood ed William Hornbeck, Charles Crichton

Sabu, Walter Hudd, Allan Jeayes, W. E. Holloway, Wilfrid Hyde-White

'Should draw anywhere in the world.' – *Variety*
'This is a fractured film, its skeleton is awry, its bones stick out through the skin.' – *Richard Griffith, 1941*
'It has gone the way of *Man of Aran*: enormous advance publicity, director out of touch with the press for months, rumours of great epics sealed in tins, and then the disappointing diminutive achievement.' – *Graham Greene*

Emil and the Detectives*

Germany 1931 80m bw
UFA

City children discover and chase a crook, who is finally arrested.

A pleasing fable for children which has survived several subsequent versions; the original is probably the best.

w Billy Wilder *novel* Erich Kästner d Gerhard Lamprecht ph Werner Brandes m Allan Grey

Fritz Rasp, Kathe Haack

† Other versions: Britain 1935, directed by Milton Rosmer, with George Hayes; West Germany 1954, directed by R. A. Stemmle, with Kurt Meisel; US 1964 (Walt Disney), directed by Peter Tewkesbury, with Walter Slezak.

The Empire Strikes Back**

US 1980 124m Eastmancolor Panavision
TCF/Lucasfilm (Gary Kurtz)
V, V(W), L

The Rebel Alliance takes refuge from Darth Vader on a frozen planet.

More exhilarating interplanetary adventures, as mindless as *Star Wars* but just as enjoyable for aficionados.

w Leigh Brackett, Lawrence Kasdan *story* George Lucas d Irvin Kershner ph Peter Suschitzky m John Williams pd Norman Reynolds

Mark Hamill, Harrison Ford, Carrie Fisher, Billy Dee Williams

'Slightly encumbered by some mythic and neo-Sophoclean overtones, but its inventiveness, humour and special effects are scarcely less inspired than those of its phenomenally successful predecessor.' – *New Yorker*
AAN: John Williams; art direction

BFA: music

Encino Man

US 1992 88m Technicolor
Warner/Hollywood Pictures/Touchwood Pacific Partners 1 (George Zaloom)
V
GB title: *California Man*

Two high-school students revive a frozen prehistoric youth who quickly adapts to the prevailing life-style.

A depressing youth comedy, though those with a Neanderthal sense of humour may be amused.

w Shawn Schepps *story* George Zaloom, Shawn Schepps d Les Mayfield ph Robert Brickmann *m* J. Peter Robinson *pd* James Allen *ed* Eric Sears, Jonathan Siegel

Sean Astin, Brendan Fraser, Pauly Shore, Megan Ward, Robin Tunney, Michael DeLuise, Patrick Van Horn, Dalton James, Rick Ducommun

'Mindless would-be comedy . . . insulting even within its own no-effort parameters.' – *Variety*
'Less funny than your own funeral.' – *Washington Post*

The End of the Golden Weather

New Zealand 1992 103m colour
Blue Dolphin/South Pacific/New Zealand Film Commission/TV New Zealand (Christina Milligan, Ian Mune)

During a summer holiday a lonely boy becomes friendly with a retarded youth with Olympic ambitions.

A slight and uninvolving movie of the dawning of maturity.

w Ian Mune, Bruce Mason *play* Bruce Mason *d* Ian Mune *ph* Alun Bollinger *m* Stephen McCurdy *pd* Ron Highfield *ed* Michael Horton

Stephen Fulford, Stephen Papps, Paul Gittins, Gabrielle Hammond, David Taylor, Alexandra Marshall

'An intimate and gentle coming-of-age comedy drama.' – *Variety*

The End of the River*

GB 1947 83m bw
GFD/The Archers (Michael Powell, Emeric Pressburger)

A South American Indian boy flees to the outside world and finds life in the city as dangerous as in the jungle.

Strange but oddly impressive departure for British film-makers at this time. A commercial and critical disaster.

w Wolfgang Wilhelm
novel Desmond Holdridge *d* Derek Twist *ph* Christopher Challis
m Lambert Williamson

Sabu, Esmond Knight, Bibi Ferreira, Robert Douglas, Antoinette Cellier, Raymond Lovell, Torin Thatcher, James Hayter

The Endless Summer

US 1966 95m Technicolor
Bruce Brown Films/Columbia

A study of surfing round the world.

A documentary which became a cult for those influenced by this Californian obsession; smashing photography hardly atones for an approach so naïve as to become fatuous.

wd/ph/ed Bruce Brown

Erik the Viking

GB 1989 108m Technicolor
UIP/Erik The Viking Productions/Prominent Features/AB Svensk Filmindustri (Terry Glinwood)
V, L

A Viking sails on an expedition to wake the Gods.

Uneasy mix of fantasy and humour.

wd Terry Jones *novel* Terry Jones *ph* Ian Wilson *m* Neil Innes *pd* John Beard *ed* George Akers

Tim Robbins, Mickey Rooney, Eartha Kitt, Terry Jones, Imogen Stubbs, John Cleese, Tsutomu Sekine, Anthony Sher, Gary Cady, Charles McKeown, Tim McInnerny, John Gordon Sinclair

'A thunderous, unfunny jumble.' – *MFB*

Ernest Saves Christmas

US 1988 91m Metrocolor
Warner/Touchstone/Silver Screen Partners III (Stacy Williams, Doug Claybourne)

Santa Claus goes to America to find someone to take over his job.

Inept and witless from start to finish.

w B. Kline, Ed Turner d John Cherry ph Peter Stein m Mark Snow ad Ian Thomas ed Sharyn L. Ross

Jim Varney, Douglas Seale, Oliver Clark, Noelle Parker, Gailard Sartain, Billie Bird, Bill Byrge, Robert Lesser, Key Howard

The Errand Boy

US 1961 92m bw
Paramount/Jerry Lewis (Ernest D. Glucksman)
V

A dimwit paperhanger causes havoc in a Hollywood studio but is eventually signed up as a comic to rival Jerry Lewis.

Feeble comedy with the star at his self-satisfied worst.

wd Jerry Lewis ph W. Wallace Kelley m Walter Scharf

Jerry Lewis, Brian Donlevy, Sig Rumann, Fritz Feld, Isobel Elsom, Iris Adrian

Escapade in Florence

US 1962 80m Technicolor
Walt Disney (Bill Anderson)

Two American students in Florence uncover art thefts.

Cheerful adventure for children, well enough produced on location, but quite unmemorable.

w Maurice Tombragel *novel The Golden Doors* by Edward Fenton d Steve Previn ph Kurt Grigoleit m Buddy Baker

Ivan Desny, Tommy Kirk, Annette Funicello, Nino Castelnuovo

The Escape Artist*

US 1982 93m Technicolor
Zoetrope Studios (Doug Claybourne, Buck Houghton)

A young boy justifies his descent from 'the world's greatest escape artist'.

Curiously unfulfilled fable, too vague to satisfy the family audience it seems to aim at, but with pleasant moments.

w Melissa Mathison, Stephen Zito. *novel* David Wagoner d Caleb Deschanel ph Stephen H. Burum m Georges Delerue pd Dean Tavoularis

Griffin O'Neal, Raul Julia, Teri Garr, Joan Hackett, Gabriel Dell, Desi Arnaz

Escape from the Dark

GB 1976 104m Technicolor
Walt Disney (Ron Miller)

In 1909 Yorkshire, two boys save pit ponies from the slaughterhouse.

Efficient family fare with plenty of suspense and good character cameos.

w Rosemary Anne Sisson d Charles Jarrott ph Paul Beeson m Ron Goodwin

Alastair Sim, Peter Barkworth, Maurice Colbourne, Susan Tebbs, Geraldine McEwan, Prunella Scales, Leslie Sands, Joe Gladwin

Escape to Witch Mountain*

US 1974 97m Technicolor
Walt Disney (Jerome Courtland)

Two mysterious orphan children have extraordinary powers, are chased by a scheming millionaire, and prove to come from another planet.

Mildly ingenious story frittered away by poor scripting and special effects. A stimulating change in children's films, however.

w Robert Malcolm Young novel Alexander Key d John Hough ph Frank Phillips m Johnny Mandel sp Art Cruickshank, Danny Lee

Ray Milland, Donald Pleasence, Eddie Albert, Kim Richards, Ike Eisenmann, Walter Barnes, Reta Shaw, Denver Pyle

Explorers
US 1985 109m Technicolor
Paramount/Edward S. Feldman/Industrial Light and Magic

Two boys make off in a space craft and encounter an alien race whose culture consists of intercepted American television programmes.

Slightly interesting but overlong fantasy spoof, probably not for popular consumption.

w Eric Luke d Joe Dante ph John Hora m Jerry Goldsmith pd Robert F. Boyle

Ethan Hawke, River Phoenix, Jason Presson, Amanda Peterson

'One of the weirdest and most endearingly offbeat alien pix to have surfaced in recent years.' – *Variety*

'Johnny never had it so good – or lost it so fast!'

Expresso Bongo*
GB 1959 111m bw
  Dyaliscope
BL/Britannia/Conquest (Val Guest)
V

A Soho agent turns a nondescript teenage singer into an international star.

Heavily vulgarized version of a stage skit on the Tommy Steele rock phenomenon, divested of most of its satirical barbs and only intermittently amusing.

w Wolf Mankowitz play Wolf Mankowitz d Val Guest ph John Wilcox md Robert Farnon m/ly David Heneker, Monty Norman

Laurence Harvey, Sylvia Syms, Yolande Donlan, Cliff Richard, *Meier Tzelniker*, Gilbert Harding, Ambrosine Philpotts, Eric Pohlmann, Wilfrid Lawson, Hermione Baddeley, Reginald Beckwith, Martin Miller

'What the cinema offers is a sardonic rattle with music . . . The approach may be satirical or flippant; and yet one finds oneself half-beginning to believe in the subject; even minding about it.' – *Dilys Powell*

F

A Family Affair*
US 1937 69m bw
MGM (Lucien Hubbard)

A small-town judge faces a few family problems.

The second feature that started the highly successful Hardy family series (qv under Hardy). In this case the judge and his wife were played by actors who did not persevere into the series, but the stage was otherwise set for a long run, and the town of Carvel came to mean home to many Americans abroad.

w Kay Van Riper play *Skidding* by Aurania Rouverol d George B. Seitz ph Lester White m David Snell

Lionel Barrymore, Spring Byington, *Mickey Rooney*, Eric Linden, Cecilia Parker, Sara Haden, Charles Grapewin, Julie Haydon

'Family trade and tops in dual locations.' – *Variety*

Fantasia****
US 1940 135m Technicolor
Walt Disney
V, L

A concert of classical music is given cartoon interpretations. The pieces are:

Bach: Toccata and Fugue in D Minor
Tchaikovsky: The Nutcracker Suite
Dukas: The Sorcerer's Apprentice
Stravinsky: The Rite of Spring
Beethoven: The Pastoral Symphony
Ponchielli: Dance of the Hours
Mussorgsky: Night on a Bare Mountain
Schubert: Ave Maria

Brilliantly inventive for the most part, the cartoons having become classics in themselves. The least part (the Pastoral Symphony) can be forgiven.
supervisor Ben Sharpsteen
md Edward H. Plumb

Leopold Stokowski, the Philadelphia Orchestra, Deems Taylor

'Dull as it is towards the end, ridiculous as it is in the bend of the knee before Art, it is one of the strange and beautiful things that have happened in the world.' – *Otis Ferguson*
'It is ambitious, and finely so, and one feels that its vulgarities are at least unintentional.' – *James Agate*
'Disney sometimes at his worst, often at his very best; and the best is on a level which no other cinematographic designer has reached. It takes over two hours, but somehow or other I'm afraid you will have to find the time.' – *Dilys Powell*

† Multiplane cameras, showing degrees of depth in animation, were used for the first time. The film was re-released in a print restored to its original freshness in 1990.

AA: Special Award to Walt Disney, Leopold Stokowski

Fantastic Voyage*
US 1966 100m DeLuxe
Cinemascope
TCF (Saul David)
V, L

When a top scientist is shot and suffers brain damage, a team of doctors and a boat are miniaturized and injected into his blood stream . . . but one is a traitor.

Engagingly absurd science fiction which keeps its momentum but is somewhat let down by its décor.

w Harry Kleiner   d Richard Fleischer   ph Ernest Laszlo
m Leonard Rosenman   ad Dale Hennesy, Jack Martin Smith   sp L. B. Abbott, Art Cruickshank, Emil Kosa Jnr

Stephen Boyd, Raquel Welch, Edmond O'Brien, Donald Pleasence, Arthur Kennedy, Arthur O'Connell, William Redfield

'The process shots are so clumsily matted . . . that the actors look as if a child has cut them out with blunt scissors.' – *Pauline Kael*

AA: art direction; special visual effects (Art Cruickshank)
AAN: Ernest Laszlo

Father Goose*
US 1964 116m Technicolor
U-I/Granox (Robert Arthur)
V

During World War II a South Seas wanderer is compelled by the Australian navy to act as sky observer on a small island, where he finds himself in charge of six refugee schoolchildren and their schoolmistress.

Eager-to-please but unsatisfactory film which wanders between farce, adventure and sex comedy, taking too long about all of them.

w Peter Stone, Frank Tarloff
d Ralph Nelson   ph Charles Lang Jnr   m Cy Coleman

Cary Grant, Leslie Caron, Trevor Howard

CARY GRANT: 'Let me tell you I am not a father figure. I am not a brother figure or an uncle figure or a cousin figure. In fact, the only figure I intend being is a total stranger figure.'

'Reasoning would indicate a made-to-order Christmas package for the family trade. However, the more sophisticated may be bored and exasperated after some of the initial brightness wears off.' – *Cue*
'Cary Grant wrings what there is to be wrung from the role, but never quite enough to conceal the fact that *Father Goose* is a waste of his talent and the audience's time.' – *Arthur Knight*

AA: Peter Stone, Frank Tarloff

Father Is a Bachelor
US 1950 85m bw
Columbia (S. Sylvan Simon)

A young tramp cares for a family of orphaned children.

Boringly sentimental semi-Western.

w Aleen Leslie, James Edward Grant   d Norman Foster, Abby Berlin   ph Burnett Guffey
m Arthur Morton

William Holden, Coleen Gray, Charles Winninger, Stuart Erwin, Sig Rumann

'Saccharine, paper thin. At least one spectator at the Palace yesterday couldn't take it – a tot of about four, wearing a cowboy suit, who aimed a toy pistol at the screen and popped off the cast one by one.' – *New York Times*

'The bride gets the thrills! Father gets the bills!'

Father of the Bride**
US 1950 93m bw
MGM (Pandro S. Berman)
V, L

A dismayed but happy father surveys the cost and chaos of his daughter's marriage.

Fragmentary but mainly delightful suburban comedy which finds Hollywood in its best light vein and benefits from a strong central performance.

w Frances Goodrich, Albert Hackett *novel* Edward Streeter *d* Vincente Minnelli *ph* John Alton *m* Adolph Deutsch

Spencer Tracy, Joan Bennett, Elizabeth Taylor, Don Taylor, Billie Burke, Moroni Olsen, Leo G. Carroll, Taylor Holmes, Melville Cooper

'The idealization of a safe sheltered existence, the good life according to MGM: 24 carat complacency.' – *New Yorker, 1980*

† Jack Benny badly wanted the role but was thought unsuitable.
AAN: best picture; Frances Goodrich, Albert Hackett; Spencer Tracy

'Love is wonderful. Until it happens to your only daughter.'

Father of the Bride
US 1991 105m Technicolor
Touchstone/Touchwood Pacific Partners I (Nancy Myers, Carol Baum, Howard Rosenman)
V, L

A father is upset by his daughter's announcement that she is engaged – and even more horrified by the arrangements for an expensive wedding.

Lacklustre remake with flat or exaggerated performances, few jokes and a great deal of sentimentality.

w Frances Goodrich, Albert Hackett, Nancy Myers, Charles Shyer *novel* Edward Streeter *d* Charles Shyer *ph* John Lindley *m* Alan Silvestri *pd* Sandy Veneziano *ed* Richard Marks

Steve Martin, Diane Keaton, Kimberley Williams, Martin Short, Kieran Culkin, George Newbern, B. D. Wong, Peter Michael Goetz

'Little more than a mildly entertaining diversion.' – *Empire*

Father's Little Dividend
US 1951 81m bw
MGM (Pandro S. Berman)

Sequel to *Father of the Bride*, in which the newlyweds have a baby.

A very flat follow-up, palatable enough at the time but quite unmemorable.

w Frances Goodrich, Albert Hackett *d* Vincente Minnelli *ph* John Alton *m* Albert Sendrey

Spencer Tracy, Joan Bennett, Elizabeth Taylor, Don Taylor, Billie Burke, Moroni Olsen, Frank Faylen, Marietta Canty, Russ Tamblyn

Feather Your Nest*
GB 1937 86m bw
ATP (Basil Dean)

A gramophone record technician substitutes his own voice for a star and becomes world famous.

The star in less farcical vein than usual; this is the one in which he sings 'Leaning on a Lamp-post'.

w Austin Melford, Robert Edmunds, Anthony Kimmins *story* Ivar and Sheila Campbell *d* William Beaudine *ph* Ronald Neame *m* Leslie Sarony, Leslie Holmes and others *ad* R. Holmers Paul *ed* Ernest Aldridge

George Formby, Polly Ward, Enid Stamp Taylor, Val Rosing, Davy Burnaby

'A thrill a minute! A laugh a second! A comedy cyclone!'

Feet First**
US 1930 88m bw
Harold Lloyd

A shoe salesman gets entangled with crooks and has a narrow escape when hanging from the side of a building.

Very funny early talkie comedy, probably the comedian's last wholly satisfactory film.

w Lex Neal, Felix Adler, Paul Gerard Smith *d* Clyde Bruckman *ph* Walter Ludin, Henry Kohler

Harold Lloyd, Robert McWade, Barbara Kent

'That Lloyd was a bit pressed for laughs may be guessed from the fact that he is again dangling from the front of a skyscraper.' – *Variety*

Felix the Cat: The Movie
US 1989 82m colour
Transatlantic/Felix The Cat Creations/ Productions Inc (Don Oriolo, Christian Schneider, Janos Schenk)
V

Felix rescues a princess from another dimension.

Laboured attempt to update the classic cartoon figure.

w Don Oriolo, Pete Brown *d* Tibor Hernadi *ph* Laszlo Radocsay *pd* Tibor A. Belay, Tibor Hernadi

voices of Chris Phillips, Maureen O'Connnell, Peter Neuman, Alice Playton, Susan Montanaro, Don Oriolo, Christian Schneider, David Kolin

'More likely to bury the ingratiating Felix beyond revival than to stimulate fresh legions of fans.' – *Philip Strick, MFB*

FernGully: The Last Rainforest
Australia 1992 76m DeLuxe
TCF/FAI/Youngheart (Wayne Young, Peter Faiman)
V

A fairy, a fruit-bat and a miniaturized lumberjack save the rainforest from the evil spirit who would destroy it.

Moderately enjoyable animated feature with an ecological moral: be kind to trees.

w Jim Cox *story* Diana Young *d* Bill Kroyer *m* Alan Silvestri *ad* Susan Kroyer *ed* Gillian Hutshing

voices of: Tim Curry, Samantha Mathis, Christian Slater, Jonathan Ward, Robin Williams, Grace Zabriskie, Geoffrey Blake, Robert Pastorelli, Cheech Marin, Tommy Chong, Tone-Loc

'As lectures on the environment go, this one is less likely to induce adult narcolepsy than most.' – *Ian Johnstone, Sunday Times*

'Pic will amply entertain tykes while feeding them an environmental lesson, and features enough amusing jokes and clever songs to make it palatable for adults.' – *Variety*

Fiddler on the Roof**
US 1971 180m Technicolor Panavision 70
UA/Mirisch (Norman Jewison)
V, L

In a pre-revolutionary Russian village, Tevye the Jewish milkman survives family and political problems and when the pogroms begin cheerfully emigrates to America.

Self-conscious, grittily realistic adaptation of the stage musical, with slow and heavy patches in its grossly overlong celebration of a vanished way of life. The big moments still come off well though the songs tend to be thrown away and the photography is unnecessarily murky.

w Joseph Stein play Joseph Stein story Tevye and his Daughters by Sholom Aleichem d Norman Jewison ph Oswald Morris md John Williams pd Robert Boyle m/ly Jerry Bock, Sheldon Harnick

Topol, Norma Crane, Leonard Frey, Molly Picon

'Jewison hasn't so much directed a film as prepared a product for world consumption.' – Stanley Kauffmann

AA: Oswald Morris; John Williams
AAN: best picture; Norman Jewison (as director); Topol; Leonard Frey

The Fifth Musketeer
Austria 1978 106m Eastmancolor
Sascha-Wien Film/Ted Richmond
aka: Behind the Iron Mask

Louis XIII and his twin brother Philippe vie for the crown of France.

Virtually a remake of The Man in the Iron Mask, with patchy style and a few excisable sex scenes added. The 1939 version was better.

w David Ambrose d Ken Annakin ph Jack Cardiff m Riz Ortolani

Beau Bridges, Sylvia Kristel, Ursula Andress, Cornel Wilde (as D'Artagnan), Lloyd Bridges, Alan Hale Jnr, José Ferrer (the ageing musketeers), Rex Harrison (Colbert), Olivia de Havilland (Queen Anne), Ian McShane, Helmut Dantine

The Fighting Prince of Donegal
GB 1966 104m Technicolor
Walt Disney (Bill Anderson)

Adventures of an Irish rebel in the reign of Elizabeth I.

Adequate Boys' Own Paper romp.

w Robert Westerby novel Red Hugh, Prince of Donegal by Robert T. Reilly d Michael O'Herlihy ph Arthur Ibbetson m George Bruns

Peter McEnery, Susan Hampshire, Tom Adams, Gordon Jackson, Andrew Keir, Norman Wooland, Richard Leech

A Fine Mess
US 1985 88m DeLuxe Panavision
Columbia/BEE/Delphi V (Tony Adams)
L

Two private eyes who accidentally know too much are chased by gangsters.

Not enough plot for a feature, and not enough comedy talent for a comedy, despite the dedication to Laurel and Hardy.

wd Blake Edwards ph Harry Stradling m Henry Mancini pd Rodger Maus ed John F. Burnett

Ted Danson, Howie Mandel, Richard

Mulligan, Stuart Margolin, Paul Sorvino

'Word of mouth is unlikely to be favourable . . . mechanically contrived funny business, most of which falls pretty flat.' – *Variety*
'The plot needn't be the thing, but then the gags and setpieces aren't much either.' – *Sight and Sound*

The Finishing Touch*
US 1928 20m bw silent
Hal Roach

Stan and Ollie accidentally destroy the house they are building.

Excellent early star slapstick with predictable but enjoyable gags.

w H. M. Walker d Clyde Bruckman ph George Stevens ed Richard Currier

Laurel and Hardy, Edgar Kennedy, Dorothy Coburn

Fire and Ice
US 1982 82m colour
Fox/PSO (Ralph Bakshi, Frank Frazetta)

Evil Lord Nekron uses black magic to subdue the good King Jarol.

Fair cartoon feature, using rotoscoping, in the mould of *Conan the Barbarian*.

w Roy Thomas, Gerry Conway d Ralph Bakshi m William Kraft ed E. Davis Marshall

voices of Susan Tyrrell, Maggie Rosewell, William Ostrander, Stephen Mendel, Clare Nono, Alan Koss

The Fire in the Stone
Australia 1983 100m colour
South Australian Film Corp (Pamela H. Vanneck)

A teenager foils a murderer, finds some opals and re-unites her parents.

Unexceptional and undemanding entertainment.

w Graeme Koetsveld novel Colin Thiele d Gary Conway ph Ross Berryman m Garry and Anita Hardman ad Derek Mills ed Philip Reid

Alan Cassell, Paul Smith, Ray Meagher, Linda Hartley, Leo Taylor, Andrew Gaston, Theo Pertsinidis

Fireman Save My Child
US 1954 80m bw
U-I (Howard Christie)

In 1910 San Francisco, incompetent firemen accidentally catch a gang of crooks.

Slapstick farce intended for Abbott and Costello, taken over by a new team which did not catch on, played like the Keystone Kops. Mildly funny during the chases.

w Lee Loeb, John Grant d Leslie Goodwins ph Clifford Stine m Joseph Gershenson

Buddy Hackett, Spike Jones and the City Slickers, Hugh O'Brian, Adèle Jergens

First Men in the Moon*
GB 1964 103m Technicolor Panavision
Columbia/Ameran (Charles H. Schneer)
V, L

A Victorian eccentric makes a voyage to the moon and is forced to stay there.

Rather slack in plot development, but an enjoyable schoolboy romp with a good eye for detail and tongue firmly in cheek.

w Nigel Kneale, Jan Read novel H. G. Wells d Nathan Juran

ph Wilkie Cooper *m* Laurie Johnson *sp* Ray Harryhausen

Lionel Jeffries, Edward Judd, Martha Hyer

† Uncredited, Peter Finch played the bit part of a process server.

The Five Thousand Fingers of Doctor T*

US 1953 88m Technicolor
Columbia/*Stanley Kramer*

A boy who hates piano lessons dreams of his teacher as an evil genius who keeps five hundred boys imprisoned in a castle of musical instruments.

Badly scripted fantasy with gleaming sophisticated dream sequences which deserve a better frame. A real oddity to come from Hollywood at this time, even though Dr Seuss' books were and are bestsellers.

w Dr Seuss (Theodore Geisel), Alan Scott *d* Roy Rowland *ph* Franz Planer *m* Frederick Hollander *ly* Dr Seuss *pd* Rudolph Sternad *ch* Eugene Loring

Hans Conried, Tommy Rettig, Peter Lind Hayes, Mary Healy
AAN: Frederick Hollander

Five Weeks in a Balloon

US 1962 101m DeLuxe Cinemascope
TCF (Irwin Allen)

In 1862 a professor is financed on a balloon trip into central Africa.

Would-be humorous semi-fantasy which strives to equal *Journey to the Center of the Earth* but unfortunately falls flat on its face despite the interesting talent available. Limp comedy situations, poor production values.

w Charles Bennett, Irwin Allen, Albert Gail *novel* Jules Verne *d* Irwin Allen *ph* Winton Hoch *m* Paul Sawtell *ad* Jack Martin Smith, Alfred Ybarra

Cedric Hardwicke, Peter Lorre, Red Buttons, Fabian, Richard Haydn, Billy Gilbert, Herbert Marshall, Reginald Owen, Henry Daniell

The Fixer Uppers

US 1935 20m bw
Hal Roach
V

Christmas card salesmen try to help a bored wife, but her jealous husband challenges Ollie to a duel.

Rather flat comedy marking a tailing-off from the stars' best period.

w uncredited *d* Charles Rogers *ph* Art Lloyd *ed* Bert Jordan

Laurel and Hardy, Mae Busch, Charles Middleton, Arthur Housman

† A remake of an early silent, *Slipping Wives*.

The Flame and the Arrow*

US 1950 88m Technicolor
Warner/Norma (Harold Hecht, Frank Ross)

In medieval Italy, a rebel leader seeks victory over a tyrant.

Good-humoured Robin Hood stuff with the star at his most acrobatic.

w Waldo Salt *d* Jacques Tourneur *ph* Ernest Haller *m* Max Steiner *ad* Edward Carrere

Burt Lancaster, Virginia Mayo, Robert Douglas, Aline MacMahon, Frank Allenby, Nick Cravat

'I never found a Technicolor costume picture so entertaining.' – *Richard Mallett, Punch*
AAN: Ernest Haller; Max Steiner

Flash Gordon
GB 1980 115m Technicolor
Todd-AO
EMI/Famous/Starling (Dino de Laurentiis)
V, L

A football hero, his girl friend, and Dr Zarkov have adventures on the planet Mongo.

Lively comic strip addition to the increasing numbers of such things being restaged at enormous expense fifty years after their prime.

w Lorenzo Semple Jnr, from characters created by Alex Raymond   d Michael Hodges   ph Gil Taylor   m Queen   pd Danilo Donati

Sam J. Jones, Melody Anderson, Topol, Max Von Sydow, Timothy Dalton, Brian Blessed, Peter Wyngarde

'An expensively irrelevant gloss on its sources.' – *Richard Combs, MFB*

Flight of the Doves*
US 1971 101m colour
Columbia/Rainbow (Ralph Nelson)

Two children run away from their bullying stepfather to join their Irish grandmother, but are chased by a wicked uncle who knows they are heirs to a fortune.

Pantomimish whimsy which works in fits and starts, but has little real humour or charm.

w Frank Gabrielson, Ralph Nelson   novel Walter Macken   d Ralph Nelson   ph Harry Waxman   m Roy Budd

Ron Moody, Dorothy McGuire, Helen Raye, Dana, Jack Wild, Stanley Holloway, William Rushton

The Flight of the Dragon
US 1982 98m colour
Rankin/Bass Productions (Arthur Rankin Jr, Jules Bass)

An author is plucked from modern times back into a mythic past to help save magic in the world.

Children's cartoon with an ecological message. By modern standards, the animation is above average.

w Romeo Muller   book *The Flight of Dragons* by Peter Dickinson   d Arthur Rankin Jr, Jules Bass   m Maury Laws   pd Wayne Anderson

voices of Victor Bueno, James Gregory, James Earl Jones, Harry Morgan, John Ritter

Flight of the Navigator*
US 1986 90m colour
Buena Vista/Walt Disney (Robby Wald, Dimitri Villard)

Kidnapped by aliens, a 12-year-old boy returns home after an eight-year absence without having grown any older.

Science fiction aimed at a family audience and providing blandly innocuous, occasionally amusing entertainment.

w Michael Burton, Matt Macmanus   story Mark H. Baker   d Randal Kleiser   ph James Glennon   m Alan Silvestri   pd William J. Creber   ed Jeff Gourson

Joey Cramer, Veronica Cartwright, Cliff DeYoung, Sarah Jessica Parker, Matt Adler, Howard Hesseman, Paul Mall (Paul Reubens)

Flipper
US 1963 87m Metrocolor
(MGM) Ivan Tors

A fisherman's son on the Florida Keys befriends a dolphin.

Harmless boy-and-animal adventure which spawned two sequels and a TV series.

w Arthur Weiss d James B. Clark ph Lamar Boren, Joseph Brun m Henry Vars

Chuck Connors, Luke Halpin, Kathleen Maguire, Connie Scott

† *Flipper's New Adventure* followed in 1964.

Fluffy

US 1964 92m Eastmancolor
U-I/Scarus (Gordon Kay)

A biologist manages to tame a lion.

Mindless, cheerful animal comedy.

w Samuel Rocca d Earl Bellamy ph Clifford Stine m Irving Gertz

Tony Randall, Shirley Jones, Edward Andrews, Ernest Truex, Howard Morris, Jim Backus, Frank Faylen

The Flying Deuces*

US 1939 67m bw
Boris Morros
V

Laurel and Hardy join the Foreign Legion.

Patchy comedy from the end of the comedians' period of glory, and showing signs of decline.

w Ralph Spence, Harry Langdon, Charles Rogers, Alfred Schiller d Edward Sutherland ph Art Lloyd, Elmer Dyer md Edward Paul m Leo Shuken ed Jack Dennis

Stan Laurel, Oliver Hardy, Jean Parker, James Finlayson, Reginald Gardiner, Charles Middleton

'Mechanical stuff . . . seemed like *Beau Hunks* and *Bonnie Scotland* all over again.' – *William K. Everson*

Flying Elephants

US 1927 20m bw silent
Hal Roach

A caveman has the toothache.

Fragmentary and generally unsatisfactory comedy starring Laurel and Hardy before they properly teamed, but released after their joint success.

w Hal Roach, H. M. Walker d Frank Butler

Laurel and Hardy, James Finlayson, Viola Richard, Dorothy Coburn

Follow a Star

GB 1959 104m bw
Rank (Hugh Stewart)

A shy amateur singer allows a fading star to mime to his voice.

Star comedy with an antique plot and a superfluity of pathos.

w Jack Davies, Henry Blyth, Norman Wisdom d Robert Asher ph Jack Asher m Philip Green

Norman Wisdom, Jerry Desmonde, June Laverick, Hattie Jacques, Richard Wattis, John Le Mesurier, Fenella Fielding, Ron Moody

'Such comedy as there is is mostly muffed by the lack of any sense of comic timing.' – *MFB*

Follow Me Boys

US 1966 132m Technicolor
Walt Disney (Winston Hibler)

The domestic trials and tribulations of a smalltown schoolmaster.

Sentimental family saga full of patriotic fervour.

w Louis Pelletier novel *God and My Country* by Mackinlay Kantor
d Norman Tokar ph Clifford Stine m George Bruns

Fred MacMurray, Vera Miles, Lillian Gish, Charlie Ruggles, Elliott Reid, Kurt Russell, Luana Patten, Ken Murray

'Demands an extremely strong stomach.' – *MFB*

For the Love of Benji
US 1977 84m colour
Mulberry Square

A small dog gets lost in the Greek islands.

Adequate follow-up to *Benji*; what more can one say?

w Ben Vaughn, Joe Camp d Joe Camp

Patsy Garrett, Cynthia Smith, Peter Bowles, Ed Nelson

For the Love of Mike*
US 1960 84m DeLuxe Cinemascope
TCF/Shergari (George Sherman)
GB title: *None But the Brave*

An Indian boy in New Mexico is helped by a priest to care for sick animals.

Sentimental outdoor film for young people with a pleasantly light touch.

w D. D. Beauchamp d George Sherman ph Alex Phillips m Raul La Vista

Richard Basehart, Stuart Erwin, Arthur Shields, Armando Silvestre

For Your Eyes Only*
GB 1981 127m Technicolor Panavision
UA/Eon (Albert R. Broccoli)
L

James Bond traces a top secret device sunk in a surveillance vehicle off the Greek coast.

Lively set-pieces can't quite redeem this wholly uninventive addition to the Bond canon. Fun while it's on, but next morning there's nothing left to remember.

w Richard Maibaum, Michael G. Wilson d John Glen ph Alan Hume m Bill Conti pd Peter Lamont

Roger Moore, Carole Bouquet, Topol, Lynn-Holly Johnson, Julian Glover, Jill Bennett, Jack Hedley, Lois Maxwell, Desmond Llewelyn, Geoffrey Keen

'Roger Moore fronts for a succession of stunt men with all the relaxed, lifelike charm of a foyer poster of himself.' – *Sunday Times*
'Pretty boring between the stunts, as if the director isn't interested in actors, and Broccoli forgot to commission a screenplay.' – *Guardian*

† The first Bond in which original author Ian Fleming doesn't even rate a credit.
AAN: title song (*m* Bill Conti, *ly* Mick Leeson)

Four Clowns**
US 1970 96m bw
Robert Youngson Productions (Herb Gelbspan)

Studies of four silent comedians. Laurel and Hardy in excerpts from *Putting Pants on Philip*, *The Second Hundred Years*, *Their Purple Moment*, *Big Business*, *Two Tars* and *Double Whoopee*; Charley Chase in *Us*, *What Price Goofy*, *Fluttering Hearts*, *The Family Group* and *Limousine Love*; Buster Keaton in *Seven Chances*.

An essential compendium, especially for the Charley Chase revaluation which was long overdue.

w Robert Youngson   m Manny Alban

Narrator: Jay Jackson

The Four Feathers****
GB 1939 130m Technicolor
London (Alexander Korda, Irving Asher)
V, L

The standard version of the above, perfectly cast and presented, with battle scenes which have since turned up in a score of other films from *Zarak* to *Master of the World*; also a triumph of early colour.

w R. C. Sherriff, Lajos Biro, Arthur Wimperis   d Zoltan Korda
ph Georges Périnal, Osmond Borradaile, Jack Cardiff   m Miklos Rozsa   ad Vincent Korda
ed William Hornbeck, Henry Cornelius

John Clements, Ralph Richardson, C. Aubrey Smith, June Duprez, Allan Jeayes, Jack Allen, Donald Gray, Henry Oscar, John Laurie

'It cannot fail to be one of the best films of the year . . . even the richest of the ham goes smoothly down, savoured with humour and satire.' – *Graham Greene*

† Remade 1956 as *Storm over the Nile* (qv). An effective TV movie, *The Four Feathers*, was made in 1977, directed by Don Sharp and starring Beau Bridges, Robert Powell, Simon Ward, Richard Johnson, Jane Seymour and Harry Andrews.

'What has eight legs, feathers, and is usually seen coming to the rescue?'

The Four Musketeers (The Revenge of Milady)*
Panama 1974 103m Technicolor
TCF/Film Trust/Este (Alexander Salkind, Michael Salkind)

Athos, Porthos, Aramis and D'Artagnan have a final battle with Rochefort.

Perfunctory sequel to the same team's *The Three Musketeers*; allegedly the two films were intended as one, but if so the first ten reels were by far the best, though this section has its regulation quota of high spirits and lusty action.

w George MacDonald Fraser
d Richard Lester   ph David Watkin   m Lalo Schifrin
pd Brian Eatwell

Michael York, Oliver Reed, Frank Finlay, Richard Chamberlain, Raquel Welch, Faye Dunaway, Charlton Heston, Christopher Lee, Simon Ward, Geraldine Chaplin, Jean-Pierre Cassel, Roy Kinnear

'The whole sleek formula has rolled over to reveal a very soft, very flabby underside.' – *Tony Rayns*

The Fox and the Hound*
US 1981 83m Technicolor
Walt Disney (Wolfgang Reitherman, Art Stevens)

A fox cub makes friends with a hound puppy, but their friendship is tested when they grow up.

Not unpleasant but somewhat heavy-going for a feature cartoon, made with some of the old Disney style but none of the old inventiveness.

w various   novel Daniel P. Mannix   d Art Stevens, Ted Berman, Richard Rich voices of Mickey Rooney, Kurt Russell, Pearl Bailey, Jack Albertson, Sandy Duncan, Jeanette Nolan

'Laughs are few and far between ... the whole enterprise lacks vitality.' – *Brenda Davies, MFB*

Francis*

US 1950 90m bw
U-I (Robert Arthur)

An army private makes friends with a talking mule who causes him some embarrassment.

Simple-minded, quite agreeable if rather slow-moving fantasy farce which was popular enough to spawn several sequels and later a TV series called *Mister Ed*.

w David Stern novel David Stern d Arthur Lubin ph Irving Glassberg m Frank Skinner

Donald O'Connor, Patricia Medina, Zasu Pitts, Ray Collins, John McIntire, Eduard Franz, Robert Warwick, and Chill Wills as Francis' voice. Sequels (the first six with Donald O'Connor):

1951: FRANCIS GOES TO THE RACES
1952: FRANCIS GOES TO WEST POINT
1953: FRANCIS COVERS BIG TOWN
1954: FRANCIS JOINS THE WACS
1955: FRANCIS IN THE NAVY
1956: FRANCIS IN THE HAUNTED HOUSE (with Mickey Rooney)

Freaky Friday

US 1976 100m Technicolor
Walt Disney (Ron Miller)
L

A 13-year-old and her mother, each discontented with their lot, express a wish to change places – and do.

A trendy update of *Vice Versa*, padded out with Disney irrelevancies and long outstaying its welcome.

w Mary Rodgers novel Mary Rodgers d Gary Nelson ph Charles F. Wheeler m Johnny Mandel

Jodie Foster, Barbara Harris, John Astin, Patsy Kelly, Dick Van Patten, Sorrell Booke, Marie Windsor

Freckles

US 1935 69m bw
RKO (Pandro S. Berman)

A mild teenager gets a job as a timber guard.

Unsensational version of a rustic classic.

w Dorothy Yost novel Gene Stratton-Porter d Edward Killy, William Hamilton

'The novel, published in 1875, is shown to have sold 2,000,000 copies. It will have a tough time making the same grade as a picture ... its appeal is of a past generation.' – *Variety*

† A 1960 remake for Fox starred Martin West.

Freddie as F.R.0.7

GB 1992 91m colour
Rank/Hollywood Road Films
V

A human-sized frog, a French secret agent, investigates the disappearance of such British institutions as Buckingham Palace and the Tower of London.

Dated, animated parody of James Bond. It was intended as the first of a series starring Freddie, but its box-office failure led to a sequel being abandoned.

w Jon Acevski, David Ashton

d Jon Acevski *ph* Rex Neville *m/ly* David Dundas, Rick Wentworth, Don Black, Jon Acevski, David Ashton *ad* Paul Shardlow *ed* Alex Rayment, Mick Manning

voices of Ben Kingsley, Jenny Agutter, Brian Blessed, Nigel Hawthorne, Michael Hordern, Edmund Kingsley, Phyllis Logan, Victor Maddern, Jonathan Pryce, Prunella Scales, John Sessions, Billie Whitelaw

'This likeable enough saga of a super-agent frog looks unlikely to hop into the big time.' – *Variety*

Free Willy*

US 1993 112m Technicolor
Warner/Canal+/Regency/Alcor (Jennie Lew Tugend, Lauren Shuler-Donner)

A young, disturbed boy forms a friendship with a killer whale threatened with death.

Sentimental animal story with a little charm and some appeal to the under-10s, but no more than a damp update of *Lassie*.

w Keith A. Walker, Corey Blechman *d* Simon Wincer *ph* Robbie Greenber *m* Basil Poledouris

Jason James Richter, Lori Petty, Jayne Atkinson, August Schellenberg, Michael Madsen, Michael Ironside

'The movie hits every emotional button with a firm fist.' – Richard Corliss, *Time*

The Freshman**

US 1925 75m (24 fps) bw silent
Harold Lloyd
V

An awkward college student accidentally becomes a star football player.

A rather slow but striking star vehicle with assured set-pieces. The football game climax was later used as the first reel of *Mad Wednesday*.

w Sam Taylor, Ted Wilde, Tim Whelan, John Grey *d* Fred Newmeyer, Sam Taylor *ph* Walter Lundin, Henry Kohler

Harold Lloyd, Jobyna Ralston, Brooks Benedict

From Russia with Love***

GB 1963 118m Technicolor
UA/Eon (Harry Saltzman, Albert Broccoli)
V

A Russian spy joins an international crime organization and develops a plan to kill James Bond and steal a coding machine.

The second Bond adventure and possibly the best, with Istanbul and Venice for backdrops and climaxes involving a speeding train and a helicopter. Arrant nonsense with tongue in cheek, on a big budget.

w Richard Maibaum, Johanna Harwood *novel* Ian Fleming *d* Terence Young *ph* Ted Moore *m* John Barry *titles* Robert Brownjohn

Sean Connery, Robert Shaw, Pedro Armendariz, Daniela Bianchi, *Lotte Lenya*, Bernard Lee, Eunice Gayson, Lois Maxwell

From Soup to Nuts*

US 1928 20m bw silent
Hal Roach

Two temporary waiters wreck a dinner party.

Very funny slapstick which the stars subsequently reworked into *A Chump at Oxford*.

w H. M. Walker *story* Leo

McCarey d Edgar Kennedy
ph Len Powers ed Richard Currier

Laurel and Hardy, Anita Garvin, Tiny Sandford

From the Mixed-Up Files of Mrs Basil E. Frankweiler
US 1973 105m colour
Cinema 5

Two children hide out in New York's Metropolitan Museum of Art and befriend a rich woman.

An unusual idea makes ho-hum entertainment for well-brought-up children.

w Blanche Hanalis novel E. L. Konigsberg d Fielder Cook

Ingrid Bergman, Sally Prager, Johnny Doran, George Rose, Richard Mulligan

The Frozen Limits*
GB 1939 84m bw
Gainsborough (Edward Black)

Six impecunious comedians hear of the Yukon gold rush, and join it . . . forty years too late.

The Crazy Gang not quite at its best, but working hard, with a few hilarious moments and a special assist from Moore Marriott.

w Marriott Edgar, Val Guest, J. O. C. Orton d Marcel Varnel
ph Arthur Crabtree md Louis Levy ad Vetchinsky ed R. E. Dearing, Alfred Roome

Flanagan and Allen, Nervo and Knox, Naughton and Gold, Moore Marriott, Eileen Bell, Anthony Hulme, Bernard Lee, Eric Clavering

'The funniest English picture yet produced . . . it can bear comparison with *Safety Last* and *The General*.' – Graham Greene

Fuddy Duddy Buddy**
US 1952 7m Technicolor
UPA

Mr Magoo mistakes a walrus for his friend the colonel.

Top drawer Magoo adventure climaxing with the celebrated line: 'I don't care if he is a walrus. I like him. I like him!'

wd John Hubley m William Lava

Fun and Fancy Free*
US 1947 73m Technicolor
Walt Disney (Ben Sharpsteen)

Cartoon stories told by and to Jiminy Cricket and Edgar Bergen.

Variable Disney ragbag including *Bongo* the Bear, and a lengthy version of *Jack and the Beanstalk*.

w various d various

The Funniest Man in the World*
US 1967 102m bw
Funnyman Inc

Moderately intelligent compilation of sequences from the films of Charlie Chaplin, including *Making a Living*, *Kid Auto Races at Venice*, *Tillie's Punctured Romance*, *The Tramp*, *A Night Out*, *The Rink*, *The Immigrant* and *Easy Street*. The later shorts and features, on which Chaplin himself claimed full copyright, are not included.

wd Vernon P. Becker

A Funny Thing Happened on the Way to the Forum**
GB 1966 99m DeLuxe
UA/Quadrangle (Melvin Frank)
V, L

In ancient Rome, a conniving slave schemes to win his freedom.

Bawdy farce from a Broadway musical inspired by Plautus but with a New

York Jewish atmosphere. The film pays scant attention to the comic numbers that made the show a hit, but adds some style of its own, including a free-for-all slapstick climax.

w Melvin Frank, Michael Pertwee *musical comedy* Burt Shevelove, Larry Gelbart d Richard Lester ph Nicolas Roeg md Ken Thorne pd Tony Walton titles Richard Williams m/ly Stephen Sondheim

Zero Mostel, Phil Silvers, Michael Crawford, Jack Gilford, *Michael Hordern*, Buster Keaton, Patricia Jessel, Leon Greene, Beatrix Lehmann

'Actors have to be very fast and very sly to make themselves felt amid the flash and glitter of a characteristic piece of Lester film-mosaic.' – *John Russell Taylor*

'He proceeds by fits and starts and leaves jokes suspended in mid-air . . . like coitus interruptus going on forever.' – *Pauline Kael*

AA: Ken Thorne

The Further Perils of Laurel and Hardy***
US 1967 99m bw
TCF/Robert Youngson

A compilation of longish extracts from the stars' silent comedies, including *Early to Bed*, *The Second Hundred Years*, *Should Married Men Go Home*, *You're Darn Tootin'*, *Habeas Corpus*, *That's My Wife*, and *Leave 'Em Laughing*. The producer is to be congratulated on refurbishing so many deteriorating negatives, though the commentary leaves much to be desired.
w/ed Robert Youngson m John Parker

G

Gasbags*
GB 1940 77m bw
Gainsborough (Edward Black)

Airmen stranded in Germany by a barrage balloon return in a captured secret weapon.

Fast-moving knockabout from the Crazy Gang; often inventive despite reach-me-down script and production.

w Val Guest, Marriott Edgar
d Marcel Varnel   ph Arthur Crabtree   md Louis Levy

Flanagan and Allen, Nervo and Knox, Naughton and Gold, Moore Marriott, Wally Patch, Peter Gawthorne, Frederick Valk

Gay Purree*
US 1962 85m Technicolor
UPA (Henry Saperstein)

A country cat goes to Paris and is Shanghaied.

Feature cartoon similar to Disney's later *The Aristocats* and about as good, i.e. not quite up to the best standards.

w Dorothy and Chuck Jones
d Abe Levitow   md Mort Lindsey
m/ly Harold Arlen, E. Y. Harburg

voices of Judy Garland, Robert Goulet, Hermione Gingold

The Geisha Boy
US 1958 98m Technicolor Vistavision
Paramount (Jerry Lewis)

A third-rate magician joins a USO entertainment tour in Japan.

Disconnected farce which amuses only fitfully, and actively displeases when it becomes sentimental with the star drooling over a baby.

wd Frank Tashlin   ph Haskell Boggs   m Walter Scharf

Jerry Lewis, Marie MacDonald, Barton MacLane, Sessue Hayakawa, Suzanne Pleshette

'Everybody laughs but Buster!'
The General****
US 1926 80m approx (24 fps)
   bw   silent
UA/Buster Keaton (Joseph M. Schenck)
V, L

A confederate train driver gets his train and his girl back when they are stolen by Union soldiers.

Slow-starting, then hilarious action comedy, often voted one of the best ever made. Its sequence of sight gags, each topping the one before, is an incredible joy to behold.

w Al Boasberg, Charles Smith
d Buster Keaton, Clyde Bruckman
ph J. Devereux Jennings, Bert Haines

Buster Keaton, Marion Mack, Glen Cavander

'It has all the sweet earnestness in the world. It is about trains, frontier America, flower-faced girls.' – *New Yorker, 1977*

'The production itself is singularly well mounted, but the fun is not exactly plentiful . . . here he is more the acrobat than the clown, and his vehicle might be described as a mixture of cast iron and jelly.' – *Mordaunt Hall, New York Times*

† The story is based on an actual incident of the Civil War, treated more seriously in *The Great Locomotive Chase* (qv).

†† The screenplay with 1,400 freeze frames was issued in 1976 in the Film Classics Library (editor, Richard Anobile).

General Spanky
US 1936 73m approx bw
MGM/Hal Roach

A small boy is instrumental in a famous Civil War victory.

Uneasy sentimental melodrama vehicle for one of the moppet stars of 'Our Gang'.

w Richard Flournoy, Hal Yates, John Guedel d Gordon Douglas, Fred Newmeyer

Spanky McFarland, Phillips Holmes, Hobart Bosworth, Ralph Morgan, Irving Pichel

'Desultory, overlong . . . built for the lesser family trade.' – *Variety*

Genevieve****
GB 1953 86m Technicolor
GFD/Sirius (Henry Cornelius)

Two friendly rivals engage in a race on the way back from the Brighton veteran car rally.

One of those happy films in which for no very good or expected reason a number of modest elements merge smoothly to create an aura of high style and memorable moments. A charmingly witty script, carefully pointed direction, attractive actors and locations, an atmosphere of light-hearted British sex and a lively harmonica theme turned it, after a slowish start, into one of Britain's biggest commercial hits and most fondly remembered comedies.

w William Rose d Henry Cornelius ph Christopher Challis md Muir Mathieson m Larry Adler (who also played it) ad Michael Stringer

Dinah Sheridan, John Gregson, Kay Kendall, Kenneth More, Geoffrey Keen, Joyce Grenfell, Reginald Beckwith, Arthur Wontner

'One of the best things to have happened to British films over the last five years.' – *Gavin Lambert*

† On American prints, Muir Mathieson was credited as the composer and with the Oscar nomination rather than Larry Adler, who was blacklisted at the time.
AAN: William Rose; Larry Adler

Gerald McBoing Boing***
US 1951 7m Technicolor
UPA

A small boy becomes famous because he can't speak words: 'he goes boing-boing instead'.

Highly influential cartoon in what was then a new style; told with a light touch which is still extremely funny. Followed less successfully by *Gerald McBoing Boing's Symphony* and *Gerald McBoing Boing On Planet Moo*.

w Dr Seuss (Theodore Geisel)
d Robert Cannon   *m* Gail Kubik
pd John Hubley

AA: best cartoon

Get Back
GB 1991 89m colour/bw
Entertainment/Allied Filmmakers/Front Page/MPL (Henry Thomas, Philip Knatchbull)

Documentary of a world tour by Paul McCartney and his band.

An extended music video that is a far cry from Lester's exuberant earlier treatment of the Beatles; he and McCartney are obviously older and staider.   *d* Richard Lester
ph Jordan Cronenweth, Robert Paynter   *ed* John Victor Smith

'Heavy on nostalgia and light on visual zap. Low-tech item will score limited biz in specialized play-off . . . By MTV standards, this is somewhere in a stone age.' – *Variety*

Get Cracking*
GB 1942 96m bw
Columbia (Ben Henry)

George joins the home guard.

Adequate star comedy.

w L. DuGarde Peach   *d* Marcel Varnel   *ph* Stephen Dade
md Harry Bidgood

George Formby, Edward Rigby, Frank Pettingell, Dinah Sheridan, Ronald Shiner, Wally Patch, Irene Handl

Ghost Chase
West Germany 1987 89m colour
Medusa/Contropolis/pro-ject Film/ Hessischer Rundfunk (Dean Heyde)
V

Horror movie-makers summon a ghost to help them find treasure.

Its convoluted plot seems designed to confuse the young audience at which it is presumably aimed, though it misses the target anyway.

w Roland Emmerich, Thomas Kubisch   *story* Roland Emmerich, Oliver Eberle   *d* Roland Emmerich   *ph* Karl Walter Lindenlaub   *pd* Ekkehard Schroeer, Sonja B. Zimmer   *sp* Joachim Grueninger, Hubert Bartholomae
ed Brigitte Pia Fritsche

Jason Lively, Jill Whitlow, Tim McDaniel, Paul Gleason, Chuck Mitchell, Leonard Lansink, Ian McNaughton, Toby Kaye, Cynthia Frost, Julian Curry

The Ghost of St Michael's**
GB 1941 82m bw
Ealing (Basil Dearden)

A school is evacuated to the Isle of Skye, and the local ghost turns out to be an enemy agent.

The star's schoolmaster character is here at its seedy best, and he is well supported in a comedy-thriller plot.

w Angus Macphail, John Dighton
d Marcel Varnel   *ph* Derek Williams

Will Hay, Claude Hulbert, Felix Aylmer, Raymond Huntley, Elliot Mason, Charles Hawtrey, John Laurie, Hay Petrie, Roddy Hughes, Manning Whiley

The Ghost Train**
GB 1931 72m bw
Gainsborough (Michael Balcon)

Passengers stranded at a haunted station in Cornwall include a detective posing as a silly ass in order to trap smugglers.

Excellent early sound version of a

comedy-thriller play which has not only been among the most commercially successful ever written but also provided the basic plot for many another comedy: *Oh Mr Porter, The Ghost of St Michael's, Back Room Boy, Hold That Ghost,* etc. Previously filmed as a silent in 1927, with Guy Newall.

w Angus Macphail, Lajos Biro
play Arnold Ridley   d Walter Forde
ph Leslie Rowson   ad Walter Murton   ed Ian Dalrymple

Jack Hulbert, Cicely Courtneidge, Donald Calthrop, Ann Todd, Cyril Raymond, Angela Baddeley, Allan Jeayes

The Ghost Train*
GB 1941 85m bw
Gainsborough (Edward Black)

Adequate remake with the lead split into two characters, which doesn't work quite so well.

w Marriott Edgar, Val Guest, J. O. C. Orton   d Walter Forde   ph Jack Cox

Arthur Askey, Richard Murdoch, Kathleen Harrison, Morland Graham, Linden Travers, Peter Murray Hill, Herbert Lomas

Ghostbusters*
US 1984 105m Metrocolor Panavision
Columbia/Delphi (Ivan Reitman)
V, L

Unemployed academic parapsychologists set themselves up as ghostbusters and destroy several monstrous apparitions on the streets of New York.

Crude farce with expensive special effects. It took more money – millions more – than *Indiana Jones and the Temple of Doom*, which must say something about the age we live in.

w Dan Aykroyd, Harold Ramis
d Ivan Reitman   ph Laszlo Kovacs, Herb Wagreitch   m Elmer Bernstein   pd John DeCuir
ed Sheldon Kahn, David Blewitt

Bill Murray, Dan Aykroyd, Harold Ramis, Sigourney Weaver, Rick Moranis, Annie Potts, William Atherton
AAN: title song (m/ly Ray Parker)

Ghostbusters II
US 1989 108m DeLuxe Panavision
Columbia TriStar (Ivan Reitman)
V, L

The disbanded Ghostbusters reform to deal with supernatural threats to New York.

Rambling, disjointed sequel of little amusement.

w Harold Ramis, Dan Aykroyd
d Ivan Reitman   ph Michael Chapman   m Randy Edelman
pd Bo Welch   ed Sheldon Kahn, Donn Cambern

Bill Murray, Dan Aykroyd, Sigourney Weaver, Harold Ramis, Rick Moranis, Ernie Hudson, Annie Potts, Peter MacNichol, Harris Yulin, David Margulies

Gidget
US 1959 95m Eastmancolor Cinemascope
Columbia (Lewis J. Rachmil)

A 16-year-old girl falls for a surfer; her parents disapprove until he turns out to be the son of their best friend.

Commercial mixture of domestic comedy and beach athletics, for nice teenagers and their moms and pops.

w Gabrielle Upton novel Frederick Kohner d Paul Wendkos ph Burnett Guffey md Morris Stoloff m George Duning

Sandra Dee, Cliff Robertson, James Darren, Arthur O'Connell

† Sequels include *Gidget Goes Hawaiian* (1961) with Deborah Walley; *Gidget Goes to Rome* (1962) with Cindy Carol; and two TV movies.

The Girl Can't Help It*
US 1956 97m Eastmancolor Cinemascope
TCF (Frank Tashlin)
V, L

A theatrical agent grooms a gangster's dumb girl friend for stardom.

Scatty, garish pop scene spoof with a plot borrowed from *Born Yesterday* and a lot of jokes about its new star's superstructure. Some scenes are funny, and it puts the first rock and roll stars in pickle for all time.

w Frank Tashlin, Herbert Baker story *Do Re Mi* by Garson Kanin d Frank Tashlin ph Leon Shamroy md Lionel Newman

Jayne Mansfield, Tom Ewell, Edmond O'Brien, Henry Jones, John Emery; and Julie London, Ray Anthony, Fats Domino, Little Richard, The Platters

Girl Happy
US 1965 96m Metrocolor Panavision
MGM/Euterpe (Joe Pasternak)
V

A pop singer in Florida is forced to chaperone a group of college girls including a gangster's daughter.

Standard star vehicle, quite professionally made and totally forgettable.

w Harvey Bullock, R. S. Allen d Boris Sagal ph Philip Lathrop m George Stoll

Elvis Presley, Harold J. Stone, Shelley Fabares, Gary Crosby, Nita Talbot

Girl of the Limberlost
US 1934 86m bw
Monogram

A girl of the swamps becomes a high school graduate.

Tearful rehash of an old sentimental warhorse.

w Adele Comandini novel Gene Stratton Porter d Christy Cabanne

Louise Dresser, Ralph Morgan, Marian Marsh, Henry B. Walthall, Helen Jerome Eddy, Betty Blythe

'Wholesome to a fault. A family film good enough for anybody to see, but the fault lies in that not everybody will want to see it.' – *Variety*

Give My Regards to Broad Street*
GB 1984 108m colour
TCF/MPL (Andros Epimanondas)

An international rock star fears that the priceless tapes of his new album have been stolen, and searches London for them.

An absurdly thin premise even for a musical which is essentially an ego trip for Paul McCartney, who at least squandered his own money on it and not the bank's. Some of the numbers have merit but the mood never connects.

w Paul McCartney d Peter Webb ph Ian McMillan m Paul McCartney pd Anthony Pratt

Paul McCartney, Bryan Brown, Ringo Starr, Barbara Bach, Tracey Ullman, Ralph Richardson, George Martin, John Bennett

Gleaming the Cube
US 1988 105m Deluxe colour
Rank/Gladden Entertainment (Lawrence Turman)

A teenage skateboarder tracks down the killers of his adopted Vietnamese brother.

Likely to appeal only to those who know what the film's title means.

w Michael Tolkin   d Graeme Clifford   ph Reed Smoot   m Jay Ferguson   pd John Muto   ed John Wright

Christian Slater, Steven Bauer, Richard Herd, Le Tuan, Min Luong, Art Chudabala, Ed Lauter, Micole Mercurio, Peter Kwong

The Gnome-Mobile*
US 1967 90m Technicolor
Walt Disney (James Algar)

A millionaire and his family go for a forest picnic and help a colony of gnomes.

Cheerful adventures for small children, with good trick work.

w Ellis Kadison   novel Upton Sinclair   d Robert Stevenson   ph Edward Colman   m Buddy Baker

Walter Brennan, Matthew Garber, Karen Dotrice, Richard Deacon, Sean McClory, Ed Wynn, Jerome Cowan, Charles Lane

'Laughter is what it has nothing else but!'

Go West*
US 1925 70m (24 fps) bw silent
Metro-Goldwyn/Buster Keaton (Joseph M. Schenck)

A tenderfoot makes friends with a cow and takes it everywhere.

Disappointingly slow star comedy with splendid moments.

w Raymond Cannon   d Buster Keaton   ph Bert Haines, E. Lessley

Buster Keaton, Howard Truesdall, Kathleen Myers

Go West**
US 1940 82m bw
MGM (Jack Cummings)
V

Three zanies tackle a Western villain.

Minor Marx comedy with a good start (the ticket office sketch) and a rousing finale as they take a moving train to bits, but some pretty soggy stuff in between.

w Irving Brecher   d Edward Buzzell   ph Leonard Smith   md Georgie Stoll   m Bronislau Kaper

Groucho Marx, Harpo Marx, Chico Marx, John Carroll, Diana Lewis, Robert Barrat

The Gods Must Be Crazy
South Africa 1980 109m colour Panavision
New Realm/Mimosa/CAT (Jamie Uys)
V, L

A Coca Cola bottle falls from a plane and becomes a religious object to Kalahari bushmen.

Unexpected throwback farce with the blacks behaving almost as stupidly as Mantan Moreland in an old Charlie Chan movie. One for the Race Relations Board.

wd Jamie Uys   ph Jamie Uys, Buster Reynolds   m John Boshoff   ad Caroline Burls

N'xau, Marius Weyers, Sandra Prinsloo, Nic de Jager, Michael Thys

The Gods Must Be Crazy II
South Africa 1988 98m colour
Fox/Elrina Investment Corp (Boet Troskie)
V

A bushman searching for his lost children finds a New York lawyer in the desert.

Implausible tale, as condescending as the first film to its black cast.

wd Jamie Uys   ph Buster Reynolds   m Charles Fox
ed Renee Engelbrecht, Ivan Hall

N'xau, Lena Farugia, Hans Strydom, Eiros, Nadies, Erick Bowen, Treasure Tshabalala, Pierre Van Pletzen, Lournes Swanepoel, Richard Loring

'The gospel according to today!'
Godspell*
US 1973 102m TVC color
Columbia/Lansbury/Duncan/Beruh (Edgar Lansbury)

The Gospel according to St Matthew played out musically by hippies in the streets of New York.

Wild and woolly film version of the successful theatrical fantasy, surviving chiefly by virtue of its gleaming photography.

w David Greene, John Michael Tebelak   play John Michael Tebelak   d David Greene
ph Richard G. Heimann   m/ly Stephen Schwartz

Victor Garber, David Haskell, Jerry Sroka, Lynne Thigpen, Robin Lamont

'A patch of terra incognita somewhere between *Sesame Street* and the gospel according to *Laugh-In*.' – Bruce Williamson

Godzilla
Japan 1955 80m (dubbed version) bw
Toho (Tomoyuki Tanaka)
original title: *Gojira*

A prehistoric monster is awakened by H-bomb tests and menaces Tokyo.

Tepid forerunner of scores of Japanese monster movies peopled by men in rubber suits.

w Takeo Murato, Inoshiro Honda
d Inoshiro Honda   ph Masao Tamai   m Akira Ifukube

Raymond Burr, Takashi Shimura, Momoko Kochi

† Sequels included *Godzilla vs the Thing, King Kong vs Godzilla, Godzilla vs the Sea Monster, Godzilla vs the Smog Monster, Destroy All Monsters*. Other monstrous creations included *Rodan, Manda* and *Mothra*.

Godzilla versus Gigan
Japan 1972 89m (dubbed) colour
Toho Productions (Tomoyuki Tanaka)
aka: *Godzilla on Monster Island*

With the aid of Godzilla and his friends, a comic-book artist foils a plot by giant alien cockroaches to take over the world.

The usual nonsense, with the novelty of talking monsters, although their dialogue is no more interesting than that of the humans.

w Shinichi Sekizawa   d Jun Fukuda   m Akira Ifukube
pd Yoshifumi Honda   sp Akiyoshi Nakano   ed Yoshio Tamura

Hiroshi Ishikawa, Tomoko Umeda, Yuriko Hishimi, Minora Takashima, Zan Fujita, Toshiaki Nishizawa, Kunio Murai

Godzilla versus Megalon
Japan 1976 80m (dubbed) colour
Toho Studios (Tomoyuki Tanaka)

Angered by nuclear tests, the ruler of an underwater world sends a monster, a sort of winged lobster, to destroy Tokyo.

Most ridiculous, and, for that reason, the most enjoyable of the *Godzilla* series, notable for the Seatopians, a submarine race given to wearing togas with knee-length boots, and the tag-team wrestling style of the monster combats.

w Shinichi Sekizawa   *d* Jun Fukuda   *ph* Yuzuru Aizawa   *m* Riichiro Manabe   *ad* Yoshibumi Honda   *sp* Akiyoshi Nakano   *ed* Michiko Ikeda

Katsuhiko Sasaki, Yutaka Hayashi, Hiroyuki Kawase

The Gold Rush***
US 1925 72m (sound version 1942) bw
Charles Chaplin
L

A lone prospector in the Yukon becomes rich after various adventures.

Essentially a succession of slowly but carefully built visual gags, this is Chaplin's finest example of comedy drawn from utter privation; as such it appealed vastly to the poor of the world. As a clown, Chaplin himself is near his best, though as usual there is rather too much straining for pathos.

wd/m Charles Chaplin   *ph* Rollie Totheroh   *md* Max Terr (1942 version)   *ad* Charles D. Hall   *ed* Harold McGhean (1942 version)

Charles Chaplin, Georgia Hale, Mack Swain, Tom Murray
AAN: Max Terr

The Golden Age of Buster Keaton**
US 1975 97m bw
Jay Ward (Raymond Rohauer)

A useful introductory package to the shorts and features of Buster Keaton, with most of the great silent scenes present.

commentary: Bill Scott

The Golden Age of Comedy****
US 1957 78m bw
Robert Youngson Productions

First of the scholarly compilations of silent comedy which saved many negatives from destruction, this is a fast-paced general survey which despite a facetious sound track does provide a laugh a minute.

It particularly brought Laurel and Hardy back into public notice, and includes sections from *Two Tars* and *The Battle of the Century*.

wd Robert Youngson
narrators Dweight Weist, Ward Wilson   *m* George Steiner

Stan Laurel, Oliver Hardy, Harry Langdon, Ben Turpin, Will Rogers, Billy Bevan, Charlie Chase, Andy Clyde

'His blade of gold, a legend in battle – her kiss of surrender, the prize of victory!'
The Golden Blade
US 1953 80m Technicolor
U-I (Richard Wilson)

With the help of a magic sword, Harun saves a princess and captures a rebel.

Standard cut-rate Arabian Nights adventure, very typical of its studio during the fifties.

w John Rich   *d* Nathan Juran   *ph* Maury Gertsman   *m* Joseph Gershenson

Rock Hudson, Piper Laurie, George Macready, Gene Evans, Kathleen Hughes

The Golden Child
US 1986 93m Metrocolor
Paramount/Feldman-Meeker/Eddie Murphy
V, L

A social worker is assigned to look for a mystic child who will bring peace to the Earth.

Astonishingly inept fantasy.

w Dennis Feldman d Michael Ritchie ph Donald E. Thorin m Michael Colombier

Eddie Murphy, Charles Dance, Charlotte Lewis, Victor Wong

The Golden Hawk
US 1952 83m Technicolor
Columbia

A pirate determines to avenge his mother's death at the hands of the governor of Cartagena.

Clean-cut period romp for boys who don't demand realism.

w Robert E. Kent novel Frank Yerby d Sidney Salkow

Sterling Hayden, Rhonda Fleming, John Sutton, Helena Carter, Paul Cavanagh

The Golden Horde
US 1951 76m Technicolor
U-I (Howard Christie)
aka: *The Golden Horde of Genghis Khan*

Crusaders meet Mongols in Samarkand, and Sir Guy wins a princess.

Rather priceless idiocies are perpetrated in this variation on the studio's favourite Arabian Nights theme, but somehow they fail to make one laugh, which should be the only possible response to such a farrago.

w Gerald Drayson Adams
d George Sherman ph Russell Metty m Hans Salter

David Farrar, Ann Blyth, George Macready, Henry Brandon, Richard Egan, Marvin Miller

The Golden Seal*
US 1983 94m Metrocolor
Samuel Goldwyn Jnr (Russell Thatcher)
L

On a bleak Aleutian island a boy stops hunters from killing a seal once thought mythical.

Rather chilling and thinly plotted moral fable for children, who may, however, be bored. The seals, the scenery and the music just about save it.

w John Groves novel *A River Ran out of Eden* by James Vance Marshall d Frank Zuniga ph Eric Saarinen m Dana Kaproff, John Barry

Steve Railsback, Michael Beck, Penelope Milford, Torquil Campbell

The Golden Voyage of Sinbad*
GB 1973 105m Eastmancolor
Columbia/Morningside (Charles H. Schneer)
V, L

Sinbad finds a strange map and crosses swords with a great magician.

Routine, rather uninspired fantasy enlivened by grotesque trick effects.

w Brian Clemens, Ray Harryhausen d Gordon Hessler ph Ted Moore m Miklos Rozsa pd John Stoll sp Ray Harryhausen

John Philip Law, Caroline Munro, Tom Baker, Douglas Wilmer, Grégoire Aslan

Goldfinger***
GB 1964 112m Technicolor
UA/Eon (Harry Saltzman, Albert R. Broccoli)
V

James Bond prevents an international gold smuggler from robbing Fort Knox.

Probably the liveliest and most amusing of the Bond spy spoofs, with a fairly taut plot between the numerous highlights. The big budget is well used.

w Richard Maibaum, Paul Dehn novel Ian Fleming   d Guy Hamilton   ph Ted Moore   m John Barry   pd Ken Adam   titles Robert Brownjohn

Sean Connery, Honor Blackman, Gert Frobe, Harold Sakata, Shirley Eaton, Bernard Lee, Lois Maxwell, Desmond Llewellyn

'A dazzling object lesson in the principle that nothing succeeds like excess.' – *Penelope Gilliatt*
'A diverting comic strip for grown-ups.' – *Judith Crist*

Good Morning Boys**
GB 1937 79m bw
GFD/Gainsborough (Edward Black)

A schoolmaster takes his troublesome pupils to Paris and becomes involved with an art theft.

Sprightly vehicle for the star's seedy schoolmaster persona: it established him as a major draw in British films.

w Marriott Edgar, Val Guest, Anthony Kimmins   d Marcel Varnel   ph Arthur Crabtree   md Louis Levy   ad Vetchinsky   ed R. E. Dearing, Alfred Roome

Will Hay, Graham Moffatt, Lilli Palmer, Mark Daly, Peter Gawthorne, Martita Hunt, Charles Hawtrey, Will Hay Jnr

† Remade with Ronald Shiner as *Top of the Form*.

The Goonies
US 1985 111m Technicolor Panavision
Warner/Steven Spielberg
V, L

Kids discover a pirate map and set out on a fantasy treasure hunt.

The bottomless pit of the Spielberg genre, a silly tale which takes forever to get going and is acted by children who have not studied elocution. The trick effects when they come are OK, but it's a long annoying haul to that point.

w Chris Columbus   story Steven Spielberg   d Richard Donner   ph Nick McLean   m Dave Grusin   pd J. Michael Riva   ed Michael Kahn

Sean Astin, Josh Brolin, Jeff Cohen, Corey Feldman, Kerri Green, Martha Plimpton, Ke Huy Kwan

The Goose Steps Out*
GB 1942 79m bw
Ealing (S. C. Balcon)

To steal a secret weapon, an incompetent teacher is sent into Germany in place of his Nazi double.

Quite amusing star vehicle, not up to his best standards.

w Angus Macphail, John Dighton d Will Hay, Basil Dearden   ph Ernest Palmer   m Bretton Byrd

Will Hay, Charles Hawtrey, Frank Pettingell, Julien Mitchell, Peter Croft,

Jeremy Hawk, Peter Ustinov, Raymond Lovell, Barry Morse

'This is the big one! Two years in the making!'

Gorgo
GB 1960 78m Technicolor
King Brothers (Wilfrid Eades)

A prehistoric monster is caught in Irish waters and brought to London, but rescued by its mother.

Amiable monster hokum with a happy ending but not much technical resource.

w John Loring, Daniel Hyatt d Eugene Lourié ph Frederick A. Young m Angelo Lavagnino sp Tom Howard

Bill Travers, William Sylvester, Vincent Winter, Christopher Rhodes, Joseph O'Conor, Bruce Seton, Martin Benson

Grandma's Boy*
US 1922 50m approx (24 fps)
bw silent
Associated Exhibitors

Inspired by the heroism of his own grandpa, a meek and mild young fellow subdues a terrifying tramp.

Modest second-feature-length comedy of a burgeoning star, no great shakes by his later standards.

d Fred Newmeyer

Harold Lloyd, Dick Sutherland, Anna Townsend

Grease**
US 1978 110m Metrocolor
Panavision
Paramount/Robert Stigwood, Allan Carr
V, V(W), L

The path of true love in a fifties high school does not run smoothly.

Amiable 'period' musical for teenagers: a highly fashionable exploitation of the new star John Travolta, its commercialism was undeniable, and it carefully built its appeal to older age groups.

w Bronte Woodard *stage musical* Jim Jacobs, Warren Casey d Randal Kleiser ch Patricia Birch ph Bill Butler md Louis St Louis pd Phil Jefferies titles John Wilson m/ly Jim Jacobs, Warren Casey ed John F. Burnett

John Travolta, Olivia Newton-John, Stockard Channing, Eve Arden, Frankie Avalon, Joan Blondell, Edd Byrnes, Sid Caesar, Alice Ghostley, Sha Na Na, Jeff Conaway, Barry Pearl, Michael Tucci

'A bogus, clumsily jointed pastiche of late fifties high school musicals, studded with leftovers from *West Side Story* and *Rebel Without A Cause*.' – New Yorker

AAN: song, 'Hopelessly Devoted to You' (*m/ly* John Farrar)

Grease 2
US 1982 114m Metrocolor
Panavision
Paramount (Robert Stigwood, Allan Carr)
V, V(W), L

In 1961 an English boy causes emotional problems when he joins the senior class of Rydell High School.

Despite the mixture as before, this sequel was a resounding flop in all departments, perhaps proving that the success of the original was only a fluke of timing.

w Ken Finkleman d Patricia Birch ph Frank Stanley md Louis St Louis songs various

Maxwell Caulfield, Michele Pfeiffer, Adrian Zmed, Lorna Luft, Eve Arden,

Sid Caesar, Tab Hunter, Connie Stevens

'It's like being cooped up for two hours inside a combination of juke box and pinball machine, with you as the ball.' – *Daily Mail*

The Great Adventure**
Sweden 1953 73m bw
Arne Sucksdorff

Two boys on a farm rescue an otter and keep it as a pet.

Superbly photographed wildlife film featuring a variety of small animals.

wd/ed/ph Arne Sucksdorff *m* Lars Erik Larsson

Anders Norberg, Kjell Sucksdorff, Arne Sucksdorff

The Great Chase
US 1963 82m bw
Continental

A compendium of chase sequences from silent films.

w Harvey Kort, Paul Killiam, Saul Turrell

William S. Hart, Douglas Fairbanks Snr and Buster Keaton (in *The General*)

Great Expectations****
GB 1946 118m bw
Rank/Cineguild (Anthony Havelock-Allan)
V, L

A boy meets an escaped convict on the Romney Marshes, with strange consequences for both of them.

Despite the inevitable simplifications, this is a superbly pictorial rendering of a much-loved novel, with all the famous characters in safe hands and masterly judgement in every department.

w Ronald Neame, David Lean, Kay Walsh, Cecil McGivern, Anthony Havelock-Allan *d* David Lean *ph* Guy Green *m* Walter Goehr *ad* John Bryan

John Mills, Bernard Miles, *Finlay Currie*, Martita Hunt, Valerie Hobson, Jean Simmons, Alec Guinness, Francis L. Sullivan, Anthony Wager, Ivor Barnard, Freda Jackson, Hay Petrie, O. B. Clarence, George Hayes, Torin Thatcher, Eileen Erskine

'The first big British film to have been made, a film that sweeps our cloistered virtues out into the open.' – *Richard Winnington*
'The best Dickens adaptation, and arguably David Lean's finest film.' – *NFT, 1969*
'It does for Dickens what *Henry V* did for Shakespeare. That is, it indicates a sound method for translating him from print to film . . . almost never less than graceful, tasteful and intelligent, and some of it better than that.' – *James Agee*

† It was remade as a less than memorable TV movie in 1974, directed by Joseph Hardy and starring Michael York, Sarah Miles and James Mason.

AA: Guy Green; John Bryan
AAN: best picture; script; David Lean (as director)

Great Guns*
US 1941 74m bw
TCF (Sol M. Wurtzel)
V

A young millionaire's retainers join the army with him.

Disappointing Laurel and Hardy comedy, their first for Fox and the beginning of their decline. A few good jokes, but no overall control or inventiveness.

w Lou Breslow *d* Monty Banks

ph Glen MacWilliams *m* Emil Newman *ed* Al de Gaetano

Stan Laurel, Oliver Hardy, Sheila Ryan, Dick Nelson, Edmund Macdonald, Charles Trowbridge, Ludwig Stossel, Mae Marsh

Great – Isambard Kingdom Brunel*
GB 1975 28m Eastmancolor
British Lion

A musical, animated biography of the great Victorian engineer.

Quite unexpected, and therefore the more delightful.

w Bob Godfrey *d* Bob Godfrey

The Great Locomotive Chase*
US 1956 76m Technicolor
  Cinemascope
Walt Disney (Lawrence Edward Watkin)

During the Civil War, Union spies steal a train and destroy track and bridges behind them.

A serious version of Buster Keaton's *The General*, based on a true incident; good sequences but no overall pace.

w Lawrence Edward Watkin *d* Francis D. Lyon *ph* Charles Boyle *m* Paul Smith

Fess Parker, Jeffrey Hunter, Jeff York, John Lupton, Kenneth Tobey

The Great Mr Handel*
GB 1942 103m Technicolor
Rank/GHW (James B. Sloan)
V

How the 18th-century composer came to write the Messiah.

Earnest, unlikely biopic, naïve but rather commendable.

w Gerald Elliott, Victor MacClure *play* L. DuGarde Peach *d* Norman Walker *ph* Claude Friese-Greene, Jack Cardiff *md* Ernest Irving

Wilfrid Lawson, Elizabeth Allan, Malcolm Keen, Michael Shepley, Hay Petrie, A. E. Matthews

'A graceful addition to the ranks of prestige pictures.' – *Kine Weekly*

The Great Mouse Detective*
US 1986 80m Technicolor
Walt Disney/Silver Screen Partners II
  (Burny Mattinson)
V, L

GB title: *Basil, The Great Mouse Detective*

A mouse who has studied Sherlock Holmes solves the mystery of a missing mouse toymaker and outwits the evil Professor Rattigan.

One of the better recent Disney cartoon features, but the texture will probably never again be so rich as in the days of *Pinocchio* and *Bambi*.

w Pete Young, Steven Hulett, John Musker, Matthew O'Callaghan, Dave Michener, Vane Gerry, Ron Clements, Bruce M. Morris, Melvin Shaw, Burny Mattinson *novel Basil of Baker Street* by Eve Titus *d* John Musker, Ron Clements, Dave Michener and Burny Mattinson *ph* Ed Austin *m* Henry Mancini *pd* Guy Vasilovich *ed* Roy M. Brewer Jr, James Melton

voices of Barrie Ingham, Vincent Price, Val Bettin, Alan Young

The Great Muppet Caper**
GB 1981 97m Technicolor
ITC (David Lazer, Frank Oz)

Kermit and Fozzie are reporters sent to solve a jewel robbery.

Considerably livelier than *The Muppet Movie* but a badly timed flop at the box-office, this genial caper has a pleasant collection of guest stars as well as showing the familiar puppets at their most typical.

w Tom Patchett, Jay Tarses, Jerry Juhl, Jack Rose   d Jim Henson
ph Oswald Morris   m Joe Raposo
pd Harry Lange

Diana Rigg, Charles Grodin, John Cleese, Robert Morley, Trevor Howard, Peter Ustinov, Jack Warden

'Large chunks are pleasingly daft.' – *Sight and Sound*
AAN: song 'The First Time It Happened' (m/ly Joe Raposo)

The Great Outdoors
US 1988 90m CFI Panavision
Universal/Hughes Entertainment (Arne L. Schmidt)
V

A family's holiday in the woods is disrupted by a surprise visit from their wealthy in-laws.

Broad and tiresome comedy in which its participants flail around noisily to no particular purpose.

w John Hughes   d Howard Deutch   ph Ric Waite   m Thomas Newman   pd John W. Corso
ed Tom Rolf, William Gordean, Seth Flaum

Dan Aykroyd, John Candy, Stephanie Faracy, Annette Bening, Chris Young, Ian Giatti, Hilary Gordon, Rebecca Gordon, Robert Prosky

'The greatest comedy ever made!'
The Great Race***
US 1965 163m Technicolor Super Panavision
Warner/Patricia/Jalem/Reynard (Martin Jurow)
L

In 1908, the Great Leslie and Professor Fate are leading contenders in the first New York to Paris car race.

Elaborate comedy spectacular with many good moments, notably the early disasters, a Western saloon brawl, and a custard pie fight. Elsewhere, there is more evidence of an oversize budget than of wit or finesse, and the entire *Prisoner of Zenda* spoof could have been omitted. Excellent production detail and general good humour.

w Arthur Ross   d Blake Edwards   ph Russell Harlan
m Henry Mancini   pd Fernando Carrere

Jack Lemmon, Tony Curtis, Peter Falk, Natalie Wood, George Macready, Ross Martin, Vivian Vance, Dorothy Provine
AAN: Russell Harlan; song 'The Sweetheart Tree' (m Henry Mancini, ly Johnny Mercer)

The Great Rupert
US 1950 87m bw
Eagle Lion (George Pal)

A family of impoverished acrobats are assisted by a pet squirrel which proves lucky in more ways than one.

Modest whimsical comedy which outstays its welcome.

w Laslo Vadnay   d Irving Pichel

Jimmy Durante, Terry Moore, Tom Drake, Sara Haden, Frank Orth

† The squirrel was part puppet.

The Great St Trinian's Train Robbery
GB 1966 94m Eastmancolor
British Lion/Braywild (Leslie Gilliat)
V

The staff of St Trinian's is infiltrated by would-be train robbers.

Flat-footed farce with a sense of strain evident from first to last shot.

w Frank Launder, Ivor Herbert
d Frank Launder, Sidney Gilliat
ph Ken Hodges   m Malcolm Arnold

Frankie Howerd, Dora Bryan, Reg Varney, Desmond Walter-Ellis, Raymond Huntley, Richard Wattis, George Benson, Eric Barker, Godfrey Winn, George Cole, Colin Gordon, Barbara Couper, Elspeth Duxbury

'What do you do when the war is over and you're the second best pilot in the world?'

The Great Waldo Pepper*
US 1975 108m Technicolor Todd-AO 35
Universal (George Roy Hill)
V, L

In the twenties, a World War I flyer becomes an aerial stuntman.

Whimsical spectacular which concentrates less on the mystique of flying than on a series of splendid stunts.

w William Goldman   d George Roy Hill   ph Robert Surtees   m Henry Mancini

Robert Redford, Bo Svenson, Bo Brundin, Susan Sarandon, Geoffrey Lewis

'Charged with enthralling balletic precision.' – Tom Milne
'One hundred per cent pure plastic adolescent male fantasy.' – New Yorker

The Greatest Show on Earth*
US 1952 153m Technicolor
Paramount/Cecil B. de Mille (Henry Wilcoxon)
V, L

Various dramas come to a head under the big top.

Moribund circus drama with bad acting, stilted production, an irrelevant train crash climax and a few genuinely spectacular and enjoyable moments.

w Fredric M. Frank, Theodore St John, Frank Cavett, Barre Lyndon
d Cecil B. de Mille   ph George Barnes, Peverell Marley, Wallace Kelley   m Victor Young   ad Hal Pereira, Walter Tyler   ed Anne Bauchens

Betty Hutton, Cornel Wilde, James Stewart, Charlton Heston, Dorothy Lamour, Gloria Grahame, Lyle Bettger, Henry Wilcoxon, Emmett Kelly, Lawrence Tierney, John Kellogg, John Ringling North

AA: best picture; original story (Fredric M. Frank, Theodore St John, Frank Cavett)
AAN: Cecil B. de Mille (as director); editing

Green Grass of Wyoming
US 1948 88m Technicolor
TCF

A rancher captures his runaway white stallion and wins the local trotting races.

Predictable, good-looking family film shot on location; a second sequel to *My Friend Flicka*.

w Martin Berkeley   novel Mary O'Hara   d Louis King
ph Charles G. Clarke   m Cyril Mockridge

Peggy Cummins, Charles Coburn, Robert Arthur, Lloyd Nolan
AAN: Charles G. Clarke

The Green Pastures***
US 1936 93m bw
Warner (Henry Blanke)

Old Testament stories as seen through simple-minded negro eyes.

Though recently attacked as setting

back the cause of black emancipation, this is a brilliantly sympathetic and humorous film, very cunningly adapted for the screen in a series of dramatic scenes which make the material work even better than it did on the stage.

w Marc Connelly   play Marc Connelly   stories Roark Bradford   d William Keighley, Marc Connelly   ph Hal Mohr   m Erich Wolfgang Korngold

Rex Ingram, Oscar Polk, Eddie Anderson, Frank Wilson, George Reed

'I imagine God has a sense of humour, and I imagine that He is delighted with *The Green Pastures*.' – *Don Herold*
'That disturbance around the Music Hall yesterday was the noise of shuffling queues in Sixth Avenue and the sound of motion picture critics dancing in the street.' – *Bosley Crowther, New York Times*
'This is as good a religious play as one is likely to get in this age from a practised New York writer.' – *Graham Greene*

The Green Years*
US   1946   127m   bw
MGM (Leon Gordon)

A young boy brought up strictly in Ireland makes friends with his mischievous grandfather.

Period family film in familiar style, sparked only by its scene-stealing star performance.

w Robert Ardrey, Sonya Levien   novel A. J. Cronin   d Victor Saville   ph George Folsey   m Herbert Stothart   ad Cedric Gibbons, Hans Peters

Charles Coburn, Dean Stockwell, Tom Drake, Beverly Tyler, Hume Cronyn, Gladys Cooper, Selena Royle, Jessica Tandy, Richard Haydn, Andy Clyde

'It has been described in the ads as "wonderful" by everyone within Louis B. Mayer's purchasing power except his horses, so I hesitate to ask you to take my word for it: the picture is awful.' – *James Agee*
AAN: George Folsey; Charles Coburn

Gregory's Girl**
GB   1980   91m   colour
Lake/NFFC/STV (Davina Belling, Clive Parsons)
V

In a Scottish new town, a school footballer becomes aware of sex.

Curiously diverting comedy peopled by dreamers but handicapped by impenetrable accents. An unexpected world-wide success.

wd Bill Forsyth   ph Michael Coulter   m Colin Tully

Gordon John Sinclair, Dee Hepburn, Jake D'Arcy, Claire Grogan

BFA: best script

Gremlins*
US   1984   106m   Technicolor
Warner/Amblin (Michael Finnell)
V, L

Small furry creatures called mogwais prove to be immensely prolific and dangerous when wet.

Juvenile horror comic, a kind of deliberate inversion of *E.T.* Slow to start, and a little too knowingly nasty, with variable special effects; but a pretty hot commercial success.

w Chris Columbus   d Joe Dante   ph John Hora   m Jerry Goldsmith   sp Gremlin designer: Chris Walas   ed Tina Hirsch

Zach Galligan, Phoebe Cates, Hoyt

Axton, Polly Holliday, Keye Luke, Scott Brady, Edward Andrews

'Don't go if you still believe in Santa Claus.' – *Roger Ebert*

Gremlins 2: The New Batch**
US 1990 105m Technicolor
Warner/Amblin (Michael Finnell)
V, L

A mogwai, captured by mad research scientists, produces hundreds of violent gremlins who run amuck in a megalomaniac property developer's skyscraper.

A sequel more entertaining than the original, stuffed with in-jokes for movie buffs.

w Charlie Haas   d Joe Dante
ph John Hora   m Jerry Goldsmith   pd James Spencer
ad Joe Lucky   sp Gremlin and mogwai effects: Rick Baker
ed Kent Beyda

Zach Galligan, Phoebe Cates, Hoyt Axton, Frances Lee McCam, Polly Holliday, Dick Miller, Keye Luke, Judge Reinhold, Corey Feldman

'An hilarious sequel featuring equal parts creature slapstick and satirical barbs for adults.' – *Variety*

Greyfriars Bobby*
GB 1960 91m Technicolor
Walt Disney (Hugh Attwooll)

A Skye terrier keeps persistent vigil over his master's grave and is made a freeman of the city of Edinburgh.

Adequately produced film of a charming old Victorian story.

w Robert Westerby   book Eleanor Atkinson   d Don Chaffey   ph Paul Beeson   m Francis Chagrin

Donald Crisp, Laurence Naismith, Alexander Mackenzie, Kay Walsh, Andrew Cruickshank, Vincent Winter, Moultrie Kelsall, Duncan Macrae

'The better Disney qualities of exact period detail and childlike directness are apparent.' – *MFB*

† The story was previously filmed as *Challenge to Lassie*.

Greystoke: The Legend of Tarzan, Lord of the Apes
GB 1984 130m Eastmancolor Panavision
Warner/WEA Records (Hugh Hudson, Stanley S. Canter)
V, L

In the 1880s, an English lord and lady are killed in Africa, and their son is brought up by apes.

An absurd attempt to treat the story seriously after 70 years of hokum, this meandering chronicle, cut down from something much longer and even less endurable, has men in ape suits, an eye for unpleasant detail, and Ralph Richardson sliding down the stairs on a tray. The attempt to moralize at the end is emetic.

w P. H. Vazak (Robert Towne), Michael Austin   novel *Tarzan of the Apes* by Edgar Rice Burroughs
d Hugh Hudson   ph John Alcott
m John Scott   pd Stuart Craig

Ralph Richardson, Ian Holm, James Fox, Christopher Lambert, Andie MacDowell, Cheryl Campbell, Paul Geoffrey, John Wells, Nigel Davenport, Ian Charleson, Richard Griffiths

'A unique mixture of pomposity and ineptitude . . . in the second half the movie simply loses its mind, and dribbles to a pathetically indecisive conclusion.' – *Pauline Kael, New Yorker*
AAN: Ralph Richardson (supporting actor); adapted screenplay

Gulliver's Travels**
US 1939 74m Technicolor
Paramount/Max Fleischer
L

Animated cartoon version which invents a Romeo-Juliet romance between Lilliput and Blefuscu and has the usual trouble with romantic humans.

At the time it represented a genuine challenge to Disney, but has not worn well in terms of pace or inventiveness. Fleischer made one more feature cartoon, *Mr Bug Goes to Town*.

d Dave Fleischer   *m* Victor Young   *m/ly* Ralph Rainger, Leo Robin

'Effective entertainment, but may not reach the grosses of *Snow White*.' – *Variety*
AAN: song 'Faithful Forever'; Victor Young

Gulliver's Travels
GB 1976 81m Eastmancolor
EMI/Valeness-Belvision (Josef Shaftel)

An ineffective treatment, again aimed at children, in which Gulliver is the only human element and all the Lilliputians are cartooned.

w Don Black   *d* Peter Hunt   *ph* Alan Hume   *m* Michel Legrand   *pd* Michael Stringer

Richard Harris, Catherine Schell, Norman Shelley

'Bonelessly inoffensive.' – *Sight and Sound*

The Gumball Rally
US 1976 107m Technicolor
Warner/First Artists (Chuck Bail)

A variety of vehicles take part in a crazy race from New York to Long Beach.

The stuntmen are the real stars of this good-looking but dramatically deficient chase and destruction extravaganza.

w Leon Capetanos   *d* Chuck Bail   *ph* Richard Glouner   *m* Dominic Frontière   *stunt coordinator* Eddie Donno

Michael Sarrazin, Normann Burton, Gary Busey, John Durren, Susan Flannery

'Thrills for a thousand movies plundered for one mighty show!'
'Romance aflame through dangerous days and nights of terror! In a land where anything can happen – most of all to a beautiful girl alone!'

Gunga Din***
US 1939 117m bw
RKO (George Stevens)
L

Three cheerful army veterans meet adventure on the North-West Frontier.

Rousing period actioner with comedy asides, one of the most entertaining of its kind ever made.

w Joel Sayre, Fred Guiol, Ben Hecht, Charles MacArthur   *poem* Rudyard Kipling   *d* George Stevens   *ph* Joseph H. August   *m* Alfred Newman   *ad* Van Nest Polglase

Cary Grant, Victor McLaglen, Douglas Fairbanks Jnr, Sam Jaffe, Eduardo Ciannelli, Joan Fontaine, Montagu Love, Robert Coote, Cecil Kellaway, Abner Biberman, Lumsden Hare

'One of the big money pictures this year . . . will recoup plenty at the box office window.' – *Variety*
'One of the most enjoyable nonsense-adventure movies of all time.' – *Pauline Kael, 1968*

'Bravura is the exact word for the performances, and Stevens' composition and cutting of the fight sequences is particularly stunning.' – *NFT, 1973*

Guns in the Heather
US 1968 90m Technicolor
Walt Disney

An American schoolboy in Ireland finds that his elder brother is a CIA agent.

Tolerable kiddie-fodder from the Disney treadmill; later desiccated for TV.

w Herman Groves   *d* Robert Butler

Glenn Corbett, Alfred Burke, Kurt Russell, Patrick Barr

Gus
US 1976 96m Technicolor
Walt Disney (Ron Miller)

A football team co-opts a mule which can kick a hundred yard ball.

Predictable Disney fantasy comedy with a direct line back to *The Absent Minded Professor*.

w Arthur Alsberg, Don Nelson
d Vincent McEveety   *ph* Frank Phillips   *m* Robert F. Brunner

Ed Asner, Don Knotts, Gary Grimes, Tim Conway, Liberty Williams, Bob Crane, Harold Gould, Tom Bosley, Dick Van Patten

'In the current comedy climate, when humour so often hinges on a four-letter word or its lengthier variant, a light-hearted football game spoof is a breath of fresh air.' – *Tatiana Balkoff Lipscomb, Films in Review*

Gypsy Colt
US 1954 72m Ansco Color
MGM

A cherished colt has to be sold, but makes its way back home.

Disguised second feature remake of *Lassie Come Home*; good for children.

w Martin Berkeley   *d* Andrew Marton

Donna Corcoran, Ward Bond, Frances Dee, Larry Keating, Lee Van Cleef

H

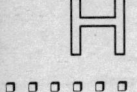

Habeas Corpus*
US 1928 20m bw silent
Hal Roach

A mad professor sends two vagabonds out to look for a body.

Unusual star comedy, more grotesque and pantomimish than any of the others.

w H. M. Walker   story Leo McCarey   d James Parrott   ph Len Powers   ed Richard Currier

Laurel and Hardy, Richard Carle

'It's everything a motion picture can be!'
Half a Sixpence*
GB 1967 148m Technicolor Panavision
Paramount/Ameran (Charles H. Schneer, George Sidney)

A draper's assistant inherits a fortune and moves into society.

Mildly likeable but limp and overlong musical which would have benefited from more intimate, sharper treatment than the wide screen can give. The period decor and lively numbers seem insufficient compensation for the longueurs.

w Beverley Cross   play Beverley Cross   novel Kipps by H. G. Wells   d George Sidney   ph Geoffrey Unsworth   pd Ted Haworth   ch Gillian Lynne   m/ly David Heneker

Tommy Steele, Julia Foster, Cyril Richard, Penelope Horner, Elaine Taylor, Hilton Edwards, Pamela Brown, James Villiers

Hambone and Hillie
US 1983 90m colour Panavision
Sandy Howard/Adams Apple (Gary Gillingham)

A small dog is lost at New York airport and tracks his aged mistress on foot to California.

Basically a revamp of *Lassie Come Home*, with a cute dog and some attractive exteriors, but made unsuitable for its presumably intended family audience by the death of a second dog and a horrific pitchfork sequence in which a heavily pregnant woman is attacked by marauders.

w Sandra K. Bailey, Michael Murphey, Joel Soisson   d Roy Watts   ph Jon Kranhouse   m George Garvarentz

Lillian Gish, Timothy Bottoms, Candy Clark, Robert Walker, O. J. Simpson, Jack Carter, Alan Hale

Hand in Hand*
GB 1960 80m bw
ABP (Helen Winston)

The friendship of two 7-year-olds is affected by racial prejudice because one is Catholic and the other Jewish; but after misunderstandings their friendship is confirmed by priest and rabbi.

Pleasant, well-meaning drama apparently intended for older children.

w Diana Morgan d Philip Leacock ph Frederick A. Young m Stanley Black

Lorette Parry, Phillip Needs, Sybil Thorndike, John Gregson, Finlay Currie

Hannibal

Italy 1959 103m Technicolor Supercinescope
Liber Film (Ottavio Poggi)

Hannibal crosses the Alps and falls for the daughter of a Roman senator.

Unhistorical farrago which totally fails to entertain on any level.

w Mortimer Braus d Carlo Ludovico Bragaglia, Edgar G. Ulmer ph Raffaele Masciocchi m Carlo Rustichelli

Victor Mature, Rita Gam, Gabriele Ferzetti, Milly Vitale, Rik Battaglia

'Not even the elephants emerge with dignity.' – *MFB*

Hans Christian Andersen*

US 1952 112m Technicolor
Samuel Goldwyn
L

A storytelling cobbler leaves his village to make shoes for the prima ballerina in Copenhagen.

Artificial, sugary confection with little humour and far too little magic of any kind; the star carries it nicely, but he is on his own apart from the songs.

w Moss Hart d Charles Vidor ph Harry Stradling md Walter Scharf *m/ly Frank Loesser* ad Richard Day ch Roland Petit

Danny Kaye, Zizi Jeanmaire, Farley Granger, John Qualen, Joey Walsh

† 16 screenplays were written before this one was chosen. Moira Shearer was signed for the role of ballerina but became pregnant. Gary Cooper was thought of for the lead, with William Wyler as director.
AAN: Harry Stradling; Walter Scharf; song 'Thumbelina'

The Happiest Days of Your Life***

GB 1950 81m bw
British Lion/Individual (Frank Launder)

A ministry mistake billets a girls' school on a boys' school.

Briskly handled version of a semi-classic postwar farce, with many familiar talents in excellent form.

w Frank Launder, John Dighton *play John Dighton* d Frank Launder ph Stan Pavey m Mischa Spoliansky

Alastair Sim, Margaret Rutherford, Joyce Grenfell, Richard Wattis, Edward Rigby, Guy Middleton, Muriel Aked, John Bentley, Bernadette O'Farrell

'Absolutely first rate fun.' – *Richard Mallett, Punch*
'Launder couldn't have knocked another laugh out of the situation if he'd used a hockey stick.' – *Sunday Express*
'The best mixed comedy pairing since Groucho Marx and Margaret Dumont.' – *Sunday Chronicle*

The Happiest Millionaire

US 1967 159m Technicolor
Walt Disney (Bill Anderson)

In 1916, a sporting millionaire has several surprising interests but finds time to sort out family problems.

Drearily inept family entertainment with a couple of good songs and an amusing alligator sequence but acres of yawning boredom in between.

w A. J. Carothers play Kyle Crichton book My Philadelphia Father by Cornelia Drexel Biddle d Norman Tokar ph Edward Colman md Jack Elliott m/ly Richard M. and Robert B. Sherman

Fred MacMurray, *Tommy Steele*, Greer Garson, John Davidson, Gladys Cooper, Lesley Anne Warren, Geraldine Page, Hermione Baddeley

The Happy Road*

US/France 1956 100m bw
MGM/Thor (Gene Kelly)

Two children run away from a Swiss school and are pursued by the American father of one of them.

Whimsical peripatetic comedy which fails to come off despite charming passages.

w Arthur Julian, Joseph Morhaim, Harry Kurnitz d Gene Kelly ph Robert Juillard m George Van Parys

Gene Kelly, Barbara Laage, Michael Redgrave, Bobby Clark, Brigitte Fossey

A Hard Day's Night****

GB 1964 85m bw
UA/Proscenium (Walter Shenson)
V, L

Harassed by their manager and Paul's grandpa, the Beatles embark from Liverpool by train for a London TV show.

Comic fantasia with music; an enormous commercial success with the director trying every cinematic gag in the book, it led directly to all the kaleidoscopic swinging London spy thrillers and comedies of the later sixties, and so has a lot to answer for; but at the time it was a sweet breath of fresh air, and the Beatles even seemed willing and likeable.

w Alun Owen d Richard Lester ph Gilbert Taylor md George Martin m/ly The Beatles

The Beatles, Wilfrid Brambell, Norman Rossington, *Victor Spinetti*

'A fine conglomeration of madcap clowning . . . with such a dazzling use of camera that it tickles the intellect and electrifies the nerves.' – *Bosley Crowther*
'All technology was enlisted in the service of the gag, and a kind of nuclear gagmanship exploded.' – *John Simon*
'The *Citizen Kane* of Jukebox movies' – *Andrew Sarris*
AAN: Alun Owen; George Martin

The Hardy Family

America's favourite fictional characters just before and during World War II were the family of a small-town judge, who seemed to personify all that everyone was fighting for, especially as the young son was always getting into amusing scrapes. Designed by a delighted MGM as low-budgeters, they paid for many an expensive failure, and introduced, as young Andy's girlfriends, a series of starlets who went on to much bigger things. The basic family was Lewis Stone, Fay Holden, Mickey Rooney, Cecilia Parker and Sara Haden (as the spinster aunt); but in the very first episode Lionel Barrymore and Spring Byington played the judge and his wife. MGM was given a special Academy Award in 1942 'for representing the American Way of Life' in the films.

A FAMILY AFFAIR (1936); 69m; d George B. Seitz; w Kay Van Riper; play Aurania Rouverol

YOU'RE ONLY YOUNG ONCE (1938); 78m; *d* George B. Seitz; *w* Kay Van Riper; introducing Ann Rutherford (who became a regular)
JUDGE HARDY'S CHILDREN (1938); 78m; *d* George B. Seitz; *w* Kay Van Riper; *with* Ruth Hussey
LOVE FINDS ANDY HARDY (1938); 90m; *d* George B. Seitz; *w* William Ludwig; *with* Judy Garland, Lana Turner
OUT WEST WITH THE HARDYS (1938); 90m; *d* George B. Seitz; *w* Kay Van Riper, Agnes Christine Johnston, William Ludwig
THE HARDYS RIDE HIGH (1939); 81m; *d* George B. Seitz; *w* as above
ANDY HARDY GETS SPRING FEVER (1939); 85m; *d* W. S. Van Dyke II; *w* Kay Van Riper
JUDGE HARDY AND SON (1939); 90m; *d* George B. Seitz; *w* Carey Wilson; *with* June Preisser, Maria Ouspenskaya
ANDY HARDY MEETS A DEBUTANTE (1940); 89m; *d* George B. Seitz; *w* Annalee Whitmore, Thomas Seller; *with* Judy Garland
ANDY HARDY'S PRIVATE SECRETARY (1941); 101m; *d* George B. Seitz; *w* Jane Murfin, Harry Ruskin; *with* Kathryn Grayson, Ian Hunter
LIFE BEGINS FOR ANDY HARDY (1941); 100m; *d* George B. Seitz; *w* Agnes Christine Johnston; *with* Judy Garland
THE COURTSHIP OF ANDY HARDY (1942); 93m; *d* George B. Seitz; *w* Agnes Christine Johnston; *with* Donna Reed
ANDY HARDY'S DOUBLE LIFE (1942); 92m; *d* George B. Seitz; *w* Agnes Christine Johnston; *with* Esther Williams, Susan Peters
ANDY HARDY'S BLONDE TROUBLE (1944); 107m; *d* George B. Seitz; *w* Harry Ruskin, William Ludwig, Agnes Christine Johnston; *with* Bonita Granville, Jean Porter, Herbert Marshall, the Wilde twins
LOVE LAUGHS AT ANDY HARDY (1946); 94m; *d* Willis Goldbeck; *w* Harry Ruskin, William Ludwig; *with* Bonita Granville
ANDY HARDY COMES HOME (1958); 80m; *d* Howard Koch; *w* Edward Everett Hutshing, Robert Morris Donley; *without* Lewis Stone

Harold Lloyd's Funny Side of Life***
US 1963 99m bw
Harold Lloyd (Duncan Mansfield)

Excerpts from twenties comedies plus a shortened version of *The Freshman* (1925).

Excellent compilation, though the mini-feature makes it a little unbalanced.

w Arthur Ross *m* Walter Scharf

Harold Lloyd

Harold Lloyd's World of Comedy****
US 1962 97m bw
Harold Lloyd

Generous clips from the comic climaxes of Lloyd's best silent and sound comedies including *Safety Last, The Freshman, Hot Water, Why Worry, Girl Shy, Professor Beware, Movie Crazy* and *Feet First*.

As Lloyd's work lends itself well to extract, this can hardly fail to be a superb anthology capsuling the appeal of one of America's greatest silent comedians. The timing is just perfect.

w Walter Scharf

commentary: Art Ross

Harry and the Hendersons
US 1987 110m DeLuxe
Universal/Amblin (Richard Vane, William Dear)

L
GB title: *Big Foot and the Hendersons*

A camping family meets a docile Big Foot.

Elementary kiddie/family pic in the wake of *E.T.*

w William Dear, William E. Martin, Ezra D. Rappaport   *d* William Dear   *m* Bruce Broughton   *pd* James Bissell   *sp* Harry designed by Rick Baker   *ed* Donn Cambern

John Lithgow, Melinda Dillon, David Suchet, Don Ameche, Margaret Langrick, Joshua Rudoy

AA: best make-up

Harvey***
US 1950 104m bw
U-I (John Beck)
V

A middle-aged drunk has an imaginary white rabbit as his friend, and his sister tries to have him certified.

An amiably batty play with splendid lines is here transferred virtually intact to the screen and survives superbly thanks to understanding by all concerned, though the star is as yet too young for a role which he later made his own.

w Mary Chase (with Oscar Brodney)   *play* Mary Chase   *d* Henry Koster   *ph* William Daniels   *m* Frank Skinner

James Stewart, Josephine Hull, *Victoria Horne*, Peggy Dow, *Cecil Kellaway*, Charles Drake, *Jesse White*, Nana Bryant, Wallace Ford

VETA LOUISE (Josephine Hull): 'Myrtle Mae, you have a lot to learn, and I hope you never learn it.'

ELWOOD (James Stewart): 'I've wrestled with reality for 35 years, and I'm happy, doctor, I finally won out over it.'

ELWOOD: 'Harvey and I have things to do . . . we sit in the bars . . . have a drink or two . . . and play the juke box. Very soon the faces of the other people turn towards me and they smile. They say: "We don't know your name, mister, but you're all right, all right." Harvey and I warm ourselves in these golden moments. We came as strangers – soon we have friends. They come over. They sit with us. They drink with us. They talk to us. They tell us about the great big terrible things they've done and the great big wonderful things they're going to do. Their hopes, their regrets. Their loves, their hates. All very large, because nobody ever brings anything small into a bar. Then I introduce them to Harvey, and he's bigger and grander than anything they can offer me. When they leave, they leave impressed. The same people seldom come back.'

ELWOOD (describing his first meeting with Harvey): 'I'd just helped Ed Hickey into a taxi. Ed had been mixing his drinks, and I felt he needed conveying. I started to walk down the street when I heard a voice saying: "Good evening, Mr Dowd". I turned, and there was this big white rabbit leaning against a lamp-post. Well, I thought nothing of that! Because when you've lived in a town as long as I've lived in this one, you get used to the fact that everybody knows your name . . .'

AA: Josephine Hull
AAN: James Stewart

Hawk the Slayer
GB 1980 93m colour
ITC/Chips (Harry Robertson)
V, L

Good and evil brothers compete for possession of a magical flying sword.

Curiously unexciting and rather gloomy sword-and-sorcery epic.

w Terry Marcel, Harry Robertson d Terry Marcel ph Paul Beeson m Harry Robertson

Jack Palance, John Terry, Bernard Bresslaw, Ray Charleson, Annette Crosbie, Cheryl Campbell, Peter O'Farrell

Hawmps
US 1976 127m colour
Mulberry Square

The Texas cavalry experiments with the use of camels in the south-western desert.

Incredibly overstretched and tedious period comedy with some bright patches.

w William Bickley, Michael Warren d Joe Camp

James Hampton, Christopher Connelly, Slim Pickens, Denver Pyle, Jennifer Hawkins, Jack Elam

Head*
US 1968 85m Technicolor
Columbia (Bert Schneider)
V, L

Fantasia on the life of a sixties pop group.

A psychedelic trip of a movie which does for the Monkees what *A Hard Day's Night* and *Yellow Submarine* did for the Beatles, and what *Monty Python* did for us all. Sometimes funny, slick and clever; often just plain silly.

w Jack Nicholson, Bob Rafaelson d Bob Rafaelson ph Michael Hugo m Ken Thorne sp Chuck Gaspar

The Monkees, Victor Mature, Annette Funicello, Timothy Carey

'Random particles tossed around in some demented jester's wind machine.' – *Richard Combs, MFB, 1978*
'A mind-blowing collage of mixed media, a free-for-all freakout of rock music and psychedelic splashes of colour.' – *Daily Variety*

Heidi*
US 1937 88m bw
TCF (Raymond Griffith)
V

An orphan is sent to stay with her crusty grandfather in a mountain village.

Star-tailored version of a favourite children's story; just what the box-office ordered at the time.

w Walter Ferris, Julian Josephson novel Johanna Spyri d Allan Dwan ph Arthur Miller md Louis Silvers

Shirley Temple, Jean Hersholt, Arthur Treacher, Helen Westley, Pauline Moore, Mary Nash, Thomas Beck, Sidney Blackmer, Mady Christians, Sig Rumann, Marcia Mae Jones, Christian Rub

'Good for the average Temple draw or better.' – *Variety*

The Hellstrom Chronicle
US 1971 90m CFI colour
David Wolper

A scientist explains the range and variety of insect life.

Odd documentary in fictional bookends; smart and quite sensational for those with strong stomachs.

w David Seltzer d Walon Green

Laurence Pressman (as Nils Hellstrom)

AA: best documentary

Hellzapoppin***
US 1942 84m bw
Universal/Mayfair (Glenn Tryon, Alex Gottlieb)

Two incompetent comics make a picture.

Zany modification of a smash burlesque revue; the crazy jokes are toned down and a romantic interest is added (and tentatively sent up). The result is patchy but often hilarious, and the whole is a handy consensus of forties humour and pop music.

w Nat Perrin, Warren Wilson
d H. C. Potter   ph Woody Bredell
md Charles Previn   m Frank Skinner

Ole Olsen, Chic Johnson, Hugh Herbert, Martha Raye, Mischa Auer, Robert Paige, Jane Frazee, Shemp Howard, Elisha Cook Jnr, Richard Lane

'Alive with good gags, mechanical surprise effects, and novelty touches.' – *CEA Report*

† The Frankenstein monster and Man Who Falls into Pool were played by Dale Van Sickel.

Help!*
GB 1965 92m Eastmancolor
UA/Walter Shenson/Suba Films
V, L

An oriental high priest chases the Beatles around the world because one of them has a sacred ring.

Exhausting attempt to outdo *A Hard Day's Night* in lunatic frenzy, which goes to prove that some talents work better on low budgets. The humour is a frantic cross between *Hellzapoppin*, the Goons, Bugs Bunny and the shade of Monty Python to come. It looks good but becomes too tiresome to entertain.

w Charles Wood, Marc Behm
d Dick Lester   ph David Watkin
m The Beatles   ad Ray Simm

The Beatles, Leo McKern, Eleanor Bron, Victor Spinetti

Helpmates***
US 1932 20m bw
Hal Roach
V

Stan helps Ollie clean up after a wild party while the wife was away.

A brilliant succession of catastrophe gags in the stars' best tradition.

w H. M. Walker   d James Parrott   ph Art Lloyd   ed Richard Currier

Laurel and Hardy, Blanche Payson, Robert Callahan

Henry VIII and His Six Wives*
GB 1972 125m Technicolor
EMI (Roy Baird)

Dullish historical account of the king's reign, staged as recollections from his deathbed but lacking any of the sparkle of *The Private Life of Henry VIII* made forty years previously.

Accurate sets and costumes fail to compensate for lack of film flair.

w Ian Thorne   d Waris Hussein
ph Peter Suschitzky   m David Munro

Keith Michell, Frances Cuka (Aragon), Charlotte Rampling (Boleyn), Jane Asher (Seymour), Jenny Bos (Cleves), Lynne Frederick (Howard), Barbara Leigh-Hunt (Parr), Donald Pleasence (Thomas Cromwell)

† The production was stimulated by a highly successful BBC TV series, *The Six Wives of Henry VIII*.

Henry V****
GB 1944 137m Technicolor
Rank/Two Cities (Laurence Olivier)
V

Shakespeare's historical play is seen in performance at the Globe Theatre in 1603; as it develops, the scenery becomes more realistic.

Immensely stirring, experimental and almost wholly successful production of Shakespeare on film, sturdy both in its stylization and its command of more conventional cinematic resources for the battle.

w Laurence Olivier, Alan Dent *play* William Shakespeare *d* Laurence Olivier *ph* Robert Krasker *m* William Walton *ad* Paul Sheriff, Carmen Dillon

Laurence Olivier, *Robert Newton, Leslie Banks, Esmond Knight,* Renée Asherson, George Robey, *Leo Genn,* Ernest Thesiger, Ivy St Helier, Ralph Truman, Harcourt Williams, Max Adrian, Valentine Dyall, Felix Aylmer, John Laurie, Roy Emerton

'His production – it was his first time out as a director – is a triumph of colour, music, spectacle, and soaring heroic poetry, and, as actor, he brings lungs, exultation, and a bashful wit to the role.' – *Pauline Kael, 70s*

AA: Special Award to Laurence Olivier
AAN: best picture; William Walton; Laurence Olivier (as actor); art direction

Henry V***
GB 1989 137m Technicolor
Curzon/Renaissance Films (Bruce Sharman)
V, V(W)

After his claim to the throne of France is refused, King Henry invades the country and wins a famous victory.

A darker film than Olivier's, with which it can stand comparison, stressing the brutality of war.

w Kenneth Branagh *play* William Shakespeare *d* Kenneth Branagh *ph* Kenneth MacMillan *m* Patrick Doyle *pd* Tim Harvey *ed* Mike Bradsell

Kenneth Branagh, Derek Jacobi, Simon Shepherd, James Larkin, Brian Blessed, James Simmons, Paul Gregory, Charles Kay, Alec McCowen, Edward Jewesbury, Ian Holm, Michael Williams, Geoffrey Hutchings, Robert Stephens, Judi Dench, Paul Scofield, Harold Innocent, Emma Thompson, Geraldine McEwan

'The film's visual tedium, vulgarity and musical mediocrity would be more bearable if Branagh himself were a more persuasive lead actor.' – *MFB*
'The more I thought about it, the more convinced I became that here was a play to be reclaimed from jingoism and its World War Two associations.' – *Kenneth Branagh*

AA: best costume design (Phyllis Dalton)
AAN: Kenneth Branagh (as best actor and best director)

Herbie Goes Bananas
US 1980 100m Technicolor
Walt Disney

Two Americans take their magical Volkswagen on a South American holiday.

Listless addition to a series which has already gone on too long.

w Don Tait *d* Vincent McEveety

Charles Martin Smith, Stephan W.

Burns, Cloris Leachman, John Vernon

Herbie Goes to Monte Carlo
US   1977   105m   Technicolor
Walt Disney (Ron Miller)

The Volkswagen with a mind of its own enters the Monte Carlo rally and routs a gang of thieves.

Utterly predictable, patchily made family comedy.

w Arthur Alsberg, Don Nelson
d Vincent McEveety   ph Leonard J. South   m Frank de Vol

Dean Jones, Don Knotts, Julie Sommars, Jacques Marin, Roy Kinnear, Bernard Fox

† Second sequel to *The Love Bug*.

Herbie Rides Again
US   1974   88m   Technicolor
Walt Disney (Bill Walsh)

A Volkswagen with a mind of its own helps an old lady to rout a property developer.

Acceptable sequel to *The Love Bug*.

w Bill Walsh   d Robert Stevenson

Helen Hayes, Ken Berry, Stefanie Powers, John McIntyre, Keenan Wynn, Huntz Hall

Hercules
Italy   1957   105m
Eastmancolor   Dyaliscope
Oscar/Galatea (Federico Teti)
L
original title: *Le Fatiche di Ercole*

Hercules helps Jason find the golden fleece.

The strong man epic which started a genre; of little interest in itself.

w Pietro Francisci, Ennio de Concini, Gaio Frattini   d Pietro Francisci
ph Mario Bava   m Enzo Masetti

Steve Reeves, Sylva Koscina, Gianna Maria Canale, Fabrizio Mione

Hercules Unchained
Italy/France   1959   105m
Eastmancolor   Dyaliscope
Lux/Galatea (Bruno Vailati)
L
original title: *Ercole e la Regina di Lidia*

Hercules has problems with the king of Thebes and the queen of Lidia.

More comic-strip versions of old legends. This item had more spent on it in publicity than in production cost, and consequently was seen by vast audiences around the world. It isn't very good.

w Pietro Francisci, Ennio di Concini   d Pietro Francisci
ph Mario Bava   m Enzo Masetti

Steve Reeves, Sylva Koscina, Sylvia Lopez, Primo Carnera

† Many sequels followed, the hero sometimes being known as Ursus or Goliath.

Hero at Large
US   1980   98m   Metrocolor
MGM (Stephen Freedman)
V

An actor playing Captain Avenger accidentally becomes a real-life hero, but his fans turn against him when they find he's just an ordinary guy.

Muddled satirical comedy-melodrama with too many pauses for love interest.

w A. J. Carothers   d Martin Davidson

John Ritter, Anne Archer, Bert Convy, Kevin McCarthy, Harry Bellaver

A High Wind in Jamaica*
GB 1965 104m DeLuxe
  Cinemascope
TCF (John Croydon)

In Victorian days, English children en route home from Jamaica are captured by pirates and influence their lives.

Semi-serious adventure story with a highly unlikely ending in which the chief pirate allows himself to be executed for a murder committed by a child. There are however pleasures along the way.

w Stanley Mann, Ronald Harwood, Denis Cannan novel Richard Hughes d Alexander Mackendrick ph Douglas Slocombe m Larry Adler

Deborah Baxter, Anthony Quinn, James Coburn, Isabel Dean, Nigel Davenport, Gert Frobe, Lila Kedrova

The Hills of Home
US 1948 95m Technicolor
MGM
GB title: *Master of Lassie*

A doctor returns to his Scottish village to practise medicine, and brings his faithful collie.

Adequate addition to the Lassie saga, with competent work all round.

w William Ludwig d Fred Wilcox

Edmund Gwenn, Tom Drake, Donald Crisp, Rhys Williams, Reginald Owen

Hog Wild***
US 1930 20m bw
Hal Roach
V

Stan helps Ollie to put a radio aerial on the roof of his house.

Brilliantly sustained slapstick makes this one of the best star comedies of Laurel and Hardy.

w H. M. Walker, Leo McCarey d James Parrott ph George Stevens ed Richard Currier

Laurel and Hardy, Fay Holderness, Dorothy Granger

Holiday for Lovers
US 1959 103m DeLuxe
  Cinemascope
TCF (David Weisbart)

To distract his teenage daughter from boys, a Boston psychiatrist organizes a family holiday in South America.

Frail old-fashioned family comedy with entirely predictable situations culminating in a drunk scene for stuffy father.

w Luther Davis d Henry Levin ph Charles G. Clarke m Leigh Harline

Clifton Webb, Jane Wyman, Paul Henreid, Carol Lynley, Jill St John, Gary Crosby, José Greco

Hollywood or Bust
US 1956 95m Technicolor
  Vistavision
Paramount/Hal Wallis

Two halfwits win a car and drive across country to Hollywood.

Dopey comedy with more misses than hits; the last film of Martin and Lewis as a team.

w Erna Lazarus d Frank Tashlin ph Daniel Fapp m Walter Scharf

Dean Martin, Jerry Lewis, Pat Crowley, Maxie Rosenbloom, Anita Ekberg

The Holy Terror
US 1936 66m bw
TCF

A child is a mischief-maker at a naval air station.

Lightweight star vehicle for Shirley Temple's only competitor.

w Lou Breslow, John Patrick d James Tinling

Jane Withers, Tony Martin, Leah Ray, Joan Davis, El Brendel, John Eldredge

'Nicely paced for laughs . . . strong dual bill attraction.' – *Variety*

Home Alone*
US   1990   102m   DeLuxe
TCF/John Hughes
V, L

A young boy, inadvertently left behind at Christmas when his parents go on holiday, foils some inept housebreakers.

Swinging uneasily between heavy-handed slapstick and sentimental domestic comedy, this unpretentious movie was, inexplicably, the biggest box-office success of 1990.

w John Hughes   d Chris Columbus   ph Julio Macat   m John Williams   pd John Muto   ed Raja Gosnell

Macauley Culkin, Joe Pesci, Daniel Stern, Catherine O'Hara, John Heard, Roberts Blossom, John Candy

'What is astonishing is that a cute family comedy which takes over an hour really to get going should have provoked such an enthusiastic audience response and gained such a phenomenal word-of-mouth reputation.' – *MFB*
AAN: John Williams; best song 'Somewhere In My Memory'

'He's Up Past His Bedtime In The City That Never Sleeps!'
Home Alone 2: Lost in New York
US   1992   120m   colour
TCF (John Hughes)

Separated from his family after boarding the wrong plane, a young boy alone in New York thwarts the same two robbers he met at home.

Virtually a re-make of the first film, though the humour has a far more unpleasantly sadistic edge to it. This undistinguished comedy was among the biggest box-office successes of 1992.

w John Hughes   d Chris Columbus   ph Julio Macat   m John Williams   pd Sandy Veneziano   ed Raja Gosnell

Macauley Culkin, Joe Pesci, Daniel Stern, Catherine O'Hara, John Heard, Devin Ratray, Hillary Wolf, Maureen Elisabeth Shay, Brenda Fricker

'An interesting example of formula film-making, making use of a higher budget than before but even lower expectations.' – *Derek Malcolm, Guardian*

A Home of Your Own*
GB   1965   44m   bw
Dormar/British Lion

Calamities pile up on a building site.

Genuinely funny silent comedy, with bits from a variety of familiar faces.

w Jay Lewis, John Whyte   d Bob Kellett

Ronnie Barker, George Benson, Richard Briers, Janet Brown, Peter Butterworth, Bernard Cribbins, Fred Emney, Bill Fraser, Ronnie Stevens

Home Sweet Homicide
US   1946   90m   bw
TCF

Children solve a murder mystery with the help of their mother, a detective novelist.

Mild family fare.

w F. Hugh Herbert novel Craig Rice d Lloyd Bacon ph John Seitz m David Buttolph

Lynn Bari, Randolph Scott, Peggy Ann Garner, Connie Marshall, Dean Stockwell, Barbara Whiting

Honey, I Blew Up the Kid
US 1992 89m Technicolor
Buena Vista/Walt Disney (Dawn Steel, Edward S. Feldman)

An inventor inadvertently exposes his two-year-old son to a ray that causes him to grow to 50 feet tall.

Predictable and dull comedy that fails to develop its central notion in interesting ways.

w Thom Eberhardt, Peter Elbling, Garry Goodrow d Randal Kleiser ph John Hora m Bruce Broughton pd Leslie Dilley ed Michael A. Stevenson, Harry Hitner, Tina Hirsch

Rick Moranis, Marcia Strassman, Robert Oliveri, Daniel Shalikar, Joshua Shalikar, Lloyd Bridges, John Shea, Keri Russell, Ron Canada, Amy O'Neill

'A romp, escapism at its breeziest.' – *Variety*
'Proclaims in its every move that particular blend of crassness and technical expertise that is so often used for Hollywood's more down-market popular successes.' – Derek Malcolm, *Guardian*

Honey, I Shrunk the Kids*
US 1989 93m Metrocolor
Warner/Walt Disney/Doric (Penny Finkelman Cox)

V

An inventor inadvertently miniaturises his children and dumps them in the garden.

Amusing comedy with Disney's winsomeness kept at bay for the most part, apart from a brave little ant.

w Ed Naha, Tom Schulman story Stuart Gordon, Brian Yuzna, Ed Naha d Joe Johnston ph Hiro Narita pd Gregg Fonseca ed Michael A. Stevenson

Rick Moranis, Matt Frewer, Marcia Strassman, Kristine Sutherland, Thomas Brown, Jared Rushton, Amy O'Neil, Robert Oliveri, Carl Steven

Hook*
US 1991 144m DeLuxe Panavision
Columbia TriStar/Amblin (Kathleen Kennedy, Frank Marshall, Gerald R. Molen)

V, L

Peter Pan, who has returned to the ordinary world to become a father and a corporate lawyer, returns to Neverland to fight Captain Hook.

Sprawling, overlong, often camp extravaganza with splendid special effects and settings that may appeal to the small child in most of us, even if it is time that Spielberg himself grew up.

w Jim V. Hart, Malia Scotch Marmo play Peter Pan by J. M. Barrie story Jim V. Hart, Nick Castle d Steven Spielberg ph Dean Cundey m John Williams pd Norman Garwood (John Napier was visual consultant) *sp* Industrial Light and Magic *ed* Michael Kahn

Dustin Hoffman, Robin Williams, Julia Roberts, Bob Hoskins, Maggie Smith, Caroline Goodall, Charlie Korsmo, Amber Scott, Laurel Cronin, Phil Collins, David Crosby

'Spirited, rambunctious, often messy and undisciplined, this determined attempt to recast the Peter Pan story in contemporary terms splashes every bit of its megabudget (between $60 and $80 million) onto the screen; commercial elements overflow in such abundance that major hit status seems guaranteed.' – *Variety*

'Peel away the expensive, special effects surface and there's nothing but formula.' – *Washington Post*

† Glenn Close appears in an uncredited role as a bearded pirate.
AAN: song 'When You're Alone' (*m* John Williams, *ly* Leslie Bricusse); Norman Garwood; visual effects

The Hoosegow**

US 1929 20m bw
Hal Roach

Stan and Ollie, in prison, contrive to fell a tree on the cook's tent and to smother the governor in boiled rice.

Splendid slapstick leading up to one of their best tit-for-tat routines.

w Leo McCarey, H. M. Walker *d* James Parrott *ph* George Stevens, Len Powers, Glenn Robert Kershner *ed* Richard Currier

Laurel and Hardy, James Finlayson, Tiny Sandford

Hopalong Cassidy

Cassidy, a creation of Clarence E. Mulford, was a fictitious gentleman cowboy who oddly enough wore black; 26 books about him were published between 1912 and 1956 when Mulford died. 66 films were made starring William Boyd as Hoppy, with either George Gabby Hayes or Andy Clyde as comic sidekick: Harry Sherman produced them, first for Paramount and then for UA, and they were later edited down for TV, in which medium Boyd became a folk hero and eventually made a further series. The films were easy-going, slow-moving second features which always pointed an admirable moral for children; their main directors were Howard Bretherton, Nate Watt, Lesley Selander and George Archainbaud.

1935: HOPALONG CASSIDY, THE EAGLE'S BROOD, BAR 20 RIDES AGAIN
1936: CALL OF THE PRAIRIE, THREE ON THE TRAIL, HEART OF THE WEST, HOPALONG CASSIDY RETURNS, TRAIL DUST
1937: BORDERLAND, HILLS OF OLD WYOMING, NORTH OF THE RIO GRANDE, RUSTLERS' VALLEY, HOPALONG RIDES AGAIN, TEXAS TRAIL
1938: HEART OF ARIZONA, BAR 20 JUSTICE, PRIDE OF THE WEST, IN OLD MEXICO, SUNSET TRAIL, THE FRONTIERSMAN, PARTNERS OF THE PLAINS, CASSIDY OF BAR 20
1939: RANGE WAR, LAW OF THE PAMPAS, SILVER ON THE SAGE, RENEGADE TRAIL
1940: SANTA FE MARSHAL, THE SHOWDOWN, HIDDEN GOLD, STAGECOACH WAR, THREE MEN FROM TEXAS
1941: DOOMED CARAVAN, IN OLD COLORADO, BORDER VIGILANTES, PIRATES ON HORSEBACK, WIDE OPEN TOWN, OUTLAWS OF THE DESERT, RIDERS OF THE TIMBERLINE, SECRETS OF THE

WASTELAND, STICK TO YOUR
GUNS, TWILIGHT ON THE TRAIL
1942: UNDERCOVER MAN
1943: COLT COMRADES, BAR 20,
LOST CANYON, HOPPY SERVES A
WRIT, BORDER PATROL, THE
LEATHER BURNERS, FALSE
COLOURS, RIDERS OF THE
DEADLINE
1944: MYSTERY MAN, FORTY
THIEVES, TEXAS MASQUERADE,
LUMBERJACK
1946: THE DEVIL'S PLAYGROUND
1947: FOOL'S GOLD, HOPPY'S
HOLIDAY, MARAUDERS,
UNEXPECTED GUEST, DANGEROUS
VENTURE
1948: SINISTER JOURNEY, SILENT
CONFLICT, STRANGE GAMBLE,
BORROWED TROUBLE, THE DEAD
DON'T DREAM, FALSE PARADISE

Hoppity Goes to Town: see
Mr Bug Goes to Town

'A scandalous record of low Marx at
college – or life among the thirsty co-eds!'
Horse Feathers***
US 1932 69m bw
Paramount (Herman J. Mankiewicz)

A college needs to win at football, and
its corrupt new president knows just
how to do it.

Possibly the Marxes' wildest yet most
streamlined kaleidoscope of high jinks
and irreverence, with at least one
bright gag or line to the minute and
lively musical interludes to boot. A
classic of zany comedy.

w Bert Kalmar, Harry Ruby, S. J.
Perelman, Will B. Johnstone
d Norman Z. McLeod   ph Ray
June   m/ly Bert Kalmar, Harry Ruby

Groucho, Chico, Harpo, Zeppo, Thelma
Todd, Robert Greig

GROUCHO: 'You have the brain of a
four-year-old child, and I'll bet he was
glad to get rid of it.'
CHICO: 'There's a man outside with
a big black moustache.'
GROUCHO: 'Tell him I've got one.'
GROUCHO (to Zeppo): 'You're a
disgrace to our family name of
Wagstaff, if such a thing is possible.'
GROUCHO:
'For years before my son was born
I used to yell from night till morn
Whatever it is – I'm against it!
And I've been yelling since I first
commenced it – I'm against it!'

'The current Marx comedy is the
funniest talkie since the last Marx
comedy, and the record it establishes
is not likely to be disturbed until the
next Marx comedy comes along. As
for comparisons, I was too busy having
a good time to make any.' – *Philip K.
Scheuer*

The Horse in the Grey Flannel Suit
US 1969 112m Technicolor
Walt Disney

A teenager's horse becomes the
central figure in an advertising
campaign for a stomach pill.

Interminable kiddie movie which in
its virtual absence of plot or
excitement is likely to bore kiddies to
death.

w Louis Pelletier   novel *The Year of
the Horse* by Eric Hatch   d Norman
Tokar

Dean Jones, Fred Clark, Diane Baker,
Lloyd Bochner, Morey Amsterdam

The Horse without a Head**
GB 1963 89m Technicolor
Walt Disney (Hugh Attwooll)

Stolen money is hidden in an old toy
horse, and crooks trying to get it back
clash with police and children.

Excellent children's adventure with scenes on trains and in a toy factory.

w T. E. B. Clarke   d Don Chaffey
ph Paul Beeson   m Eric Rogers

Leo McKern, Jean-Pierre Aumont, Herbert Lom, Pamela Franklin, Vincent Winter

Hot Lead and Cold Feet
US   1978   90m   colour
Buena Vista (Ron Miller)

Twin brothers, one a tough gunfighter, the other a pacifist, compete in a race to inherit a Western town.

Comic Western showcasing Dale in three differing roles – as the father and his two sons – but with a script that runs out of ideas long before the end.

w Arthur Alsberg, Joe McEveety, Don Nelson   story Rod Piffath
d Robert Butler   ph Frank Phillips   m Buddy Baker   ad John Mansbridge, Frank T. Smith   ed Ray de Leuw

Jim Dale, Karen Valentine, Don Knots, Jack Elam, Darren McGaven, John Williams, Warren Vanders

'There's Something Funny In The Air.'
Hot Shots!
US   1991   85m   DeLuxe
TCF (Bill Badalato)
V

A young disturbed pilot joins an élite group to take part in a raid on a nuclear plant or, as secondary target, an accordion factory.

A hit-and-miss send-up of *Top Gun* and other Hollywood hits, in which most of the targets are missed.

w Jim Abrahams, Pat Proft   d Jim Abrahams   ph Bill Butler

m Sylvester Levay   pd William A. Elliott   ed Jane Kurson, Eric Sears

Charlie Sheen, Cary Elwes, Valeria Golino, Lloyd Bridges, Jon Cryer, Kevin Dunn, Bill Irwin, William O'Leary, Kristy Swanson, Efrem Zimbalist Jnr

Hot Water*
US   1924   50m approx (24 fps)
   bw   silent
Harold Lloyd

A young husband has trouble with a turkey, a new car and his in-laws.

Casually structured star comedy with brilliant sequences.

w Harold Lloyd, Sam Taylor
d Fred Newmeyer, Sam Taylor

Harold Lloyd, Jobyna Ralston, Josephine Crowell

The Hound of the Baskervilles**
US   1939   80m   bw
(TCF) Gene Markey
L

Sherlock Holmes solves the mystery of a supernatural hound threatening the life of a Dartmoor baronet.

Basil Rathbone's first appearance as Sherlock Holmes is in a painstaking studio production which achieves good atmosphere and preserves the flavour if not the letter of the book but is let down by a curious lack of pace.

w Ernest Pascal   novel Arthur Conan Doyle   d Sidney Lanfield   ph Peverell Marley   m Cyril Mockridge   ad Thomas Little

Basil Rathbone, Nigel Bruce, Richard Greene, Wendy Barrie, Lionel Atwill, Morton Lowry, John Carradine, Barlowe Borland, Beryl Mercer,

Ralph Forbes, E. E. Clive, Eily Malyon, Mary Gordon

'A startling mystery-chiller . . . will find many bookings on top spots of key duallers.' – *Variety*
'Lush dialogue, stagey sets and vintage supporting cast make it a delectable Hollywood period piece.' – *Judith Crist, 1980*

† For Rathbone's other appearances as Holmes see under *Sherlock Holmes*.

The Hound of the Baskervilles*
GB 1959 86m Technicolor
UA/Hammer (Anthony Hinds)
V

Spirited remake let down by dogged Hammer insistence on promises of horror and sex; good atmosphere also let down by poor colour.

w Peter Bryan *novel* Arthur Conan Doyle *d* Terence Fisher
ph Jack Asher *m* James Bernard *ad* Bernard Robinson
ed James Needs

Peter Cushing, André Morell, Christopher Lee, Marla Landi, Ewen Solon, Francis de Wolff, Miles Malleson, John Le Mesurier

Houseboat
US 1958 110m Technicolor Vistavision
Paramount/Scribe (Jack Rose)
V, L

A widower with three children engages a maid who is really a socialite, and they all set up house on a boat.

Artificial sentimental comedy with A-1 credits but little style or bite.

w Melville Shavelson, Jack Rose
d Melville Shavelson *ph* Ray June *m* George Duning

Cary Grant, Sophia Loren, Martha Hyer, Eduardo Ciannelli, Harry Guardino

'The kind of picture to which you can take your stuffy maiden aunt, your wicked sophisticated uncle and your ten-year-old child, and they will all have a wonderful time.' – *Ruth Waterbury, Los Angeles Examiner*
AAN: script; song 'Almost In Your Arms' (*m/ly* Jay Livingston, Ray Evans)

Housekeeping*
US 1987 115m colour
Columbia (Robert F. Colesberry)

Two orphaned sisters are brought up by their wayward aunt.

In his first American feature, Forsyth's pawky humour is overlaid with a bleaker view and his characters seem more conventional and less well-observed.

wd Bill Forsyth *novel* Marilynne Robinson *ph* Michael Coulter
m Michael Gibbs *pd* Adrienne Atkinson *ed* Michael Ellis

Christine Lahti, Sara Walker, Andrea Burchill, Anne Pitoniak, Barbara Reese, Bill Smillie, Margo Pinvidic, Wayne Robson

'Rich is their humor! Deep are their passions! Reckless are their lives! Mighty is their story!'
'"What are you? A man or a saint? I don't want him, I want you!" Her desire scorched both their lives with the vicious breath of scandal!'

How Green Was My Valley***
US 1941 118m bw
TCF (Darryl F. Zanuck)
V, L

Memories of childhood in a Welsh mining village.

Prettified and unconvincing but

dramatically very effective tearjerker in the style which lasted from Cukor's *David Copperfield* to *The Green Years*. High production values here add a touch of extra class, turning the result into a Hollywood milestone despite its intrinsic inadequacies.

w Philip Dunne novel Richard Llewellyn d John Ford ph Arthur Miller m Alfred Newman ad Richard Day, Nathan Juran ed James B. Clark

Walter Pidgeon, Maureen O'Hara, Roddy McDowall, Donald Crisp, Sara Allgood, Anna Lee, John Loder, Barry Fitzgerald, Patric Knowles, Morton Lowry, Arthur Shields, Frederic Worlock

'Perfection of cinematic narrative . . . pure visual action, pictures powerfully composed, dramatically photographed, smoothly and eloquently put together.' – *James Shelley Hamilton*

† The unseen narrator was Irving Pichel.

AA: best picture; John Ford; Arthur Miller; Donald Crisp; art direction
AAN: Philip Dunne; Alfred Newman; Sara Allgood; James B. Clark

How the West Was Won*

US 1962 162m Technicolor
 Cinerama
MGM/Cinerama (Bernard Smith)
V

Panoramic Western following the daughter of a pioneering family from youth (1830) to old age, with several half-relevant stories along the way.

Muddled spectacular with splendid set-pieces but abysmal dullness in between, especially if not seen in three-strip Cinerama (the Cinemascope prints are muddy and still show the dividing lines). An all-star fairground show of its time.

w James R. Webb d Henry Hathaway (first half), John Ford (Civil War), George Marshall (train) ph William Daniels, Milton Krasner, Charles Lang Jnr, Joseph LaShelle m Alfred Newman ad George W. Davis, William Ferrari, Addison Hehr

Debbie Reynolds, Carroll Baker, Lee J. Cobb, Henry Fonda, Carolyn Jones, Karl Malden, Gregory Peck, George Peppard, Robert Preston, James Stewart, Eli Wallach, John Wayne, Richard Widmark, Brigid Bazlen, Walter Brennan, David Brian, Andy Devine, Raymond Massey, Agnes Moorehead, Henry Morgan, Thelma Ritter, Russ Tamblyn, Spencer Tracy (narrator)

'That goddamned Cinerama . . . do you know a waist shot is as close as you could get with that thing?' – *Henry Hathaway*

AA: James R. Webb
AAN: best picture; photography; music

Howard the Duck

US 1986 111m DeLuxe
Universal/Gloria Katz/George Lucas
V
GB title: *Howard, a New Breed of Hero*

A duck from outer space comes to Earth and has various uncomfortable adventures.

Toned down from an adult comic strip, this peculiar film has nowhere to go because it's too sexy for kids and too stupid for adults.

w Willard Huyck, Gloria Katz from Steve Gerber's character d Willard Huyck ph Richard H. Kline m John Barry pd Peter Jamison

Lea Thompson, Jeffrey Jones, Paul Guilfoyle

Huckleberry Finn**
US 1939 90m bw
MGM (Joseph L. Mankiewicz)

Solidly competent remake with excellent production values and several entertaining sequences.

w Hugo Butler d Richard Thorpe ph John Seitz m Franz Waxman

Mickey Rooney, Walter Connolly, William Frawley, Rex Ingram

Huckleberry Finn*
US 1960 107m Metrocolor Cinemascope
MGM (Samuel Goldwyn Jnr)
aka: *The Adventures of Huckleberry Finn*

Another patchy remake.

w James Lee d Michael Curtiz ph Ted McCord m Jerome Moross

Eddie Hodges, Tony Randall, Archie Moore, Neville Brand, Judy Canova, Buster Keaton, Andy Devine

Huckleberry Finn
US 1974 118m DeLuxe Panavision
UA/Apjac/Readers Digest (Robert Greenhut)

Ambitious but lustreless version of the famous story, with songs.

w/m/ly Richard M. Sherman, Robert B. Sherman d J. Lee-Thompson ph Laszlo Kovacs pd Philip Jeffries

Jeff East, Paul Winfield, David Wayne, Harvey Korman, Arthur O'Connell, Gary Merrill, Natalie Trundy

'It expires in a morass of treacle.' – *Tom Milne*
'It transforms a great work of fiction into something bland, boring and tasteless.' – *Michael Billington, Illustrated London News*

Hue and Cry***
GB 1946 82m bw
Ealing (Michael Balcon)

East End boys discover that their favourite boys' paper is being used by crooks to pass information.

The first 'Ealing comedy' uses vivid London locations as background for a sturdy comic plot with a climax in which the criminals are rounded up by thousands of boys swarming over dockland.

w T. E. B. Clarke d Charles Crichton ph Douglas Slocombe, John Seaholme m Georges Auric

Alastair Sim, Jack Warner, Harry Fowler, Valerie White, Frederick Piper

'Refreshing, bloodtingling and disarming.' – *Richard Winnington*

Hugo the Hippo
US 1975 78m colour
Brut (Robert Halmi)

An independently-minded hippo combats a Zanzibar magician.

Uninventive cartoon feature, endearing neither in characterization nor in draughtsmanship.

w Thomas Baum d William Feigenbaum md Bert Keyes

voices of Burl Ives, Marie Osmond, Jimmy Osmond, Robert Morley, Paul Lynde

The Hunchback of Notre Dame****
US 1939 117m bw
RKO (Pandro S. Berman)
V, L

This superb remake is one of the best examples of Hollywood expertise at work: art direction, set construction, costumes, camera, lighting and above all direction brilliantly support an irresistible story and bravura acting.

w Sonya Levien, Bruno Frank d William Dieterle ph Joseph H. August m Alfred Newman ad Van Nest Polglase

Charles Laughton, Cedric Hardwicke, Maureen O'Hara, Edmond O'Brien, Thomas Mitchell, Harry Davenport, Walter Hampden, Alan Marshal, George Zucco, Katherine Alexander, Fritz Leiber, Rod la Rocque

'A super thriller-chiller. Will roll up healthy grosses at the ticket windows.' – *Variety*

'Has seldom been bettered as an evocation of medieval life.' – *John Baxter, 1968*

'It exceeds in sheer magnificence any similar film in history. Sets are vast and rich in detail, crowds are immense, and camera uses of both are versatile, varied and veracious.' – *Motion Picture Herald*

† Other versions: *Esmeralda* (1906, French); *Notre Dame de Paris* (1911, French); *The Darling of Paris* (1917, US, with Theda Bara).
AAN: Alfred Newman

I Wanna Hold Your Hand

US 1978 104m Technicolor
Universal/Steven Spielberg (Tamara Asseyev, Alex Rose)

A day in 1964 finds assorted New Jersey teenagers eagerly awaiting the Beatles' appearance on the Ed Sullivan Show.

Modest period comedy utilizing fresh young talent.

w Robert Zemeckis, Bob Gale
d Robert Zemeckis ph Donald M. Morgan m Meredith Willson

Nancy Allen, Bobby diCicco, Marc McClure, Susan Kendall Newman

Ichabod and Mr Toad**

US 1949 68m Technicolor
Walt Disney
aka: *The Adventures of Ichabod and Mr Toad*

Cartoon versions of stories by Washington Irving and Kenneth Grahame.

An uncomfortable double bill; the story of Ichabod, though well narrated by Bing Crosby, is macabre without being very interesting; *The Wind in the Willows*, however, is charmingly pictured, and Mr Toad is splendidly voiced by Eric Blore. d Jack Kinney, Clyde Geronimi, James Algar supervisor Ben Sharpsteen

The Idle Class*

US 1922 30m approx bw
silent
First National/Charles Chaplin
V

A tramp dreams of the rich life and is mistaken for the husband of a lady.

Rather slight later Chaplin without the full-blooded farcical elements which made him so popular around 1917.

wd Charles Chaplin ph Rollie Totheroh

Charles Chaplin, Edna Purviance, Mack Swain

The Immigrant**

US 1917 20m approx bw
silent
Mutual

A penniless immigrant befriends a girl on the boat and later helps her in a café.

One of the most inventive early Chaplins, with touches of sentiment and social comment which for once only strengthen and do not antagonize.

wd *Charles Chaplin* ph William C. Foster, Rollie Totheroh

Charles Chaplin, Edna Purviance, Albert Austin, Henry Bergman, Eric Campbell

'In its roughness and apparent simplicity it is as much a jewel as a story by O. Henry.' – *Photoplay*

'A thousand thrills ... and Hayley Mills'

In Search of the Castaways***
GB 1961 100m Technicolor
Walt Disney (Hugh Attwooll)

With the aid of an eccentric professor, three children seek their lost explorer father in some geographically fantastic regions of South America.

Engaging Victorian fantasy which starts realistically but builds up to sequences in the manner of *The Wizard of Oz* and concludes in *Treasure Island* vein. Jaunty juvenile fare.

w Lowell S. Hawley *novel Captain Grant's Children* by Jules Verne d Robert Stevenson ph Paul Beeson m William Alwyn ad Michael Stringer

Maurice Chevalier, Hayley Mills, George Sanders, Wilfrid Hyde White, *Wilfrid Brambell*

In Society*
US 1944 74m bw
Universal (Edmund Hartmann)

Two incompetent plumbers ruin a mansion.

One of the better A & C romps, with little padding between the comedy highlights, though the trimmings are fearsomely dated.

w John Grant, Hal Fimberg, Edmund L. Hartmann d Jean Yarbrough ph Jerome Ash m Edgar Fairchild

Bud Abbott, Lou Costello, Kirby Grant, Ann Gillis, Arthur Treacher, Steve Geray, George Dolenz, Marion Hutton

In the Doghouse
GB 1961 93m bw
Rank (Hugh Stewart)

Misadventures of a newly qualified vet.

Easy-going farce with animal interest and a great many familiar faces.

w Michael Pertwee *novel It's a Vet's Life* by Alex Duncan d Darcy Conyers ph Alan Hume m Philip Green

Leslie Phillips, Peggy Cummins, Hattie Jacques, James Booth, Dick Bentley, Colin Gordon, Joan Heal, Fenella Fielding, Esma Cannon, Richard Goolden, Joan Hickson, Vida Hope, Harry Locke, Kynaston Reeves

The Incredible Journey**
US 1963 80m Technicolor
Walt Disney (James Algar)

Two dogs and a cat, separated from their owners, escape and travel 250 miles home.

A novelty attraction which keeps going purely on its animal interest, which is considerable.

w James Algar *book* Sheila Burnford d Fletcher Markle ph Kenneth Peach, Jack Couffer, Lloyd Beebe m Oliver Wallace

The Incredible Mr Limpet
US 1964 102m Technicolor
Warner (John C. Rose)

A meek but patriotic clerk is turned down by the navy and turns into a fish. In this form he becomes a radar assistant to a warship.

Sentimental sub-Disney goo, part animated.

w Jameson Bewer, John C. Rose *novel* Theodore Pratt d Arthur Lubin ph Harold Stine m Frank Perkins

Don Knotts, Andrew Duggan, Larry Keating, Jack Weston

Indiana Jones and the Last Crusade**

US 1989 127m DeLuxe
UIP/Paramount/Lucasfilm (Robert Watts)
V, L

Indiana Jones goes in search of his father who disappeared while looking for the Holy Grail.

The formula as before, which still works thanks to some splendid set-pieces and the genial interplay between Ford and Connery.

w Jeffrey Boam   story George Lucas, Menno Meyjes   d Steven Spielberg   ph Douglas Slocombe   m John Williams   pd Elliot Scott   ed Michael Kahn

Harrison Ford, Sean Connery, Denholm Elliott, Alison Doody, John Rhys-Davies, Julian Glover, River Phoenix, Michael Byrne, Kevork Malikyan, Robert Eddison, Richard Young, Alexei Sayle

'The hero is back!'

Indiana Jones and the Temple of Doom*

US 1984 118m Rank/DeLuxe Panavision
Paramount/Lucasfilm (Robert Watts)
V, L

A prequel to *Raiders of the Lost Ark*: Jones in 1935 finds the sacred Sankara stone.

Slow-starting adventure romp with much ingenuity and too much brutality and horror. In the US it caused the creation of a new censor certificate: PG(13).

w Willard Huyck, Gloria Katz   story George Lucas   d Steven Spielberg   ph Douglas Slocombe, Allan Daviau   m John Williams   pd Elliot Scott

Harrison Ford, Kate Capshaw, Ke Huy Kwan, Philip Stone

'One of the most sheerly pleasurable physical comedies ever made.' – *Pauline Kael, New Yorker*
'A thin, arch, graceless affair.' – *Observer*
'A two-hour series of none too carefully linked chase sequences . . . sitting on the edge of your seat gives you a sore bum but also a numb brain.' – *Guardian*
AAN: music

Innerspace*

US 1987 120m Technicolor
Warner/Amblin/Steven Spielberg/Guber-Peters (Michael Finnell)
V, L

A miniaturized air force flyer is injected into the body of a grocery clerk.

Derivative comedy with clever twists; very tolerable of its kind, but no *Back to the Future*.

w Jeffrey Boam, Chip Proser   d Joe Dante   ph Andrew Laszlo   m Jerry Goldsmith   pd James H. Spencer

Dennis Quaid, Martin Short, Meg Ryan, Kevin McCarthy, Fiona Lewis

AA: special visual effects (Dennis Muren)

International Velvet

GB 1978 125m Metrocolor
MGM (Bryan Forbes)

A hostile orphan becomes an international horsewoman.

Disappointing attempt to produce a sequel to 1944's *National Velvet*; none of it coheres, one is not clear to whom it is intended to appeal, and some of the dialogue is fearsome.

wd Bryan Forbes *ph* Tony Imi
m Francis Lai *pd* Keith Wilson

Nanette Newman, Tatum O'Neal, Anthony Hopkins, Christopher Plummer, Peter Barkworth, Dinsdale Landen

'Where myth and magic walk the earth.'
Into the West*
Eire 1992 102m Technicolor
Entertainment/Little Bird/Parallel/Majestic/ Miramax/Film Four/Newcomm (Jonathan Cavendish, Tim Palmer)

V

A father, a former traveller, hunts for his two sons who have run away from their Dublin home with a magical white horse, Tir na nOg.

An odd, likeable film, despite its not always successful mythic overtones, and one that should have an appeal to the young.

w Jim Sheridan, David Keating
story Michael Pearce *d* Mike Newell *ph* Tom Sigel *m* Patrick Doyle *pd* Jamie Leonard
ed Peter Boyle

Gabriel Byrne, Ellen Barkin, Ciarán Fitzgerald, Ruaidhri Conroy, David Kelly, Johnny Murphy, Colm Meaney, John Kavanagh, Brendan Gleeson, Jim Norton

'Its heady mix of Irish myth and gritty realism will effortlessly capture the imaginations of all ages.' – *Empire*

'From out of space – came hordes of green monsters!'
Invaders from Mars
US 1953 82m Cinecolor
Edward L. Alperson

Martian invaders use hypnotized humans as saboteurs.

Poverty Row sci-fi partly redeemed by its erratic but talented designer who provides flashes of visual imagination.

w Richard Blake *d/pd* William Cameron Menzies *ph* John Seitz
m Raoul Kraushaar

Helena Carter, Arthur Franz, Leif Erickson, Hillary Brooke

Invaders from Mars
US 1986 100m TVC colour
Panavision
Cannon (Menahem Golan, Yoram Globus)

A boy one night sees a space ship land in his back yard.

Astonishingly witless remake of a show that was a cheap second feature in 1953.

w Dan O'Bannon, Don Jakoby
d Tobe Hooper *ph* Daniel Pearl *m* Christopher Young

Karen Black, Hunter Carson, Timothy Bottoms, Louise Fletcher, Bud Cort

Invasion of the Astro-Monsters
Japan 1967 90m (dubbed) colour
Toho/Henry G. Saperstein Enterprises (Tomoyuki Tanaka)
aka: *Monster Zero; Invasion of Planet X; Godzilla vs Monster Zero*

Aliens program three monsters, Godzilla, Rodan and Ghidrah, to attack the Earth.

Dull monster movie, its only novelty being its American leading man.

w Shinichi Sekizawa *d* Inoshiro Honda *ph* Hajime Koizumi
m Akira Ifukube *ad* Takeo Kita
sp Eiji Tsuburaya *ed* Rhyohei Fujii

Nick Adams, Akira Takarada, Kumi Mizuno, Keiki Sawai, Jun Tazaki, Yoshio Tsuchiya, Akira Kubo

Invasion of the Saucermen

US 1957 90m bw
AIP/Malibu (James H. Nicholson, Robert J. Gurney Jnr)

Little green aliens who land on Earth in a flying saucer are defeated by teenagers.

Science fiction with comic overtones, though done with so little finesse that it is difficult to know what is intentionally funny and what is accidentally so.

w Robert J. Gurney Jnr, Al Martin story Paul Fairman d Edward L. Cahn ph Fred West m Ronald Stein ad Don Ament ed Ronald Sinclair

Steve Terrell, Gloria Castillo, Frank Gorshin

Invisible Boy

US 1957 89m bw
MGM/Pan (Nicholas Nayfack)

A scientist allows his 10-year-old son to repair a robot, which comes under the control of an alien force.

Minor sci-fi utilizing the robot from *Forbidden Planet*.

w Cyril Hume d Herman Hoffman ph Harold Wellman m Les Baxter

Richard Eyer, Philip Abbott, Harold J. Stone, Diane Brewster

Invitation to the Dance**

GB 1954 92m Technicolor
MGM (Arthur Freed)

Three stories in dance and mime.

Unsuccessful ballet film which closed its star's great period and virtually ended the heyday of the Hollywood musical. The simple fact emerged that European ballet styles were not Kelly's forte; yet there was much to enjoy in *Circus*, *Ring around the Rosy* and *The Magic Lamp*.

wd/ch Gene Kelly ph Frederick A. Young m Jacques Ibert, André Previn, Rimsky-Korsakov ad Alfred Junge

Gene Kelly, Igor Youskevitch, Tommy Rall, Belita, Tamara Toumanova

Ishtar

US 1987 107m Technicolor
Columbia/Delphi V (Warren Beatty)
V

Two untalented songwriters get involved with Middle Eastern turmoil.

Bitty rehash of old jokes and situations, vaguely resembling a Hope-Crosby Road picture of long ago, but far less funny despite costing 50 million dollars.

wd Elaine May ph Vittorio Storaro pd Paul Sylbert

Dustin Hoffman, Warren Beatty, Isabelle Adjani, Charles Grodin, Jack Weston, Tess Harper

'One can't help but wonder whether the camel was the only blind creature who had something to do with this picture.' – *Daily Variety*

The Island at the Top of the World**

US 1974 93m Technicolor
Walt Disney (Winston Hibler)

In 1907, a rich Englishman commissions an airship to take him to a mythical arctic Shangri-La in search of his lost son.

Generally brisk and effective adventure fantasy whose trick effects are sufficiently splendid to redeem a sag in the middle and an overplus of Viking chatter which has to be laboriously translated.

w John Whedon novel *The Lost*

Ones by Ian Cameron d Robert
Stevenson ph Frank Phillips
m Maurice Jarre pd Peter
Ellenshaw sp Art Cruickshank,
Danny Lee

Donald Sinden, David Hartman,
Jacques Marin, Mako

Island of the Blue Dolphins
US 1964 93m Eastmancolor
U-I/Robert B. Radnitz

Two orphaned children grow up alone
on a Californian island, protected by
wild dogs.

Pleasant if unconvincing family film
based on a true story.

w Ted Sherdeman, Jane Klove
novel Scott O'Dell d James B.
Clark ph Leo Tover m Paul
Sawtell

Celia Kaye, Larry Dornasin, George
Kennedy

Island of the Lost
US 1968 92m colour
Ivan Tors

An anthropologist sets sail for an
uncharted island and is shipwrecked
on it.

Good-looking but singularly plotless
action adventure.

w Richard Carlson, Ivan Tors
d Richard Carlson

Richard Greene, Luke Halpin, Mark
Hulswit

It Shouldn't Happen to a Vet
GB 1976 93m Technicolor
EMI/Talent Associates/Readers Digest
US title: *All Things Bright and Beautiful*

Adventures of a Yorkshire vet just
before World War II.

Competent sequel to *All Creatures
Great and Small* (qv).

w Alan Plater books James
Herriot d Eric Till ph Arthur
Ibbetson m Laurie Johnson

John Alderton, Colin Blakely, Lisa
Harrow, Bill Maynard, Richard
Pearson, Raymond Francis, John
Barrett, Paul Shelley

It's a Mad Mad Mad Mad World**
US 1963 192m Technicolor
  Ultra Panavision 70
UA/Stanley Kramer
V, L

An assortment of people including a
frustrated cop are overcome by greed
when they hear of buried loot.

Three hours of frantic chasing and
violent slapstick is too much even
when done on this scale and with this
cast, but one must observe that scene
for scene it is extremely well done and
most of the players are in unusually
good form though they all outstay
their welcome and are upstaged by
the stunt men.

w William and Tania Rose
d Stanley Kramer ph Ernest
Laszlo m Ernest Gold,
stunts Carey Loftin titles Saul Bass

Spencer Tracy, Jimmy Durante, *Milton
Berle*, Sid Caesar, Ethel Merman,
Buddy Hackett, Mickey Rooney, Dick
Shawn, *Phil Silvers*, *Terry-Thomas*,
Jonathan Winters, Edie Adams,
Dorothy Provine, Eddie Anderson,
Jim Backus, William Demarest, Peter
Falk, Paul Ford, Leo Gorcey, Ben
Blue, Edward Everett Horton, Buster
Keaton, Joe E. Brown, Carl Reiner,
the Three Stooges, Zasu Pitts, Sterling
Holloway, Jack Benny, Jerry Lewis

'To watch on a Cinerama screen in full
colour a small army of actors inflict

mayhem on each other with cars, planes, explosives and other devices for more than three hours with stereophonic sound effects is simply too much for the human eye and ear to respond to, let alone the funny bone.' – *Dwight MacDonald*
AAN: Ernest Laszlo; Ernest Gold; title song (*m* Ernest Gold, *ly* Mack David)

It's Great to Be Young*
GB 1956 93m Technicolor
AB-Pathé/Marble Arch (Victor Skutezky)

A popular teacher falls foul of the new headmaster who tries to disband the school orchestra.

Very acceptable but totally forgettable star comedy.

w Ted Willis *d* Cyril Frankel
ph Gilbert Taylor *m* Ray Martin, Lester Powell, John Addison

John Mills, Cecil Parker, Jeremy Spenser, Dorothy Bromiley, John Salew, Derek Blomfield, Eleanor Summerfield, Bryan Forbes

Ivanhoe*
GB 1952 106m Technicolor
MGM (Pandro S. Berman)
V

Derring-do among the knights of medieval England.

Tolerable, big-budget spectacular based on Sir Walter Scott's novel.

w Noel Langley, Aeneas Mackenzie *d* Richard Thorpe
ph F. A. Young *m* Miklos Rozsa

Robert Taylor, Joan Fontaine, Elizabeth Taylor, Emlyn Williams, George Sanders, Robert Douglas, Finlay Currie, Felix Aylmer, Francis de Wolff, Guy Rolfe, Norman Wooland, Basil Sydney
AAN: best picture; F. A. Young; Miklos Rozsa

J

Jabberwocky
GB 1977 101m Technicolor
Umbrella (John Goldstone, Sandy Lieberson)
L

A medieval cooper's apprentice is mistaken for a prince and slays the dragon which is terrorizing the neighbourhood.

An intellectual Carry On film, with very little more taste and a great deal more unpleasant imagery. Despite much re-editing, the laughs are very intermittent.

w Charles Alverson, Terry Gilliam
d Terry Gilliam   ph Terry Bedford
m De Wolfe   pd Roy Smith

Michael Palin, Max Wall, Deborah Fallender, Warren Mitchell, John Le Mesurier, Harry H. Corbett, Rodney Bewes, Bernard Bresslaw

'The constant emphasis on blood, excrement, dismemberment and filth ultimately becomes rather wearing.' – *Michael Billington, Illustrated London News*

Jack and the Beanstalk
US 1952 78m Supercinecolor
Warner/Alex Gottlieb

A babysitter dreams the story he is reading aloud.

Rather feeble star comedy aimed entirely at the kiddie set, and with none of the familiar routines. The 'bookends', as is customary, are in black and white.

w Nat Curtis   d Jean Yarbrough
ph George Robinson   m Heinz Roemheld

Bud Abbott, Lou Costello, Buddy Baer, Dorothy Ford, William Farnum

Jack the Giant Killer**
US 1961 94m Technicolor
Zenith/Edward Small (Robert E. Kent)

Demon Pendragon kidnaps the princess of Cornwall but she is rescued by a farmer's son.

Very creditable fairy tale, with the right style and atmosphere assisted by vigorous acting, good pace and excellent trick effects. Unfortunately it turned out rather scary for a child audience and so fell between two stools.

w Orville Hampton, Nathan Juran
d Nathan Juran   ph David S. Horsley   m Paul Sawtell, Bert Shefter   ad Fernando Carere, Frank McCoy   sp Howard Anderson

Kerwin Mathews, Judi Meredith, *Torin Thatcher, Don Beddoe*, Walter Burke, Barry Kelley

'A love story every woman would die a thousand deaths to live!'

Jane Eyre***
US 1943 96m bw
TCF (William Goetz)
V

In Victorian times, a harshly treated orphan girl becomes governess in a mysterious Yorkshire mansion with a brooding master.

Sharply paced, reasonably faithful and superbly staged Hollywood version of Charlotte Brontë's archetypal romantic novel which stimulated so many imitations, including *Rebecca*.

w Aldous Huxley, Robert Stevenson, John Houseman   d Robert Stevenson   ph George Barnes   m Bernard Herrmann   ad Wiard B. Ihnen, James Basevi   sp Fred Sersen

Joan Fontaine, Orson Welles, Margaret O'Brien, *Henry Daniell*, John Sutton, Agnes Moorehead, Elizabeth Taylor, Peggy Ann Garner, Sara Allgood, Aubrey Mather, Hillary Brooke, Edith Barrett, Ethel Griffies, Barbara Everest, John Abbott

'A careful and tame production, a sadly vanilla-flavoured Joan Fontaine, and Orson Welles treating himself to broad operatic sculpturings of body, cloak and diction, his eyes glinting in the Rembrandt gloom, at every chance, like side orders of jelly.' – *James Agee*
'The essentials are still there; and the non-essentials, such as the gloom, the shadows, the ground mist, the rain and the storms, have been expanded and redoubled and magnified to fill up the gaps.' – *Richard Mallett, Punch*

Janie
US   1944   106m   bw
Warner (Brock Pemberton)

The teenage daughter of a middle-class American household gets into innocent scrapes with the army.

Deafening tomboy farce.

w Agnes Christine Johnston, Charles Hoffman   play Josephine Bentham, Herschel V. Williams Jnr   d Michael Curtiz   ph Carl Guthrie   m/ly Lee David, Sammy Cahn, Jule Styne   ed Owen Marks

Joyce Reynolds, Robert Hutton, Ann Harding, Edward Arnold, Robert Benchley, Claire Foley, Hattie McDaniel

† *Janie Gets Married*, made the following year and running 89m, had almost identical credits except that Joan Leslie replaced Joyce Reynolds and Dorothy Malone joined the cast.
AAN: Owen Marks

Jason and the Argonauts***
GB   1963   104m   Technicolor
Columbia/Charles H. Schneer
V, L

With help and hindrance from the gods, Jason voyages in search of the Golden Fleece and meets all kinds of monsters.

Rambling semi-classic mythological fantasy which keeps its tongue firmly in its cheek and provides a framework for some splendid stop-frame animation.

w Jan Read, Beverley Cross   d Don Chaffey   ph Wilkie Cooper   m Bernard Herrmann   sp Ray Harryhausen

Todd Armstrong, Honor Blackman, Niall MacGinnis, Andrew Faulds, Nancy Kovack

Jaws**
US   1975   125m   Technicolor
Panavision
Universal/Zanuck-Brown (William S. Gilmore Jnr)
V, L

A man-eating shark causes havoc off the Long Island coast.

In the exploitation-hungry seventies this film took more money than any other. In itself, despite genuinely suspenseful and frightening sequences, it is a slackly narrated and sometimes flatly handled thriller with an over-abundance of dialogue and, when it finally appears, a pretty unconvincing monster.

w Peter Benchley, Carl Gottlieb
novel Peter Benchley   d Steven
Spielberg   ph Bill Butler   m John
Williams   ad Joseph Alves Jnr
ed Verna Fields

Robert Shaw, Roy Scheider, Richard Dreyfuss, Lorraine Gary, Murray Hamilton, Carl Gottlieb

'A mind-numbing repast for sense-sated gluttons. Shark stew for the stupefied.' – *William S. Pechter*
'The opening sequences have few parallels in modern cinema; like the shower scene in *Psycho* they will haunt a whole generation.' – *Les Keyser, Hollywood in the Seventies*

AA: John Williams; Verna Fields; sound
AAN: best picture

Jaws 2
US   1978   117m   Technicolor
    Panavision
Universal/Richard Zanuck, David Brown
    (Joe Alves)
V, L

Another man-eating shark menaces teenagers in the Long Island resort of Amity.

Repetitive and feeble sequel aimed directly at the popcorn market.

w Carl Gottlieb, Howard Sackler, Dorothy Tristan   d Jeannot Szwarc
ph Michael Butler, David Butler, Michael McGowan   m John Williams

Roy Scheider, Lorraine Gary, Murray Hamilton, Joseph Mascolo, Collin Wilcox

'A manipulation of the audience, in the best sense of the term' – *Jeannot Szwarc, director*

Jean de Florette**
France   1986   121m
    Eastmancolor   Technovision
Renn/Films A2/RAI2/DD
V, L

Elemental story of feuding over water supplies in rural France in the 20s.

Stunning performances and detailed depiction of Provençal farming life made it a wild success in France, repeated to a remarkable extent abroad.

w Claude Berri, Gérard Brach
novel Marcel Pagnol   d Claude Berri
ph Bruno Nuytten   m Jean-Claude Petit   pd Bernard Vezat

Yves Montand, Gérard Depardieu, Daniel Auteuil, Elisabeth Depardieu

† The saga continued in *Manon des Sources* (qv), from Pagnol's sequel *L'eau de collines*.

Jeannie*
GB   1941   101m   bw
GFD/Tansa (Marcel Hellman)
US title: *Girl in Distress*

A Scots girl comes into money and takes a European holiday.

Mildly astringent, generally amusing comedy which overcomes shaky production. Remade as *Let's Be Happy* in 1952.

w Anatole de Grunwald, Roland Pertwee   *play* Aimée Stuart
d Harold French   ph Bernard Knowles   m Mischa Spoliansky

Barbara Mullen, Michael Redgrave, Albert Lieven, Wilfrid Lawson, Kay Hammond, Edward Chapman, Googie Withers, Gus MacNaughton

'One of the easiest, sweetest of light comedies.' – *James Agee*
'As enchanting a bit of rue and nonsense as we've succumbed to in many a month.' – *New York Times*

'Some say he's dead ... some say he never will be!'
Jeremiah Johnson**
US 1972 107m Technicolor Panavision
Warner (Joe Wizan)
V, L

In the 1850s an ex-soldier becomes a mountain trapper.

Splendidly made if rather desultorily plotted adventure story with the feel of raw reality.

w John Milius, Edward Anhalt
d *Sydney Pollack* ph Andrew Callaghan m John Rubinstein, Tim McIntire

Robert Redford, Will Geer, Allyn McLerie

Jesus Christ Superstar*
US 1973 107m Technicolor Todd-AO 35
Universal (Norman Jewison, Robert Stigwood)
V, V(W), L

Young tourists in Israel re-enact episodes of the life of Christ.

Location-set fantasia based on the phenomenally successful rock opera; some of it works, but the original concept was a theatrical one.

w Melvyn Bragg, Norman Jewison d Norman Jewison
ph *Douglas Slocombe* md André Previn m/ly *Andrew Lloyd Webber*, Tim Rice

Ted Neeley, Carl Anderson, Yvonne Elliman, Barry Dennen

'One of the true fiascos of modern cinema.' – *Paul D. Zimmerman*
AAN: André Previn

Jetsons: The Movie
US 1990 83m CFI color
UIP/Universal/Hanna-Berbera/Wang/ Cuckoo's Nest Studios (Bruce David Johnson)

The Jetson family solve the problem of alien saboteurs who object to their asteroid being the site of a mining factory.

Poorly animated situation comedy that would be better suited to television and best suited to the nearest garbage disposal unit.

w Dennis Marks, Carl Sautter
d William Hanna, Joseph Barbera
ph Daniel Bunn m John Debney

voices of George O'Hanlon, Mel Blanc, Penny Singleton, Tiffany, Patric Zimmerman, Don Messick, Jean Vanderpyl

'This exercise in high-tech tedium might prove more bewildering than charming to its pre-teen audience.' – *MFB*

'When the going gets tough, the tough get going!'
Jewel of the Nile*
US 1985 104m Technicolor
TCF/Michael Douglas
V, L

A lady novelist gets into trouble when she accepts an invitation from a Middle Eastern potentate.

Moderate sequel to *Romancing the Stone*; plenty of action, but dull spots in between.

w Mark Rosenthal, Lawrence Konner d Lewis Teague ph Jan DeBont m Jack Nitzsche
pd Richard Dawking, Terry Knight

Michael Douglas, Kathleen Turner, Danny DeVito, Spiros Focas

'Mass destruction, endless gunfire and a fiery finish ... the only box office question is whether the film comes late in the cycle for Saturday matinee revivals.' – *Variety*

Jitterbugs*
US 1943 75m bw
TCF (Sol M. Wurtzel)

Laurel and Hardy help a night-club singer to fight off gangsters.

The last Laurel and Hardy film to contain any good scenes, and almost the only one of their TCF films that did.

w Scott Darling *d* Mal St Clair *ph* Lucien Andriot *md* Emil Newman *m/ly* Charles Newman, Lew Pollack *ed* James Bashevi, Chester Gore

Stan Laurel, Oliver Hardy, Vivian Blaine, Bob Bailey, Douglas Fowley, Noel Madison, Lee Patrick

Johann Mouse***
US 1952 8m Technicolor
MGM (Fred Quimby)

Strauss's mouse dances to his master's music; the cat, to lure him out, learns to play the piano.

Splendid Tom and Jerry cartoon from the great period of this neglected art.

AA: best cartoon

Johnny Tremain
US 1957 81m Technicolor
Walt Disney

In 1773 Boston an apprentice silversmith joins the Sons of Liberty and helps start the War of Independence.

Schoolbook history with little vitality.

w Tom Blackburn *novel* Esther Forbes *d* Robert Stevenson *ph* Charles B. Boyle *m* George Bruns

Hal Stalmaster, Luana Patten, Jeff York, Sebastian Cabot, Richard Beymer, Walter Sande

'Everyone's book is now everyone's motion picture!'

Jonathan Livingston Seagull
US 1973 114m DeLuxe Panavision
Paramount/JLS Partnership/Hall Bartlett
V

The life of a seagull who aims to fly faster than any of his peers and eventually arrives in a perfect world.

Weird 'family' fantasy based on a phenomenally successful book which clearly could not translate easily to the screen. The bird photography is much more successful than the mysticism.

w Richard Bach *novel* Richard Bach *d* Hall Bartlett *ph* Jack Couffer *ph* Boris Leven *m* Neil Diamond, Lee Holdridge

'A parable couched in the form of a nature film of overpowering beauty and strength in which, perhaps to our horror, we are forced to recognize ourselves in a seagull obsessed with the heights.' – *Michael Korda*
'It may be that the creature best qualified to review it is another seagull.' – *Benny Green, Punch*
'If one must spend two hours following the adventures of a bird, far better that the hero be Donald Duck.' – *Jay Cocks, Time*
'The sort of garbage that only a seagull could love.' – *Judith Crist*
AAN: Jack Couffer

The Jones Family

Less human, more farcical than the Hardy films (qv), this series was TCF's second feature answer to MGM's money-makers, and pleased a lot of people at the time. Pop was Jed Prouty, Mom was Spring Byington, Grandma was Florence Roberts, and the youngsters included Kenneth Howell, George Ernest, Billy Mahan, June Carlson and June Lang. The first script was from a play by Katharine Cavanaugh, and the principal director was Frank Strayer.

1936: EVERY SATURDAY NIGHT, EDUCATING FATHER, BACK TO NATURE
1937: OFF TO THE RACES, BORROWING TROUBLE, HOT WATER
1938: LOVE ON A BUDGET, TRIP TO PARIS, SAFETY IN NUMBERS, DOWN ON THE FARM
1939: EVERYBODY'S BABY, QUICK MILLIONS, THE JONES FAMILY IN HOLLYWOOD, TOO BUSY TO WORK
1940: ON THEIR OWN

† An earlier series with different actors was abandoned after two episodes: *Young as You Feel* (1931), *Business and Pleasure* (1932).

Jour de Fête***
France 1948 87m bw
Francinex (Fred Orain)
V, L

A village postman sees a film about the efficiency of the American postal service and decides to smarten himself up.

First, and some say best, of Tati's comedy vehicles: two-thirds superb local colour, one-third hilarious slapstick.

w Jacques Tati, Henri Marquet
d *Jacques Tati* ph Jacques Mercanton m Jean Yatove

Jacques Tati, Guy Decomble, Paul Fankeur, Santa Relli

'You could watch it with a bout of toothache and it would make you laugh.' – *Daily Express*

† A reissue version had colour items hand-painted in each frame, and proved quite effective.

Journey Back to Oz*
US 1964 (released 1974) 90m colour
Norm Prescott and Lou Scheimer/ Filmation

Dorothy makes a return journey over the rainbow to fight the wicked witch's sister.

Competent cartoon version of Frank Baum themes from *The Wizard of Oz*.

d Hal Sutherland

voices of Liza Minnelli, Milton Berle, Ethel Merman, Margaret Hamilton, Mickey Rooney, Paul Ford

The Journey of Natty Gann
US 1985 105m colour
Walt Disney (Michael Lobell)

During the Chicago depression, a girl follows her father west and hitch-hikes across America.

A kind of human *Lassie Come Home*: doggedly watchable but not inspiring, especially since it was shot in Canada.

w Jeanne Rosenberg d Jeremy Kagan ph Richard Bush
m James Horner

Meredith Salenger, John Cusack, Ray Wise, Scatman Crothers

'Cut to an hour, it would make a fine Disney telepic.' – *Variety*
AAN: costumes (Albert Wolsky)

Journey to the Center of the Earth***
US 1959 132m DeLuxe Cinemascope

TCF (Charles Brackett)
V, L

An Edinburgh professor and assorted colleagues follow an explorer's trail down an extinct Icelandic volcano to the Earth's centre.

Enjoyable hokum which gets more and more fantastic but only occasionally misses its footing; it ends splendidly with the team being catapulted out of Stromboli on a tide of lava.

w *Walter Reisch, Charles Brackett novel* Jules Verne   d *Henry Levin* ph Leo Tover   m *Bernard Herrmann*   ad Lyle R. Wheeler, Franz Bachelin, Herman A. Blumenthal

James Mason, Arlene Dahl, Pat Boone, Peter Ronson, Diane Baker, Thayer David

'The attraction of a Jules Verne fantasy ... is in the endearing contrast between the wildest adventures and the staidest Victorian propriety on the part of those undergoing them ... There is about the whole film a good-natured enjoyment of its own excesses.' – *Penelope Houston*
AAN: art direction

'Caught in a fantastic time trap.'
Journey to the Center of Time
US   1967   82m   colour
Ember/Flamingo/Borealis-Dorad (Ray Dorn, David L. Hewitt)

Scientists inadvertently send themselves to the year 5000 AD, at a time of a war with aliens, and then travel to 1,000,000 BC where they are attacked by monsters.

Low budget, unexciting sf, with the prehistoric world represented by one medium-sized lizard, dry ice and coloured lights.

w *David Prentiss*   d *David L. Hewitt*   ph Robert Caramico   pd Edward D. Engoron   sp Modern Film Effects   ed Bill Welburn

Scott Brady, Gigi Perreau, Anthony Eisley, Abraham Sofaer, Poupee Gamin

'Greater than Ivanhoe!'
'Thrill to ruthless men and their goddess-like women in a sin-swept age!'
'Thrill to traitors and heroes, killings and conspiracies, passions and violence in Rome's most exciting age!'
Julius Caesar**
US   1953   121m   bw
MGM (John Houseman)
V

Cassius and Brutus lead the conspirators who murder Caesar, but are themselves routed by Mark Antony.

Straightforward, rather leaden presentation of Shakespeare's play, lit by effective moments in the acting, but the sudden change from talk to battle is not smoothed over.

wd *Joseph L. Mankiewicz*
ph *Joseph Ruttenberg*   m *Miklos Rozsa*   ad Cedric Gibbons, Edward Carfagno

John Gielgud, James Mason, Marlon Brando, Greer Garson, Deborah Kerr, Louis Calhern, Edmond O'Brien, George Macready, Michael Pate, John Hoyt, Alan Napier

AA: art direction
AAN: best picture; Joseph Ruttenberg; Miklos Rozsa; Marlon Brando

Jumbo*
US   1962   124m   Metrocolor
Panavision
MGM (Joe Pasternak, Martin Melcher)
aka: *Billy Rose's Jumbo*

In 1910, the daughter of the owner of a shaky circus prevents a take-over bid.

Hoary circus story with music. General effect disappointing: the elephant steals the show.

w Sidney Sheldon play Ben Hecht, Charles MacArthur d Charles Walters ph William H. Daniels md George Stoll ch Busby Berkeley m/ly Richard Rodgers, Lorenz Hart

Doris Day, *Jimmy Durante*, Stephen Boyd, Martha Raye, Dean Jagger
AAN: George Stoll

Jumping Jacks*
US 1952 96m bw
Paramount/Hal B. Wallis

Two cabaret comedians join the paratroops.

Standard star farce, one of Martin and Lewis' best.

w Robert Lees, Fred Rinaldo, Herbert Baker d Norman Taurog ph Daniel L. Fapp m Joseph J. Lilley

Dean Martin, *Jerry Lewis*, Mona Freeman, Robert Strauss, Don Defore

'More thrilling than the deeds of man ... more beautiful than the love of woman ... more wonderful than the dreams of children!'

The Jungle Book*
US 1942 109m Technicolor
Alexander Korda (W. Howard Greene)
L
aka: *Rudyard Kipling's Jungle Book*

Growing up with animals in an Indian forest, a boy forestalls the getaway of three thieves.

High-budgeted but rather boring live action version with stiff-jointed model animals.

w Laurence Stallings
stories Rudyard Kipling d Zoltan Korda, André de Toth ph Lee Garmes, W. Howard Greene
m Miklos Rozsa ad Vincent Korda

Sabu, Joseph Calleia, John Qualen, Frank Puglia, Rosemary de Camp
AAN: cinematography; Miklos Rozsa; Vincent Korda

Jungle Book*
US 1967 78m Technicolor
Walt Disney

Cartoon version relying less on action than on songs and voices; patchily successful but no classic.

d Wolfgang Reitherman m/ly Richard and Robert Sherman, Terry Gilkyson

voices of George Sanders, Phil Harris, Louis Prima, Sebastian Cabot, Sterling Holloway
AAN: song 'The Bare Necessities' (*m/ly* Terry Gilkyson)

Junior Miss*
US 1945 94m bw
TCF (William Perlberg)

A teenager causes trouble by meddling in the lives of her family.

Amusing family comedy from a hit play.

w George Seaton play Jerome Chodorov, Joseph Fields
stories Sally Benson d George Seaton ph Charles Clarke m David Buttolph

Peggy Ann Garner, Allyn Joslyn, Faye Marlowe, Mona Freeman, Michael Dunne, John Alexander

Jupiter's Darling*
US 1954 96m Eastmancolor Cinemascope
MGM (George Wells)

Advancing on Rome, Hannibal falls in love with the dictator's fiancée.

A splendid example of the higher lunacy, with coloured elephants decorating an MGM musical about the fall of the Roman Empire. Small elements can be salvaged, and the gall is enough to be divided into three parts.

w Dorothy Kingsley play The Road to Rome by Robert E. Sherwood d George Sidney ph Paul C. Vogel, Charles Rosher m David Rose ch Hermes Pan m/ly Burton Lane, Harold Adamson ad Cedric Gibbons, Uric McCleary

Esther Williams, Howard Keel, George Sanders, Marge and Gower Champion, Richard Haydn, William Demarest

'An adventure 65 million years in the making.'

Jurassic Park*
US 1993 127m colour
UIP/Universal/Amblin (Kathleen Kennedy, Gerald R. Molen)

Genetically re-created from blood taken from ancient mosquitoes, Dinosaurs run amok in a theme park.

The dinosaurs are amazing: living, breathing, believable creatures, which is more than you can say for the actors in this otherwise cardboard creation, hung up on toilet jokes and often seeming no more than an elongated commercial for all the merchandise associated with the movie, which includes a long, shameless pan along shelves of the toys and books available. The film was distributed with a warning that it might upset sensitive children. Sensitive adults are likely to be disappointed, too.

w Michael Crichton, David Koepp novel Michael Crichton d Steven Spielberg ph Dean Cundey m John Williams pd Rick Carter sp Industrial Light and Magic, Stan Winston, Dennis Muren, Phil Tippett, Michael Lantieri ed Michael Kahn

Sam Neill, Laura Dern, Jeff Goldblum, Richard Attenborough, Bob Peck, Martin Ferrero, B. D. Wong, Joseph Mazello, Ariana Richards, Samuel L. Jackson

'Doesn't have the imagination – or the courage – to take us any place we haven't been a thousand times before. It's just a creature feature on amphetamines.' – Terrence Rafferty, New Yorker

† Among the many inconsistencies in the narrative, Sam Neill warns that the Tyrannosaurus Rex reacts to movement when he can have no knowledge or experience of this fact. The film topped the box-office charts in virtually every country (France being the exception).
AAN: visual effects

Just Around the Corner
US 1938 70m bw
TCF (David Hempstead)

A little girl helps her dad to get on in business.

Tedious Little Miss Fixit tale from the period when Shirley's star was sliding.

w Ethel Hill, J. P. McEvoy, Darrel Ware d Irving Cummings ph Henry Sharp md Louis Silvers

Shirley Temple, Charles Farrell, Bert Lahr, Joan Davis, Amanda Duff, Bill Robinson, Franklin Pangborn, Cora Witherspoon

'Top flight for general all-round entertainment.' – Variety

K

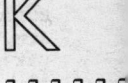

The Karate Kid*
US 1984 127m Metrocolor
Columbia/Delphi II (Jerry Weintraub)
V, L

A teenage boy, new to California, joins a karate club and defeats the local bullies.

A kind of amateur *Rocky*, not bad in its way, but its huge commercial success in the US remains mystifying.

w Robert Mark Kamen   d John G. Avildsen   ph James Crabe   m Bill Conti   pd William J. Cassidy   ed Bud Smith, Walt Mulconery

Ralph Macchio, Noriyuki 'Pat' Morita, Elizabeth Shue, Martin Kove, Randee Heller, William Zabka

AAN: Pat Morita (supporting actor)

The Karate Kid Part II
US 1986 113m DeLuxe
Columbia/Delphi II (Jerry Weintraub)
V, L

Daniel's teacher heads back to Okinawa where his father is gravely ill.

Tedious attempt to spin out a surprise hit; no surprises this time.

w Robert Mark Kamen   d John G. Avildsen   ph James Crabe   m Bill Conti   pd William J. Cassidy   ed David Garfield, Jane Kurson, John G. Avildsen

Pat Morita, Ralph Macchio, Nobu McCarthy, Danny Kamekona

AAN: song 'Glory of Love'

Karate Kid III
US 1989 112m DeLuxe
Columbia TriStar (Jerry Weintraub)
V, L

The karate kid defeats villains who attempt to humiliate him.

Even less interesting than Part II.

w Robert Mark Kamen   d John G. Avildsen   ph Stephen Yaconelli   m Bill Conti   pd William F. Matthews   ed John Carter, John G. Avildsen

Ralph Macchio, Noriyuki 'Pat' Morita, Robyn Lively, Thomas Ian Griffith, Martin L. Kove, Sean Kanan, Jonathan Avildsen

'Young love, meanwhile, has rarely been shown so boringly on screen.' – *MFB*

Keep 'Em Flying
US 1941 86m bw
Universal (Glenn Tryon)

Two incompetents in the Army Air Corps get mixed up with identical twin girls.

A big moneymaker of its day, this comedy now seems especially resistible.

w True Boardman, Nat Perrin, John Grant   d Arthur Lubin   ph Joseph Valentine   m Frank Skinner

Bud Abbott, Lou Costello, Martha Raye, Carol Bruce, William Gargan, Dick Foran, Charles Lang
AAN: song 'Pig Foot Pete' (*m* Gene de Paul, *ly* Don Raye)

Kentucky Moonshine*
US 1938 87m bw
TCF (Darryl F. Zanuck)

In the hope of a radio contract, the Ritz Brothers masquerade as hillbillies and find themselves in the middle of a feud.

One of the trio's best solo vehicles.

w Art Arthur, M. M. Musselman *d* David Butler *ph* Robert Planck *md* Louis Silvers *m/ly* Lew Pollack, Sidney Mitchell

The Ritz Brothers, Tony Martin, Marjorie Weaver, Slim Summerville, John Carradine, Wally Vernon, Berton Churchill, Eddie Collins

'It's crazy and it's wild, but it's funny and grand entertainment.' – *Variety*

Kes**
GB 1969 109m Technicolor
UA/Woodfall (Tony Garnett)
V

In a northern industrial town, a boy learns about life from the fate of his pet bird.

Realistic family drama that is one of the key British films of its period.

w Barry Hines, Ken Loach, Tony Garnet *novel* A Kestrel for a Knave by Barry Hines *d* Ken Loach *ph* Chris Menges *m* John Cameron

David Bradley, Lynne Perrie, Colin Welland, Freddie Fletcher, Brian Glover

'There emerges a most discouraging picture of life in the industrial north ... infinitely sad in its total implications, it is also immensely funny in much of its detail.' – *Brenda Davies*
'Particularly to be admired is the way in which the dialogue has been kept flowing, as if it were always spontaneous, something proceeding from the moment.' – *Dilys Powell*

'Where the Nile divides, their mighty conflict begins!'
Khartoum*
GB 1966 134m Technicolor Ultra Panavision
UA/Julian Blaustein

The last years of General Gordon.

Dullish history book stuff which fails to explain Gordon the man but occasionally erupts into glowing action.

w Robert Ardrey *d* Basil Dearden *ph* Edward Scaife, Harry Waxman *m* Frank Cordell

Charlton Heston, Laurence Olivier, Ralph Richardson, Richard Johnson, Hugh Williams, Alexander Knox, Johnny Sekka, Nigel Green, Michael Hordern

'Academic accuracy and spectacular battles are unhappy partners.' – *MFB*
'Beautifully photographed, lavishly mounted, intelligently acted, but ultimately dull.' – *Sight and Sound*
AAN: Robert Ardrey

The Kid***
US 1921 52m approx (24 fps) bw silent
First National/Charles Chaplin
V

A tramp brings up an abandoned baby, and later loses him to his mother; but there is a happy ending.

Sentimental comedy set in the slums.

The comedy is very sparingly laid on, but the effect of the whole is much less painful than the synopsis would suggest, the production is comparatively smooth, the child actor is sensational, and the film contains much of the quintessential Chaplin.

wd Charles Chaplin   ph Rollie Totheroh

Charles Chaplin, Jackie Coogan, Edna Purviance

The Kid Brother****
US 1927 83m bw silent
Paramount/Lloyd (Harold Lloyd)

The youngest son in the family proves that he is more than the household drudge.

Lively, slapstick comedy with the star at his best.

w John Grey, Tom Crizer, Ted Wilde   d Ted Wilde, J. A. Howe, Lewis Milestone   ph Walter Lundin, Henry N. Kohler   ad Liell K. Vedder   ed Allen McNeil

Harold Lloyd, Jobyna Ralston, Walter James, Leo Willis, Olin Francis, Constantine Romanoff

'As gaggy a gag picture as he has ever done.' – *Variety*

A Kid for Two Farthings*
GB 1955 96m Eastmancolor
London Films (Carol Reed)

Among the colourful characters of London's Petticoat Lane market moves a boy whose pet goat seems to have the magical power of a unicorn.

Whimsical character comedy-drama made with some style but too insubstantial and unconvincing to be affectionately remembered.

w Wolf Mankowitz   d Carol Reed   ph Ted Scaife   m Benjamin Frankel

Celia Johnson, Diana Dors, David Kossoff, Brenda de Banzie, Sidney Tafler, Primo Carnera, Joe Robinson, Jonathan Ashmore

Kidnapped*
US 1938 93m bw
TCF (Kenneth MacGowan)

During the Jacobite rebellion a young boy is sold by his wicked uncle as a slave, and is helped by an outlaw.

Much altered version of a classic adventure story, exciting enough in its own right, and well made in the thirties tradition.

w Sonya Levien, Richard Sherman, Walter Ferris   novel Robert Louis Stevenson   d Alfred L. Werker   ph Bert Glennon   m Arthur Lange

Warner Baxter, Freddie Bartholomew, Arleen Whelan, John Carradine, C. Aubrey Smith, Nigel Bruce, Reginald Owen

'Strange modifications have been wrought ... ambitious effort which misses top rating.' – *Variety*

Kidnapped*
GB 1959 95m Technicolor
Walt Disney (Hugh Attwooll)
L

A remake fairly faithful to the book, which results in a few *longueurs;* but in general the action is spirited.

wd Robert Stevenson   ph Paul Beeson   m Cedric Thorpe Davie

Peter Finch, James MacArthur, Bernard Lee, John Laurie, Finlay Currie, Niall MacGinnis, Peter O'Toole, Miles Malleson, Oliver Johnston, Duncan Macrae, Andrew Cruickshank

Kidnapped*
GB 1971 107m Movielab Panavision
Omnibus (Frederick H. Brogger)

Remake incorporating sections of *Catriona*. Not particularly exciting, but the acting helps.

w Jack Pulman d Delbert Mann ph Paul Beeson m Roy Budd

Michael Caine, Lawrence Douglas, Trevor Howard, Jack Hawkins, Donald Pleasence, Gordon Jackson, Freddie Jones, Jack Watson

The Kidnappers*
GB 1953 95m bw
Rank/Nolbandov-Parkyn
US title: *The Little Kidnappers*

In a Nova Scotian village at the turn of the century a stern old man denies his young grandchildren a pet, so they borrow a baby and hide it in the woods.

Fairly pleasing and popular whimsy for family audiences.

w Neil Paterson d Philip Leacock ph Eric Cross m Bruce Montgomery

Duncan Macrae, Vincent Winter, Jon Whiteley, Theodore Bikel, Jean Anderson

Kim*
US 1950 112m Technicolor
MGM (Leon Gordon)
V

The orphaned son of a British soldier in India has adventures with his horseman friend who belongs to the British secret service.

Colourful *Boys' Own Paper* high jinks, quite lively but never convincing.

w Leon Gordon, Helen Deutsch, Richard Schayer novel Rudyard Kipling d Victor Saville ph William Skall m André Previn

Errol Flynn, Dean Stockwell, Paul Lukas, Robert Douglas, Thomas Gomez, Cecil Kellaway, Arnold Moss, Reginald Owen

'Ornate, lavish, but curiously lacking in genuine atmosphere, vitality or period sense.' – *Penelope Houston*

The King and I*
US 1956 133m Eastmancolor Cinemascope 55
TCF (Charles Brackett)
V, V(W), L

Musical remake of *Anna and the King of Siam* (qv), from the highly successful stage production.

The film is opulent in lush detail but quite lacking in style.

w Ernest Lehman d Walter Lang ph Leon Shamroy md Alfred Newman, Ken Darby m Richard Rodgers book/ly Oscar Hammerstein II ad Lyle Wheeler, John DeCuir

Deborah Kerr, Yul Brynner, Rita Moreno, Martin Benson, Alan Mowbray, Geoffrey Toone, Terry Saunders

'Gaiety has something of a struggle to survive.' – *Penelope Houston*

AA: Yul Brynner; Alfred Newman, Ken Darby; art direction
AAN: best picture; Walter Lang; Leon Shamroy; Deborah Kerr

King Kong****
US 1933 100m bw
RKO (Merian C. Cooper)
V, L

A film producer on safari brings back a giant ape which terrorizes New York.

The greatest monster movie of all, a miracle of trick work and suspense, with some of the most memorable moments in film history.

w James Creelman, Ruth Rose story Edgar Wallace d Merian C. Cooper, Ernest Schoedsack ph Edward Linden, Vernon Walker, L. O. Taylor sound effects Murray Spivak chief technician Willis J. O'Brien m Max Steiner

Robert Armstrong, Fay Wray, Bruce Cabot, Frank Reicher

CARL DENHAM (Robert Armstrong): 'It wasn't the airplanes. It was beauty killed the beast.'

'If properly handled, should gather good grosses in a walk . . . and may open up a new medium for scaring babies via the screen.' – *Variety*
'Just amusing nonsense punctuated by such reflections as why, if the natives wanted to keep the monster on the other side of the wall, they should have built a door big enough to let him through.' – *James Agate*

'The most exciting motion picture event of all time!'
King Kong
US 1976 135m Metrocolor Panavision
Dino de Laurentiis
V, L

Semi-spoof remake with added sexual overtones; though launched on a massive wave of publicity, it lacks both the charm and the technical resources of its predecessor.

w Lorenzo Semple Jnr d John Guillermin ph Richard H. Kline m John Barry pd Dale Hennesy, Mario Chiari

Jeff Bridges, Charles Grodin, Jessica Lange, John Randolph, René Auberjonois, Julius Harris, Ed Lauter

'The one and original lovable monster is lost amid all the hydraulic manipulations in what now emerges as the story of a dumb blonde who falls for a huge plastic finger.' – *Judith Crist, Saturday Review*
'Even with colour, the settings of Kong II are no match for the rich black-and-white chiaroscuro of Kong I, with its echoes of artists like Gustave Doré and Max Ernst and its sensitivity to the emotional values of tone and texture.' – *Jack Kroll, Newsweek*

† *King Kong Lives* (L) crept out minimally in 1986.

AA: visual effects (Carlo Rambaldi, Glen Robinson, Frank Van Der Veer)
AAN: Richard H. Kline

'A story of the Christ! The glory of his spoken words!'
King of Kings*
US 1961 161m Super Technirama
MGM/Samuel Bronston

The life of Jesus Christ.

Known in the trade as *I Was a Teenage Jesus*, this good-looking but rather tedious film is neither vulgar nor very interesting; a solemn, decent, bible-in-pictures pageant.

w Philip Yordan d Nicholas Ray ph Franz Planer, Manuel Berenger m Miklos Rozsa ad Georges Wakhevitch

Jeffrey Hunter, Robert Ryan, Siobhan McKenna, Frank Thring, Hurd Hatfield, Rip Torn, Harry Guardino, Viveca Lindfors, Rita Gam

'Body of a Greek god! Strength of a Hercules!'
King of the Jungle
US 1933 73m bw
Paramount

A small boy grows up with lions; he is captured with them and sold to an American circus.

Sub-Tarzan hokum which cheered up the kids.

w Philip Wylie, Fred Niblo Jnr, C. T. Stoneham d H. Bruce Humberstone, Max Marcin

Buster Crabbe, Frances Dee, Douglass Dumbrille, Robert Adair, Robert Barrat

'Minus any help from the marquee it will have to attract on merit alone, and on merit it rates fair business.' – *Variety*

King of the Khyber Rifles

US 1954 100m Technicolor
  Cinemascope
TCF (Frank Rosenberg)

In 1857 a British garrison in India is threatened by the forces of Kuuram Khan but saved by a half-caste officer.

Standard North-West Frontier adventure, old-fashioned and rather dull.

w Ivan Goff, Ben Roberts d Henry King ph Leon Shamroy m Bernard Herrmann

Tyrone Power, Terry Moore, Michael Rennie, Guy Rolfe, John Justin

King of the Wind

US 1989 102m Technicolor
Enterprise/Davis Panzer/HTV International
  (Michael Guest, Paul Sarony, Peter S. Davis, William Panzer)
V

Adventures in France and England of a young Arab groom and his horse.

Lamely told and a waste of everyone's time.

w Phil Frey novel Marguerite Henry d Peter Duffell ph Brian Morgan m John Scott pd Ken Sharp ed Lyndon Matthews

Frank Finlay, Jenny Agutter, Nigel Hawthorne, Navin Chowdhry, Ralph Bates, Neil Dickson, Barry Foster, Jill Gascoine, Joan Hickson, Anthony Quayle, Ian Richardson, Norman Rodway, Peter Vaughan, Richard Harris, Glenda Jackson

King Ralph

US 1991 97m Eastmancolor
UIP/Universal/Mirage/Ibro (Jack Brodsky)
V, L

A Las Vegas entertainer becomes King of England when the Royal Family is electrocuted.

Witless farce, set in an England that even P.G. Wodehouse would have found quaintly old hat.

wd David S. Ward novel Headlong by Emlyn Williams ph Kenneth MacMillan m James Newton Howard pd Simon Holland ed John Jympson

John Goodman, Peter O'Toole, John Hurt, Camille Coduri, Richard Griffiths, Leslie Phillips, James Villiers, Joely Richardson, Niall O'Brian, Julian Glover, Judy Parfitt

'As the man who wouldn't be King if he could help it, Goodman redeems what might have been just another high-concept comedy for the party of humanity.' – *Richard Schickel, Time*

King Richard and the Crusaders

US 1954 113m Warnercolor
  Cinemascope
Warner (Henry Blanke)

During the Crusades, the dreaded Saladin arrives in England in disguise and falls in love with Lady Edith . . .

Crudely confected comic strip version of Sir Walter Scott's *The Talisman*, ineptly written and cast, with poor production values.

w John Twist d David Butler
ph Peverell Marley m Max Steiner

Rex Harrison (as Saladin), Virginia Mayo, George Sanders, Laurence Harvey, Robert Douglas

LADY EDITH (Virginia Mayo): 'Fight, fight, fight! That's all you think of, Dick Plantagenet!'

'Do not adjust your set – the sound you hear is Sir Walter Scott turning in his grave.' – *Sunday Express*
'It shows why the Crusades never really amounted to much.' – *Time*

King Solomon's Mines*
GB 1937 80m bw
Gainsborough (Geoffrey Barkas)

Explorers in Africa persuade an exiled chief to help them find a diamond mine.

Rather somnolent though well-cast version of a favourite adventure novel, with a splendid final reel.

w Michael Hogan, A. R. Rawlinson, Roland Pertwee, Ralph Spence, Charles Bennett novel H. Rider Haggard d Robert Stevenson
ph Glen MacWilliams m Mischa Spoliansky

Cedric Hardwicke, *Paul Robeson*, Roland Young, John Loder, Anna Lee, Sydney Fairbrother, Robert Adams

'If the pop houses can accept its half-throttle speed, they'll get all the thrills and entertainment they want.' – *Variety*
'They kept the eye of the camera open for every form of wild and savage life and crammed it all into the picture, so one gets the impression that Allan Quartermain is delivering a lecture with illustrations rather than taking part in an adventure.' – *Richard Mallett, Punch*

King Solomon's Mines*
US 1950 102m Technicolor
MGM (Sam Zimbalist)

A remake which is largely travelogue with the merest trimmings of story.

w Helen Deutsch d Compton Bennett ph Robert Surtees
ed Ralph E. Winters, Conrad A. Nervig

Stewart Granger, Deborah Kerr, Richard Carlson, Hugo Haas, Lowell Gilmore

† Andrew Marton directed the second unit sequences.

AA: Robert Surtees; editing
AAN: best picture

King Solomon's Mines
US 1985 100m colour
  Cinemascope
Cannon

Quartermain is hired by a girl who wants to find her kidnapped father.

Adaptation in the vein of *Indiana Jones* and then some: the leading characters are almost boiled in a pot. Enjoyment depends on your sense of humour.

w Gene Quintano, James R. Silke
d J. Lee-Thompson

Richard Chamberlain, Sharon Stone, Herbert Lom, John Rhys-Davies, Ken Gampu

'The cinema's equivalent to junk food.' – *Sunday Mail*

'The king's ships ... the king's gold ... the king's girls ... were the treasure!'
The King's Pirate
US 1967 100m Technicolor
Universal (Robert Arthur)

An American in the 18th-century British navy infiltrates a pirate stronghold in Madagascar.

Tatty remake of *Against All Flags*, rising to a few minor heights of swashbuckling.

w Paul Wayne   d Don Weis
ph Clifford Stine   m Ralph Ferraro

Doug McClure, Jill St John, Guy Stockwell, Kurt Kasznar, Torin Thatcher, Richard Deacon, Sean McClory

The King's Thief
US 1955 79m Eastmancolor Cinemascope
MGM (Edwin H. Knopf)

The Duke of Brampton plots treason against Charles II but a highwayman robs him of an incriminating notebook.

Dismal swashbuckler with neither zest nor style, just a cast of unhappy-looking actors.

w Charles Knopf   d Robert Z. Leonard   ph Robert Planck
m Miklos Rozsa

David Niven, Edmund Purdom, Ann Blyth, George Sanders, Roger Moore

Kipps***
GB 1941 112m bw
TCF (Edward Black)
US title: *The Remarkable Mr Kipps*

In 1906, a draper's assistant comes into money and tries to crash society.

Charming, unassuming film of a well-loved novel, later musicalized as *Half a Sixpence*.

w Sidney Gilliat   novel H. G. Wells   d Carol Reed   ph Arthur Crabtree   m Charles Williams

Michael Redgrave, Phyllis Calvert, Diana Wynyard, *Arthur Riscoe*, Max Adrian, Helen Haye, Michael Wilding, Lloyd Pearson, Edward Rigby, Hermione Baddeley, Frank Pettingell, Beatrice Varley, Kathleen Harrison, Felix Aylmer

'It has the old fashioned charm of wax roses under a glass bell.' – *New York Times*

Kismet
US 1955 113m Eastmancolor Cinemascope
MGM (Arthur Freed)
V, L

Unlucky musical remake from the stage show with Borodin music.

w Charles Lederer, Luther Davis
musical play Charles Lederer, Luther Davis   d Vincente Minnelli
ph Joseph Ruttenberg   ch Jack Cole   ad Cedric Gibbons, Preston Ames

Howard Keel, Ann Blyth, Dolores Gray, Vic Damone, Monty Woolley, Sebastian Cabot, Jay C. Flippen, Mike Mazurki, Jack Elam

Kiss Me Kate**
US 1953 111m Anscocolor 3-D
MGM (Jack Cummings)
V, L

The married leading players of a musical version of *The Taming of the Shrew* lead an equally tempestuous life backstage.

Brisk, bright screen version of the Broadway musical hit.

w Dorothy Kingsley   play Samuel and Bella Spewack   d George Sidney   ph Charles Rosher
md André Previn, Saul Chaplin
m/ly Cole Porter   ch Hermes Pan

Howard Keel, Kathryn Grayson, Ann

Miller, Keenan Wynn, Bobby Van, Tommy Rall, James Whitmore, Bob Fosse, Kurt Kasznar

AAN: André Previn, Saul Chaplin

Knights and Emeralds

GB 1986 94m colour

Warner/Goldcrest/Enigma (Susan Richards, Raymond Day)

A young white drummer joins a rival black band for the national marching bands championship.

Dull teen drama of racial relationships, accompanied by a great deal of uninteresting music.

wd Ian Emes *ph* Richard Greatrex *m* Colin Towns *ad* Deborah Gillingham *ed* John Victor-Smith

Christopher Wild, Beverley Hills, Warren Mitchell, Bill Leadbitter, Rachel Davies

Knights of the Round Table*

GB 1953 115m Eastmancolor Cinemascope

MGM (Pandro S. Berman)

Lancelot, banished from King Arthur's court for loving Guinevere, returns to defeat the evil Modred.

Disappointingly flat, pageant-like adaptation of the legends, with a few lively strands insufficiently firmly drawn together.

w Talbot Jennings, Jan Lustig, Noel Langley *d* Richard Thorpe *ph* Frederick A. Young, Stephen Dade *m* Miklos Rozsa *ad* Alfred Junge, Hans Peters

Robert Taylor, Mel Ferrer, Ava Gardner, Anne Crawford, Stanley Baker, Felix Aylmer, Robert Urquhart, Niall MacGinnis

AAN: art direction

Krull

GB 1983 121m Metrocolor

Columbia/Ted Mann-Ron Silverman

V

Prince Colwyn's bride-to-be is abducted by the Beast of the Black Fortress.

Old-fashioned derring-do taking place on a somewhat unattractive planet; nevertheless fairly lively in its action and trick effects.

w Stanford Sherman *d* Peter Yates *ph* Peter Suschitzky *m* James Horner *pd* Stephen Grimes

Ken Marshall, Lysette Anthony, Freddie Jones, Francesca Annis, Alun Armstrong, David Battley, Bernard Bresslaw, John Welsh, Tony Church, Bernard Archard

'Nearly everything in it has been done before, in some cases rather better, but rarely quite so likeably.' – *Nick Roddick, MFB*

'Not really thrilling enough to be a blockbuster and not light enough to be anything else.' – *Sight and Sound*

L

Labyrinth
US 1986 101m colour
Tri-Star/Eric Rattray, George Lucas
V, L

A young girl embarks on a fantasy adventure to save her stepbrother from the clutches of the Goblin King.

Bizarre but tedious attempt to create a new *Alice in Wonderland*, with the inventor of the Muppets in charge. Unfortunately his creatures become less attractive with each attempt, and the script is emaciated.

w Terry Jones, from script by Dennis Less and Jim Henson *d* Jim Henson *ph* Alex Thomson *m* Trevor Jones *pd* Elliot Scott *conceptual design* Brian Froud

David Bowie, Jennifer Connelly, Toby Froud, Shelley Thompson

'A crashing bore . . . no real charm or texture to capture the imagination.' – *Variety*

Lady and the Tramp**
US 1955 76m Technicolor Cinemascope
Walt Disney (Erdmann Penner)

A pedigree spaniel falls foul of two Siamese cats and has a romantic adventure with a mongrel who helps her.

Pleasant cartoon feature in Disney's cutest and most anthropomorphic vein.

d Hamilton Luske, Clyde Geronimi, Wilfred Jackson *m* Oliver Wallace *m/ly* Peggy Lee, Sonny Burke

voices of Peggy Lee, Barbara Luddy, Bill Thompson, Bill Baucon, Stan Freberg

Lady for a Day***
US 1933 95m bw
Columbia (Frank Capra)
V, L

Gangsters help an old apple seller to pose as a rich woman when her daughter visits.

Splendid sentimental comedy full of cinematic resource; the best translation of Runyon to the screen.

w Robert Riskin *story* Madame La Gimp by Damon Runyon *d* Frank Capra *ph* Joseph Walker

May Robson, Warren William, Guy Kibbee, Glenda Farrell, Ned Sparks, Jean Parker, Walter Connolly, Nat Pendleton

'Exceptionally adroit direction and scenario . . . sell it with plenty of adjectives as it will please everybody.' – *Variety*
AAN: best picture; Robert Riskin; Frank Capra; May Robson

The Lady Vanishes****
GB 1938 97m bw
Gaumont British/Gainsborough (Edward Black)
L

En route back to England by train from Switzerland, an old lady disappears and two young people investigate.

The disappearing lady trick brilliantly refurbished by Hitchcock and his screenwriters, who even get away with a horrid model shot at the beginning. Superb, suspenseful, brilliantly funny, meticulously detailed entertainment.

w Sidney Gilliat, Frank Launder, novel *The Wheel Spins* by Ethel Lina White d Alfred Hitchcock ph Jack Cox md Louis Levy

Margaret Lockwood, Michael Redgrave, Dame May Whitty, Paul Lukas, Basil Radford, Naunton Wayne, Catherine Lacey, Cecil Parker, Linden Travers, Googie Withers, Mary Clare, Philip Leaver

'If it were not so brilliant a melodrama, we should class it as a brilliant comedy.' – *Frank S. Nugent*
'No one can study the deceptive effortlessness with which one thing leads to another without learning where the true beauty of this medium is to be mined.' – *Otis Ferguson*
'Directed with such skill and velocity that it has come to represent the very quintessence of screen suspense.' – *Pauline Kael, 70s*

† Hitchcock was actually second choice as director. The production was ready to roll as *Lost Lady*, directed by Roy William Neill, with Charters and Caldicott already in place, when Neill became unavailable and Hitch stepped in.

The Lady Vanishes
GB 1979 97m Eastmancolor Panavision
Rank/Hammer (Michael Carreras, Tom Sachs)

A remake of the above in which everything goes wrong: wrong shape, wrong actors, wrong style (or lack of it).

Reasonable adherence to the original script can't save it.

w George Axelrod d Anthony Page ph Douglas Slocombe m Richard Hartley pd Wilfred Shingleton

Cybill Shepherd, Elliott Gould, Angela Lansbury, Herbert Lom, Arthur Lowe, Ian Carmichael, Gerald Harper, Jenny Runacre, Jean Anderson

The Lady with a Lamp*
GB 1951 110m bw
British Lion/Imperadio (Herbert Wilcox)

The life of Florence Nightingale and her work in reforming the nursing service in 19th-century England.

Solid biopic, not quite in accord with history.

w Warren Chetham Strode play Reginald Berkeley d Herbert Wilcox ph Max Greene m Anthony Collins ad William C. Andrews

Anna Neagle, Michael Wilding, Gladys Young, Felix Aylmer, Julian D'Albie, Arthur Young, Edwin Styles, Barbara Couper, Cecil Trouncer, Rosalie Crutchley

'A slow, sedate, refined chronicle . . . Herbert Wilcox is a good deal more at ease with the balls and dinners, than with anything that happens later.' – *Penelope Houston*
'It may please fans of Anna Neagle

and Michael Wilding, but not fans of Florence Nightingale.' – *Richard Mallett, Punch*

'Cursed for eternity! No force in heaven will release them ... no power on earth can save them!'

Ladyhawke

US 1985 124m Technicolor Panavision
Warner/Richard Donner, Lauren Schuler
V, L

Medieval boy and girl lovers have been changed respectively into a wolf and a hawk, never simultaneously to resume their true forms.

Unpersuasive legend, dolefully told at excessive length.

w Edward Khmara, Michael Thomas, Tom Mankiewicz   d Richard Donner   ph Vittorio Storaro   m Andrew Powell   pd Wolf Kroeger   ed Stuart Baird

Matthew Broderick, Rutger Hauer, Michelle Pfeiffer, Leo McKern, John Wood

The Ladykillers*

GB 1955 97m Technicolor
Ealing (Seth Holt)
V

An old lady takes in a sinister lodger, who with his four friends commits a robbery. When she finds out, they plot to kill her, but are hoist with their own petards.

Overrated comedy in poor colour; those who made it quite clearly think it funnier than it is.

w William Rose   d Alexander Mackendrick   ph Otto Heller   m Tristam Cary

Alec Guinness, *Katie Johnson*, Peter Sellers, Cecil Parker, Herbert Lom, Danny Green, Jack Warner, Frankie Howerd, Kenneth Connor

'To be frivolous about frivolous matters, that's merely boring. To be frivolous about something that's in some way deadly serious, that's true comedy.' – *Alexander Mackendrick*
AAN: William Rose

Lancelot and Guinevere*

GB 1962 117m Eastmancolor Panavision
Emblem (Cornel Wilde)
US title: *Sword of Lancelot*

Sir Lancelot covets the wife of his beloved King Arthur, but after Arthur's death she takes the veil.

Decently made, rather tame transcription of the legends, with all concerned doing quite creditably but not brilliantly.

w Richard Schayer, Jefferson Pascal   d Cornel Wilde   ph Harry Waxman   m Ron Goodwin

Cornel Wilde, Jean Wallace, Brian Aherne, George Baker, John Barrie

The Land before Time

US 1988 69m Technicolor
UIP/Universal/Amblin (Don Bluth, Gary Goldman, John Pomeroy)
L

An orphaned dinosaur sets out with friends to find the way to a valley of plenty.

Over-cute, immensely sentimental animated feature.

w Stu Krieger   story Judy Freudberg, Tony Geiss   d Don Bluth   ph Jim Mann   m James Horner

Voices of Gabriel Damon, Helen Shaver, Bill Erwin, Candice Houston, Pat Hingle, Burke Barnes, Judith Barsi, Will Ryan

The Land that Time Forgot*
GB 1974 91m Technicolor
Amicus (John Dark)
V

In 1916, survivors from a torpedoed supply ship find themselves on a legendary island full of prehistoric monsters.

Lively old-fashioned adventure fantasy with good technical credits.

w James Cawthorne, Michael Moorcock novel Edgar Rice Burroughs d Kevin Connor ph Alan Hume m Douglas Gamley pd Maurice Carter sp Derek Meddings, Roger Dicken

Doug McClure, John McEnery, Susan Penhaligon, Keith Barron, Anthony Ainley

The Land Unknown*
US 1957 78m bw Cinemascope
U-I (William Alland)

A plane is forced down into a strange Antarctic valley where dinosaurs still roam.

Efficient adventure fantasy on *King Kong* lines but without any of that film's panache.

w Laslo Gorog d Virgil Vogel ph Ellis Carter m Hans Salter sp Roswell Hoffman, Fred Knoth, Orien Ernest, Jack Kevan

Jock Mahoney, Shawn Smith, William Reynolds, Henry Brandon

Lassie

The official Lassie series, made by MGM, was as follows:

1943: LASSIE COME HOME (qv)
1945: SON OF LASSIE (d S. Sylvan Simon with Peter Lawford, Donald Crisp, Nigel Bruce)
1946: COURAGE OF LASSIE (d Fred M. Wilcox with Elizabeth Taylor, Frank Morgan, Tom Drake)
1948: THE HILLS OF HOME* (d Fred M. Wilcox with Edmund Gwenn, Donald Crisp, Tom Drake)
1949: THE SUN COMES UP (d Richard Thorpe with Jeanette MacDonald, Lloyd Nolan)
1949: CHALLENGE TO LASSIE (d Richard Thorpe with Edmund Gwenn, Donald Crisp)
1951: THE PAINTED HILLS (d Harold F. Kress with Paul Kelly, Bruce Cowling)

† Later 'Lassie' features were taken from episodes of the long-running TV series.
*GB title: *Master of Lassie*.

Lassie Come Home*
US 1943 88m Technicolor
MGM (Samuel Marx)

A poor family is forced to sell its beloved dog, but she makes a remarkable journey to return to them.

First of the Lassie films and certainly the best: an old-fashioned heartwarmer.

w Hugo Butler novel Eric Knight d Fred M. Wilcox ph Leonard Smith m Daniele Amfitheatrof

Roddy McDowall, Elizabeth Taylor, Donald Crisp, Edmund Gwenn, Dame May Whitty, Nigel Bruce, Elsa Lanchester, J. Pat O'Malley

'The late Eric Knight wrote this immortal essay in Doggery-Woggery. MGM finished it off.' – *Richard Winnington*
AAN: Leonard Smith

'Pompeii ... drunk with wealth and power ... rotten with pagan pleasures ... doomed to fiery death from the skies!'

The Last Days of Pompeii*
US 1935 96m bw
RKO (Merian C. Cooper)

In ancient Pompeii, various personal dramas are submerged in the eruption of Vesuvius.

Starchy melodrama capped by a reel of spectacular disaster.

w Ruth Rose, Boris Ingster *novel* Lord Lytton d Merian C. Cooper, Ernest Schoedsack ph Eddie Linden Jnr, J. Roy Hunt m Roy Webb sp Vernon Walker, Harry Redmond

Preston Foster, Basil Rathbone, Alan Hale, Dorothy Wilson

'Well-done spectacle minus romance and cast names. Should do all right generally.' – *Variety*

The Last Dinosaur
US 1977 100m colour
Rankin-Bass Productions

An oil-drilling team discovers a *tyrannosaurus rex* while probing the polar oil-cap.

Inept monster saga with poorish special effects from a Japanese team.

w William Overgard d Alex Grasshof, Tom Kotani ph Shoshi Ueda m Maury Laws

Richard Boone, Joan Van Ark, Steven Keats

The Last Flight of Noah's Ark
US 1980 98m Technicolor
Walt Disney

An impecunious pilot reluctantly flies an orphanage worker and a cargo of animals across the Pacific, only to be stranded with them on a desert island.

It must have sounded like a good idea, but if it was to work at all it needed much sharper handling.

w Steven W. Carabatsos, Sandy Glass, George Arthur Bloom *story* The Gremlin's Castle by Ernest K. Gann d Charles Jarrott ph Charles F. Wheeler m Maurice Jarre

Elliott Gould, Geneviève Bujold, Ricky Schroder, Tammy Lauren, Vincent Gardenia

The Last of the Mohicans
US 1936 91m bw
Edward Small
L

Incidents during colonial America's French-Indian war.

Vigorous if rough-and-ready Western, later remade (poorly) as *Last of the Redmen* and as a Canadian TV series.

w Philip Dunne, John Balderston, Paul Perez, Daniel Moore *novel* James Fenimore Cooper d George B. Seitz ph Robert Planck m Roy Webb

Randolph Scott, Binnie Barnes, Bruce Cabot, Henry Wilcoxon, Heather Angel, Hugh Buckler

The Last of the Mohicans*
US 1992 122m colour Scope
Warner/Morgan Creek (Michael Mann, Hunt Lowry)

The white, adopted son of an Indian rescues a British officer's two daughters from hostile Indians and falls in love with one of them.

An ambitious but flawed epic adventure: the characterization is as shallow as the photography, the action is repetitious, the narrative lacks suspense and the romance is unconvincing, with Cooper's self-reliant woodsman here tamed into domesticity.

w Michael Mann, Christopher Crowe novel James Fenimore Cooper story screenplay by Philip Dunne d Michael Mann ph Dante Spinotti m Trevor Jones, Randy Edelman pd Wolf Kroeger ed Dov Hoenig, Arthur Schmidt

Daniel Day-Lewis, Madeleine Stowe, Russell Means, Eric Schweig, Jodhi May, Steven Waddington, Wes Studi, Maurice Roeves, Patrice Chereau

'Whether it was because we were young or the movies were young or the world was at least youngish, old-fashioned Hollywood history was exhilarating. In retrospect there is something alarming about its simplicities and the enthusiasm we brought to it. It is the great virtue of this grandly scaled yet deliriously energetic movie that it reanimates that long-ago feeling without patronizing it – and without making us think we will wake up some day once again embarrassed by it.' – *Richard Schickel, Time*
'Michael Mann has been aiming all along at two very different targets, trying to turn an adventure story into a responsible account of Native American life, while also making it lovey-dovey enough for the market place.' – *Adam Mars-Jones, Independent*
AAN: sound

'A different kind of love story!'
The Last Remake of Beau Geste
US 1977 85m Technicolor
Universal (William S. Gilmore Jnr)

The Geste brothers find themselves in the Foreign Legion after the theft of the Blue Water sapphire.

Woebegone spoof of a romantic original, with most of the jokes totally irrelevant to the purpose and seldom at all funny.

w Marty Feldman, Chris J. Allen d Marty Feldman ph Gerry Fisher m John Morris

Marty Feldman, Michael York, Ann-Margret, Peter Ustinov, Trevor Howard, James Earl Jones, Henry Gibson, Terry-Thomas, Roy Kinnear, Spike Milligan, Hugh Griffith, Irene Handl

'A ragbag of a film which looks like nothing so much as a Monty Python extravaganza in which inspiration has run dry and the comic timing gone sadly awry.' – *Tom Milne, MFB*

The Last Starfighter*
US 1984 101m Technicolor Panavision
Lorimar/Universal (Gary Adelson, Edward O. Denault)
L

A teenage whiz at video games is abducted by the survivors of a distant planet who need his skills if they are to outwit their enemies.

A surprisingly pleasant variation on the *Star Wars* boom, with sharp and witty performances from two reliable character actors and some elegant gadgetry to offset the teenage mooning.

w Jonathan Betuel d Nick Castle ph King Baggot m Craig Safan pd Ron Cobb ed C. Timothy O'Meara

Lance Guest, *Robert Preston, Dan O'Herlihy,* Catherine Mary Stewart, Barbara Bosson, Norman Snow

Laugh with Max Linder**
France 1963 88m bw
Films Max Linder
original title: *En Compagnie de Max Linder*

Excerpts from three of the dapper comedian's most famous American comedies: *Be My Wife* (1921), *The Three Must-Get-Theres* (1922), *Seven Years' Bad Luck* (1923).

A compilation which must serve as a consensus of this almost forgotten comedian's work. The gag with a broken mirror in particular was borrowed by innumerable other comedians, notably the Marx Brothers in *Duck Soup*. Audiences new to Linder's work will find him not especially sympathetic but capable of many felicities. He wrote, produced and directed all three films.

compiler Maud Max Linder

Laughing Gravy***
US 1931 20m bw
Hal Roach
V(C)

Stan and Ollie retrieve their dog when the landlord throws it out into the snow.

One of the most endearing comedies of these stars, and one of the simplest.

w H. M. Walker   *d* James W. Horne

Laurel and Hardy, Charlie Hall

Laughterhouse*
GB 1984 93m colour
Greenpoint/Film Four International (Ann Scott)

A Norfolk farmer decides to walk his fattened geese to market.

An attempt to revive the tradition of Ealing comedy lands up somewhere on the wrong side of Group Three. Not enough plot, almost no jokes, and the geese are almost the only pleasant creatures.

w Brian Glover   *d* Richard Eyre
ph Clive Tickner   *m* Dominic Muldowney

Ian Holm, Penelope Wilton, Bill Owen, Richard Hope, Stephen Moore, Rosemary Martin

The Laurel and Hardy Murder Case
US 1930 30m bw
Hal Roach

Heirs to a fortune are menaced by a mad murderer.

Empty spoof on *The Cat and the Canary* which affords little scope to Laurel and Hardy.

w H. M. Walker   *d* James Parrott

Laurel and Hardy's Laughing Twenties**
US 1965 90m bw
MGM/Robert Youngson
V, L

Excerpts from lesser comedians of the period – Max Davidson, Charlie Chase – are interspersed with highlights from Laurel and Hardy's silent two-reelers.

A hilarious and craftsmanlike compilation, perhaps a little too long for its own good.

w/ed Robert Youngson   *m* Skeets Alquist   *commentator* Jay Jackson

† Films extracted include *Putting Pants on Philip*, *From Soup to Nuts*, *Wrong Again*, *The Finishing Touch*, *Liberty*, *Double Whoopee*, *Leave 'Em Laughing*, *You're Darn Tooting* and the custard pie climax from *The Battle of the Century*.

The Lavender Hill Mob****
GB 1951 78m bw
Ealing (Michael Truman)
V, L

A timid bank clerk conceives and executes a bullion robbery.

Superbly characterized and inventively detailed comedy, one of the best ever made at Ealing or in Britain.

w T.E.B. Clarke   d Charles Crichton   ph Douglas Slocombe   m Georges Auric

Alec Guinness, Stanley Holloway, Sidney James, Alfie Bass, Marjorie Fielding, Edie Martin, John Gregson, Gibb McLaughlin

'Amusing situations and dialogue are well paced and sustained throughout: the climax is delightful.' – *MFB*

AA: T. E. B. Clarke
AAN: Alec Guinness

Lawrence of Arabia***
GB 1962 221m Technicolor Super Panavision 70
Columbia/Horizon (Sam Spiegel)
V(W), L

An adventurer's life with the Arabs, told in flashbacks after his accidental death in the thirties.

Sprawling epic which manages after four hours to give no insight whatever into the complexities of character of this mysterious historic figure, but is often spectacularly beautiful and exciting along the way.

w Robert Bolt   d David Lean   ph Frederick A. Young   m Maurice Jarre   pd John Box   ad John Stoll

Peter O'Toole, Omar Sharif, Arthur Kennedy, Jack Hawkins, Donald Wolfit, Claude Rains, Anthony Quayle, Alec Guinness, Anthony Quinn, Jose Ferrer, Michel Ray, Zia Mohyeddin

'Grandeur of conception is not up to grandeur of setting.' – *Penelope Houston*

'Lean has managed to market epics as serious entertainment rather than as the spectacles they are.' – *Time Out, 1980*

† Albert Finney turned down the role before O'Toole was offered it.

AA: best picture; David Lean; Frederick A. Young; Maurice Jarre
AAN: Robert Bolt; Peter O'Toole; Omar Sharif

Leave 'Em Laughing*
US 1928 20m bw silent
Hal Roach

Stan has toothache, visits the dentist, and accidentally causes all concerned to inhale an overdose of laughing gas.

The earlier sequences are only mildly funny, but the laughing finale is irresistible.

w Hal Roach and Reed Heustis   d Clyde Bruckman

Laurel and Hardy, Edgar Kennedy, Charlie Hall

Legend*
GB 1985 94m Fujicolour Panavision
(TCF/Universal) Legend Productions (Arnon Milchan)
V

Young peasant Jack takes his sweetheart on a quest to see the last surviving unicorns, but Satan uses them as pawns in his own game.

Elegant fairy tale for the few grown-ups who have use for such a thing. More to look at than to listen to.

w William Hjortsberg   d Ridley Scott   ph Alex Thomson   m Jerry Goldsmith   pd Assheton Gorton   ed Terry Rawlings

Tim Curry, Mia Sara, Tom Cruise, David Bennent

'The dying gasp of the sword and sorcery cycle.' – *Philip French, Observer*

'The enchanted forests constantly threaten to sell us something – most frequently soft toilet paper.' – *Ibid.*

AAN: make-up (Rob Bottin, Peter Robb-King)

The Legend of Lobo*
US 1962 67m Technicolor
Walt Disney (James Algar)

The life of a forest wolf.

Anthropomorphic entertainment in which a dreaded animal becomes something of a hero and finally saves his mate from bounty hunters. Impeccably contrived, like a live-action *Bambi*.

w Dwight Hauser, James Algar
story Ernest Thompson Seton
d James Algar *ph* Jack Couffer, Lloyd Beebe *m* Oliver Wallace

'The film where you hiss the villain and cheer the hero!'
The Legend of the Lone Ranger
US 1981 98m Technicolor Panavision
ITC/Jack Wrather (Walter Coblenz)

A much-betrayed young Texan, almost killed in an ambush, is nursed back to health by an Indian and becomes a masked avenger.

Extremely ill-constructed and moody western, apparently photographed through brown windsor soup, which doesn't slip into the right gear until twenty minutes before the end.

w Ivan Goff, Ben Roberts, Michael Kane, William Roberts *d* William A. Fraker *ph* Laszlo Kovacs
m John Barry

Klinton Spilsbury, Michael Horse, Christopher Lloyd, Matt Clark

'Wallows in endless sentiment before switching to what may possibly have been intended as parody.' – *Sight and Sound*

'Tedious hokum ... the kind of film that closes cinemas.' – *Sunday Times*

Legend of the Lost
US 1957 107m Technirama
UA/Batjac/Robert Haggiag/Dear (Henry Hathaway)

Two adventurers and a slave girl seek a lost city in the Sahara.

Tediously vague and underplotted desert adventure with a few attractive moments.

w Robert Presnell Jnr, Ben Hecht
d Henry Hathaway *ph* Jack Cardiff *m* A. F. Lavagnino

John Wayne, Sophia Loren, Rossano Brazzi

Let George Do It**
GB 1940 82m bw
Ealing (Basil Dearden)

A ukelele player accidentally goes to Bergen instead of Blackpool and is mistaken for a spy.

Generally thought to be the best George Formby vehicle, with plenty of pace, good situations and catchy tunes.

w John Dighton, Austin Melford, Angus MacPhail, Basil Dearden
d Marcel Varnel *ph* Gordon Dines, Ronald Neame

George Formby, Phyllis Calvert, Garry Marsh, Romney Brent, Bernard Lee, Coral Browne, Torin Thatcher, Hal Gordon

Liberty**
US 1929 20m bw silent
Hal Roach
V

Two convicts escape and have adventures high on a construction site.

Amusing gags are succeeded by breathtaking thrills in the Harold Lloyd style.

w Leo McCarey and H. M. Walker d Leo McCarey

Laurel and Hardy, James Finlayson

Licence to Kill*
US 1989 133m Technicolor Panavision
UIP/United Artists/Danjaq (Albert R. Broccoli, Michael G. Wilson)
V

James Bond goes after a drug dealer who has injured his best friend.

The mixture is much as usual, though the action is more violent and Bond has become more of a free agent.

w Michael G. Wilson, Richard Maibaum d John Glen ph Alec Mills m Michael Kamen pd Peter Lamont ed John Grover

Timothy Dalton, Carey Lowell, Robert Davi, Talisa Soto, Anthony Zerbe, Frank McRae, Everett McGill, Wayne Newton, Benicio del Toro

Lt Robin Crusoe USN
US 1966 114m Technicolor
Walt Disney (Bill Walsh, Ron Miller)

A navy pilot parachutes on to a Pacific island and gets involved in the local women's lib movement.

Slow-paced family comedy with very few laughs.

w Bill Walsh, Don da Gradi d Byron Paul ph William Snyder m Bob Brunner

Dick Van Dyke, Nancy Kwan, Akim Tamiroff

Life Is a Circus
GB 1958 84m bw
Vale Film (M. Smedley Aston)

An odd-job man in a rundown circus finds Aladdin's lamp.

Feeble comedy by the Crazy Gang in a state of geriatric disrepair, simply going through the motions, which is an understandable reaction given the script. Chesney Allen makes a brief appearance to sing 'Underneath the Arches' with his old partner, Bud Flanagan.

wd Val Guest m Philip Green ad Tony Masters ed Bill Lenny

Bud Flanagan, Nervo and Knox, Naughton and Gold, Monsewer Eddie Gray, Shirley Eaton, Michael Holliday, Joseph Tomelty, Lionel Jeffries

'Take your cookie to see the picture that takes the cake for laughs!'

Life with Father*
US 1947 118m Technicolor
Warner (Robert Buckner)

Turn-of-the-century anecdotes of an irascible well-to-do paterfamilias who won't be baptized.

Well-upholstered screen version of a long-running play; oddly tedious considering the talent involved.

w Donald Ogden Stewart play Howard Lindsay, Russel Crouse d Michael Curtiz ph Peverell Marley, William V. Skall m Max Steiner ad Robert Haas

William Powell, Irene Dunne, Edmund Gwenn, Zasu Pitts, Elizabeth Taylor, Martin Milner, Jimmy Lydon, Emma Dunn, Moroni Olsen, Elizabeth Risdon

'Everybody seems to be trying too

hard ... the director is totally out of his element in this careful, deadly version.' – *New Yorker, 1978*

† Censorship of the day absurdly clipped Father's famous last line: 'I'm going to be baptized, damn it!'
AAN: Peverell Marley, William V. Skall; Max Steiner; William Powell; Robert Haas

The Light at the Edge of the World
US/Spain/Liechtenstein 1971 120m Eastmancolor Panavision
Bryna/Jet/Triumfilm (Kirk Douglas, Ilya Salkind)

A lighthouse keeper near Cape Horn resists a band of wreckers.

Pretentious, disaster-prone version of a simple adventure story; one wonders not so much what went wrong as whether anything went right in this international venture.

w Tom Rowe novel Jules Verne
d Kevin Billington ph Henri Decaë m Piero Piccioni

Kirk Douglas, Yul Brynner, Samantha Eggar, Jean-Claude Drouot, Fernando Rey, Renato Salvatori

The Light in the Forest
US 1958 92m Technicolor
Walt Disney

Kidnapped by Indians as an infant, a teenager is returned to his parents but finds the white man's ways disturbing.

Modest frontier drama with a moral.

w Lawrence Edward Watkin
novel Conrad Richter d Herschel Daugherty ph Ellsworth Fredericks m Paul Smith

James MacArthur, Carol Lynley, Jessica Tandy, Wendell Corey, Fess Parker, Joanne Dru, Joseph Calleia

Li'l Abner*
US 1959 113m Technicolor Vistavision
Paramount/Panama-Frank (Norman Panama)

The hillbilly town of Dogpatch, tagged the most useless community in America, fights being used as a test site for A-bombs.

Set-bound, intrinsically American, but bright and cheerful film of a stage show about Al Capp's famous comic strip characters.

wd Norman Panama, Melvin Frank from the musical show (ly Johnny Mercer, words Gene de Paul)
ph Daniel L. Fapp md Joseph Lilley, Nelson Riddle m Gene de Paul ch Dee Dee Wood, Michael Kidd

Peter Palmer, Leslie Parrish, Billie Hayes, Howard St John, Stubby Kaye, Stella Stevens, Julie Newmar, Robert Strauss

'As joyous, screwy, dancin' and jokin' a musical show as Hollywood has sent us for a long time.' – *Sunday Dispatch*
AAN: Joseph Lilley, Nelson Riddle

Limelight***
US 1952 144m bw
Charles Chaplin
V

A broken-down music hall comedian is stimulated by a young ballerina to a final hour of triumph.

Sentimental drama in a highly theatrical London East End setting. In other hands it would be very hokey, but Chaplin's best qualities, as well as his worst, are in evidence, and in a way the film sums up his own career.

wd Charles Chaplin ph Karl Struss m Charles Chaplin, Raymond Rasch, Larry Russell ad Eugene

*Lourié   photographic
consultant* Rollie Totheroh

Charles Chaplin, Claire Bloom, Buster Keaton, Sydney Chaplin, Nigel Bruce, Norman Lloyd

'From the first reel it is clear that he now wants to talk, that he loves to talk ... where a development in the story line might easily be conveyed by a small visual effect, he prefers to make a speech about it ... it is a disturbing rejection of the nature of the medium itself.' – *Walter Kerr*

'Surely the richest hunk of self-gratification since Huck and Tom attended their own funeral.' – *New Yorker, 1982*

'His exhortations about life, courage, consciousness and "truth" are set in a self-pitying, self-glorifying story.' – *Pauline Kael, 70s*

AA: Charles Chaplin, Raymond Rasch, Larry Russell

The Lion

GB   1962   96m   DeLuxe
  Cinemascope
TCF (Samuel G. Engel)

An American lawyer goes to Africa to visit his ex-wife and their child.

Unabsorbing marital drama with child and animal interest.

w Irene and Louis Kamp
novel Joseph Kessel   *d* Jack Cardiff   *ph* Ted Scaife
m Malcolm Arnold

William Holden, Trevor Howard, Capucine, Pamela Franklin

'The main fault must be attributed to the spiritless direction of Jack Cardiff, whose recent change of métier has resulted in the industry losing a great lighting cameraman.' – *John Gillett*

Lionheart

US   1987   104m   colour
Orion (Stanley O'Toole, Talia Shire)
V, L

On his way to join King Richard the Lionheart's crusade, a young knight rescues a band of children from a slave trader.

Aimed at a family audience, it lacks excitement and pace and is best treated as a soporific.

w Menno Meyjes, Richard Outten
d Franklin J. Schaffner   *ph* Alec Mills   *m* Jerry Goldsmith   *pd* Gil Parrondo   *ed* David Bretherton, Richard Haines

Eric Stoltz, Gabriel Byrne, Nicola Cowper, Dexter Fletcher, Deborah Barrymore, Nicholas Clay, Bruce Purchase, Neil Dickson, Chris Pitt

'High on heart-warming ideals, but low in every other department.' – *Empire*

The Little Ark

US   1971   86m   DeLuxe
  Panavision
Cinema Center/Robert B. Radnitz

Two war orphans and their pets, trapped in a flood, sail to safety in a houseboat.

Well-meaning, somewhat allegorical family film, too desultory to maintain interest and rather too frightening for children.

w Joanna Crawford   *novel* Jan de Hartog   *d* James B. Clark
ph Austin Dempster, Denys Coop
m Fred Karlin

Theodore Bikel, Philip Frame, Genevieve Ambas
AAN: song 'Come Follow Follow Me' (*m* Fred Karlin, *ly* Marsha Karlin)

A Little Bit of Heaven

US 1940 87m bw
Universal (Joe Pasternak)

A 12-year-old girl becomes a singing sensation but runs into family opposition.

Predictable vehicle for a young star being built up as a stop-gap Deanna Durbin.

w Daniel Taradash, Gertrude Purcell, Harold Goldman story Grover Jones d Andrew Marton ph John Seitz m Charles Previn

Gloria Jean, Robert Stack, Hugh Herbert, C. Aubrey Smith, Stuart Erwin, Nan Grey, Eugene Pallette, Billy Gilbert, Butch and Buddy

The Little Colonel**

US 1935 80m bw (colour sequence)
Fox (B. G. De Sylva)

In a southern household after the Civil War, a little girl ends a family feud, plays Cupid to her sister, routs a few villains and mollifies her cantankerous grandfather.

First-class Temple vehicle, the first to boast an expensive production.

w William Conselman novel Annie Fellows Johnson d David Butler ph Arthur Miller md Arthur Lange

Shirley Temple, Lionel Barrymore, Evelyn Venable, John Lodge, Bill Robinson, Hattie McDaniel, Sidney Blackmer

Little Dorrit**

GB 1987 Part 1 176m/Part 2 181m Technicolor
Sands/Cannon (John Brabourne)
V, L

Faithful adaptation of classic novel.

Lovingly made by a large team, economically and authentically re-creating Dickens's London, with a starry cast giving their all. Adored by audiences who could take the length.

wd Christine Edzard, novel Charles Dickens ph Bruno De Keyzer m Giuseppe Verdi

Derek Jacobi, Joan Greenwood, Max Wall, *Alec Guinness*, Cyril Cusack, Sarah Pickering, Eleanor Bron, Robert Morley
AAN: Alec Guinness; best adapted screenplay

Little Lord Fauntleroy*

US 1936 98m bw
David O. Selznick

A sound remake which did surprisingly well at the box-office and is still very watchable.

w Richard Schayer, Hugh Walpole, David O. Selznick d John Cromwell ph Charles Rosher m Max Steiner

Freddie Bartholomew, C. Aubrey Smith, Mickey Rooney, Dolores Costello, Jessie Ralph, Guy Kibbee

† A TV movie version appeared in 1980, with Ricky Schroder and Alec Guinness.

The Little Mermaid**

US 1989 83m
Warner/Walt Disney/Silver Screen Partners IV (Howard Ashman, John Musker)
V

A mermaid falls in love with a prince and longs to be human.

A return to Disney's classic manner, with some excellent animation, though sentimentality is rampant.

wd John Musker, Ron Clements story Hans Christian Andersen

m Alan Menken *m/ly* Howard Ashman, Alan Menken

Voices of Rene Auberjonois, Christopher Daniel Barnes, Jodi Benson, Pat Carroll, Paddi Edwards, Buddy Hackett, Jason Marin, Kenneth Mars, Edie McClurg, Will Ryan, Ben Wright, Samuel E. Wright

AA: best original score; best song

Little Miss Broadway
US 1938 70m bw
TCF (David Hempstead)

A small girl is adopted by the owner of a hotel for vaudeville artistes.

One of the child star's more casual vehicles, but quite pleasing.

w Harry Tugend, Jack Yellen *d* Irving Cummings *ph* Arthur Miller *md* Louis Silvers

Shirley Temple, George Murphy, Jimmy Durante, Edna May Oliver, Phyllis Brooks, George Barbier, Edward Ellis, Jane Darwell, El Brendel, Donald Meek, Claude Gillingwater, Russell Hicks

'It can't be old age, but it does look like weariness.' – *New York Times*
'Shirley is better than her new vehicle, which in turn is better than her last one.' – *Variety*

Little Miss Marker**
US 1934 80m bw
Paramount (B. P. Schulberg)
GB title: *The Girl in Pawn*

A cynical racetrack gambler is forced to adopt a little girl, who not only softens him but saves him from his enemies.

The twin appeals of Temple (a new hot property) and Runyon made this a big hit of its time.

w William R. Lipman, Sam Hellman, Gladys Lehman *story* Damon Runyon *d* Alexander Hall *ph* Alfred Gilks *songs* Leo Robin, Ralph Rainger

Shirley Temple, Adolphe Menjou, Dorothy Dell, Charles Bickford, Lynne Overman, Frank McGlynn Snr, Willie Best

'A good response to that element which claims there is nothing good in pictures. Clean, funny, with thrills and heart appeal all nicely blended.' – *Variety*
'No one can deny that the infant was a trouper: she delivers her lines with a killer instinct.' – *Pauline Kael, 70s*

† Remade as *Sorrowful Jones* (qv).

Little Miss Marker
US 1980 103m Technicolor
Universal (Jennings Lang)

Mainly glutinous remake of the above, with acerbic asides from the star.

wd Walter Bernstein *ph* Philip Lathrop *m* Henry Mancini

Walter Matthau, Julie Andrews, Tony Curtis, Bob Newhart, Sara Stimson, Lee Grant, Brian Dennehy

The Little Prince
US 1974 89m Technicolor
Paramount/Stanley Donen

A small boy leaves the asteroid he rules to learn of life on Earth.

A whimsical bestseller turns into an arch musical which falls over itself early on and never recovers; in any case it fatally lacks the common touch, though it has pleasing moments.

w Alan Jay Lerner *novel* Antoine de St-Exupery *d* Stanley Donen *ph* Christopher Challis *pd* John

Barry   m/ly Frederick Loewe, Alan Jay Lerner

Richard Kiley, Steven Warner, *Bob Fosse*, Gene Wilder, Joss Ackland, Clive Revill, Victor Spinetti, Graham Crowden

'Handsome production cannot obscure limited artistic achievement.' – *Variety*

† Kiley replaced Frank Sinatra, who backed out.
AAN: title song; musical adaptation (Angela Morley, Douglas Gamley)

The Little Princess**
US   1939   93m   Technicolor
TCF (Gene Markey)

In Victorian London a little girl is left at a harsh school when her father goes abroad.

One of the child star's plushest vehicles, a charming early colour film complete with dream sequence and happy ending.

w Ethel Hill, Walter Ferris   *novel* Frances Hodgson Burnett   d Walter Lang   ph Arthur Miller, William Skall   md Louis Silvers

Shirley Temple, Richard Greene, Anita Louise, Ian Hunter, Cesar Romero, Arthur Treacher, Mary Nash, Sybil Jason, Miles Mander, Marcia Mae Jones, Beryl Mercer, E. E. Clive

Little Shop of Horrors*
US   1986   88m   Technicolor
Warner (David Geffen)
V, L

Workers in a flower shop are menaced by a plant with sinister intent.

Transcript of the off-Broadway musical curiously inspired by a 1961 Roger Corman horror flick which few people saw. A strange item with occasional effective moments.

w Howard Ashman   *play* Howard Ashman   d Frank Oz   ph Robert Paynter   m Alan Menken   pd Roy Walker   ed John Jympson, Derek Trigg, Bob Gavin

Rick Moranis, Ellen Greene, Vincent Gardenia, Steve Martin

'The best movie ever made about a man-eating plant.' – *People*
AAN: song 'Mean Green Mother from Outer Space'

'They leap from the book and live!'
Little Women***
US   1933   115m   bw
RKO (David O. Selznick, Merian C. Cooper, Kenneth MacGowan)

The growing up of four sisters in pre-Civil War America.

Charming 'big picture' of its day, with excellent production and performances.

w Sarah Y. Mason, Victor Heerman   *novel* Louisa May Alcott   d George Cukor   ph Henry Gerrard   m Max Steiner

Katharine Hepburn, Paul Lukas, Joan Bennett, Frances Dee, Jean Parker, *Spring Byington*, Edna May Oliver, Douglass Montgomery, Henry Stephenson, Samuel S. Hinds, John Lodge, Nydia Westman

'If to put a book on the screen with all the effectiveness that sympathy and good taste and careful artifice can devise is to make a fine motion picture, then *Little Women* is a fine picture.' – *James Shelley Hamilton*
'One of the most satisfactory pictures I have ever seen.' – *E. V. Lucas, Punch*
'A reminder that emotions and vitality and truth can be evoked from lavender and lace as well as from machine

guns and precision dances.' – *Thornton Delehanty, New York Post*

AA: script
AAN: best picture; George Cukor

Little Women*
US 1949 122m Technicolor
MGM (Mervyn Le Roy)
V, L

Syrupy Christmas-card remake, notably lacking the light touch.

w Andrew Solt, Sarah Y. Mason, Victor Heerman   d Mervyn Le Roy   ph Robert Planck, Charles Schoenbaum   m Adolph Deutsch (after Max Steiner)   ad Cedric Gibbons, Paul Groesse

June Allyson, Elizabeth Taylor, Peter Lawford, Margaret O'Brien, Janet Leigh, Mary Astor

'It will raise a smile and draw a tear from the sentimental.' – *MFB*

AA: art direction
AAN: cinematography

The Littlest Rebel*
US 1935 70m bw
TCF (B. G. De Sylva)
V

A small southern girl persuades President Lincoln to release her father.

Charming, archetypal early Temple vehicle, very well produced.

w Edwin Burke   play Edward Peple   d David Butler   ph John Seitz   m Cyril Mockridge

Shirley Temple, John Boles, Jack Holt, Karen Morley, *Bill Robinson*, Guinn Williams, Willie Best, Frank McGlynn Snr

'Shirley Temple as the public likes her . . . which means money.' – *Variety*

Live and Let Die*
GB 1973 121m Eastmancolor
UA/Eon (Harry Saltzman)
L

James Bond chases a black master criminal and becomes involved in West Indian Voodoo.

Standard tongue-in-cheek spy adventure with a new lightweight star and an air of *déjà vu*. Professional standards high.

w Tom Mankiewicz   novel Ian Fleming   d Guy Hamilton   ph Ted Moore   m George Martin   titles Maurice Binder

Roger Moore, Yaphet Kotto, Jane Seymour, Clifton James, David Hedison, Bernard Lee, Lois Maxwell

'Plot lines have descended further to the level of the old Saturday afternoon serial, and the treatment is more than ever like a cartoon.' – *Variety*
'A Bond movie is not made. It is packaged. Like an Almond Joy. So much coconut to this much chocolate and a dash of raisins.' – *Joseph Gelmis*
AAN: title song (*m/ly* Paul and Linda McCartney)

The Live Ghost
US 1934 20m bw
Hal Roach

Two reluctant sailors think they have murdered one of their mates.

Somewhat unyielding material for Stan and Ollie, but still funnier than any of their rivals at the time.

w H. M. Walker   d Charles Rogers

Laurel and Hardy, Walter Long, Arthur Housman

'1750 to 1! Always outnumbered! Never outfought!'

Lives of a Bengal Lancer**
US 1934 119m bw
Paramount (Louis D. Lighton)

Adventures on the North-West Frontier.

British army heroics are here taken rather solemnly, but the film is efficient and fondly remembered.

w Waldemar Young, John F. Balderston, Achmed Abdullah, Grover Jones, William Slavens McNutt   book Francis Yeats-Brown   d Henry Hathaway   ph Charles Lang   m Milan Roder   ad Hans Dreier, Roland Anderson   ed Ellsworth Hoagland

Gary Cooper, *Franchot Tone, Richard Cromwell*, Sir Guy Standing, C. Aubrey Smith, Monte Blue, Kathleen Burke, Colin Tapley, *Douglass Dumbrille*, Akim Tamiroff, Noble Johnson

'The best army picture ever made.' – *Daily Telegraph*

AAN: best picture; script; Henry Hathaway; art direction; editing

The Living Daylights**
GB 1987 130m Technicolor Panavision
MGM-UA/Eon (Albert R. Broccoli, Michael G. Wilson)
V, L

James Bond helps the Soviets chase a KGB defector with sinister intent.

25th-anniversary Bond heroics with more adult style than usual, and all technical aspects up to par.

w Richard Maibaum, Michael G. Wilson   d John Glen   ph Alec Mills   m John Barry   pd Peter Lamont

Timothy Dalton, Maryam d'Abo, Jeroen Krabbe, Joe Don Baker, John Rhys-Davies, Art Malik, Robert Brown

The Living Desert***
US 1953 72m Technicolor
Walt Disney (James Algar)

A light-hearted documentary showing the animals and insects which live in American desert areas.

The aim is entertainment and Disney is not above faking, i.e. the famous sequence in which scorpions appear to do a square dance, but on its level the thing is brilliantly done.

w James Algar, Winston Hibler, Ted Sears   d James Algar   ph N. Paul Kenworthy Jnr, Robert H. Grandall   m Paul Smith   special processes Ub Iwerks

'The film has the same cosy anthropomorphism as a Disney cartoon and its facetious commentary and vulgar music score are typical of others in the series.' – *Georges Sadoul*

† The other 'True Life Adventures' were: *Seal Island* 49 (2 reels), *Beaver Valley* 50 (2 reels), *Nature's Half Acre* 51 (2 reels), *Water Birds* 52 (2 reels), *Bear Country* 53, *Prowlers of the Everglades* 53, *The African Lion* 55, *Secrets of Life* 56, *White Wilderness* 58, *Jungle Cat* 60.

AA: Documentary

Living Free
GB 1972 92m colour
Columbia/Open Road/High Road (Paul Radin)
V

On the death of Elsa the lioness, George and Joy Adamson capture her three cubs and transfer them for their own safety to Serengeti.

Sloppy sequel to *Born Free*, depending very heavily on the appeal of the cubs.

w Millard Kaufman *d* Jack Couffer *ph* Wolfgang Suschitzky *m* Sol Kaplan

Susan Hampshire, Nigel Davenport, Geoffrey Keen

Local Hero**
GB 1983 111m colour
Enigma/Goldcrest (David Puttnam)
V, L

A young American executive meets various difficulties when he is sent to a Scottish coastal village to arrange for the building of a new refinery.

Reminiscent of various Ealing comedies, especially *Whisky Galore* and *The Maggie*, this ambitious comedy is really not funny enough for its great length.

wd Bill Forsyth *ph* Chris Menges *m* Mark Knopfler

Burt Lancaster, Peter Riegert, *Denis Lawson*, Peter Capaldi, Fulton Mackay, Jenny Seagrove

'Little in the way of obvious commercial hooks ... dominated by a constantly surprising sense of whimsicality.' – *Variety*

BFA: direction

The Lone Ranger
US 1955 85m Warnercolor
Jack Wrather

The masked do-gooder foils a ranchers' plot to destroy an Indian reservation.

Tolerably watchable adventures.

w Herb Meadow *d* Stuart Heisler

Clayton Moore, Jay Silverheels, Lyle Bettger, Bonita Granville, Perry Lopez

The Lone Ranger and the Lost City of Gold
US 1958 81m colour
Jack Wrather

The masked rider solves murders which have been committed for a mysterious medallion.

Lively Western for kids.

w Robert Schaefer and Eric Freiwald *d* Lesley Selander

Clayton Moore, Jay Silverheels, Douglas Kennedy, Charles Watts

Long John Silver
Australia 1953 106m Eastmancolor Cinemascope
TI Pictures (Joseph Kaufman)

Back from Treasure Island, Silver and Hawkins plan a return visit with fresh clues to the treasure.

Cheaply produced, bitsy-piecy adventure fragments with no one to restrain the star from eye-rolling.

w Martin Rackin *d* Byron Haskin *ph* Carl Guthrie *m* David Buttolph

Robert Newton, Connie Gilchrist, Kit Taylor, Rod Taylor

'A classic of the bashful age!'
Long Pants*
US 1927 58m (24 fps) bw silent
First National/Harry Langdon

A country bumpkin has trouble in the city.

Far from the best Langdon comedy, but funny in flashes.

w Arthur Ripley *d* Frank Capra *ph* Elgin Lessley

Harry Langdon, Gladys Brockwell, Alan Roscoe, Alma Bennett

HALLIWELL'S GUIDE TO THE BEST CHILDREN'S FILMS

The Long Ships
GB/Yugoslavia 1963 126m Technirama
Columbia/Warwick/Avila (Irving Allen)
V

A Viking adventurer and a Moorish prince fall out over a golden bell.

Stilted medieval epic with some visual compensations but more chat than action.

w Berkely Mather, Beverley Cross *novel* Frank G. Bengtsson *d* Jack Cardiff *ph* Christopher Challis *m* Dusan Radic

Richard Widmark, Sidney Poitier, Russ Tamblyn, Rosanna Schiaffino, Oscar Homolka, Colin Blakely

'To say it was disastrous is a compliment.' – *Sidney Poitier*

Lord Jeff
US 1938 78m bw
MGM (Frank Davis)
GB title: *The Boy from Barnardo's*

A well-brought-up boy gets into trouble and is sent under supervision to a naval school.

Adequate family film with absolutely no surprises.

w James K. McGuinness *story* Bradford Ropes, Val Burton, Endré Bohem *d* Sam Wood *ph* John Seitz *m* Edward Ward

Freddie Bartholomew, Mickey Rooney, Charles Coburn, Herbert Mundin, Terry Kilburn, Gale Sondergaard, Peter Lawford

Lord of the Flies
GB 1963 91m bw
Allen-Hogdon Productions/Two Arts (Lewis M. Allen)

After a plane crash, a party of English schoolboys are stranded on an uncharted tropical island and gradually turn savage.

Semi-professional production of a semi-poetic novel which worked well on the printed page but on screen seems crude and unconvincing.

wd Peter Brook *novel* William Golding *ph* Tom Hollyman, Gerald Feil *m* Raymond Leppard

James Aubrey, Tom Chapin, Hugh Edwards, Roger Elwin, Tom Gaman

'A Classic Story of Conflict and Survival'

Lord of the Flies
US 1990 90m DeLuxe Panavision
Columbia/Castle Rock/Nelson/Jack's Camp/Signal Hill (Ross Milloy)
V, L

Boys from a US military school, survivors of an air crash on an uninhabited tropical island, revert to savagery.

Dull remake, with crude melodrama substituting for the subtle social disintegration of the original.

w Sara Schiff *novel* William Golding *d* Harry Hook *ph* Martin Fuhrer *m* Philippe Sarde *pd* Jamie Leonard *ed* Harry Hook

Balthazar Getty, Chris Furth, Danuel Pipoly, Badgett Dale, Edward Taft, Andrew Taft, Bob Peck, Bill Schoppert, Michael Greene

'Individual performances mostly never rise above the semi-amateur level.' – *Variety*

'A Technicolor travel brochure in which a pack of already uncivilized kids act rough and talk dirty like children temporarily freed from the vigilance of their parents.' – *Alexander Walker, London Evening Standard*

Lord of the Rings*
US 1978 133m DeLuxe
UA/Fantasy (Saul Zaentz)

In Middle Earth the Dark Lord loses a powerful ring, and a Hobbit tries to prevent him from getting it back.

Disappointingly stolid, overlong and confused cartoon version of a modern classic which may well deserve all those adjectives. Parts of it are charming, and the method of making cartoons from film of actors photographed in the ordinary way is certainly ingenious though it denies the cartoon characters their own full richness.

w Chris Conkling, Peter S. Beagle
books J. R. R. Tolkien   d Ralph Bakshi   ph Timothy Galfas
m Leonard Rosenman
voices Christopher Guard, John Hurt, William Squire, Michael Scholes

Lorna Doone**
GB 1934 90m bw
ATP (Basil Dean)

In 1625 on Exmoor, a farmer comes to love an outlaw's daughter who proves to be in reality a kidnapped heiress.

Simple, straightforward, effective version of the famous romance, with refreshing use of exteriors.

w Dorothy Farnum, Miles Malleson, Gordon Wellesley   novel R. D. Blackmore   d Basil Dean
ph Robert Martin

Victoria Hopper, John Loder, Margaret Lockwood, *Roy Emerton*, Edward Rigby, Mary Clare, Roger Livesey, George Curzon, D. A. Clarke-Smith, Lawrence Hanray, Amy Veness, Eliot Makeham

'It has polish, but it lacks drama and grip.' – *Variety*

Lorna Doone
US 1951 89m Technicolor
Columbia (Edward Small)

Grotesque remake which treats the story like a cheap Western.

w Jesse L. Lasky Jnr, Richard Schayer   d Phil Karlson
ph Charles Van Enger   m George Duning

Barbara Hale, Richard Greene, Anne Howard, William Bishop, Carl Benton Reid, Ron Randell, Sean McClory, Onslow Stevens, Lester Matthews, John Dehner

The Lost Continent*
GB 1968 98m Technicolor
Hammer (Michael Carreras)

The captain of a tramp steamer illegally carries dynamite, and he and his passengers are stranded in a weird Sargasso Sea colony run by the Spanish Inquisition.

Hilariously imaginative hokum with splendid art direction and some of the grottiest monsters on film; but memorable moments do not quite add up to a classic of the genre.

w Michael Nash   novel Uncharted Seas by Dennis Wheatley   d Michael Carreras   ph Paul Beeson
m Gerard Schurmann   ad Arthur Lawson   sp Robert A. Mattey, Cliff Richardson

Eric Porter, Hildegarde Neff, Suzanna Leigh, Tony Beckley, Nigel Stock, Neil McCallum, Jimmy Hanley, James Cossins, Victor Maddern

'One of the most ludicrously enjoyable bad films since *Salome Where She Danced*.' – *MFB*

Lost Horizon****
US 1937 130m (released at 118m) bw
Columbia (Frank Capra)
V, L

Escaping from a Chinese revolution, four people are kidnapped by plane and taken to an idyllic civilization in a Tibetan valley, where the weather is always kind and men are not only gentle to each other but live to a very advanced age.

Much re-cut romantic adventure which leaves out some of the emphasis of a favourite Utopian novel but stands up pretty well on its own, at least as a supreme example of Hollywood moonshine, with perfect casting, direction and music. If the design has a touch of Ziegfeld, that's Hollywood.

w Robert Riskin, novel James Hilton d Frank Capra ph Joseph Walker m Dmitri Tiomkin ad Stephen Goosson

Ronald Colman, H. B. Warner, Thomas Mitchell, Edward Everett Horton, Sam Jaffe, Isabel Jewell, Jane Wyatt, Margo, John Howard

'One of the most impressive of all thirties films, a splendid fantasy which, physically and emotionally, lets out all the stops.' – John Baxter, 1968
'One is reminded of a British critic's comment on Mary of Scotland, "the inaccuracies must have involved tremendous research".' – Robert Stebbins
'The best film I've seen for ages, but will somebody please tell me how they got the grand piano along a footpath on which only one person can walk at a time with rope and pickaxe and with a sheer drop of three thousand feet or so?' – James Agate
'If the long dull ethical sequences had been cut to the bone there would have been plenty of room for the real story: the shock of western crudity and injustice on a man returned from a more gentle and beautiful way of life.' – Graham Greene

† A 1943 reissue trimmed down the negative still further, to 109 minutes; but in 1979 the American Film Institute restored a print of the original length.

AA: Stephen Goosson
AAN: best picture; Dmitri Tiomkin; H. B. Warner

'The adventure that will live forever has been transformed into spectacular musical drama!'
'Come to Shangri-La and a new world of love!'

Lost Horizon*
US 1972 143m Panavision Technicolor
Columbia/Ross Hunter

Torpid remake with a good opening followed by slabs of philosophizing dialogue and an unbroken series of tedious songs.

w Larry Kramer d Charles Jarrott ph Robert Surtees m Burt Bacharach songs Burt Bacharach, Hal David ad Preston Ames

Peter Finch, Liv Ullmann, Sally Kellerman, Bobby Van, George Kennedy, Michael York, Olivia Hussey, James Shigeta, John Gielgud, Charles Boyer

'It will never play again outside of Shangri-La.' – Les Keyser, Hollywood in the Seventies
'Only Ross Hunter would remake a 1937 movie into a 1932 one.' – Judith Crist
'It can't even be enjoyed as camp.' – Newsweek
'The narrative has no energy, and the

pauses for the pedagogic songs are so awkward that you feel the director's wheelchair needs oiling.' – *Pauline Kael*

Lost in a Harem**
US 1944 89m bw
MGM (George Haight)

Two travelling entertainers in the Middle East get mixed up with a conniving sultan, who hypnotizes them.

Lively, well-staged romp which shows the comedians at their best and uses astute borrowings from burlesque, pantomime, and Hollywood traditions of fantasy and running jokes.

w Harry Ruskin, John Grant, Harry Crane   d Charles Reisner
ph Lester White   m David Snell

Bud Abbott, Lou Costello, Douglass Dumbrille, Marilyn Maxwell, John Conte, Jimmy Dorsey and his Orchestra

'In the middle of the twentieth century you fall off the brink of time!'

The Lost World
US 1960 98m DeLuxe Cinemascope
TCF/Saratoga (Irwin Allen)

Professor Challenger is financed by a newspaper to confirm the report of prehistoric life on a South African plateau.

Pitiful attempt to continue the success of *Journey to the Center of the Earth*, with the story idiotically modernized, unconvincing monsters, a script which inserts conventional romance and villainy, and fatal miscasting of the central part.

w Irwin Allen, Charles Bennett
novel Sir Arthur Conan Doyle
d Irwin Allen   ph Winton C. Hoch   m Bert Shefter, Paul Sawtell

Claude Rains, *Michael Rennie*, David Hedison, *Richard Haydn*, Fernando Lamas, Jill St. John, Ray Stricklyn

'Resembles nothing so much as a ride on a rundown fairground Ghost Train.' – *MFB*

† There had been a silent version in 1924, with Wallace Beery as Challenger and primitive models by Willis O'Brien.

Louisiana Story*
US 1948 77m bw
Standard Oil Company (Robert Flaherty)

In the Louisiana bayous a young native boy watches as oil drillers make a strike.

Quite beautiful but over-extended semi-documentary.

w Robert and Frances Flaherty
d Robert Flaherty   ph Richard Leacock   m Virgil Thomson
ed Helen Van Dongen

Joseph Boudreaux, Lionel Leblanc, Frank Hardy

'The film will be remembered, not for its content, but for the sustained beauty of photography and music, harmonised in shots recalling the delicacy of Chinese landscape painting.' – *Campbell Dixon*
AAN: original story

The Love Bug**
US 1968 107m Technicolor
Walt Disney (Bill Walsh)
L

An unsuccessful racing driver finds that his small private Volkswagen has a mind of its own.

Amusing, pacy period fantasy in the best Disney style.

w Bill Walsh, Don da Gradi
d Robert Stevenson *ph* Edward Colman *m* George Bruns
sp Eustace Lycett

David Tomlinson, Dean Jones, Michele Lee, Buddy Hackett, Joe Flynn, Benson Fong, Joe E. Ross

Love Happy*
US 1949 85m bw
Lester Cowan/Mary Pickford
V, L

A group of impoverished actors accidentally gets possession of the Romanov diamonds.

The last dismaying Marx Brothers film, with Harpo taking the limelight and Groucho loping in for a couple of brief, tired appearances. A roof chase works, but Harpo tries too hard for sentiment, and the production looks shoddy.

w Ben Hecht, Frank Tashlin, Mac Benoff *d* David Miller
ph William Mellor *m* Ann Ronell

Groucho, Harpo, Chico, Eric Blore, Ilona Massey, Marilyn Monroe, Vera-Ellen

Loving You
US 1957 101m Technicolor Vistavision
Paramount/Hal B. Wallis
V, L

A press agent signs a young hillbilly singer to give zest to her husband's band.

Empty-headed, glossy star vehicle.

w Herbert Baker, Hal Kanter *d* Hal Kanter *ph* Charles Lang Jnr
m Walter Scharf

Elvis Presley, Lizabeth Scott, Wendell Corey, Dolores Hart, James Gleason

M

Mac and Me
US 1988 99m
Guild/R. J. Louis
L

A family of aliens is inadvertently dumped in California.

A cardboard confection, copying much of the plot of *E.T.*, that is little more than a dull and extended commercial for fast foods.

w Steven Feke, Stewart Raffill d Stewart Raffill ph Nick McLean m Alan Silvestri pd W. Stewart Campbell ed Tom Walls

Christine Ebersole, Jonathan Ward, Tina Caspary, Lauren Stanley, Jade Calegory, Vinnie Torrente, Martin West

Mad about Music*
US 1938 98m bw
Universal (Joe Pasternak)

A girl at a Swiss school adopts a personable visitor as her father.

Pleasing star vehicle with charm and humour.

w Bruce Manning, Felix Jackson d Norman Taurog ph Joseph Valentine m Frank Skinner, Charles Previn m/ly Harold Adamson, Jimmy McHugh

Deanna Durbin, Herbert Marshall, Gail Patrick, Arthur Treacher, Helen Parrish, Marcia Mae Jones, William Frawley

'Another Durbin smash . . . will mop up at the b.o.' – *Variety*
AAN: original story (Marcella Burke, Frederick Kohner); Joseph Valentine; Frank Skinner, Charles Previn

The Maggie**
GB 1953 93m bw
Ealing (Michael Truman)
US title: *High and Dry*

An American businessman is tricked into sending his private cargo to a Scottish island on an old puffer in need of repair.

Mildly amusing comedy about the wily Scots; not the studio at its best, but pretty fair.

w William Rose d Alexander Mackendrick ph Gordon Dines m John Addison

Paul Douglas, *Alex Mackenzie*, James Copeland, Abe Barker, Dorothy Alison, Hubert Gregg, Geoffrey Keen, Andrew Keir, Tommy Kearins

The Magic Carpet
US 1951 84m Supercinecolor
Sam Katzman/Columbia

The caliph's son returns as the Scarlet Falcon to rout the usurper.

Hopeless kid's matinée rubbish, not even performed with verve.

w David Matthews d Lew Landers

Lucille Ball, Raymond Burr, John Agar, Patricia Medina, George Tobias

The Magic of Lassie
US 1978 99m colour
Lassie Productions (Bonita Granville Wrather, William Beaudine)

A collie dog is sold but makes its way back home.

Downright peculiar revamp of *Lassie Come Home* with music and an ageing all-star cast.

w Jean Holloway, Richard B. Sherman, Robert M. Sherman *d* Don Chaffey *m* Irwin Kostal *songs* Richard and Robert Sherman

James Stewart, Alice Faye, Mickey Rooney, Pernell Roberts, Stephanie Zimbalist, Gene Evans
AAN: song 'When You're Loved'

The Magic Sword
US 1962 80m Eastmancolor
UA/Bert I. Gordon

The son of a well-meaning witch rescues a princess from the clutches of an evil sorcerer.

Shaky medieval fantasy on too low a budget.

w Bernard Schoenfeld *d* Bert I. Gordon *ph* Paul Vogel *m* Richard Markowitz *sp* Milt Rice

Basil Rathbone, Estelle Winwood, Gary Lockwood, Anne Helm

The Magnet
GB 1950 79m bw
Ealing (Sidney Cole)

A small boy steals a magnet and accidentally becomes a hero.

Very mild Ealing comedy, not really up to snuff.

w T. E. B. Clarke *d* Charles Frend *ph* Lionel Banes *m* William Alwyn

Stephen Murray, Kay Walsh, William Fox, Meredith Edwards, Gladys Henson, Thora Hird, Wylie Watson

Maid to Order
US 1987 96m DeLuxe
Vista/New Century (Herb Jaffe, Mort Engelberg)
V, L

A spoiled rich girl takes work as a maid but finds she has a fairy godmother.

Weird semi-fantasy which wasn't wanted in the 80s, Cinderella being out of fashion.

wd Amy Jones (co-writers Perry and Randy Howze) *ph* Shelly Johnson *m* Georges Delerue *pd* Jeffrey Townsend *ed* Sidney Wolinski

Ally Sheedy, Michael Ontkean, Beverly D'Angelo, Valerie Perrine, Dick Shawn, Tom Skerritt

Make a Wish
US 1937 75m bw
(RKO) Sol Lesser

A composer discovers a boy singer at a summer camp.

Acceptable family entertainment.

w Gertrude Berg, Bernard Schubert, Earle Snell *d* Kurt Neumann *ph* John Mescall *songs* Oscar Straus *m* Hugo Riesenfeld

Basil Rathbone, Bobby Breen, Marion Claire, Leon Errol, Henry Armetta, Ralph Forbes, Donald Meek
AAN: Hugo Riesenfeld

Make Mine Music**
US 1946 74m Technicolor
Walt Disney (Joe Grant)

A programme of cartoon shorts:
JOHNNY FEDORA, ALL THE CATS
JOIN IN, WITHOUT YOU, TWO
SILHOUETTES, CASEY AT THE BAT,
THE MARTINS AND THE COYS,
BLUE BAYOU, AFTER YOU'VE
GONE, WILLIE THE SINGING
WHALE, PETER AND THE WOLF

An insubstantial banquet, sometimes
arty and sometimes chocolate boxy,
which occasionally rises to the
expected heights.

w various *d* various

'There is enough genuine charm and
imagination and humour to make up
perhaps one good average Disney
short.' – *James Agee*

Malachi's Cove
GB 1973 75m Technicolor
Penrith/Impact Quadrant Films (Andrew
 Sinclair, Kent Walwin)
aka: *The Seaweed Children*

In 1880 Cornwall, a 14-year-old girl
lives by selling seaweed.

Slimly-plotted film for the family,
pleasant without being very
interesting.

wd Henry Herbert *story* Anthony
Trollope *ph* Walter Lassally
m Brian Gascoigne

Donald Pleasence, Dai Bradley,
Veronica Quilligan, Arthur English,
David Howe

'She'll coax the blues right out of your
heart'
Mame*
US 1974 131m Technicolor
 Panavision
Warner/ABC (Robert Fryer, James
 Cresson)
V, L

In 1928, a 10-year-old boy goes to live
with his eccentric, sophisticated aunt.

Old-fashioned and rather bad film of
a much overrated Broadway musical,
inept in most departments but with
occasional show-stopping moments.

w Paul Zandel *play* Jerome
Lawrence, Robert E. Lee
book Patrick Dennis *d* Gene
Saks *ph* Philip Lathrop
pd Robert F. Boyle *m/ly* Jerry
Herman

Lucille Ball, Beatrice Arthur, Robert
Preston, Bruce Davison, Jane Connell,
Joyce Van Patten, John McGiver

'It makes one realize afresh the
parlous state of the Hollywood
musical, fighting to survive against
misplaced superstars and elephantine
budgets matched with minuscule
imagination.' – *Geoff Brown*
'The cast seem to have been
handpicked for their tone-deafness,
and Lucille Ball's close-ups are shot
blatantly out of focus.' – *Sight and
Sound*
'So terrible it isn't boring; you can get
fixated staring at it and wondering
what Lucille Ball thought she was
doing.' – *New Yorker, 1977*

The Man from Snowy River
Australia 1982 104m
 Eastmancolor Panavision
Cambridge Films/Michael Edgley
 International (Geoff Burrowes)
V, L

In 1888, an orphan boy grows up with
an obsession about wild horses.

Essentially no more than an Audie-
Murphy-style Western given full
down-under treatment. An
Australian smash, a programmer
elsewhere.

w John Dixon, Fred Cullen
poem A. B. Paterson *d* George
Miller *ph* Keith Wagstaff
m Bruce Rowland

Kirk Douglas, Jack Thompson, Sigrid Thornton, Tom Burlinson, Terence Donovan, Lorraine Bayly

The Man in the Iron Mask**
US 1939 110m bw
Edward Small

King Louis XIV keeps his twin brother prisoner.

Exhilarating swashbuckler based on a classic novel, with a complex plot, good acting and the three musketeers in full cry.

w George Bruce, novel Alexandre Dumas d James Whale ph Robert Planck m Lucien Moraweck, Lud Gluskin

Louis Hayward, Warren William (as D'Artagnan), Alan Hale, Bert Roach, Miles Mander, Joan Bennett, Joseph Schildkraut, Walter Kingsford, Marion Martin, Montagu Love, Albert Dekker

'Substantial entertainment for general appeal and satisfaction.' – Variety
'A sort of combination of The Prisoner of Zenda and The Three Musketeers, with a few wild west chases thrown in ... not unentertaining.' – Richard Mallett, Punch

† Remade 1976 as a TV movie with Richard Chamberlain, and 1978 as The Fifth Musketeer (qv).
AAN: Lucien Moraweck, Lud Gluskin

Man of La Mancha*
US 1972 132m DeLuxe
UA/PEA (Arthur Hiller)
V

Arrested by the Inquisition and thrown into prison, Miguel de Cervantes relates the story of Don Quixote.

Unimaginative but generally good-looking attempt to recreate on the screen an essentially theatrical experience.

w Dale Wasserman play Dale Wasserman d Arthur Hiller ph Goffredo Rotunno md Laurence Rosenthal m Mitch Leigh ly Joe Darion ad Luciano Damiani

Peter O'Toole, Sophia Loren, James Coco, Harry Andrews, John Castle, Brian Blessed

'Needful of all the imagination the spectator can muster.' – Variety
AAN: Laurence Rosenthal

The Man with the Golden Gun*
GB 1974 125m Eastmancolor
UA/Eon (Harry Saltzman, Albert R. Broccoli)
V, L

James Bond goes to the Far East to liquidate a professional assassin named Scaramanga.

Thin and obvious Bond extravaganza with conventional expensive excitements.

w Richard Maibaum, Tom Mankiewicz novel Ian Fleming d Guy Hamilton ph Ted Moore, Oswald Morris m John Barry pd Peter Murton

Roger Moore, Christopher Lee, Britt Ekland, Maud Adams, Hervé Villechaize, Clifton James, Richard Loo, Marc Lawrence

'The script lacks satiric insolence and the picture grinds on humourlessly.' – New Yorker

'She'll find a home in every heart! She'll reach the heart of every home!'
Mandy***
GB 1952 93m bw
Ealing (Leslie Norman)
V
US title: The Crash of Silence

A little girl, born deaf, is sent to a special school.

Carefully wrought and very sympathetic little semi-documentary film in which all the adults underplay in concession to a new child star who alas did not last long at the top.

w Nigel Balchin, Jack Whittingham *novel This Day Is Ours* by Hilda Lewis d Alexander Mackendrick ph Douglas Slocombe m William Alwyn

Jack Hawkins, Terence Morgan, Phyllis Calvert, *Mandy Miller*, Godfrey Tearle, Dorothy Alison

'An extremely touching film, in spite of occasional obviousness in a plot never dull, and in spite of its subject never saccharine.' – *Dilys Powell*

Mannequin
US 1987 89m DuArt
TCF/Gladden (Art Levinson)
V, L

A window dresser falls in love with a mannequin who changes into a real live girl.

Feeble and never less than idiotic fantasy.

w Edward Rugoff, Michael Gottlieb d Michael Gottlieb ph Tim Suhrstedt m Sylvester Levay pd Josan Russo ed Richard Halsey, Frank Jiminez

Andrew McCarthy, Kim Cattrall, Estelle Getty, James Spader, G. W. Bailey, Carole Davis, Stephen Vinovich, Christopher Maher, Meshach Taylor

Mannequin Two: On the Move
US 1991 95m colour
Rank/Gladden (Edward Rugoff)
V, L

A window dresser discovers that a mannequin holds the imprisoned spirit of a bewitched peasant girl.

Even less enjoyable than the original, if that's possible.

w Edward Rugoff, David Isaacs, Ken Levine, Betty Israel d Stewart Raffill ph Larry Pizer m David McHugh ad Norman B. Dodge Jnr ed Joan Chapman

Kristy Swanson, William Ragsdale, Meshach Taylor, Terry Kizer, Stuart Pankin, Cynthia Harris, Andrew Hill Newman

'If this stiff ever shows any life, it will be a wonder indeed.' – *Variety*
'A messy rehash of clichés and tired jokes.' – *Empire*

Manon des Sources***
France 1986 114m colour
Renn Productions/A2/RAI 2/DD Productions (Roland Thenot)
V, L

A young girl avenges the wrong done to her father by a farmer and his nephew.

Absorbing drama of rural life, impeccably performed and directed.

w Claude Berri, Gérard Brach *novel* Marcel Pagnol d Claude Berri ph Bruno Nuytten m Jean-Claude Petit pd Bernard Vizat ed Geneviève Louveau, Hervé de Luze

Yves Montand, Daniel Auteuil, Emmanuelle Béart, Hippolyte Girardot, Margarita Lozano, Gabriel Bacquier

The Mark of Zorro***
US 1940 94m bw
TCF (Raymond Griffith)

After being educated in Spain, Diego de Vega returns to California and finds the country enslaved and his father half-corrupted by tyrants. Disguising himself as a masked bandit, he leads the country to expel the usurpers.

Splendid adventure stuff for boys of all ages, an amalgam of *The Scarlet Pimpernel* and *Robin Hood* to which in this version the director adds an overwhelming pictorial sense which makes it stand out as the finest of all.

w John Taintor Foote, Garrett Fort, Bess Meredyth   d Rouben Mamoulian   ph Arthur Miller   m Alfred Newman   ad Richard Day, Joseph C. Wright

Tyrone Power, Basil Rathbone, J. Edward Bromberg, Linda Darnell, Eugene Pallette, Montagu Love, Janet Beecher, Robert Lowery
AAN: Alfred Newman

Mary Poppins***
US 1964 139m Technicolor
Walt Disney (Bill Walsh)
V

In Edwardian London a magical nanny teaches two slightly naughty children to make life enjoyable for themselves and others.

Sporadically a very pleasant and effective entertainment for children of all ages, with plenty of brightness and charm including magic tricks, the mixing of live with cartoon adventures, and just plain fun. It suffers, however, from a wandering narrative in the second half (when Miss Poppins scarcely appears) and from Mr Van Dyke's really lamentable attempt at Cockney.

w Bill Walsh, Don da Gradi   novel P. L. Travers   d Robert Stevenson   ph Edward Colman   md Irwin Kostal   pd Tony Walton   m/ly Richard M. and Robert B. Sherman   ad Carroll Clark, William H. Tuntke   sp Eustace Lycett, Peter Ellenshaw, Robert A. Mattey   ed Cotton Warburton

Julie Andrews, David Tomlinson, Glynis Johns, Dick Van Dyke, Reginald Owen, Ed Wynn, Matthew Garber, Karen Dotrice, Hermione Baddeley, Elsa Lanchester, Arthur Treacher, Jane Darwell

AA: Richard M. and Robert B. Sherman; Julie Andrews; song 'Chim Chim Cheree'; special visual effects; editing
AAN: best picture; script; Robert Stevenson; Edward Colman; Irwin Kostal; art direction

'They used every passion in their incredible duel, and every man in their savage games of intrigue!'
Mary Queen of Scots
GB 1971 128m Technicolor
    Panavision
Universal/Hal B. Wallis

The story of Mary Stuart's opposition to Elizabeth I, her imprisonment and execution.

Schoolbook history in which none of the characters comes to life; dramatic movement is almost entirely lacking despite the liberties taken with fact.

w John Hale   d Charles Jarrott   ph Christopher Challis   m John Barry

Vanessa Redgrave, Glenda Jackson, Trevor Howard, Patrick McGoohan, Nigel Davenport

'Without a better script, Hercules couldn't lift this story off the ground.'
– *Pauline Kael, New Yorker*
AAN: John Barry; Vanessa Redgrave

The Master of Ballantrae

GB 1953 89m Technicolor
Warner
V

Two brothers toss to decide which shall join Bonnie Prince Charlie's 1745 rebellion.

Half-hearted version of a classic adventure novel.

w Herb Meadow novel R. L. Stevenson d William Keighley ph Jack Cardiff m William Alwyn

Errol Flynn, Anthony Steel, Roger Livesey, Beatrice Campbell, Felix Aylmer, Mervyn Johns, Jacques Berthier, Yvonne Furneaux, Ralph Truman

'All that can be salvaged from this rather unforgivable Anglo-American junket are some pleasant exteriors.' – *Gavin Lambert*

Master of the World

US 1961 104m Magnacolor
AIP/Alta Vista (James H. Nicholson, Anthony Carras)

In 1848 a mad inventor takes to the air in his magnificent flying machine in the hope of persuading men to stop war.

Aerial version of *Twenty Thousand Leagues under the Sea*, with cheap sets and much use of stock footage; some scenes however have a certain vigour.

w Richard Matheson novel Jules Verne d William Witney ph Gil Warrenton m Les Baxter

Vincent Price, Charles Bronson, Henry Hull, Mary Webster, David Frankham

Masters of the Universe

US 1987 106m Metrocolor
Edward R. Pressman/Cannon
L

He-Man defends the planet Eternia from the evil Skeletor.

Live action version of the TV cartoons of the toys of the comic strip. Pretty weak stuff, even for 5-year-olds.

w David Odell d Gary Goddard

Dolph Lundgren, Frank Langella, Meg Foster, Billy Barty

Matilda

US 1978 105m Movielab
AIP/Albert S. Ruddy

A down-at-heel theatrical agent finds success with a boxing kangaroo.

Damon Runyon meets Walt Disney in an old-fashioned family audience picture for which there may no longer be an audience.

w Albert S. Ruddy, Timothy Galfas novel Paul Gallico d Daniel Mann ph Jack Woolf m Jerrold Immel pd Boris Leven

Elliott Gould, Robert Mitchum, Harry Guardino, Clive Revill, Karen Carlson, Lionel Stander, Art Metrano, Roy Clark

Maya

US 1966 91m Technicolor Panavision
MGM/King Brothers (Mary P. Murray, Herman King)

A teenage American boy arrives in India to visit his disillusioned father, who finally comes to understand him only after he has run away.

Good-looking but otherwise uninteresting animal drama which served as the pilot for a TV series.

w John Fante   d John Berry
ph Gunter Senftleben   m Riz Ortolani

Clint Walker, Jay North, I. S. Johar, Sajid Khan

Me and My Pal*
US 1933 20m bw
Hal Roach

Ollie becomes engrossed in a jigsaw puzzle and forgets to get married.

Oddball star comedy which nearly comes off but simply doesn't provide enough jokes.

w Stan Laurel   d Charles Rogers, Lloyd French

Laurel and Hardy, James Finlayson, Eddie Dunn

Meet Me in St Louis***
US 1944 113m Technicolor
MGM (Arthur Freed)
V, L

Scenes in the life of an affectionate family at the turn of the century.

Patchy but generally highly agreeable musical nostalgia with an effective sense of the passing years and seasons.

w Irving Brecher, Fred F. Finklehoffe   novel Sally Benson   d Vincente Minnelli   ph George Folsey   md Georgie Stoll

Judy Garland, Margaret O'Brien, Tom Drake, Leon Ames, Mary Astor, Lucille Bremer, June Lockhart, Harry Davenport, Marjorie Main, Joan Carroll, Hugh Marlowe, Robert Sully, Chill Wills

'A family group framed in velvet and tinsel ... it has everything a romantic musical should have.' – Dilys Powell, 1955

AAN: script; George Folsey; Georgie Stoll; song 'The Trolley Song' (m/ly Ralph Blane, Hugh Martin)

Melody
GB 1971 106m Eastmancolor
Hemdale/Sagittarius/Goodtimes (David Puttnam)
aka: S.W.A.L.K.

Calf love at school causes jealousy between two boys.

Tough-sentimental teenage comedy-drama of little interest to adults.

w Alan Parker   d Waris Hussein
ph Peter Suschitsky   m Richard Hewson

Jack Wild, Mark Lester, Tracy Hyde

Melody Time*
US 1948 75m Technicolor
Walt Disney (Ben Sharpsteen)

An unlinked variety show of cartoon segments.

A mainly mediocre selection with the usual moments of high style: *Once upon a Wintertime, Bumble Boogie, Johnny Appleseed, Little Toot, Trees, Blame it on the Samba, Pecos Bill.*

wd various.

'There seems to be an obvious connection between the Disney artists' increasing insipidity and their increasing talent for fright, but I will leave it to accredited sado-masochists to make the discovery.' – James Agee

'Women want him for his wit. The C.I.A. wants him for his body. All Nick wants is his molecules back.'
'An adventure like you've never seen.'

Memoirs of an Invisible Man*
US 1992 99m Technicolor Panavision
Warner/Le Studio Canal Plus/Regency Enterprises/Alcor (Bruce Bodner, Dan Kolsrud)
V

A CIA agent pursues a stock analyst

who has turned invisible after an accident.

Clever special effects fail to compensate for the lacklustre script and uninspired performances.

w Robert Collector, Dana Olsen, William Goldman novel H. F. Saint d John Carpenter ph William A. Fraker m Shirley Walker pd Lawrence G. Paull sp Industrial Light and Magic ed Marion Rothman

Chevy Chase, Daryl Hannah, Sam Neill, Michael McKean, Stephen Tobolowsky, Jim Norton

'Where's the wit? It fades into invisibility while you're watching it.' – *Los Angeles Times*

Men of Sherwood Forest
GB 1954 77m Eastmancolor
Hammer (Michael Carreras)

Robin Hood frees King Richard from bondage.

Fairly lively adventure romp on a low level.

w Allan MacKinnon d Val Guest ph Jimmy Harvey m Doreen Corwithen

Don Taylor, Reginald Beckwith, Eileen Moore, David King-Wood, Patrick Holt, John Van Eyssen

Men o' War*
US 1929 20m bw
Hal Roach
V

Two sailors and two girls have adventures in a park.

Simple-minded early talkie star comedy featuring their famous soda fountain routine.

w H. M. Walker d Lewis R. Foster

Laurel and Hardy, James Finlayson

Merry Andrew
US 1958 103m Metrocolor
  Cinemascope
MGM/Sol C. Siegel

A stuffy teacher in search of an ancient statue joins a travelling circus.

Deliberately charming star comedy which plumps too firmly for whimsy and, despite its professionalism, provokes barely a smile, let alone a laugh.

w Isobel Lennart, I. A. L. Diamond story Paul Gallico d/ch Michael Kidd ph Robert Surtees m Saul Chaplin ly Johnny Mercer

Danny Kaye, Pier Angeli, Baccaloni, Noel Purcell, Robert Coote, Patricia Cutts, Rex Evans, Walter Kingsford, Tommy Rall, Rhys Williams

Mickey's Christmas Carol***
US 1983 26m Technicolor
Disney
V, L

A cartoon version of Dickens with the parts played by familiar Disney characters; and a supreme re-establishment of the old Disney production values.

d Burney Mattinson

'For anyone over 35, this little jewel of a film is truly the Ghost of Christmas Past.' – *Gilbert Adair, MFB*
AAN: animated film

Midnight Patrol*
US 1933 20m bw
Hal Roach
V

Incompetent policemen arrest their own chief as a burglar.

Good standard star slapstick.

w uncredited   d Lloyd French

Laurel and Hardy, Charlie Hall, Walter Plinge

Midshipman Easy
GB 1935 77m bw
ATP (Basil Dean, Thorold Dickinson)
US title: *Men of the Sea*

In 1790, young naval officers rescue a girl from Spanish bandits.

Stilted adventure story with interesting credits.

w Anthony Kimmins
novel Frederick Marryat   d Carol Reed   ph John W. Boyle

Hughie Green, Margaret Lockwood, Harry Tate, Robert Adams, Roger Livesey, Lewis Casson

'Three centuries in the making!'
A Midsummer Night's Dream*
US 1935 133m bw
Warner (Max Reinhardt)
L

Two pairs of lovers sort out their problems with fairy help at midnight in the woods of Athens.

Shakespeare's play is treated with remarkable respect in this super-glamorous Hollywood adaptation based on the Broadway production by Max Reinhardt. Much of it comes off, and visually it's a treat.

w Charles Kenyon, Mary McCall Jnr   play William Shakespeare
d Max Reinhardt, William Dieterle
ph Hal Mohr, Fred Jackman, Byron Haskin, H. F. Koenekamp   md Erich Wolfgang Korngold   ch Bronislawa Nijinska   m Mendelssohn
ad Anton Grot   ed Ralph Dawson

James Cagney, Dick Powell, Jean Muir, Ross Alexander, Olivia de Havilland, Joe E. Brown, Hugh Herbert, Arthur Treacher, Frank McHugh, Otis Harlan, Dewey Robinson, *Victor Jory*, Verree Teasdale, *Mickey Rooney*, Anita Louise, Grant Mitchell, Ian Hunter, Hobart Cavanaugh

'General b.o. chances could be improved by judicious pruning and appreciative selling . . . a fine prestige picture not only for Warners but for the industry as a whole.' – *Variety*
'You must see it if you want to be in a position to argue about the future of the film!' – *Picturegoer*
'The publicity push behind the film is tremendous – it is going to be a success or everyone at Warner Brothers is going to get fired.' – *Robert Forsythe*
'Its assurance as a work of film technique is undoubted.' – *John Baxter, 1968*
'Its worst contradiction lies in the way Warners first ordered up a whole batch of foreign and high-sounding names to handle music, dances, general production – and then turned around and handed them empty vessels for actors.' – *Otis Ferguson*

AA: photography; editing
AAN: best picture

'The ten most terrific thrills ever pictured!'
Mighty Joe Young*
US 1949 94m bw
RKO (Merian C. Cooper)

A little girl brings back from Africa a pet gorilla which grows to enormous size and causes a city to panic.

Rather tired comic-sentimental follow-up to *King Kong*, with a tedious plot and variable animation but a few endearing highlights.

w Ruth Rose   d Ernest Schoedsack   ph J. Roy Hunt
m Roy Webb   sp Willis O'Brien, Ray Harryhausen

Terry Moore, Ben Johnson, Robert Armstrong, Frank McHugh, Douglas Fowley

The Milky Way*
US 1936 88m bw
Paramount/Harold Lloyd (Edward Sheldon)

A milkman becomes a prizefighter and overcomes a gang of crooks.

Modest Harold Lloyd comedy towards the end of his career; remade as *The Kid from Brooklyn* (qv).

w Grover Jones, Frank Butler, Richard Connell play Lynn Root, Harry Clork d Leo McCarey ph Alfred Gilks

Harold Lloyd, Adolphe Menjou, Verree Teasdale, Helen Mack, William Gargan, George Barbier, Lionel Stander

'The work of many hands, all laid on expertly.' – *Otis Ferguson*
'One is more amazed than ever at the good fortune of this youngish man whose chief talent is not to act at all, to do nothing, to serve as a blank wall for other people to scrawl their ideas on.' – *Graham Greene*

Million Dollar Duck
US 1971 92m Technicolor
Walt Disney (Bill Anderson)

A duck lays eggs with solid gold yolks, which provoke interest from gangsters as well as the government.

Minor Disney fantasy borrowed without permission from *Mr Drake's Duck* (qv).

w Roswell Rogers d Vincent McEveety ph William Snyder m Buddy Baker

Dean Jones, Sandy Duncan, Joe Flynn, Tony Roberts

The Miracle of the White Stallions*
US 1963 118m Technicolor
Walt Disney (Peter V. Herald)
GB title: *The Flight of the White Stallions*

During World War II the Nazis occupy Vienna and the owner of the Spanish Riding School guides his stallions to safety.

Adequate family adventure fare with a dull hero but interesting backgrounds.

w A. J. Carothers d Arthur Hiller ph Gunther Anders m Paul Smith

Robert Taylor, Lilli Palmer, Eddie Albert, Curt Jurgens

Miracle on 34th Street***
US 1947 94m bw
TCF (William Perlberg)
V, L
GB title: *The Big Heart*

A department store Santa Claus claims to be the real thing.

Mainly charming comedy fantasy which quickly became an American classic but does suffer from a few dull romantic stretches.

wd George Seaton, story Valentine Davies ph Charles Clarke, Lloyd Ahern m Cyril Mockridge

Edmund Gwenn, Maureen O'Hara, John Payne, Natalie Wood, Gene Lockhart, Porter Hall, William Frawley, Jerome Cowan, Thelma Ritter

'Altogether wholesome, stimulating and enjoyable.' – *Motion Picture Herald*

AA: George Seaton (as writer); Valentine Davies; Edmund Gwenn
AAN: best picture

Les Misérables****
US 1935 109m bw
Twentieth Century (Darryl F. Zanuck)
L

Unjustly convicted and sentenced to years in the galleys, Jean Valjean emerges to build up his life again but is hounded by a cruel and relentless police officer.

Solid, telling, intelligent version of a much-filmed classic novel; in adaptation and performance it is hard to see how this film could be bettered.

w W. P. Lipscomb, novel Victor Hugo d Richard Boleslawski ph Gregg Toland m Alfred Newman ed Barbara McLean

Fredric March, Charles Laughton, Cedric Hardwicke, Rochelle Hudson, Frances Drake, John Beal, Jessie Ralph, Florence Eldridge

'Brilliant filmization, sure fire for heavy money.' – *Variety*
'Unbelievably thrilling in all the departments of its manufacture . . . a memorable experience in the cinema.' – *New York Times*
'A superlative effort, a thrilling, powerful, poignant picture.' – *New York Evening Post*
'Deserving of rank among the cinema's finest achievements.' – *New York World Telegram*

† Other versions of the story: 1909, 1913 (French); 1917 (William Farnum); 1923 (French: Gabriel Gabrio); 1929 as *The Bishop's Candlesticks* (Walter Huston); 1934 (French: Harry Baur); 1946 (Italian: Gino Cervi; 1952 (see below); 1956 (French: Jean Gabin); 1978 (British: Richard Jordan).
AAN: best picture; Gregg Toland; editing

Les Misérables**
US 1952 106m bw
TCF (Fred Kohlmar)

Solemn remake, well done but lacking the spark of inspiration.

w Richard Murphy d Lewis Milestone ph Joseph LaShelle m Alex North

Michael Rennie, Robert Newton, Edmund Gwenn, Debra Paget, Cameron Mitchell, Sylvia Sidney, Elsa Lanchester, James Robertson Justice, Joseph Wiseman, Rhys Williams

Mr Bug Goes to Town*
US 1941 78m Technicolor
Max Fleischer
aka: *Hoppity Goes to Town*

An urban community of insects is in danger from developers.

A cartoon feature which failed to make its mark despite clever detail; perhaps because insects make poor heroes, or because there simply wasn't enough plot. d Dave Fleischer m Leigh Harline

Mr Drake's Duck**
GB 1950 85m bw
Daniel M. Angel/Douglas Fairbanks

A duck lays a uranium egg, and a gentleman farmer finds himself at the centre of international military disagreement.

Brisk and amusing minor comedy deploying British comic types to good purpose.

wd Val Guest, radio play Ian Messiter ph Jack Cox m Philip Martell

Douglas Fairbanks Jnr, Yolande Donlan, Wilfrid Hyde White, A. E. Matthews, Jon Pertwee, Reginald

Beckwith, Howard Marion-Crawford, Peter Butterworth, Tom Gill

'One of the funniest films I have ever seen.' – *News of the World*

Mr Forbush and the Penguins*

GB 1971 101m Technicolor
EMI/PGV/Henry Trettin

A biologist is sent to the Antarctic to study penguins, and gets a new understanding of life.

Rather broken-backed animal film with a moral; pleasant enough, its two halves don't fit together.

w Anthony Shaffer   *novel* Graham Billey   d Roy Boulting, Arne Sucksdorff   ph Harry Waxman, Ted Scaife   m John Addison

John Hurt, Hayley Mills, Tony Britton, Thorley Walters, Judy Campbell, Joss Ackland, Sally Geeson, Cyril Luckham

Mr Mom

US 1983 91m Metrocolor
Fox/Sherwood (Lynn Loring)
V, L
GB title: *Mr Mum*

Dad loses his executive job and stays home to mind the kids while his wife works.

Obvious farce with too much messy slapstick and no real development.

w John Hughes   d Stan Dragoti   ph Victor J. Kemper   m Lee Holdridge   pd Alfred Sweeney   ed Patrick Kennedy

Michael Keaton, Teri Garr, Frederick Koehler, Martin Mull, Ann Jillian

'The jokes almost sink without trace in a hazy domestic setting straight from the hoariest sitcom.' – *Geoff Brown, MFB*

Mister Quilp

GB 1975 119m Technicolor Panavision
Reader's Digest (Helen M. Straus)
aka: *The Old Curiosity Shop*

In 1840 London, an antique-shop owner is in debt to a hunchback moneylender who has designs on his business.

The novel, with its villainous lead, is a curious choice for musicalizing, and in this treatment falls desperately flat, with no sparkle of imagination visible anywhere.

w Louis Kamp, Irene Kamp
novel The Old Curiosity Shop by Charles Dickens   d Michael Tuchner   ph Christopher Challis   md Elmer Bernstein   m Anthony Newley   pd Elliot Gould   ch Gillian Lynne

Anthony Newley, Michael Hordern, David Hemmings, Sarah-Jane Varley, David Warner, Paul Rogers, Jill Bennett

'Another soggy piece of family entertainment from Reader's Digest, who produced the toothless screen musicals of *Tom Sawyer* and *Huckleberry Finn*.' – *Philip French*
'Dickens shorn of sentiment, melodrama or love ... Mr Newley's Quilp, a galvanized Quasimodo on a permanent high, is something of a strain to watch.' – *Michael Billington, Illustrated London News*

Mr Scoutmaster

US 1953 87m bw
TCF

A TV personality wants to understand children and is persuaded to take over a scout troop.

A star vehicle which starts

promisingly enough in the *Sitting Pretty* vein but quickly falls headlong into an abyss of sentimentality.

w Leonard Praskins, Barney Slater d Henry Levin ph Joseph LaShelle md Lionel Newman m Cyril Mockridge

Clifton Webb, Edmund Gwenn, George Winslow, Frances Dee, Veda Ann Borg

Mr Skitch

US 1933 70m bw
Fox

A Missouri family heads for California.

Very passable star family entertainment.

w Anne Cameron novel *Green Dice* by Anne Cameron d James Cruze

Will Rogers, Zasu Pitts, Florence Desmond, Rochelle Hudson

'Enough laughs to please in general.' – *Variety*

Mr Soft Touch

US 1949 93m bw
Columbia
GB title: *House of Settlement*

A gangster is reformed at Christmas by a social worker.

Dewy-eyed romance with Damon Runyonish asides; only for soft touches.

w Orin Jannings d Henry Levin and Gordon Douglas

Glenn Ford, Evelyn Keyes, John Ireland, Beulah Bondi, Percy Kilbride, Roman Bohnen

Mrs Brown, You've Got a Lovely Daughter

GB 1968 95m Metrocolor Panavision
MGM/Allen Klein

A young singer inherits a prize greyhound.

Inoffensive comedy musical with a swinging London background.

w Thaddeus Vane d Saul Swimmer

Peter Noone and Herman's Hermits, Stanley Holloway, Mona Washbourne, Lance Percival, Marjorie Rhodes

'You'll never laugh as long and as loud again as long as you live! The laughs come so fast and so furious you'll wish it would end before you collapse!'

Modern Times***

US 1936 87m bw
Charles Chaplin
V, L

An assembly-line worker goes berserk but can't get another job.

Silent star comedy produced in the middle of the sound period; flashes of genius alternate with sentimental sequences and jokes without punch.

wd Charles Chaplin ph Rollie Totheroh, Ira Morgan m Charles Chaplin

Charles Chaplin, Paulette Goddard, Henry Bergman, Chester Conklin, Tiny Sandford

'A natural for the world market ... box office with a capital B.' – *Variety*
'A feature picture made out of several one- and two-reel shorts, proposed titles being *The Shop*, *The Jailbird*, *The Singing Waiter*.' – *Otis Ferguson*

Molly

Australia 1983 82m colour
NSW Film Corp./Greater Union/M&L
(Hilary Linstead)

A little girl, with the help of some circus children, looks after a singing dog when its owner is taken ill.

Amusing, although slow-moving, family film that will appeal most to soft-hearted sub-teens.

w Phillip Roope, Mark Thomas, Hilary Linstead, Ned Lander   d Ned Lander   ph Vincent Monton   md Graeme Isaac   ad Robert Dein   ed Stewart Young

Claudia Karvan, Garry McDonald, Reg Lye, Melissa Jaffer, Ruth Cracknell

Mon Oncle*

France 1956 116m Eastmancolor
Specta/Gray/Alterdel-Centaure (Louis Dolivet)

V

A small boy has less affection for his parents than for his vague, clumsy uncle.

Tiresomely long star vehicle, with Tati harping on his theory of detachment, i.e. keeping his comic character on the fringes of the action. It really doesn't work in a film of this length, and the jokes are thin.

w Jacques Tati, Jacques Lagrange   d Jacques Tati   ph Jean Bourgoin   m Alain Romains, Franck Barcellini

Jacques Tati, Jean-Pierre Zola, Adrienne Servatie, Alain Becourt, Yvonne Arnaud

'Deft, elusive, full of heart.' – *Brenda Davies, MFB*

'Cinema humour at its brilliant best.' – *Daily Worker*

AA: best foreign film

'The 1931 nut crop is ready!'

Monkey Business***

US 1931 81m bw
Paramount (Herman J. Mankiewicz)

V, L

Four ship's stowaways crash a society party and catch a few crooks.

The shipboard part of this extravaganza is one of the best stretches of Marxian lunacy, but after the Chevalier impersonations it runs out of steam. Who's grumbling?

w S. J. Perelman, Will B. Johnstone, Arthur Sheekman   d Norman Z. McLeod.   ph Arthur L. Todd

Groucho, Chico, Harpo, Zeppo, Thelma Todd, Rockcliffe Fellowes, Ruth Hall, Harry Woods

'Surefire for laughs despite working along familiar lines ... picture has started off by doing sweeping business all over, and no reason why it shouldn't continue to tickle wherever it plays.' – *Variety*

Monkeys Go Home

US 1966 101m Technicolor
Walt Disney (Ron Miller)

An American inherits a French olive farm and trains chimpanzees to harvest the crop.

Footling comedy with not much of an idea, let alone a plot.

w Maurice Tombragel   *novel The Monkeys* by G. K. Wilkinson   d Andrew V. McLaglen   ph William Snyder   m Robert F. Brunner

Maurice Chevalier, Dean Jones, Yvette Mimieux, Bernard Woringer, Jules Munshin, Alan Carney

'Innocuous, extrovertly cheerful and good-humoured – and very dull.' – *MFB*

Monsieur Hulot's Holiday****
France 1953 91m bw
Cady/Discina (Fred Orain)
V, L
original title: *Les Vacances de Monsieur Hulot*

An accident-prone bachelor arrives at a seaside resort and unwittingly causes havoc for himself and everyone else.

Despite lame endings to some of the jokes, this is a film to set the whole world laughing, Hulot himself being an unforgettable character and some of the timing magnificent. One feels that it could very nearly happen.

w Jacques Tati, Henri Marquet d Jacques Tati ph Jacques Mercanton, Jean Mouselle m Alain Romans

Jacques Tati, Nathalie Pascaud, Michèle Rolla, Valentine Camax

'The casual, amateurish air of his films clearly adds to their appeal: it also appears to explain their defects.' – *Penelope Houston, MFB*
'It had me laughing out loud with more enjoyment than any other comedy film this year.' – *Daily Express*
AAN: script

The Monster Squad*
Canada 1987 81m
  Metrocolor Panavision
Keith Barish/Taft/Tri-Star
V

Dracula, Frankenstein's monster, the Wolf Man, the Gill Man and the Mummy take refuge in a small American town.

Mildly amusing spoof for the teenage audience.

w Shane Black, Fred Dekker
d Fred Dekker

Stephen Macht, Duncan Regehr, Andre Gower, Robby Kiger, Tom Noonan

The Monster that Challenged the World
US 1957 83m bw
Levy-Gardner-Laven/United Artists

A giant caterpillar lays eggs in California's Salton Sea: one hatches . . .

Overlong shocker for kids.

w Pat Fielder d Arnold Laven

Tim Holt, Audrey Dalton, Hans Conried, Milton Parsons

Monsters from an Unknown Planet (dubbed)
Japan 1975 80m colour
Miracle/Toho (Tomoyuki Tanaka)
original title: *Mekagojira No Gyakushu*; aka: *The Escape of Mechagodzilla; Terror of Mechagodzilla*

Godzilla is outclassed when aliens reanimate Mechagodzilla and loose Titanosaurus on Tokyo with the help of a renegade scientist and his cyborg daughter.

The usual nonsense from one of the later Godzilla movies, with the monsters inactive for much of the time.

w Yukiko Takayama d Ishiro Honda

Katsuhiko Sasaki, Tomoko Ai, Akihiko Mirata, Tadao Nakamura, Katsumasu Uchida

Moon Pilot**
US 1961 98m Technicolor
Walt Disney (Ron Miller)

A reluctant astronaut falls in love with a girl from outer space, who finally accompanies him on his mission.

Engaging science-fiction spoof with good performances.

w Maurice Tombragel
serial Robert Buckner   d James Neilson   ph William Snyder
m Peter Smith   sp Eustace Lycett

Edmond O'Brien, Tom Tryon, Brian Keith

The Moon Spinners*
GB   1964   119m   Technicolor
Walt Disney (Bill Anderson)

A young girl holidaying in Crete becomes involved with jewel robbers.

Teenage adventure against attractive locations; quite agreeable but overlong.

w Michael Dyne   novel Mary Stewart   d James Neilson
ph Paul Beeson   m Ron Grainer

Hayley Mills, Peter McEnery, Eli Wallach, Joan Greenwood, John Le Mesurier, *Pola Negri*

Moonfleet*
US   1955   87m   Eastmancolor Cinemascope
MGM (John Houseman)

In Dorset in 1770 an orphan boy finds that his elegant guardian leads a gang of smugglers.

Period gothic melodrama which nearly, but not quite, comes off; the script simply doesn't build to the right climax, and too many characters come to nothing. But there are splendid moments.

w Margaret Fitts, Jan Lustig
novel J. Meade Faulkner   d Fritz Lang   ph Robert Planck
m Miklos Rozsa

Stewart Granger, Jon Whiteley, George Sanders, Joan Greenwood, Viveca Lindfors, Liliane Montevecchi, Melville Cooper, Sean McClory, John Hoyt, Alan Napier

Moonraker
GB   1979   126m   Technicolor Panavision
UA/Eon (Albert S. Broccoli)
V, L

James Bond investigates the disappearance of a space shuttle during a test flight.

Adventures in Venice, Rio and the upper Amazon; all very repetitive and no longer more than faintly amusing.

w Christopher Wood   novel Ian Fleming   d Lewis Gilbert
ph Jean Tournier   m John Barry   pd Ken Adam

Roger Moore, Lois Chiles, Michael Lonsdale, Richard Kiel, Geoffrey Keen, Lois Maxwell, Bernard Lee

'Conspicuously expensive production values but an unmistakably cut price plot.' – *Sight and Sound*

Moonwalker
US   1988   93m
Warner/Ultimate Productions
V, L

Episodic look at the life and performances of Michael Jackson, culminating in a fantasy in which he stops a gangster turning children into junkies.

Strictly for fans.

w David Newman   story Michael Jackson   d Colin Chilvers, Jerry Kramer   ph John Hora, Tom Ackerman, Bob Collins, Fred Elmes, Crescenzo Notarile   m Bruce Broughton   pd Michael Ploog
ed David E. Blewitt, Mitchell Sinoway, Dale Beldin

Michael Jackson, Joe Pesci, Sean

Lennon, Kellie Parker, Brandon Adams

Morons from Outer Space
GB 1985 91m colour
Thorn EMI (Barry Hanson)

Dopey space travellers arrive on Earth.

Spoofy comedy which, apart from staging a spectacular motorway landing and mocking various popular film genres, never decides where to go.

w Griff Rhys Jones, Mel Smith d Michael Hodges ph Phil Meheux m Peter Brewis

Mel Smith, Griff Rhys Jones, Paul Bown, Joanne Pearce, Jimmy Nail, Dinsdale Landen, James B. Sikking

'It remains stuck on the launch pad.' – *Variety*

Mother Riley Meets the Vampire
GB 1952 74m bw
Renown (John Gilling)
US title: *My Son the Vampire*

An old washerwoman accidentally catches a robot-wielding crook called The Vampire.

Childish farce notable for Lucan's last appearance in his dame role, and Lugosi's last substantial appearance of any kind – two pros at the end of their tether.

w Val Valentine d John Gilling ph Stan Pavey m Linda Southworth

Arthur Lucan, Bela Lugosi, Dora Bryan, Richard Wattis

'Stupid, humourless and repulsive.' – *MFB*

The Mouse on the Moon
GB 1963 85m Eastmancolor
UA/Walter Shenson

The tiny duchy of Grand Fenwick discovers that its home-made wine makes excellent rocket fuel.

Piddling sequel to *The Mouse that Roared*, suffering from a hesitant script, too few jokes, and overacting.

w Michael Pertwee d Richard Lester ph Wilkie Cooper m Ron Grainer

Margaret Rutherford, Ron Moody, Bernard Cribbins, David Kossoff, Terry-Thomas, Michael Crawford

The Mouse that Roared**
GB 1959 85m Technicolor
Columbia/Open Road (Carl Foreman)
V

The tiny duchy of Grand Fenwick is bankrupt, and its minister decides to declare war on the United States, be defeated, and receive Marshall Aid.

Lively comedy which sounds rather better than it plays, but has bright moments.

w Roger Macdougall, Stanley Mann novel Leonard Wibberley d Jack Arnold ph John Wilcox m Edwin Astley

Peter Sellers (playing three parts), Jean Seberg, David Kossoff, William Hartnell, Leo McKern, Macdonald Parke, Harold Kasket

'The kind of irrepressible topical satire whose artistic flaws become increasingly apparent but whose merits outlast them.' – *Peter John Dyer*

Movie Crazy**
US 1932 82m bw
Harold Lloyd

A filmstruck young man is mistakenly invited to Hollywood for a film test.

The silent comedian is not quite at his best in this early sound comedy, but it contains his last really superb sequences and its picture of Hollywood is both amusing and nostalgic.

w Harold Lloyd and others   d Clyde Bruckman   ph Walter Lundin

Harold Lloyd, Constance Cummings

'A corking comedy, replete with wow belly laughs. Sure-fire.' – *Variety*

The Mudlark**
GB 1950 98m bw
TCF (Nunnally Johnson)

A scruffy boy from the docks breaks into Windsor Castle to see Queen Victoria and ends her fifteen years of seclusion.

A pleasant whimsical legend which could have done without the romantic interest, but which despite an air of unreality provides warm-hearted, well upholstered entertainment for family audiences.

w *Nunnally Johnson*
novel Theodore Bonnet   d Jean Negulesco   ph Georges Périnal
m William Alwyn   ad C. P. Norman

Alec Guinness, Irene Dunne, *Andrew Ray*, Anthony Steel, Constance Smith, *Finlay Currie, Edward Rigby*

Münchausen**
Germany 1943 134m Agfacolor
UFA (Eberhard Schmidt)
aka: *The Adventures of Baron Münchausen*

In the 1940s Baron Münchausen tells stories of his fabulous ancestor who, it is soon clear, is himself, having been given immortality by a magician.

Lavish but somewhat stilted spectacle, produced on the orders of Nazi propagandist Joseph Goebbels to mark the studio's twenty-fifth anniversary. His influence is evident in the way that all other nationalities are shown as comic.

w Berthold Bürger (Erich Kästner)   d Josef von Baky
ph Werner Krien   m Georg Haentzschel   ad Emil Hasler, Otto Gulstorff

Hans Albers, Wilhelm Bendow, Michael Bohnen, Marina Von Ditmar, Hans Brausewetter, Brigitte Horney, Käthe Haack

† Kästner used a pseudonym because his writings had been banned since 1933. After the film was released, Hitler ordered that he should receive no further commissions.

The Muppet Christmas Carol*
US 1992 86m colour
Buena Vista/Walt Disney/Jim Henson (Brian Henson, Martin G. Baker)

A Christmas-hating miser is reformed by the visitations of five ghosts.

Cheerful adaptation of the perennial story, in a version that should appeal to the young.

w Jerry Juhl   story *A Christmas Carol* by Charles Dickens   d Brian Henson   ph John Fenner
m Miles Goodman   pd Val Strazovec   m/ly Paul Williams
sp The Computer Film Company
ed Michael Jablow

Michael Caine, Steven MacKintosh, Meredith Brown, Robin Weaver, Kermit the Frog, Miss Piggy, The Great Gonzo, Fozzie Bear

'The film sinks into a quagmire of sentimentality; the Muppets withdraw discreetly during Scrooge's ghostly visitations and the dominant flavour is more saccharine than humbug. Nice try, though.' – *Sheila Johnston, Independent*

'More entertainment than humanly possible!'

The Muppet Movie**
GB 1979 97m Eastmancolor
ITC (Jim Henson)

Kermit the Frog and friends travel across America to Hollywood and are offered a film contract by Lew Lord, the famous impresario.

Technically an adroit transfer of the celebrated puppets from their TV backstage milieu to a wider canvas; but the latter tends to dwarf them, the material is very variable, the guest stars look embarrassed and the show goes on too long.

w Jerry Juhl, Jack Burns   d James Frawley   ph Isidore Mankofsky
m Paul Williams, Kenny Ascher
pd Joel Schiller

Charles Durning, Edgar Bergen, Bob Hope, Milton Berle, Mel Brooks, James Coburn, Dom DeLuise, Elliott Gould, Cloris Leachman, Telly Savalas, Orson Welles
AAN: Paul Williams, Kenny Ascher; song 'The Rainbow Connection'

The Muppets Take Manhattan*
US 1984 94m Technicolor
Tri-Star (David Lazer)
L

The Muppets' varsity show is promised a New York opening.

Probably the best of the Muppet features, but by the time of its arrival the early brilliance had been forgotten and even Miss Piggy had worn out her welcome.

w Frank Oz, Tom Patchett, Jay Tarses   d Frank Oz
AAN: Jeffrey Moss (music)

The Music Box****
US 1932 30m bw
Hal Roach
V

Two delivery men take a piano to a house at the top of a flight of steps.

Quintessential Laurel and Hardy, involving almost all their aspects including a slight song and dance. With Billy Gilbert.

w H. M. Walker   d James Parrott

AA: best short

The Music Man***
US 1962 151m Technirama
Warner (Morton da Costa)
V, L

A confidence trickster persuades a small-town council to start a boys' band, with himself as the agent for all the expenses.

Reasonably cinematic, thoroughly invigorating transference to the screen of a hit Broadway musical. Splendid period 'feel', standout performances, slight sag in second half.

w Marion Hargrove   book Meredith Willson   d Morton da Costa
ph Robert Burks   md Ray Heindorf   ch Onna White
songs Meredith Willson

Robert Preston, Shirley Jones, Buddy Hackett, *Hermione Gingold*, Pert Kelton, Paul Ford

'This is one of those triumphs that only a veteran performer can have; Preston's years of experience and his love of performing come together joyously.' – *Pauline Kael*

AA: Ray Heindorf
AAN: best picture

My Fair Lady***
US 1964 175m Technicolor Super Panavision 70
CBS/Warner (Jack L. Warner)
V, L

Musical version of *Pygmalion*, about a flower girl trained by an arrogant elocutionist to pass as a lady.

Careful, cold transcription of a stage success; cinematically quite uninventive when compared with *Pygmalion* itself, but a pretty good entertainment.

w Alan Jay Lerner play Pygmalion by Bernard Shaw d George Cukor ph Harry Stradling md André Previn m Frederick Loewe ch Hermes Pan ad Gene Allen costumes Cecil Beaton ed William Ziegler

Rex Harrison, Audrey Hepburn, *Stanley Holloway*, Wilfrid Hyde White, Gladys Cooper, Jeremy Brett, Theodore Bikel, Isobel Elsom, Mona Washbourne, Walter Burke

'The property has been not so much adapted as elegantly embalmed.' – *Andrew Sarris*

AA: best picture; George Cukor; Harry Stradling; Rex Harrison; André Previn (scoring of music); costumes; sound
AAN: Alan Jay Lerner; Stanley Holloway; Gladys Cooper; editing

My Friend Flicka*
US 1943 89m Technicolor
TCF

Adventures of a young boy and his pet colt.

Winsome boy-and-horse story, one of the most popular family films of the forties. Sequel 1945 with virtually the same cast: *Thunderhead Son of Flicka*.

w Mary O'Hara novel Mary O'Hara d Harold Schuster m Alfred Newman

Roddy McDowall, Preston Foster, Rita Johnson, James Bell, Jeff Corey

'Mac's back and he's not alone...'
My Girl
US 1991 102m Technicolor
Columbia TriStar/Imagine (Brian Grazer)
V

In the 1970s, the 11-year-old daughter of an undertaker comes to terms with her widowed father's romance and the death of a friend.

Slick, over-sentimental account of growing up, part of Hollywood's early 90s cycle of films centred on children. It provided the first screen kiss for Culkin.

w Laurice Elehwany d Howard Zieff ph Paul Elliott m James Newton Howard pd Joseph T. Garrity ed Wendy Green Bricmont

Dan Aykroyd, Jamie Lee Curtis, Macaulay Culkin, Anna Chlumsky, Richard Masur, Griffin Dunne, Ann Nelson

'As pleasant as a warm summer day and as ephemeral.' – *Variety*
'A hilarious mix of schmaltz, angst and shlock. In other words a joy to watch. One asks hopefully, it can't get worse, surely, can it? But it does.' – *Alexander Walker, London Evening Standard*

My Little Pony
US 1986 100m Technicolor
Sunbow/Hasbro

The inhabitants of Ponyland fear the wicked witch Hydia.

Immensely distended cartoon meant

to plug a fashionable line of children's dolls.

w George Arthur Bloom
d Michael Jones

† Animated in Japan.

My Pal Trigger

US 1946 79m bw
Armand Schaefer/Republic

A cowboy tracks down the man who killed his horse's sire.

Folksy Western drama, a cut above the usual Rogers episode.

w Jack Townley, John K. Butler
d Frank McDonald

Roy Rogers, Dale Evans, Jack Holt, George 'Gabby' Hayes, Roy Barcroft

Mysterious Island*

GB 1961 101m Technicolor
Columbia/Ameran (Charles Schneer)
L

Confederate officers escape by balloon and join shipwrecked English ladies on a strange island where they are menaced by prehistoric monsters and helped by Captain Nemo.

Rambling, lively juvenile adventure with good moments and excellent monsters.

w John Prebble, Dan Ullman, Crane Wilbur novel Jules Verne d Cy Endfield ph Wilkie Cooper
m Bernard Herrmann sp Ray Harryhausen

Joan Greenwood, Michael Craig, Herbert Lom, Michael Callan, Gary Merrill

† An early sound version was made by MGM in 1929, directed by Lucien Hubbard. Despite Technicolor and a cast which included Lionel Barrymore it was judged unsatisfactory, and concentrated less on stop-frame monsters than on the submarine elements ignored in the above but remade in *Captain Nemo and the Underwater City* (qv).

The Naked Gun: From the Files of Police Squad*

US 1988 85m Technicolor
UIP/Paramount (Robert K. Weiss)
V, L

A bungling detective foils attempts to assassinate the Queen in Los Angeles.

A barrage of gags, some good, some dreadful, is harnessed to a limp narrative. Not as funny as it should be.

w Jerry Zucker, Jim Abrahams, David Zucker, Pat Profit   d David Zucker   ph Robert Stevens   m Ira Newborn   pd John J. Lloyd   ed Michael Jablow

Leslie Nielsen, Priscilla Presley, Ricardo Montalban, George Kennedy, O. J. Simpson, Susan Beaubian, Nancy Marchand, Raye Birk, Jeannette Charles

'Quickly and efficiently establishes its pattern of wildly escalating absurdity within each scene, combined with a series of gags related to each character throughout the film.' – *Philip Strick, MFB*

Naked Gun 2½: The Smell of Fear

US 1991 85m Technicolor
UIP/Paramount/Zucker/Abrahams/Zucker (Robert K. Weiss)
V, L

A clumsy police lieutenant investigates an attempt to kill a solar energy expert.

The mixture as before, although this time around the slapstick comedy is enlivened with fewer good jokes.

w David Zucker, Pat Proft   d David Zucker   ph Robert Stevens   m Ira Newborn   pd John J. Lloyd   ed James Symons, Chris Greenbury

Leslie Nielsen, Priscilla Presley, George Kennedy, O.J. Simpson, Robert Goulet, Richard Griffiths, Jacqueline Brookes, Anthony James, Lloyd Bochner

'At least two-and-a-half times less funny than its hilarious progenitor.' – *Variety*
'An appealing rag-bag of the ribald and the ridiculous, showing only the slightest signs of running out of steam.' – *Philip Strick, Sight and Sound*

Nancy Drew

This series of second features starring Bonita Granville as a teenage small-town detective was moderately well received but quickly forgotten. The character was created in novels by Edward Stratemeyer and his daughter Harriet Evans; the films were all directed by William Clemens for Warner.

1938: NANCY DREW, DETECTIVE
1939: NANCY DREW, REPORTER; NANCY DREW, TROUBLE SHOOTER; NANCY DREW AND THE HIDDEN STAIRCASE

Napoleon and Samantha

US 1972 91m Technicolor
Walt Disney (Winston Hibler)

When his old guardian dies, a small boy and his girl friend run away with their pet lion.

Patchy, episodic action drama for older children, with a very sleepy lion.

w Stewart Raffil d Bernard McEveety ph Monroe Askins m Buddy Baker

Michael Douglas, Will Geer

AAN: Buddy Baker

National Lampoon's Christmas Vacation

US 1989 97m colour
Warner/Hughes Entertainment (John Hughes, Tom Jacobson)
V, L

A father decides to give the family an old-fashioned Christmas at home.

Unsubtle comedy that always goes for the easy laugh.

w John Hughes d Jeremiah S. Chechik ph Thomas Ackerman m Angelo Badalmenti pd Stephen Marsh ed Jerry Greenberg

Chevy Chase, Beverly D'Angelo, Randy Quaid, Diane Ladd, E. G. Marshall, Doris Roberts, Julia Louis-Dreyfus, Mae Questel, William Hickey

National Lampoon's European Vacation

US 1985 94m Technicolor
Warner (Matty Simmons)
V, L

An American family determines to see Europe.

Hopelessly unfunny and simple-minded comedy, lacking even the usual schoolboy smut.

w John Hughes, Robert Klane d Amy Heckerling ph Bob Paynter m Charles Fox pd Bob Cartwright ed Paul Herring

Chevy Chase, Beverly D'Angelo, Jason Lively, Dana Hill, Eric Idle

National Velvet*

US 1945 125m Technicolor
MGM (Pandro S. Berman)
V, L

Children train a horse to win the Grand National.

A big bestseller from another era; its flaws of conception and production quickly became evident.

w Theodore Reeves, Helen Deutsch novel Enid Bagnold d Clarence Brown ph Leonard Smith m Herbert Stothart ed Robert J. Kern

Mickey Rooney, Elizabeth Taylor, Anne Revere, Donald Crisp, Angela Lansbury, Jackie Jenkins, Reginald Owen, Terry Kilburn, Norma Varden, Alec Craig, Arthur Shields, Dennis Hoey

† Sequel 1978: *International Velvet*.

AA: Anne Revere; Robert J. Kern
AAN: Clarence Brown; Leonard Smith

The Navigator***

US 1924 63m approx (24 fps)
bw silent
Metro-Goldwyn/Buster Keaton (Joseph M. Schenck)
V

A millionaire and his girl are the only people on a transatlantic liner marooned in mid-ocean.

A succession of hilarious sight gags: the star in top form.

w Jean Havez, Clyde Bruckman, J. A. Mitchell   d Buster Keaton, Donald Crisp   ph Elgin Lessley, Byron Houck

Buster Keaton, Kathryn McGuire

'Studded with hilarious moments and a hundred and one adroit gags.' – *Photoplay*

Nearly a Nasty Accident
GB   1961   91m   bw
British Lion/Britannia/Marlow (Bertram Ostrer)

A mild-mannered aircraftman causes disaster wherever he goes.

Familiar faces just about save from disaster this underscripted comedy for indulgent audiences.

w Jack Davies, Hugh Woodruff   play *Touch Wood* by David Stringer, David Carr   d Don Chaffey   ph Paul Beeson   m Ken Jones

Kenneth Connor, Jimmy Edwards, Shirley Eaton, Richard Wattis, Ronnie Stevens, Jon Pertwee, Eric Barker, Peter Jones, Jack Watling, Joyce Carey, Terry Scott

Never a Dull Moment
US   1967   100m   Technicolor
Walt Disney (Ron Miller)
L

An unsuccessful actor is mistaken for a notorious gangster.

Slapstick romp with vigour but not much flair.

w A. J. Carothers   novel John Godey   d Jerry Paris   ph William Snyder   m Robert F. Brunner

Dick Van Dyke, Edward G. Robinson, Dorothy Provine, Henry Silva, Joanna Moore, Tony Bill, Slim Pickens, Jack Elam

'They thought he couldn't do the job: that's why they chose him!'
Never Cry Wolf
US   1983   105m   Technicolor
Walt Disney

A scientist is dumped alone in the Arctic to collect evidence against wolves.

Weird fable whose comic asides diminish its serious intent, and whose leading characterization is so eccentric as to bewilder any audience.

w Curtis Hanson, Sam Hamm, Richard Kletter   book Farley Mowat   d Carroll Ballard

Charles Martin Smith, Brian Dennehy, Samson Jorah

Never Say Never Again*
GB   1983   134m   Technicolor   Panavision
Warner/Woodcote/Taliafilm (Jack Schwartzman)
V

James Bond foils a world domination attempt by Blofeld.

Reasonably enjoyable mishmash of Bondery; the plot is technically a remake of *Thunderball*, not that it matters much until the end, when the underwater stuff becomes tiresome because one hardly knows who is under the masks.

w Lorenzo Semple Jnr   d Irvin Kershner   ph Douglas Slocombe   m Michel Legrand   pd Philip Harrison, Stephen Grimes

Sean Connery, Klaus Maria Brandauer, Max Von Sydow, Barbara Carrera, Kim Basinger, Bernie Casey, Alec McCowen, Edward Fox, Rowan Atkinson

'Q' (Alec McCowen): 'Good to see you again, Mr Bond. Let's get back to some gratuitous sex and violence, I say.'

Never Take No for an Answer*
GB 1951 82m bw
Constellation (Anthony Havelock-Allan)

A small boy goes to Rome to get permission from the Pope to take his sick donkey to be blessed in the church.

Slight, easy-going whimsy with attractive sunlit locations.

w Paul and Pauline Gallico novel *The Small Miracle* by Paul Gallico d Maurice Cloche, Ralph Smart ph Otto Heller m Nino Rota

Vittorio Manunta, Denis O'Dea, Guido Cellano, Nerio Bernardi

'The main pleasures of this slender film are visual ones.' – *MFB*

† Remade as a TV movie *Small Miracle*.

'A boy who needs a friend finds a world that needs a hero in a land beyond imagination!'

The Neverending Story*
West Germany 1984 94m Technicolor Technovision
Warner/Bavaria Studios/WDR/Neue Constantin Filmproduktion (Bernd Eichinger, Dieter Geissler)
V, L

A reluctant student reads a book instead: dealing with mystical monsters and make believe, it takes him back into their world.

Slow-starting fantasy with agreeable enough creations but not a lot of humour despite its intended stimulus to the imagination.

wd Wolfgang Petersen novel Michael Ende ph Jost Vacano m Klaus Doldinger, Giorgio Moroder pd Rolf Zehetbauer ed Jane Seitz

Barret Oliver, Gerald McRaney, Moses Gunn, Patricia Hayes

The Neverending Story II: The Next Chapter
Germany 1990 89m Eastmancolor Panavision
Warner/Soriba & Dehle (Dieter Geissler)
V, L

A boy and his fantasy alter-ego search for an imprisoned empress in a fairytale land of dreams.

Sequel that does little to expand the imagination.

w Karin Howard novel Michael Ende d George Miller ph Dave Connell m Robert Folk pd Bob Laing, Götz Weidner sp creature effects Colin Arthur ed Peter Hollywood, Chris Blunden

Jonathan Brandis, Kenny Morrison, Clarissa Burt, Alexandra Johnes, Martin Umbach, John Wesley Shiff, Helena Michell, Chris Burton, Thomas Hill

Newsboys' Home
US 1939 73m bw
Universal

A girl inherits a newspaper which sponsors a home for boys.

Modest debut for the East Side Kids, a spin-off group from the Dead End Kids.

w Gordon Kahn d Harold Young

Jackie Cooper, Edmund Lowe, Wendy Barrie, Edward Norris, Samuel S. Hinds; and Elisha Cook Jnr, Hally Chester, Harris Berger, David Gorcey, Billy Benedict, Charles Duncan

'Another in the tough kid cycle. Will easily handle its end of dual depots.' – *Variety*

Newsies

US 1992 121m Technicolor Panavision
Warner/Walt Disney/Touchwood Pacific Partners I (Michael Finnell)

In the 1890s news boys in New York call a strike when a newspaper publisher charges them more for his papers.

Unsuccessful attempt to create a youthful musical – the model seems to be *Oliver!* but it lacks any Dickensian dimension despite its subplot of the exploitation of child labour.

w Bob Tzudiker, Noni White d Kenny Ortega ph Andrew Laszlo m Alan Menken pd William Sandell ch Kenny Ortega, Peggy Holmes ed William Reynolds

Christian Bale, Bill Pullman, Ann-Margret, Robert Duvall, David Moscow, Ele Keats, Kevin Tighe, Luke Edwards

'With many catchy if forgettable ditties littered throughout, one is led to the inevitable conclusion that nine-year-old girls will just love it.' – *Angie Errigo, Empire*

Nicholas Nickleby**

GB 1947 108m bw
Ealing (John Croydon)
V

The adventures of a Victorian schoolmaster, deprived of his rightful fortune, who joins a band of travelling entertainers.

Quite tasteful and expert but too light-handed potted version of Dickens, which suffered by comparison with the David Lean versions.

w John Dighton novel Charles Dickens d Alberto Cavalcanti ph Gordon Dines m Lord Berners

Derek Bond, Cedric Hardwicke, Alfred Drayton, Sybil Thorndike, Stanley Holloway, James Hayter, Sally Ann Howes, Jill Balcon, Cyril Fletcher, Fay Compton

'Here's richness! Not all the novel, perhaps, but enough to make a film full of the Dickens spirit.' – *Star*

A Night at the Opera****

US 1935 96m bw
MGM (Irving Thalberg)
V, L

Three zanies first wreck, then help an opera company.

Certainly among the best of the Marxian extravaganzas, and the first to give them a big production to play with as well as musical interludes by other than themselves for a change of pace. The mix plays beautifully.

w George S. Kaufman, Morrie Ryskind d Sam Wood ph Merritt Gerstad md Herbert Stothart

Groucho, Chico, Harpo (Zeppo absented himself from here on), Margaret Dumont, Kitty Carlisle, Allan Jones, Walter Woolf King, Sig Rumann

'Corking comedy with the brothers at par and biz chances excellent . . . songs in a Marx picture are generally at a disadvantage because they're more or less interruptions, the customers awaiting the next laugh.' – *Variety*

Night Crossing

US 1982 106m Technicolor
Walt Disney (Tom Leetch)

East Germans escape to the west via air balloon.

Well-meaning melodrama which sadly lacks plot development and suspense, and is also rather miserable to look at.

w John McGreevey d Delbert Mann ph Tony Imi m Jerry Goldsmith

John Hurt, Jane Alexander, Doug McKeon, Frank McKeon, Beau Bridges, Glynnis O'Connor, Ian Bannen

A Night in Casablanca**
US 1946 85m bw
David L. Loew

Three zanies rout Nazi refugees in a North African hotel.

The last authentic Marxian extravaganza; it starts uncertainly, builds to a fine sustained frenzy, then peters out in some overstretched airplane acrobatics.

w Joseph Fields, Roland Kibbee, Frank Tashlin d Archie Mayo ph James Van Trees m Werner Janssen pd Duncan Cramer

Groucho, Chico, Harpo, Sig Rumann, Lisette Verea, Charles Drake, Lois Collier, Dan Seymour

KORNBLOW (Groucho Marx): 'I don't mind being killed, but I resent hearing it from a character whose head comes to a point.'

KORNBLOW: 'From now on the essence of this hotel will be speed. If a customer asks you for a three-minute egg, give it to him in two minutes. If he asks you for a two-minute egg, give it to him in one minute. If he asks you for a one-minute egg, give him the chicken and let him work it out for himself.'

BEATRICE (Lisette Verea): 'My name's Beatrice Ryner. I stop at the hotel.'

KORNBLOW: 'My name's Ronald Kornblow. I stop at nothing.'

'It is beside the main point to add that it isn't one of their best movies; for the worst they might ever make would be better worth seeing than most other things I can think of.' – *James Agee*

Night Owls*
US 1930 20m bw
Hal Roach

A policeman wanting to record an arrest bribes two tramps to burgle a house.

The stars at their most hilariously incompetent, unable even to get through a doorway efficiently.

w Leo McCarey, H. M. Walker d James Parrott

Laurel and Hardy, Edgar Kennedy, James Finlayson

Nikki, Wild Dog of the North*
US 1961 74m Technicolor
Walt Disney (Winston Hibler)

The life of a Canadian trapper's wolf dog.

Pleasing 'true life fiction' which didn't quite reach top feature status.

w Ralph Wright, Winston Hibler novel James Oliver Curwood d Jack Couffer m Oliver Wallace

Emile Genest, Jean Coutu

1941*
US 1979 118m Metrocolor
Panavision
Columbia/Universal/A-Team (John Milius)
V, L

Just after Pearl Harbor, a stray Japanese submarine terrorizes Hollywood.

Absurdly over-budgeted manic farce which substitutes noise for wit and slapstick for comedy; it fails on every level.

w Robert Zemeckis, Bob Gale
d Steven Spielberg   ph William A. Fraker   m John Williams
pd Dean Edward Mitzner

Dan Aykroyd, Ned Beatty, John Belushi, Lorraine Gary, Murray Hamilton, Christopher Lee, Tim Matheson, Toshiro Mifune, Warren Oates, Robert Stack, Elisha Cook Jnr

'So overloaded with visual humour of rather monstrous nature that the feeling emerges that once you've seen ten explosions, you've seen them all.' – *Variety*
'Aimed at young audiences, who deserve better fun.' – *New Yorker*
'Its sheer relentless physicality, its elaborately orchestrated pointlessness on every other level, make it probably the purest demonstration of what it means to have two of the all-time commercial blockbusters to one's record and one's hands firmly on the fantasy machine.' – *Richard Combs, MFB*
'Spielberg intended it as "a stupidly outrageous celebration of paranoia" ... audiences found it curiously unfunny and elephantine.' – *Les Keyser, Hollywood in the Seventies*
AAN: William A. Fraker

No Kidding
GB   1960   86m   bw
Peter Rogers/GHW/Anglo Amalgamated
US title: *Beware of Children*

An old house is turned into a holiday home for deprived rich children.

Strained comedy with agreeable cast.

w Norman Hudis, Robin Estridge
novel Verity Anderson   d Gerald Thomas

Leslie Phillips, Geraldine McEwan, Julia Lockwood, Noel Purcell, Irene Handl, Joan Hickson, Cyril Raymond

No Time for Sergeants
US   1958   111m   bw
Warner (Mervyn Le Roy)
L

Adventures of a hillbilly army conscript.

Heavy-handed adaptation of the stage success, a real piece of filmed theatre with not much sparkle to it.

w John Lee Mahin   play Ira Levin   novel Mac Hyman
d Mervyn Le Roy   ph Harold Rosson   m Ray Heindorf

Andy Griffith, William Fawcett, Murray Hamilton, Nick Adams, Myron McCormick, Bartlett Robinson

The Norseman
US   1978   90m   Movielab
AIP/Charles B. Pierce/Fawcett Majors

A Viking heads across the sea to America in search of his long lost father.

Low grade hokum for the easily pleased.

wd Charles B. Pierce   ph Robert Bethard   m Jaime Mendoza-Nava

Lee Majors, Cornel Wilde, Mel Ferrer, Jack Elam, Chris Connelly

Nothing but Trouble
US   1944   70m   bw
MGM (B. F. Ziedman)
V

A chef and butler accidentally prevent a poison plot against a young king.

Feebly-devised star comedy, their last for a big studio.

w Russel Rouse, Ray Golden

d Sam Taylor *ph* Charles Salerno Jnr *m* Nathaniel Shilkret

Stan Laurel, Oliver Hardy, Mary Boland, Henry O'Neill, David Leland

Now You See Him Now You Don't
US 1972 88m Technicolor
Walt Disney

Two students discover an elixir of invisibility and help prevent a gangster from taking over the college.

Flat Disney frolic with fair trick effects.

w Joseph L. McEveety *d* Robert Butler *ph* Frank Phillips *m* Robert F. Brunner *sp* Eustace Lycett, Danny Lee

Kurt Russell, Cesar Romero, Joe Flynn, Jim Backus, William Windom, Edward Andrews, Richard Bakalyan

Nuns on the Run
GB 1990 92m Technicolor
Palace/Handmade Films (Michael White)
V, L

Two petty criminals disguise themselves as nuns to escape capture.

Broad, slapstick comedy that provides scant amusement, although it went down well in America.

wd Jonathan Lynn *ph* Michael Garfath *m* Hidden Faces *pd* Simon Holland *ed* David Martin

Eric Idle, Robbie Coltrane, Camille Coduri, Janet Suzman, Doris Hare, Lila Kaye, Robert Patterson, Robert Morgan, Winston Dennis, Tom Hickey

Nutcracker – The Motion Picture*
US 1986 85m colour
Entertainment/Hyperion/Kushner/Locke
V

A movie based on the Pacific Northwest Ballet company's version of the classic ballet.

The restless and moody direction does not always do justice to the dancing, although it effectively conjures a slightly sinister atmosphere.

d Carroll Ballard *ph* Stephen M. Burum *m* Tchaikovsky *pd* Maurice Sendak *ed* John Nutt, Michael Silvers

Hugh Bigney, Vanessa Sharp, Patricia Barker, Wade Walthall

The Nutty Professor
US 1963 107m Technicolor
Paramount/Jerry Lewis (Ernest D. Glucksman)
L

An eccentric chemistry professor discovers an elixir which turns him into a pop idol.

Long dreary comedy which contains patches of its star at somewhere near his best; but even *Dr Jekyll and Mr Hyde* is funnier.

w Jerry Lewis, Bill Richmond *d* Jerry Lewis *ph* W. Wallace Kelley *m* Walter Scharf

Jerry Lewis, Stella Stevens, Howard Morris, Kathleen Freeman

O. C. and Stiggs
US 1987 109m Metrocolor
MGM (Robert Altman, Peter Newman)

Two teenagers spend their summer playing practical jokes, particularly on their obnoxious neighbour.

Tedious comedy with an air of desperate improvisation about it.

w Donald Cantrell, Ted Mann story Tod Carroll, Ted Mann d Robert Altman ph Pierre Mignot m King Sunny Ade and his African Beats pd Scott Bushnell ed Elizabeth Kling

Daniel H. Jenkins, Neill Barry, Paul Dooley, Jane Curtin, Jon Cryer, Ray Walston, Louis Nye, Tina Louise, Dennis Hopper, Melvin Van Peebles

Octopussy
GB 1983 131m Technicolor Panavision
Eon/Danjaq (Albert R. Broccoli)
V, L

James Bond takes on an evil Afghan prince and a glamorous woman who plan between them to plunder Tsarist treasures.

Bond at the end of his tether: such far-stretched adventures have become merely a tedious way of passing the time.

w George MacDonald Fraser, Richard Maibaum, Michael G. Wilson d John Glen ph Alan Hume m John Barry pd Peter Lamont

Roger Moore, Maud Adams, Louis Jourdan, Kristina Wayborn, Kabir Bedi, Desmond Llewelyn, Lois Maxwell

'As the films drift further and further into self-parody, no one seems to notice and no one (at any rate in box office terms) seems to mind.' – *Nick Roddick, MFB*

Odongo
GB 1956 85m Technicolor Cinemascope
Warwick/Columbia

A collector of animals for zoos runs into various kinds of trouble during an African safari.

Elementary jungle adventure centring on a small Sabu-like jungle boy. For the now extinct family audience.

wd John Gilling

Macdonald Carey, Rhonda Fleming, Juma, Eleanor Summerfield, Francis de Wolff, Earl Cameron

'It's an almighty laugh!'
Oh, God*
US 1977 104m Technicolor
Warner (Jerry Weintraub)
V, L

A bewildered supermarket manager is enlisted by God to prove to the world that it can only work if people try.

Overlong but generally amiable reversion to the supernatural farces of the forties: its success seems to show that people again need this kind of comfort.

w Larry Gelbart   novel Avery Corman   d Carl Reiner   ph Victor Kemper   m Jack Elliott

George Burns, John Denver, Ralph Bellamy, Donald Pleasence, Teri Garr, William Daniels, Barnard Hughes, Paul Sorvino, Barry Sullivan, Dinah Shore, Jeff Corey, David Ogden Stiers

'Undeniably funny and almost impossible to dislike.' – Tom Milne, MFB
'Basically a single-joke movie: George Burns is God in a football cap.' – Pauline Kael, New Yorker
AAN: Larry Gelbart

Oh God Book Two

US 1980 94m Technicolor
Warner (Gilbert Cates)
V

God enlists a child to remind people that he is still around.

Crass sequel with sentiment replacing jokes.

w Josh Greenfeld, Hal Goldman, Fred S. Fox, Seaman Jacobs, Melissa Miller   d Gilbert Cates   ph Ralph Woolsey   m Charles Fox   pd Preston Ames   ed Peter E. Bergher

George Burns, Suzanne Pleshette, David Birney, Louanne, Howard Duff, Hans Conried, Wilfrid Hyde White

Oh Mr Porter****

GB 1937 84m bw
GFD/Gainsborough (Edward Black)

The stationmaster of an Irish halt catches gun-runners posing as ghosts.

Marvellous star comedy showing this trio of comedians at their best, and especially Hay as the seedy incompetent. The plot is borrowed from *The Ghost Train*, but each line and gag brings its own inventiveness. A delight of character comedy and cinematic narrative.

w Marriott Edgar, Val Guest, J. O. C. Orton,   story Frank Launder   d Marcel Varnel   ph Arthur Crabtree   md Louis Levy

Will Hay, Moore Marriott, Graham Moffatt, Dave O'Toole, Dennis Wyndham

'That rare phenomenon: a film comedy without a dud scene.' – Peter Barnes, 1964
'Behind it lie the gusty uplands of the British music hall tradition, whose rich soil the British film industry is at last beginning to exploit.' – Basil Wright

'A picture straight from the heart of America!'

Oklahoma!**

US 1955 143m Technicolor Todd-AO
Magna/Rodgers and Hammerstein (Arthur Hornblow Jnr)
V, V(W), L

A cowboy wins his girl despite the intervention of a sinister hired hand.

Much of the appeal of the musical was in its simple timeworn story and stylized sets; the film makes the first merely boring and the latter are replaced by standard scenery, not even of Oklahoma. The result is efficient rather than startling or memorable.

w Sonya Levien, William Ludwig   book Oscar Hammerstein   play Green Grow the Rushes by Lynn Riggs   d Fred Zinnemann

ph Robert Surtees   *songs* Richard Rodgers, Oscar Hammerstein II
m Robert Russell Bennett, Jay Blackton, Adolph Deutsch
pd Oliver Smith   *ed* Gene Ruggiero, George Boemler

Gordon Macrae, Shirley Jones, Rod Steiger, Gloria Grahame, Charlotte Greenwood, Gene Nelson, Eddie Albert

AA: music score
AAN: Robert Surtees; editing

The Old Curiosity Shop*
GB   1934   95m   bw
BIP (Walter C. Mycroft)

The lives of a gambler and his granddaughter are affected by a miserly dwarf.

Heavy-going Dickens novel given reasonably rich production and well enough acted; sentimentality prevented a remake until the unsuccessful *Mister Quilp* (qv) in 1975.

w Margaret Kennedy, Ralph Neale   *novel* Charles Dickens   *d* Thomas Bentley   *ph* Claude Friese-Greene

Hay Petrie, Ben Webster, Elaine Benson, Beatrice Thompson, Gibb McLaughlin, Reginald Purdell, Polly Ward

Old Mother Riley

This Irish washerwoman with flailing arms and a nice line in invective was a music hall creation of Arthur Lucan, a variation of a pantomime dame. His wife Kitty Macshane played Mother Riley's daughter, and despite personal difficulties they were top of the bill for nearly 30 years. Their first film was *Stars on Parade*, a collection of music-hall acts, in 1935.

The films were very cheaply made and the padding is difficult to sit through, but Lucan at his best is a superb comedian: they were made for small independent companies such as Butcher's and usually directed by Maclean Rogers.

1937: OLD MOTHER RILEY
1938: OLD MOTHER RILEY IN PARIS
1939: OLD MOTHER RILEY MP, OLD MOTHER RILEY JOINS UP
1940: OLD MOTHER RILEY IN BUSINESS, OLD MOTHER RILEY'S GHOSTS
1941: OLD MOTHER RILEY'S CIRCUS
1942: OLD MOTHER RILEY IN SOCIETY
1943: OLD MOTHER RILEY DETECTIVE
1943: OLD MOTHER RILEY OVERSEAS
1944: OLD MOTHER RILEY AT HOME
1945: OLD MOTHER RILEY HEADMISTRESS
1947: OLD MOTHER RILEY'S NEW VENTURE
1949: OLD MOTHER RILEY'S JUNGLE TREASURE
1952: MOTHER RILEY MEETS THE VAMPIRE

Old Yeller*
US   1957   83m   Technicolor
Walt Disney

The love of a boy for his dog.

Archetypal family movie set in a remote rural area.

w Fred Gipson, William Tunberg   *novel* Fred Gipson   *d* Robert Stevenson   *ph* Charles P. Boyle   *m* Oliver Wallace

Dorothy McGuire, Fess Parker, Tommy Kirk, Kevin Corcoran, Jeff York, Chuck Connors

'Much much more than a musical!'
Oliver!***
GB 1968 146m Technicolor
Panavision 70
Columbia/Warwick/Romulus (John Woolf)

A musical version of *Oliver Twist*.

The last, perhaps, of the splendid film musicals which have priced themselves out of existence; it drags a little in spots but on the whole it does credit both to the show and the original novel, though eclipsed in style by David Lean's straight version.

w Vernon Harris   *play* Lionel Bart   *novel* Charles Dickens   d Carol Reed   ph Oswald Morris   md John Green   m Lionel Bart   pd John Box   ch Onna White   ed Ralph Kemplen

Ron Moody, Oliver Reed, Harry Secombe, Mark Lester, Shani Wallis, Jack Wild, Hugh Griffith, Joseph O'Conor, Leonard Rossiter, Hylda Baker, Peggy Mount, Megs Jenkins

'Only time will tell if it is a great film but it is certainly a great experience.' – *Joseph Morgenstern*
'There is a heightened discrepancy between the romping jollity with which everyone goes about his business and the actual business being gone about ... such narrative elements as the exploitation of child labour, pimping, abduction, prostitution and murder combine to make *Oliver!* the most non-U subject ever to receive a U certificate.' – *Jan Dawson*

AA: best picture; Carol Reed; John Green; Onna White; sound
AAN: Vernon Harris; Oswald Morris; Ron Moody; Jack Wild; costumes (Phyllis Dalton); editing

Oliver and Company*
US 1988 74m Metrocolor
Warner/Walt Disney/Silver Screen Partners III

A kitten becomes friends with a gang of criminal dogs and their human master.

Episodic film, short on charm, that only now and then provides glimpses of stylish animation.

w Jim Cox, Timothy J. Disney, James Mangold   *novel Oliver Twist* by Charles Dickens   d George Scribner   m J. A. C. Redford   ad Dan Hansen   ed Jim Melton, Mark Hester

voices of Joey Lawrence, Bill Joel, Cheech Marin, Richard Mulligan, Roscoe Lee Browne, Sheryl Lee Ralph, Dom DeLuise, Taurean Blacque, Carl Weintraub, Robert Loggia, Natalie Gregory, William Glover, Bette Midler

Oliver Twist****
GB 1948 116m bw
GFD/Cineguild (Ronald Neame)
V, L

A foundling falls among thieves but is rescued by a benevolent old gentleman.

Simplified, brilliantly cinematic version of a voluminous Victorian novel, beautiful to look at and memorably played, with every scene achieving the perfect maximum impact.

w David Lean, Stanley Haynes, *novel* Charles Dickens   d David Lean   ph Guy Green   m Arnold Bax   pd John Bryan

Alec Guinness, Robert Newton, Francis L. Sullivan, John Howard Davies, Kay Walsh, Anthony Newley, Henry

Stephenson, Mary Clare, Gibb
McLaughlin, Diana Dors

'A thoroughly expert piece of movie
entertainment.' – *Richard Winnington*
'A brilliant, fascinating movie, no less
a classic than the Dickens novel which
it brings to life.' – *Time*

Olly Olly Oxen Free
US 1978 93m Metrocolor
Rico Lion (Richard A. Colla)

A junkyard proprietress helps two
young children to launch a decrepit
hot-air balloon.

Simpleminded children's adventure
with a surprising star.

w Eugene Poinc   d Richard A.
Colla   ph Gayne Rescher   m Bob
Alcivar   pd Peter Wooley

Katharine Hepburn, Kevin McKenzie,
Dennis Dimster

'One thousand years ago, Omar Khayyam
was a poet, a scientist and military leader
so great that an army of Assassins
dedicated to world domination fell before
his genius!'

Omar Khayyam
US 1956 101m Technicolor
Vistavision
Paramount (Frank Freeman Jnr)

The Persian poet and philosopher
defends his Shah against the
Assassins.

Clean but dull Arabian Nights fantasy
with pantomime sets and no humour.

w Barre Lyndon   d William
Dieterle   ph Ernest Laszlo
m Victor Young

Cornel Wilde, Michael Rennie,
Raymond Massey, John Derek, Yma
Sumac, Sebastian Cabot, Debra Paget

On Her Majesty's Secret Service**
GB 1969 140m Technicolor
Panavision
UA/Eon/Danilaq (Harry Saltzman, Albert R.
Broccoli)
V, L

James Bond tracks down master
criminal Blofeld in Switzerland.

Perhaps to compensate for no Sean
Connery and a tragic ending, the
producers of this sixth Bond opus
shower largesse upon us in the shape
of no fewer than four protracted and
spectacular climaxes. Splendid stuff,
but too much of it, and the lack of a
happy centre does show.

w Richard Maibaum   novel Ian
Fleming   d Peter Hunt
ph Michael Reed, Egil Woxholt, Roy
Ford, John Jordan   m John
Barry   pd Syd Cain

George Lazenby, Diana Rigg, Telly
Savalas, Ilse Steppat, Gabriele
Ferzetti, Yuri Borienko, Bernard Lee,
Lois Maxwell

On the Beat
GB 1962 105m bw
Rank (Hugh Stewart)

A Scotland Yard car park attendant
manages to capture some crooks and
become a policeman.

Busy but flat comedy vehicle, never
very likeable.

w Jack Davies   d Robert Asher
ph Geoffrey Faithfull   m Philip
Green

Norman Wisdom, Jennifer Jayne,
Raymond Huntley, David Lodge

On the Buses
GB 1971 88m Technicolor
EMI/Hammer (Ronald Woolfe, Ronald
Chesney)
V

Women drivers cause trouble at a bus depot.

Grotesque, ham-handed farce from a TV series which was sometimes funny; this is merely vulgar.

w Ronald Woolfe, Ronald Chesney d Harry Booth
ph Mark MacDonald m Max Harris

Reg Varney, Doris Hare, Anna Karen, Michael Robbins, Stephen Lewis

† *Mutiny on the Buses* followed in 1972 and *Holiday on the Buses* in 1973. Both were deplorably witless.

On the Town****
US 1949 98m Technicolor
MGM (Arthur Freed)
V

Three sailors enjoy 24 hours' leave in New York.

Most of this brash location musical counts as among the best things ever to come out of Hollywood; the serious ballet towards the end tends to kill it, but it contains much to be grateful for.

w Betty Comden, Adolph Green, *ballet* Fancy Free by Leonard Bernstein d/ch Gene Kelly, Stanley Donen ph Harold Rosson
md Lennie Hayton, Roger Edens
songs various

Gene Kelly, Frank Sinatra, Jules Munshin, Vera-Ellen, Betty Garrett, Ann Miller, Tom Dugan, Florence Bates, Alice Pearce

'A film that will be enjoyed more than twice.' – *Lindsay Anderson*
'So exuberant that it threatens at moments to bounce right off the screen.' – *Time*
'The speed, the vitality, the flashing colour and design, the tricks of timing by which motion is fitted to music, the wit and invention and superlative technical accomplishment make it a really exhilarating experience.' – *Richard Mallett, Punch*

AA: Lennie Hayton, Roger Edens

Once Upon a Time*
US 1944 89m bw
Columbia (Louis Edelman)

A luckless producer makes a sensation out of a boy and his dancing caterpillar.

Thin whimsical comedy, too slight to come off given such standard treatment, but with nice touches along the way.

w Lewis Meltzer, Oscar Saul *radio play* My Client Curley by Norman Corwin, Lucille F. Herrmann
d Alexander Hall ph Franz Planer m Frederick Hollander

Cary Grant, Janet Blair, James Gleason, Ted Donaldson, Howard Freeman, William Demarest, Art Baker, John Abbott

'There just isn't enough material here for a full-length feature.' – *Philip T. Hartung*
'It would be nice to see some screen fantasy if it were done by anyone with half a heart, mind and hand for it. But when the studios try to make it, duck and stay hid till the mood has passed.' – *James Agee*

The One and Only Genuine Original Family Band
US 1968 110m Technicolor
Disney

Adventures of a Republican family at the 1888 convention.

Long and rather muddled family comedy with politics and music; not a winner anywhere.

w Lowell S. Hawley book Laura

Bower Van Nuys d Michael O'Herlihy

Walter Brennan, Buddy Ebsen, John Davidson, Lesley Ann Warren, Janet Blair, Kurt Russell, Richard Deacon

One Good Turn
GB 1954 90m bw
GFD/Two Cities (Maurice Cowan)

An orphan stays on to become an odd job man, and tries to raise money to buy an old car.

The star's second comedy is an almost unmitigated disaster, disjointed and depending too much on pathos.

w Maurice Cowan, John Paddy Carstairs, Ted Willis d John Paddy Carstairs ph Jack Cox m John Addison

Norman Wisdom, Joan Rice, Shirley Abicair, Thora Hird, William Russell, Richard Caldicot

One Hundred and One Dalmatians***
US 1961 79m Technicolor
Walt Disney

The dogs of London help save puppies which are being stolen for their skins by a cruel villainess.

Disney's last really splendid feature cartoon, with the old flexible style cleverly modernized and plenty of invention and detail in the story line. The London backgrounds are especially nicely judged.

w Bill Peet novel Dodie Smith
d Wolfgang Reitherman, Hamilton S. Luske, Clyde Geronimi m George Bruns

voices of Rod Taylor, Cate Bauer, Betty Lou Gerson, J. Pat O'Malley

'It has the freshness of the early short colour-cartoons without the savagery which has often disfigured the later feature-length stories.' – *Dilys Powell*

One Hundred Men and a Girl***
US 1937 84m bw
Universal (Joe Pasternak)

A young girl persuades a great conductor to form an orchestra of unemployed musicians.

Delightful and funny musical fable, an instance of the Pasternak formula of sweetness and light at its richest and best.

w Bruce Manning, Charles Kenyon, Hans Kraly d Henry Koster
ph Joseph Valentine m Charles Previn songs various ed Bernard W. Burton

Deanna Durbin, Adolphe Menjou, Leopold Stokowski, Alice Brady, Mischa Auer, Eugene Pallette, Billy Gilbert, Alma Kruger, Jed Prouty, Frank Jenks, Christian Rub

'Smash hit for all the family . . . something new in entertainment.' – *Variety*
'Apart from its value as entertainment, which is considerable, it reveals the cinema at its sunny-sided best.' – *New York Times.*
'An original story put over with considerable skill.' – *MFB*

AA: Charles Previn
AAN: best picture; original story (Hans Kraly); editing

One in a Million**
US 1936 94m bw
TCF (Raymond Griffith)

The daughter of a Swiss innkeeper becomes an Olympic ice-skating champion.

Sonja Henie's film debut shows Hollywood at its most professional, making entertainment out of the purest moonshine with considerable injections of novelty talent.

w Leonard Praskins, Mark Kelly d Sidney Lanfield ph Edward Cronjager md Louis Silvers songs Sidney Mitchell, Lew Pollack ch Jack Haskell

Sonja Henie, Don Ameche, The Ritz Brothers, Jean Hersholt, Ned Sparks, Arline Judge, Dixie Dunbar, Borrah Minnevitch and his Rascals, Montagu Love

'A very entertaining, adroitly mixed concoction of romance, music, comedy and skating ... Miss Henie is a screen find.' – *Variety*
AAN: Jack Haskell

One Little Indian
US 1973 91m Technicolor
Walt Disney (Winston Hibler)

A cavalry corporal escapes from jail and falls in with a ten-year-old Indian.

Sentimental semi-Western, a bit dull for Disney apart from a camel.

w Harry Spalding d Bernard McEveety ph Charles F. Wheeler m Jerry Goldsmith

James Garner, Vera Miles, Pat Hingle, Morgan Woodward, John Doucette

One Magic Christmas
Canada 1985 88m DeLuxe
Silver Screen/Telefilm Canada/Walt Disney (Peter O'Brian, Fred Roos)

An angel interferes in the lives of a family with problems.

Decidedly downbeat Christmas fantasy: daddy gets drowned, mother is a nut, and the angel looks like a tramp. Santa Claus puts in an appearance for a happy finale, but *It's a Wonderful Life* should sue for plagiarism.

w Thomas Meecham d Philip Borsos ph Frank Tidy m Michael Conway pd Bill Brodie ed Sidney Wolinksy

Mary Steenburgen, Gary Basaraba, Harry Dean Stanton, Arthur Hill

'This is the way it was!'
One Million Years BC*
GB 1966 100m Technicolor
Hammer (Michael Carreras)
V

A vague remake of a 1940 film, with animated monsters.

Not badly done, with some lively action.

w Michael Carreras d Don Chaffey ph Wilkie Cooper m Mario Nascimbene

John Richardson, Raquel Welch, Robert Brown, Percy Herbert, Martine Beswick

'Very easy to dismiss the film as a silly spectacle; but Hammer production finesse is much in evidence and Don Chaffey has done a competent job of direction. And it is all hugely enjoyable.' – *David Wilson*

One of Our Dinosaurs Is Missing*
US 1975 94m Technicolor
Walt Disney (Bill Walsh)

In the 1920s a strip of secret microfilm is smuggled out of China and hidden in a dinosaur's skeleton in the Natural History Museum.

Unexceptional family comedy with everyone trying hard; somehow it just misses, perhaps because it is told through talk rather than cinematic narrative.

w Bill Walsh novel The Great

Dinosaur Robbery by David Forrest
d Robert Stevenson *ph* Paul Beeson *m* Ron Goodwin

Helen Hayes, Peter Ustinov, Derek Nimmo, Clive Revill, Joan Sims, Bernard Bresslaw, Roy Kinnear, Deryck Guyler, Richard Pearson

Ooh, You Are Awful*

GB 1972 97m Eastmancolor
British Lion/Quintain (E. M. Smedley Aston)
V
US title: *Get Charlie Tully*

A London con man seeks a fortune, the clue to which is tattooed on the behind of one of several girls.

Amusing star vehicle with plenty of room for impersonations and outrageous jokes.

w John Warren, John Singer
d Cliff Owen *ph* Ernest Stewart
m Christopher Gunning

Dick Emery, Derren Nesbitt, Ronald Fraser, Pat Coombs, William Franklyn, Brian Oulton, Norman Bird

The Optimists of Nine Elms*

GB 1973 110m Eastmancolor
Cheetah/Sagittarius (Adrian Gaye, Victor Lyndon)

Children of a London slum make friends with an old busker.

Gentle, sentimental, quite well-observed piece of wistful melancholia, falsified by its star performance.

wd Anthony Simmons, *co-w* Tudor Gates *novel* Anthony Simmons
ph Larry Pizer *m* George Martin

Peter Sellers, Donna Mullane, John Chaffey, David Daker, Marjorie Yates

The Oracle

GB 1952 83m bw
Group Three (Colin Lesslie)
US title: *The Horse's Mouth*

A reporter discovers that a village well in Ireland contains an oracle which can predict the future.

Weak sub-Ealing comedy which aims to please and gets a few laughs. All very British.

w Patrick Campbell *d* C. M. Pennington-Richards *ph* Wolfgang Suschitzky *m* Temple Abady

Robert Beatty, Virginia McKenna, Mervyn Johns, Gilbert Harding

Orca – Killer Whale

US 1977 92m Technicolor Panavision
Famous Films/Dino de Laurentiis (Luciano Vincenzoni)
V, L

Off Newfoundland, a killer whale takes revenge for its mate's death.

A rather unpleasant attempt to mix horror and thrills with ecology: not very entertaining, and not for the squeamish.

w Luciano Vincenzoni, Sergio Donati *d* Michael Anderson
ph Ted Moore, J. Barry Herron
m Ennio Morricone

Richard Harris, Charlotte Rampling, Will Sampson, Keenan Wynn

'The biggest load of cod imaginable.' – *Philip Bergson, Sunday Times*
'There are more thrills to be had in the average dolphinarium.' – *Sight and Sound*

Oscar

US 1991 109m Technicolor
Warner/Touchstone/Silver Screen Partners IV (Leslie Belzberg)
V, L

A gangster who is trying to reform attempts to sort out the marital problems of his daughters.

Leaden attempt at a screwball comedy, and one that sinks under its own witlessness.

w Michael Barrie, Jim Mulholland play Claude Magnier d John Landis ph Mac Ahlberg m Elmer Bernstein pd Bill Kenney ed Dale Beldin, Michael R. Miller

Sylvester Stallone, Ornella Muti, Kirk Douglas, Peter Riegert, Chazz Palminteri, Vincent Spano, Marisa Tomei, Tim Curry, Don Ameche, Yvonne DeCarlo, Linda Gray

'Zany farce generates a fair share of laughs but still probably remains too creaky a conceit for modern audiences to go for in a big way.' – *Variety*

† Magnier's play was first filmed in France in 1967, directed by Eduardo Molinaro and starring Louis de Funes.

Our Little Girl
US 1935 63m bw
Fox (Edward Butcher)

A doctor's daughter brings her parents together.

One of the child star's thinner and more sentimental vehicles.

w Stephen Morehouse Avery, Allen Rivkin, Jack Yellen story *Heaven's Gate* by Florence Leighton Pfalzgraf d John Robertson ph John Seitz md Oscar Bradley

Shirley Temple, Joel McCrea, Rosemary Ames, Lyle Talbot, Erin O'Brien-Moore

'She should easily satisfy her following and assure business.' – *Variety*

Our Relations***
US 1936 65m bw
Hal Roach/Stan Laurel Productions
V, V(C), L

Two sailors entrusted with a diamond ring get mixed up with their long lost and happily married twin brothers.

A fast-moving comedy which contains some of Laurel and Hardy's most polished work as well as being their most satisfying production.

w Richard Connell, Felix Adler, Charles Rogers, Jack Jevne story *The Money Box* by W. W. Jacobs d Harry Lachman ph Rudolph Maté

Stan Laurel, Oliver Hardy, James Finlayson, Alan Hale, Sidney Toler, Daphne Pollard, Iris Adrian, Noel Madison, Ralf Harolde, *Arthur Housman*

Our Wife*
US 1931 20m bw
Hal Roach

Stan helps Ollie to elope.

Good standard star comedy with a rather disappointing third sequence as three people try to get into a car designed for one.

w H. M. Walker d James W. Horne

Laurel and Hardy, James Finlayson, Jean London

The Outsiders
US 1983 91m Technicolor Panavision
Zoetrope/Warner
V, L

A young punk leads a high school gang against another rather higher in the social scale.

Oddball youth melodrama, a curious choice for a director with big successes behind him.

w Katherine Knutsen Rowell novel S. E. Hinton d Francis Ford Coppola

Matt Dillon, Ralph Macchio, C. Thomas Howell, Patrick Swayze, Rob Lowe, Emilio Estevez, Tom Cruise

'No more than a well-acted teen film.' – Motion Picture Guide

Overboard

US 1987 112m colour
UIP/MGM (Alexandra Rose, Anthea Sylbert)
V, L

An heiress suffering from amnesia is claimed as a wife by a carpenter with three kids.

Mild amusement is provided by a predictable comedy.

w Leslie Dixon d Garry Marshall ph John A. Alonzo m Alan Silvestri ad James Shanahan, Jim Dultz ed Dov Hoenig, Sonny Baskin

Goldie Hawn, Kurt Russell, Edward Herrmann, Katherine Helmond, Roddy McDowall, Michael Hagerty, Jeffrey Wiseman

The Overlanders**

Australia 1946 91m bw
Ealing (Ralph Smart)

In 1943 a drover saves a thousand head of cattle from the Japanese by taking them two thousand miles across country.

Attractive, easy-going semi-Western, the first and best of several films made by Ealing Studios in Australia.

wd Harry Watt ph Osmond Borradaile m John Ireland

Chips Rafferty, John Heyward, Daphne Campbell

Owd Bob*

GB 1938 78m bw
GFD/Gainsborough (Edward Black)
US title: *To the Victor*

A Cumberland farmer's faithful dog is accused of killing sheep.

Sentimental yarn with good location backgrounds; the plot was later reused as *Thunder in the Valley*.

w Michael Hogan, J. B. Williams novel Alfred Olivant d Robert Stevenson ph Jack Cox md Louis Levy

Will Fyffe, John Loder, Margaret Lockwood, Moore Marriott, Graham Moffatt, Wilfred Walter, Elliot Mason

P

Pack Up Your Troubles*
US 1931 68m bw
Hal Roach
V

Two World War I veterans try to look after their late pal's orphan daughter.

Patchy comedy vehicle in which too many gags are not fully thought out or timed.

w H. M. Walker   d George Marshall, Ray McCarey   ph Art Lloyd

Stan Laurel, Oliver Hardy, Donald Dillaway, Mary Carr, Charles Middleton, Dick Cramer, James Finlayson, Tom Kennedy, Billy Gilbert

'Ben and pardner shared everything – even their wife!'

Paint Your Wagon*
US 1969 164m Technicolor
 Panavision 70
Paramount/Alan Jay Lerner (Tom Shaw)
V, V(W), L

During the California Gold Rush, two prospectors set up a Mormon menage with the same wife.

Good-looking but uncinematic and monumentally long version of an old musical with a new plot and not much dancing. There are minor pleasures, but it really shouldn't have been allowed.

w Paddy Chayevsky   musical play Alan Jay Lerner, Frederick Loewe   d Joshua Logan
ph William A. Fraker   md Nelson Riddle   pd John Truscott

Lee Marvin, Clint Eastwood, Jean Seberg, Harve Presnell, Ray Walston

'One of those big movies in which the themes are undersized and the elements are juggled around until nothing fits together right and even the good bits of the original show you started with are shot to hell.' – *Pauline Kael*
AAN: Nelson Riddle

The Pajama Game*
US 1957 101m Warnercolor
Warner/George Abbott
V, L

Workers in a pajama factory demand a pay rise, but their lady negotiator falls for the new boss.

Brilliantly conceived musical on an unlikely subject, effectively concealing its Broadway origins and becoming an expert, fast-moving, hard-hitting piece of modern musical cinema.

w George Abbott, Richard Bissell, book *Seven and a Half Cents* by Richard Bissell   d Stanley Donen,
ph Harry Stradling   songs Richard Adler, Jerry Ross   ch Bob Fosse

Doris Day, John Raitt, Eddie Foy Jnr, Reta Shaw, Carol Haney

The Paleface***
US 1948 91m Technicolor
Paramount (Robert L. Welch)

Calamity Jane undertakes an undercover mission against desperadoes, and marries a timid dentist as a cover.

Splendid wagon train comedy Western with the stars in excellent form.

w Edmund Hartman, Frank Tashlin d Norman Z. McLeod ph Ray Rennahan m Victor Young

Bob Hope, Jane Russell, Robert Armstrong, Iris Adrian, Robert Watson, Jack Searle, Joe Vitale, Clem Bevans, Charles Trowbridge

† Sequel: *Son of Paleface* (qv); remake, *The Shakiest Gun in the West* (1968).

AA: song 'Buttons and Bows' (m Jay Livingston, ly Ray Evans)

The Paper Chase**
US 1973 111m DeLuxe Panavision
TCF (Robert C. Thompson, Rodrick Paul)
L

A Harvard law graduate falls in love with the divorced daughter of his tetchiest professor.

A thoughtful analysis of attitudes to learning turns into just another youth movie.

wd James Bridges novel John Jay Osborn Jnr ph Gordon Willis m John Williams

Timothy Bottoms, Lindsay Wagner, John Houseman, Graham Bickel

'A slightly unfocused account of conformism and milk-mild rebellion on the campus.' – *Sight and Sound*
'A worthy film which engages the eye and the brain.' – *Benny Green, Punch*

AA: John Houseman
AAN: James Bridges (as writer)

'As P. T. Barnum put it, "There's a sucker born every minute".'

Paper Moon**
US 1973 103m bw
Paramount/Saticoy (Peter Bogdanovich)

In the American midwest in the thirties, a bible salesman and a plain little girl make a great con team.

Unusual but overrated comedy, imperfectly adapted from a very funny book, with careful but disappointing period sense and photography. A lot more style and gloss was required.

w Alvin Sargent novel *Addie Pray* by *Joe David Brown* d Peter Bogdanovich ph Laszlo Kovacs m popular songs and recordings

Ryan O'Neal, Tatum O'Neal, Madeline Kahn, John Hillerman

'I've rarely seen a film that looked so unlike what it was about.' – *Stanley Kauffmann*
'At its best the film is only mildly amusing, and I'm not sure I could recall a few undeniable highlights if pressed on the point.' – *Gary Arnold*
'Bogdanovich once again deploys the armoury of nostalgia with relentless cunning to evoke the threadbare side of American life forty years ago ... one of those rare movies which engages at least two of the senses.' – *Benny Green, Punch*
'It is so enjoyable, so funny, so touching that I couldn't care less about its morals.' – *Daily Telegraph*

AA: Tatum O'Neal
AAN: Alvin Sargent; Madeline Kahn

Paper Tiger
GB 1975 99m Technicolor
Maclean and Co (Euan Lloyd)
V

An ageing Englishman becomes tutor to the son of the Japanese ambassador in a Pacific state, and finds he has to live his heroic fantasies in reality.

Uneasy adventure comedy drama which might, given more skilled handling, have been much better than it is.

w Jack Davies   d Ken Annakin
ph John Cabrera   m Roy Budd

David Niven, Toshiro Mifune, Hardy Kruger, Ando, Ivan Desny, Irene Tsu, Miiko Taka, Ronald Fraser, Jeff Corey

'Makes no demands, except on 99 minutes of our time.' – *Michael Billington, Illustrated London News*

Parade*
France/Sweden   1974   85m Technicolor
Gray Film/Sveriges Radio

Jacques Tati introduces a series of acts in a small-scale circus.

Pleasant, sometimes boring variety show, to be included in the Tati canon for completeness; it does include some of his unique pieces of mime.

wd Jacques Tati

'A curious, unresolved *envoi*.' – *John Pym, MFB*
'Moments of great good humour and flashes of incomparable magic.' – *Sight and Sound*

Paradise*
US   1991   110m   Technicolor
Buena Vista/Touchstone/Touchwood Pacific Partners I/Interscope/Jean-François Lepetit (Scott Kroopf, Patrick Palmer)

A ten-year-old boy makes friends with a young girl when he goes to spend the summer with a childless couple.

Sentimentality is kept at bay for the most part and charm predominates in a gently effective narrative.

wd Mary Agnes Donoghue
ph Jerzy Zielinksi   m David Newman   pd Evelyn Sakash, Marcia Hinds   ed Eva Gardos, Debra McDermott

Melanie Griffith, Don Johnson, Elijah Wood, Thora Birch, Sheila McCarthy, Eve Gordon, Louis Latham, Greg Travis, Sarah Trigger, Richard K. Olsen

'Excellent ensemble acting and a feel-good payoff to this bittersweet tale could produce a sleeper hit.' – *Variety*

† A remake of *Le Grand Chemin* (qv), directed in 1987 by Jean-Loup Hubert.

Les Parapluies de Cherbourg**
France/West Germany   1964   92m   Eastmancolor
Parc/Madeleine/Beta
aka: *The Umbrellas of Cherbourg*

A shopgirl loves a gas station attendant. He goes on military service; she finds she is pregnant and marries for security. Years later they meet briefly by accident.

Unexpected, charming, pretty successful screen operetta with only sung dialogue. Careful acting and exquisite use of colour and camera movement paste over the thinner sections of the plot.

wd Jacques Demy   ph Jean Rabier
m Michel Legrand, Jacques Demy
ad Bernard Evein

Catherine Deneuve, Anne Vernon, Nino Castelnuovo

'Poetic neo-realism.' – *Georges Sadoul*
'We are told that in Paris the opening night audience wept and the critics were ecstatic. It would have made a

little more sense the other way round.' – *John Simon*
AAN: best foreign film; script; Michel Legrand, Jacques Demy; song 'I Will Wait for You'; scoring

Pardners
US 1956 88m Technicolor Vistavision
Paramount (Paul Jones)

An incompetent idiot goes west and accidentally cleans up the town.

Stiff Western star burlesque, a remake of *Rhythm on the Range*.

w Sidney Sheldon *d* Norman Taurog *ph* Daniel Fapp *songs* Sammy Cahn, Jimmy Van Heusen

Dean Martin, Jerry Lewis, Agnes Moorehead, Lori Nelson, John Baragrey, Jeff Morrow, Lon Chaney Jnr

Pardon Us*
US 1931 55m bw
Hal Roach
V, V(C), L
aka: *Jailbirds*

Two zany bootleggers find themselves in and out of prison.

Patchy star comedy which finds the boys on the whole not in quite their best form.

w H. M. Walker *d* James Parrott *ph* Jack Stevens

Stan Laurel, Oliver Hardy, Wilfred Lucas, Walter Long, James Finlayson

'Their first full-length, with not over two reels of value.' – *Variety*

The Parent Trap*
US 1961 129m Technicolor
Walt Disney (George Golitzen)

Twin daughters of separated parents determine to bring the family together again.

Quite bright but awesomely extended juvenile romp.

wd David Swift *novel Das Doppelte Lottchen* by Erich Kästner *ph* Lucien Ballard *m* Paul Smith

Hayley Mills, Maureen O'Hara, Brian Keith, Charles Ruggles, Leo G. Carroll, Una Merkel, Joanna Barnes, Cathleen Nesbitt, Ruth McDevitt, Nancy Kulp

The Party*
US 1968 98m DeLuxe Panavision
UA/Mirisch/Geoffrey (Blake Edwards)
L

An accident-prone Indian actor is accidentally invited to a swank Hollywood party and wrecks it.

Would-be Tatiesque comedy of disaster, occasionally well-timed but far too long for all its gloss.

w Blake Edwards, Tom and Frank Waldman *d* Blake Edwards *ph* Lucien Ballard *m* Henry Mancini *pd* Fernando Carrere

Peter Sellers, Claudine Longet, Marge Champion, Fay McKenzie, Steve Franken, Buddy Lester

'One thing the old movie makers did know is that two reels is more than enough of this stuff.' – *Wilfred Sheed*
'It is only rarely that one laughs or even smiles; mostly one just chalks up another point for ingenuity.' – *Tom Milne*

Passport to Pimlico****
GB 1949 84m bw
Ealing (E. V. H. Emmett)

Part of a London district is discovered to belong to Burgundy, and the inhabitants find themselves free of rationing restrictions.

A cleverly detailed little comedy which inaugurated the best period of Ealing, its preoccupation with suburban man and his foibles. Not exactly satire, but great fun, and kindly with it.

w T. E. B. Clarke d Henry Cornelius ph Lionel Banes m Georges Auric

Stanley Holloway, *Margaret Rutherford*, Basil Radford, Naunton Wayne, Hermione Baddeley, John Slater, Paul Dupuis, Jane Hylton, Raymond Huntley, Betty Warren, Barbara Murray, Sidney Tafler

† The film was based on a genuine news item. The Canadian government presented to the Netherlands the room in which Princess Juliana was to bear a child.
AAN: T. E. B. Clarke

Pathfinder**

Norway 1987 86m colour
Guild/Filmkameratene/Norsk Film (John M. Jacobson)
V, L
original title: *Ofelas*

A gang of ruthless raiders capture a 16-year-old boy and force him to lead them to his village so that they may plunder it.

Based on an ancient Lapp folk-tale, this is a simple, direct, marvellously exciting adventure shot in a snow- and ice-bound landscape.

wd Nils Gaup ph Erling Thurmann-Andersen m Nils-Aslak Valkeapaa pd Harald Egede-Nissen ed Niels Pagh Andersen

Mikkel Gaup, Nils Utsi, Svein Scharffenberg, Helgi Skulason, Sverre Porsanger, Svein Birger Olsen

AAN: best foreign film

Peck's Bad Boy

US 1934 70m bw
Sol Lesser/Fox

Adventures of a well-intentioned but accident-prone boy in a midwestern town.

Old-fashioned American juvenile classic, modestly well done.

w Bernard Schubert, Marguerite Roberts story G. W. Peck d Edward Cline

Jackie Cooper, Jackie Searle, Dorothy Peterson, Thomas Meighan

† Previously made in 1921 with Jackie Coogan. Cline also directed a sequel, *Peck's Bad Boy with the Circus* starring Tommy Kelly, in 1938.

Pee-wee's Big Adventure*

US 1985 92m colour
Mainline/Aspen Film Society/Robert Shapiro
V, L

Pee-wee Herman loses his red bicycle and goes looking for it.

Starring an American TV comedian who acts like a small child, this offbeat, episodic comedy has some amusing moments.

w Phil Hartman, Paul Reubens, Michael Varhol d Tim Burton ph Victor J. Kemper m Danny Elfman pd David L. Snyder ed Billy Weber

Paul Reubens, Elizabeth Daily, Mark Holton, Diane Salinger, Judd Omen, Jon Harris, Carmen Filpi, Tony Bill, James Brolin, Morgan Fairchild

'This slapstick fantasy has the bouncing-along inventiveness of a good cartoon.' – *Pauline Kael, New Yorker*

The People That Time Forgot

GB 1977 90m Technicolor
AIP/Amicus (John Dark)

Major McBride tries to rescue his old friend from a prehistoric island on which he disappeared in 1916.

Tepid sequel to *The Land That Time Forgot*: even the dinosaurs don't rise to the occasion.

w Patrick Tilley d Kevin Connor ph Alan Hume m John Scott pd Maurice Carter

Patrick Wayne, Sarah Douglas, Dana Gillespie, Doug McClure, Thorley Walters, Shane Rimmer, Tony Britton

Pepe

US 1960 195m Eastmancolor Cinemascope
Columbia/George Sidney (Jacques Gelman)

A Mexican peasant in Hollywood gets help from the stars.

Feeble and seemingly endless extravaganza in which the boring stretches far outnumber the rest, and few of the guests have anything worthwhile to do.

w Dorothy Kingsley, Claude Binyon d George Sidney ph Joe MacDonald md Johnny Green ed Viola Lawrence, Al Clark

Cantinflas, Dan Dailey, Shirley Jones, Ernie Kovacs, Jay North, William Demarest, Michael Callan, Maurice Chevalier, Bing Crosby, Richard Conte, Bobby Darin, Sammy Davis Jnr, Jimmy Durante, Zsa Zsa Gabor, Judy Garland, Hedda Hopper, Joey Bishop, Peter Lawford, Janet Leigh, Jack Lemmon, Kim Novak, André Previn, Donna Reed, Debbie Reynolds, Greer Garson, Edward G. Robinson, Cesar Romero, Frank Sinatra, Billie Burke, Tony Curtis, Dean Martin, Charles Coburn

AAN: Joe MacDonald; Johnny Green; song 'Faraway Part of Town' (*m* André Previn, *ly* Dory Langdon); editing

Perfect Day*

US 1929 20m bw
Hal Roach
V

Various problems delay a family's departure for a picnic.

Technically a most adept star comedy but its repetition can annoy.

w Hal Roach, Leo McCarey, H. M. Walker d James Parrott

Laurel and Hardy, Edgar Kennedy

† The picnic was originally to have occupied the second reel, but the departure gags swelled to occupy the entire footage.

The Perils of Pauline*

US 1947 96m Technicolor
Paramount (Sol C. Siegel)

The career of silent serial queen Pearl White.

An agreeable recreation of old time Hollywood, with plenty of slapstick chases but a shade too much sentiment also.

w P. J. Wolfson d George Marshall ph Ray Rennahan md Robert Emmett Dolan

Betty Hutton, John Lund, Billy de Wolfe, William Demarest, Constance Collier, Frank Faylen, William Farnum, Paul Panzer, Snub Pollard, Creighton Hale, Chester Conklin, James Finlayson, Hank Mann, Bert Roach, Francis McDonald, Chester Clute

'People who can accept such stuff as solid gold have either forgotten a lot, or never knew first-rate slapstick

when they saw it, twenty or thirty years ago, when it was one of the wonders of the world.' – *James Agee*
AAN: song 'I Wish I Didn't Love You So' (m/ly Frank Loesser)

Perri**

US 1957 75m Technicolor
Walt Disney (Winston Hibler)

The life of a squirrel.

Disney's first True Life Fantasy, in which live footage of animals is manipulated against artificial backgrounds to produce an effect as charming and unreal as a cartoon.

w Ralph Wright, Winston Hibler *novel* Felix Salten   d Ralph Wright   ph various   m Paul Smith

AAN: Paul Smith

Peter Pan***

US 1953 76m Technicolor
Walt Disney

Three London children are taken into fairyland by a magic flying boy who cannot grow up.

Solidly crafted cartoon version of a famous children's play; not Disney's best work, but still miles ahead of the competition.

supervisor Ben Sharpsteen
d Wilfred Jackson, Clyde Geronimi, Hamilton Luske   m Oliver Wallace

voices of Bobbie Driscoll, Kathryn Beaumont, Hans Conried, Bill Thompson, Heather Angel

Pete's Dragon

US 1977 127m Technicolor
Walt Disney (Ron Miller, Jerome Courtland)
V

In Maine in 1900, a nine-year-old boy escapes from grasping foster-parents with his pet dragon, which no one but himself can see.

A kind of juvenile rewrite of *Harvey*. The dragon is drawn (rather poorly) and the human characters are not exactly three-dimensional. A long way from *Mary Poppins*.

w Malcolm Marmorstein *story* Seton I. Miller, S. S. Field   d Don Chaffey   ph Frank Phillips   *animation* Ken Anderson   md Irwin Kostal *songs* Al Kasha, Joel Hirschhorn ch Onna White

Sean Marshall, Mickey Rooney, Jim Dale, Helen Reddy, Red Buttons, Shelley Winters, Jim Backus, Joe E. Ross, Ben Wrigley

'For a Disney film it's terribly badly made, in parts so clumsy that it looks like the work of the Burbank Amateur Camera Club.' – *Barry Took, Punch*
AAN: music; song 'Candle on the Water'

La Petite Bande**

France 1983 91m colour
Squirrel/Gaumont-Stand'Art/FR3/Hamster Productions (Denis Mermet)

A gang of English children stow away to France where they cause mayhem and save the world from a gang of wicked adults before ending up on a desert island.

Lively and subversive entertainment intended for children.

w Gilles Perrault, Michel Deville, Yan Appas, Joan Népami   d Michel Deville   ph Claude Lecompte m Edgar Cosma   pd Michel Guyot, Régis Des Plas   ed Raymonde Guyot

Andrew Chandler, Hélène Dassule, Nicole Palmer, Hamish Scrimgeour, Katherine Scrimgeour, Nicolas Sireau, Rémi Usquin, Valérie Gauthier

The Phantom of the Opera*
US 1943 92m Technicolor
Universal (George Waggner)
V

This version is more decorous and gentlemanly, with much attention paid to the music, but it certainly has its moments.

w Erich Taylor, Samuel Hoffenstein d Arthur Lubin
ph Hal Mohr, W. Howard Greene
m Edward Ward ad John B. Goodman, Alexander Golitzen

Claude Rains, Nelson Eddy, Susanna Foster, Edgar Barrier, Leo Carrillo, J. Edward Bromberg, Jane Farrar, Hume Cronyn

'A grand and gaudy entertainment.' – *Manchester Guardian*

AA: Hal Mohr, W. Howard Greene; John B. Goodman, Alexander Golitzen; Edward Ward

Phantom of the Opera
GB 1962 90m Technicolor
U-I/Hammer (Anthony Hinds)
V

Stodgy remake with the accent on shock.

w John Elder d Terence Fisher
ph Arthur Grant m Edwin Astley

Herbert Lom, Edward de Souza, Heather Sears, Thorley Walters, Michael Gough, Ian Wilson, Martin Miller, John Harvey, Miriam Karlin

'The only shock is that the British, who could have had a field day with this antique, have simply wafted it back with a lick and a promise.' – *New York Times*

The Phantom Tollbooth**
US 1969 90m Metrocolor
MGM/Animation Visual Arts

A bored boy goes through a magic tollbooth to a land beyond his wildest imagination, rescues Rhyme and Reason, and defeats the Demons of Ignorance.

Ambitious and well-devised, though rather slow-starting, cartoon feature which falls in style somewhere between *Alice in Wonderland* and *The Wizard of Oz* but is more intellectual than either and would be beyond the reach of most children. Discerning adults may have a ball.

w Chuck Jones, Sam Rosen
novel Norton Juster d Chuck Jones, Abe Levitow ph Maurice Noble

Butch Patrick

Phar Lap
Australia 1983 118m colour Panavision
TCF/Michael Edgley International (John Sexton)
V
GB title: *Phar Lap – Heart of a Nation*

The story of a crack racehorse which was the talk of the world in the early thirties but died of a mysterious disease.

The film, though adequately textured, won't win any races.

w David Williamson d Simon Wincer ph Russell Boyd
m Bruce Rowland

Tom Burlinson, Martin Vaughan, Judy Morris, Celia de Burgh, Ron Liebman, Vincent Ball

The Pickwick Papers*
GB 1952 115m bw
George Minter (Bob McNaught)
V

Various adventures of the Pickwick Club culminate in Mrs Bardell's suit for breach of promise.

Flatly conceived and loosely constructed Dickensian comedy; good humour and lots of well-known faces do not entirely atone for lack of artifice.

wd Noel Langley ph Wilkie Cooper m Antony Hopkins ad Fred Pusey

James Hayter, James Donald, Donald Wolfit, Hermione Baddeley, Hermione Gingold, Kathleen Harrison, *Nigel Patrick*, Alexander Gauge, Lionel Murton

'As welcome as the sun in the morning and as British as a cup of tea.' – *Daily Mirror*

The Picture Show Man*
Australia 1977 98m Eastmancolor
Limelight (Joan Long)

Adventures of a travelling picture show troupe in the 1920s.

Agreeably nostalgic incidents, not very dramatically connected.

w Joan Long d John Power ph Geoffrey Burton m Peter Best

Rod Taylor, John Meillon, John Ewart, Harold Hopkins, Judy Morris, Patrick Cargill

The Pied Piper**
US 1942 86m bw
TCF (Nunnally Johnson)

An elderly man who hates children finds himself smuggling several of them out of occupied France.

Smart, sentimental, occasionally funny war adventure.

w Nunnally Johnson *novel* Nevil Shute d Irving Pichel ph Edward Cronjager m Alfred Newman

Monty Woolley, Anne Baxter, Roddy McDowall, Otto Preminger, J. Carrol Naish, Lester Matthews, Jill Eastmond, Peggy Ann Garner

AAN: best picture; Edward Cronjager; Monty Woolley

The Pied Piper
GB 1971 90m Eastmancolor Panavision
Sagittarius/Goodtimes (David Puttnam, Sanford Lieberson)

In 1349 a strolling minstrel rids Hamelin of a plague of rats.

Paceless, slightly too horrific, and generally disappointing fantasy, especially from this director; poor sets and restricted action.

w Jacques Demy, Mark Peploe, Andrew Birkin d Jacques Demy ph Peter Suschitsky m Donovan pd Assheton Gorton

Donovan, Donald Pleasence, Michael Hordern, Jack Wild, Diana Dors, John Hurt

The Pink Panther**
US 1963 113m Technirama
UA/Mirisch (Martin Jurow)
V, L

An incompetent *Sûreté* inspector is in Switzerland on the trail of a jewel thief called The Phantom.

Sporadically engaging mixture of pratfalls, *Raffles*, and *Monsieur Hulot*, all dressed to kill and quite palatable for the uncritical.

w Maurice Richlin, Blake Edwards d Blake Edwards ph Philip Lathrop m Henry Mancini ad Fernando Carrere animation De Patie-Freleng

David Niven, Peter Sellers, Capucine, Claudia Cardinale, Robert Wagner, Brenda de Banzie, Colin Gordon

† Inspector Clouseau later became a cartoon character and also provoked five sequels: *A Shot in the Dark, Inspector Clouseau, The Return of the Pink Panther, The Pink Panther Strikes Again* and *The Revenge of the Pink Panther*.
AAN: Henry Mancini

The Pink Panther Strikes Again*
GB 1976 103m DeLuxe Panavision
United Artists/Amjo (Blake Edwards)
V, L

After a nervous breakdown, Chief Inspector Dreyfus builds up a vast criminal organization devoted to the extermination of Inspector Clouseau.

Zany pratfall farce with signs of over-confidence since the success of *The Return of the Pink Panther*. But some gags are funny, despite a rather boring star.

w Frank Waldman, Blake Edwards d Blake Edwards ph Harry Waxman m Henry Mancini

Peter Sellers, Herbert Lom, Colin Blakely, Leonard Rossiter, Lesley-Anne Down, Burt Kwouk
AAN: song 'Come To Me' (m Henry Mancini, ly Don Black)

'Out of a dream world into yours!'
Pinocchio****
US 1940 77m Technicolor
Walt Disney

The blue fairy breathes life into a puppet, which has to prove itself before it can turn into a real boy.

Charming, fascinating, superbly organized and streamlined cartoon feature without a single second of boredom.

supervisors Ben Sharpsteen, Hamilton Luske m/ly Leigh Harline, Ned Washington, Paul J. Smith

voices of Dickie Jones, Christian Rub, Cliff Edwards, Evelyn Venable, Walter Catlett, Frankie Darro

'A film of amazing detail and brilliant conception.' – *Leonard Maltin*
'A work that gives you almost every possible kind of pleasure to be got from a motion picture.' – *Richard Mallett, Punch*
'The limits of the animated cartoon have been blown so wide open that some of the original wonder of pictures has been restored.' – *Otis Ferguson*

AA: Leigh Harline, Ned Washington, Paul J. Smith (m); song 'When You Wish Upon a Star' (m Leigh Harline, ly Ned Washington)

Pinocchio and the Emperor of the Night
US 1987 90m colour
Palace/Filmation (Lou Scheimer)

Pinocchio continues his adventures as a real boy.

Sugary confection that cannot stand comparison with Disney's classic.

w Robby London d Hal Sutherland m Anthony Marinelli, Brian Banks songs Will Jennings, Barry Mann, Steve Tyrell

voices of Ed Asner, Lana Beeson, Tom Bosley, Linda Gary, Scott Grimes, James Earl Jones, Rickie Lee Jones, Don Knotts

The Pirate**
US 1948 102m Technicolor
MGM (Arthur Freed)
V, L

In a West Indian port, a girl imagines that a wandering player is a famous pirate, who in fact is her despised and elderly suitor.

Minor MGM musical with vivid

moments and some intimation of the greatness shortly to come; all very set-bound, but the star quality is infectious.

w Albert Hackett, Frances Goodrich play S. N. Behrman d Vincente Minnelli ph Harry Stradling md Lennie Hayton m/ly Cole Porter

Gene Kelly, Judy Garland, Walter Slezak, Gladys Cooper, Reginald Owen, George Zucco, the Nicholas Brothers
AAN: Lennie Hayton

The Pirate Movie
Australia 1982 105m Colorfilm
Fox/Joseph Hamilton International

A girl dreams herself back into *The Pirates of Penzance* but changes some of the details.

Galumphing fantasy which suggests that Australian film-makers had better stick to *Botany Bay*, *Gallipoli* and sheep shearing.

w Trevor Farrant d Ken Annakin ph Robin Copping pd Tony Woollard ed Kenneth W. Zemke

Kristy McNichol, Christopher Atkins, Ted Hamilton, Bill Kerr, Maggie Kirkpatrick, Garry Macdonald

'The slapstick and the swordplay are as ineptly choreographed as the production numbers.' – *Kim Newman, MFB*

Pirates
France/Tunisia 1986 124m Eclaircolor Panavision
Cannon/Carthago/Accent Dominco (Tarak Ben Ammar)

A British buccaneer, cast adrift on a raft, is taken aboard a Spanish galleon and causes mayhem.

A disaster from a director who should never be allowed to attempt comedy. This one is revolting when it is not a crashing bore.

w Gerard Brach, Roman Polanski d Roman Polanski ph Witold Sobocinski m Philippe Garde

Walter Matthau, Damien Thomas, Richard Pearson, Roy Kinnear, Ferdy Mayne, Charlotte Lewis

† The galleon, which cost 8 million dollars, was not wasted. It was given to the municipality of Cannes and became a tourist attraction.
AAN: costumes (Anthony Powell)

Pirates of Blood River*
GB 1961 84m Technicolor Hammerscope
Hammer (Anthony Nelson Keys)

Pirates in search of gold terrorize a Huguenot settlement.

Land-locked blood and thunder for tough schoolboys.

w John Hunter, John Gilling d John Gilling ph Arthur Grant

Christopher Lee, Andrew Keir, Kerwin Mathews, Glenn Corbett, Peter Arne, Oliver Reed, Marla Landi, Michael Ripper

Pirates of Tortuga
US 1961 97m DeLuxe Cinemascope
Sam Katzman/TCF

In the 17th-century Caribbean, a privateer is ordered by the king to go undercover and rout Sir Henry Morgan.

Listless swashbuckler with inferior talent.

w Melvin Levy, Jesse L. Lasky Jnr, Pat Silver d Robert D. Webb

Ken Scott, Dave King, Letitia Roman, John Richardson, Robert Stephens, Edgar Barrier

Pirates of Tripoli
US 1955 72m Technicolor
Sam Katzman/Columbia

A pirate captain comes to the aid of an oriental princess.

More akin to the Arabian Knights than Blackbeard, but not bad for a double-biller.

w Allen March   d Felix Feist

Paul Henreid, Patricia Medina, Paul Newland, John Miljan, Lillian Bond

The Plague Dogs
GB/US 1982 103m Technicolor
Nepenthe Productions

Two dogs escape from a research laboratory and are in danger of infecting the country with a deadly virus.

Misguided and woefully overlong attempt to preach a message through a cartoon. Like *Watership Down*, it needs the printed word and is deflected by the inevitably cuddly look of the animated animals.

wd Martin Rosen   novel Richard Adams

voices of John Hurt, James Bolam, Christopher Benjamin, Judy Geeson, Barbara Leigh-Hunt

'Somewhere in the universe, there must be something better than man!'
Planet of the Apes*
US 1968 119m DeLuxe
  Panavision
TCF/Apjac (Mort Abrahams)
V, L

Astronauts caught in a time warp land on a planet which turns out to be Earth in the distant future, when men have become beasts and the apes have taken over.

Stylish, thoughtful science fiction which starts and finishes splendidly but suffers from a sag in the middle. The ape make-up is great.

w Michael Wilson, Rod Serling, novel *Monkey Planet* by Pierre Boulle   d Franklin Schaffner
ph Leon Shamroy   m Jerry Goldsmith

Charlton Heston, Roddy McDowall, *Kim Hunter*, Maurice Evans, James Whitmore, James Daly, Linda Harrison

'One of the most telling science fiction films to date.' – *Tom Milne*

† Sequels, in roughly descending order of interest, were BENEATH THE PLANET OF THE APES (1969), ESCAPE FROM THE PLANET OF THE APES (1970), CONQUEST OF THE PLANET OF THE APES (1972) and BATTLE FOR THE PLANET OF THE APES (1973). A TV series followed in 1974, and a cartoon series in 1975.

AA: make-up (John Chambers)
AAN: Jerry Goldsmith; costumes (Morton Haack)

Playtime*
France 1968 152m
  Eastmancolor 70mm
Specta Films (René Silvera)
V

Hulot and a group of American tourists are bewildered by life in an airport, a business block and a restaurant.

Incredibly extended series of sketches, none of which is devastatingly funny. The irritation is that the talent is clearly there but needs control.

w Jacques Tati, Jacques Lagrange
d Jacques Tati *ph* Jean Badal,
Andreas Winding *m* Francis
Lemarque *pd* Eugène Roman

*Jacques Tati, Barbara Dennek,
Jacqueline Lecomte, Henri Piccoli*

'Tati still seems the wrong distance from his audience: not so far that we cannot see his gifts, not close enough so that they really touch.' – *Stanley Kauffmann*

'How sad that the result of all this, though it includes a great deal of intermittent pleasure, comes at times so dangerously close to boredom.' – *Brenda Davies, MFB*

'A series of brilliant doodles by an artist who has earned the right to indulge himself on such a scale.' – *Alexander Walker*

Please Sir

GB 1971 101m Eastmancolor
Rank/LWI/Leslie Grade (Andrew Mitchell)

The masters and pupils of Fenn Street school go on an annual camp.

Grossly inflated, occasionally funny big-screen version of the TV series.

w John Esmonde, Bob Larbey
d Mark Stuart *ph* Wilkie Cooper *m* Mike Vickers

John Alderton, Deryck Guyler, Joan Sanderson, Noel Howlett, Eric Chitty, Richard Davies

Police Academy 3: Back in Training

US 1986 82m colour
Warner (Paul Maslansky)
V

Rival police academies vie for survival.

Plodding comedy that recycles a few familiar, unfunny routines.

w Gene Quintano *d* Jerry Paris
ph Robert Saad *m* Robert Folk
pd Trevor Williams *ed* Bud Malin

Steve Guttenberg, Bubba Smith, David Graf, Michael Winslow, Marion Ramsey, Leslie Easterbrook, George Gaynes, Bobcat Goldthwait, Art Metrano

Police Academy 4: Citizens on Patrol

US 1987 87m colour
Warner (Paul Maslansky)
V

A police commandant attempts to involve ordinary people in law enforcement.

A feeble comedy that makes it impossible to understand the apparent popularity of this turgid series.

w Gene Quintano *d* Jim Drake
ph Robert Saad *m* Robert Folk
pd Trevor Williams *ed* David Rawlins

Steve Guttenberg, Bubba Smith, David Graf, Michael Winslow, Sharon Stone, Leslie Easterbrook, Bobcat Goldthwait, George Gaynes

'Carries the banner of tasteless humor ... to new heights of insipidness.' – *Variety*

Police Academy 5: Assignment: Miami Beach

US 1988 90m colour
Warner (Paul Maslansky)
V

Cops on holiday in Miami help foil a gang of jewel thieves.

Witlessness reaches a new low in a comedy devoid of laughs.

w Stephen J. Curwick *d* Alan Myerson *ph* Jim Pergola
m Robert Folk *pd* Trevor Williams *ed* Hubert de la Bouillerie

Matt McCoy, Janet Jones, George Gaynes, G. W. Bailey, Rene Auberjonois, Bubba Smith, David Graf, Michael Winslow, Leslie Easterbook

Police Academy 6: City Under Siege
US 1989 84m Technicolor
Warner (Paul Maslansky)
V, L

The police squad track down a criminal mastermind responsible for a massive crime wave.

Farcical, broadly acted comedy that does raise an occasional smile.

w Stephen J. Curwick   *d* Peter Bonerz   *ph* Charles Rosher Jr   *m* Robert Folk   *pd* Tho E. Azzari   *ed* Hubert de la Bouillerie

Bubba Smith, David Graf, Michael Winslow, Leslie Easterbrook, Marion Ramsey, Lance Kinsey, Matt McCoy, Bruce Mahler, G. W. Bailey, George Gaynes, Kenneth Mars

Pollyanna*
US 1960 134m Technicolor
Walt Disney (George Golitzen)

A 12-year-old orphan girl cheers up the grumps of the small town where she comes to live.

Well cast but overlong and rather humourless remake of a children's classic from an earlier age.

wd David Swift   *novel* Eleanor Porter   *ph* Russell Harlan   *m* Paul Smith   *ad* Carroll Clark, Robert Clatworthy

Hayley Mills, Jane Wyman, Karl Malden, Nancy Olson, Adolphe Menjou, Donald Crisp, Agnes Moorehead, Richard Egan, Kevin Corcoran, James Drury, Reta Shaw, Leora Dana

'Even Hayley Mills can neither prevent one from sympathizing with the crusty aunts, hermits, vicars and hypochondriacs who get so forcibly cheered up, nor from feverishly speculating whether films like this don't run the risk of inciting normally kind and gentle people into certain excesses of violent crime – child murder, for instance.' – *MFB*

AA: special award to Hayley Mills for 'the most outstanding juvenile performance'

Popeye
US 1980 114m colour
Paramount/Disney (Robert Evans)
L

Popeye returns to Sweethaven in search of the father who abandoned him.

Lamentable attempt by an ill-chosen director to humanize and sentimentalize a celebrated cartoon character who doesn't get into the expected physical action until the film is nearly over.

w Jules Feiffer, from characters created by E. C. Segar   *d* Robert Altman   *ph* Giuseppe Rotunno   *pd* Wolf Kroeger   *m/ly* Harry Nilsson

Robin Williams, Shelley Duvall, Ray Walston, Paul Dooley

'The picture doesn't come together, and much of it is cluttered, squawky, and eerily unfunny.' – *Pauline Kael, New Yorker*

Postman's Knock*
GB 1961 88m bw
MGM (Ronald Kinnoch)

A village postman is transferred to London, finds life and work bewildering, but captures some crooks and ends up a hero.

Mildly amusing star vehicle rising to good comic climaxes.

w John Briley, Jack Trevor Story d Robert Lynn ph Gerald Moss m Ron Goodwin

Spike Milligan, Barbara Shelley, Wilfrid Lawson

The Pride and the Passion*
US 1957 131m Technicolor Vistavision
UA/Stanley Kramer

In 1810 Spain a British naval officer helps Spanish guerrillas, by reactivating an old cannon, to win their fight against Napoleon.

Stolid, miscast adventure spectacle, its main interest being the deployment of the gun across country by surging throngs of peasants.

w Edna and Edward Anhalt novel The Gun by C. S. Forester d Stanley Kramer ph Franz Planer m Georges Antheil

Cary Grant, Sophia Loren, Frank Sinatra, Theodore Bikel, John Wengraf, Jay Novello, Philip Van Zandt

'The whirr of the cameras often seems as loud as the thunderous cannonades. It evidently takes more than dedication, cooperative multitudes and four million dollars to shoot history in the face.' – Time

The Prince and the Pauper*
US 1937 118m bw
Warner (Robert Lord)

In Tudor London, young Edward VI changes places with a street urchin who happens to be his double.

Well-produced version of a famous story; it never quite seems to hit the right style or pace, but is satisfying in patches.

w Laird Doyle novel Mark Twain d William Keighley ph Sol Polito m Erich Wolfgang Korngold

Errol Flynn, Claude Rains, Billy and Bobby Mauch, Henry Stephenson, Barton MacLane, Alan Hale, Eric Portman, Montagu Love (as Henry VIII), Lionel Pape, Halliwell Hobbes, Fritz Leiber

'Lavish but not convincing. Doubtful box office: the commercial aspect seems wholly concerned in the timeliness of a Coronation sequence and the name of Errol Flynn. It is not enough.' – Variety

The Prince and the Pauper*
Panama 1977 121m Technicolor Panavision
International Film Production/Ilya and Alexander Salkind (Pierre Spengler)
US title: Crossed Swords

Young Edward VI changes place with a beggar, who helps to expose a traitor.

Moderately well-made swashbuckler with an old-fashioned air, not really helped by stars in cameo roles or by the poor playing of the title roles.

w George MacDonald Fraser novel Mark Twain d Richard Fleischer ph Jack Cardiff m Maurice Jarre pd Anthony Pratt

Mark Lester, Oliver Reed, Raquel Welch, Ernest Borgnine, George C. Scott, Rex Harrison, David Hemmings, Charlton Heston (as Henry VIII), Harry Andrews, Murray Melvin, Julian Orchard

Prince of Pirates
US 1953 80m Technicolor
Columbia

A young prince of the Netherlands turns pirate when his brother allies with the Spanish invader.

Fast-moving costume potboiler with lavish use of action scenes from *Joan of Arc*.

w John O'Dea, Samuel Newman d Sidney Salkow

John Derek, Barbara Rush, Carla Balenda, Whitfield Connor, Edgar Barrier

Prince of Thieves
US 1948 72m bw
Sam Katzman/Columbia

Robin Hood saves a nobleman's intended from Baron Tristram.

Tatty second-feature version of a legendary figure.

w Maurice Tombragel d Howard Bretherton

Jon Hall, Patricia Morison, Alan Mowbray, Michael Duane, Adele Jergens

Prince Valiant*
US 1954 100m Technicolor Cinemascope
TCF (Robert L. Jacks)

The son of the exiled king of Scandia seeks King Arthur's help against the usurper, and becomes involved in a court plot.

Agreeable historical nonsense for teenagers, admittedly and sometimes hilariously from a comic strip.

w Dudley Nichols *comic strip* Harold Foster d Henry Hathaway ph Lucien Ballard m Franz Waxman

Robert Wagner, James Mason, Debra Paget, Janet Leigh, Sterling Hayden, Victor McLaglen, Donald Crisp, Brian Aherne, Barry Jones, Primo Carnera

The Prince Who Was a Thief
US 1951 88m Technicolor
U-I (Leonard Goldstein)

An Arabian Nights prince is lost as a baby and brought up by thieves, but finally fights back to his rightful throne.

Given the synopsis, any viewer can write the script himself. Standard eastern Western romp.

w Gerald Drayson Adams, Aeneas Mackenzie *story* Theodore Dreiser d Rudolph Maté ph Irving Glassberg m Hans Salter

Tony Curtis, Piper Laurie, Everett Sloane, Jeff Corey

The Princess and the Goblin
GB/Hungary 1992 111m colour
Entertainment/Siriol/Pannonia/SC4/NHK Enterprises (Robin Lyons)

A miner's son saves a princess from being kidnapped by goblins.

Uninteresting animated feature, with a dull fairy-tale plot dully executed.

w Robin Lyons *novel* George MacDonald d József Gémes ph Arpad Lessecry, Gyergy Verga, Ede Pagner, Nick Smith, Pete Turner, Steve Turner, Andreas Klawsz m István Lerch ed Magda Hap

voices of: Joss Ackland, Claire Bloom, Roy Kinnear, Sally Ann Marsh, Rik Mayall, Peggy Mount, Peter Murray, Victor Spinetti, Mollie Sugden

'A potentially charming medieval cartoon let down by so-so technique and unimaginative plotting.' – *Variety*

The Princess and the Pirate*
US 1944 94m Technicolor
Samuel Goldwyn (Don Hartman)
L

An impostor is on the run from a vicious pirate.

Typical star costume extravaganza with fewer laughs than you'd expect.

w Don Hartman, Melville Shavelson, Everett Freeman d David Butler ph William Snyder, Victor Milner m David Rose ad Ernst Fegte

Bob Hope, Virginia Mayo, Victor McLaglen, Walter Slezak, Walter Brennan, Marc Lawrence, Hugo Haas, Maude Eburne

'From start to finish, Hope dominates the action with well-timed colloquial nifties.' – *Variety*
AAN: David Rose; Ernst Fegte

The Princess Bride*
US 1987 98m DeLuxe
Act III (Andrew Scheinmann, Rob Reiner)
V, L

Grandfather tells a fairy tale of good and evil.

Rather strained fantasy with occasional bright moments.

w William Goldman *novel* William Goldman d Rob Reiner ph Adrian Biddle m Mark Knopfler pd Norman Garwood

Cary Elwes, Mandy Patinkin, Chris Sarandon, Christopher Guest, Peter Falk, Wallace Shawn
AAN: song 'Storybook Love'

Princess of the Nile
US 1954 71m Technicolor
TCF

An Egyptian princess of the middle ages leads her country against the invasion of a bedouin prince.

Lethargic costume piece with hopelessly miscast actors.

w Gerald Drayson Adams
d Harmon Jones

Debra Paget, Michael Rennie, Jeffrey Hunter, Dona Drake, Edgar Barrier, Jack Elam, Lee Van Cleef

The Prisoner of Zenda****
US 1937 101m bw
David O. Selznick

An Englishman on holiday in Ruritania finds himself helping to defeat a rebel plot by impersonating the kidnapped king at his coronation.

A splendid schoolboy adventure story is perfectly transferred to the screen in this exhilarating swashbuckler, one of the most entertaining films to come out of Hollywood.

w John Balderston, Wills Root, Donald Ogden Stewart, *novel* Anthony Hope d John Cromwell ph James Wong Howe m Alfred Newman ad Lyle Wheeler

Ronald Colman, Douglas Fairbanks Jnr, Madeleine Carroll, David Niven, Raymond Massey, Mary Astor, C. Aubrey Smith, Byron Foulger, Montagu Love

'The most pleasing film that has come along in ages.' – *New York Times*
'One of those rare movies that seem, by some magic trick, to become more fascinating and beguiling with each passing year.' – *John Cutts, 1971*

† Previously filmed in 1913 and 1922.
AAN: Alfred Newman; Lyle Wheeler

The Prisoner of Zenda*
US 1952 100m Technicolor
MGM (Pandro S. Berman)
V

A costly scene-for-scene remake

which only goes to show that care and discretion are no match for the happy inspiration of the original.

w John Balderston, Noel Langley d Richard Thorpe ph Joseph Ruttenberg m Alfred Newman

Stewart Granger, James Mason, Deborah Kerr, Robert Coote, Robert Douglas, Jane Greer, Louis Calhern, Francis Pierlot, Lewis Stone

The Prisoner of Zenda
US 1979 108m Technicolor
Universal (Walter Mirisch)

Palpably uneasy version of the above which teeters between comedy and straight romance, with barely a moment of real zest creeping in. The star is way off form in both roles.

w Dick Clement, Ian La Frenais d Richard Quine ph Arthur Ibbetson m Henry Mancini pd John J. Lloyd

Peter Sellers, Lynne Frederick, Lionel Jeffries, Elke Sommer, Gregory Sierra, Stuart Wilson, Jeremy Kemp, Catherine Schell, Simon Williams, Norman Rossington, John Laurie

'Flatly directed, leadenly unfunny.' – Paul Taylor, MFB

Prisoners of the Casbah
US 1953 78m Technicolor
Sam Katzman/Columbia

An Eastern princess and her lover take refuge from the evil Grand Vizier in the Casbah, a haven for outcasts.

Inept sword and sandal actioner; you can almost smell the Turkish delight.

w DeVallon Scott d Richard Bare

Gloria Grahame, Cesar Romero, Turhan Bey, Nestor Paiva

'The things I do for England!'
The Private Life of Henry VIII***
GB 1933 97m bw
London Films (Alexander Korda)
V, L

How Henry beheaded his second wife and acquired four more.

This never was a perfect film, but certain scenes are very funny and its sheer sauciness established the possibility of British films making money abroad, as well as starting several star careers. It now looks very dated and even amateurish in parts.

w Lajos Biro, Arthur Wimperis d Alexander Korda ph Georges Périnal m Kurt Schroeder

Charles Laughton, Elsa Lanchester, Robert Donat, Merle Oberon, Binnie Barnes, Franklin Dyall, Miles Mander, Wendy Barrie, Claud Allister, Everly Gregg

'Among the best anywhere and by far the top British picture . . . figures a sock entry, especially for the best houses.' – Variety

AA: Charles Laughton
AAN: best picture

The Private Lives of Elizabeth and Essex**
US 1939 106m Technicolor
Warner (Robert Lord)
V
reissue title: Elizabeth the Queen

Elizabeth I falls in love with the Earl of Essex, but events turn him into a rebel and she has to order his execution.

Unhistorical history given the grand treatment; a Hollywood picture book, not quite satisfying dramatically despite all the effort.

w Norman Reilly Raine, Aeneas

Mackenzie   *play Elizabeth the Queen by Maxwell Anderson*   d Michael Curtiz   ph Sol Polito, W. Howard Greene   m Erich Wolfgang Korngold   ad Anton Grot

Bette Davis, Errol Flynn, Olivia de Havilland, Donald Crisp, Vincent Price, Alan Hale, Henry Stephenson, Henry Daniell, Leo G. Carroll, Nanette Fabray, Robert Warwick, John Sutton

'Solid box office material, with fine grosses and holdovers indicated ... in all technical departments, picture has received topnotch investiture.' – *Variety*

'A rather stately, rigorously posed and artistically technicolored production.' – *Frank S. Nugent*

AAN: Sol Polito, W. Howard Greene; Erich Wolfgang Korngold; Anton Grot

Problem Child

US   1990   81m   DeLuxe
UIP/Universal/Imagine Entertainment (Robert Simonds)
V, L

A badly behaved boy is adopted by a small-town couple.

Broadly played, predictable comedy of mayhem and misunderstandings.

w Scott Alexander, Larry Karaszewski   d Dennis Dugan   ph Peter Lyons Collister   m Miles Goodman   pd George Costello   ed Daniel Hanley, Michael Hill

John Ritter, Jack Warden, Michael Oliver, Gilbert Gottfried, Amy Yasbeck, Michael Richards, Peter Jurasik, Charlotte Akin

'Universal took a step in the right direction by whittling it down to just 81 minutes but didn't go far enough. The studio should have excised another 75 minutes and released this unbelievable mess as a short.' – *Variety*

'Now, Junior has a brand new friend. He's bad. She's worse.'

Problem Child 2

US   1991   91m   DeLuxe
UIP/Universal/Imagine (Robert Simonds)
V

An ill-behaved boy decides that his father should marry the mother of his friend, a badly behaved girl.

Nasty-minded, witless slapstick with an anal fixation. -

w Scott Alexander, Larry Karaszewski   d Brian Levant   ph Peter Smokler   m David Kitay   pd Maria Caso   ed Lois Freeman-Fox, Robert P. Seppey

John Ritter, Michael Oliver, Jack Warden, Laraine Newman, Amy Yasbeck, Ivyann Schwan, Gilbert Gottfried, Paul Wilson

'No seam of bad taste is left unmined as the screenwriters sink to impossibly low depths in pursuit of anything vaguely resembling a laugh.' – *Mark Salisbury, Empire*

Pufnstuf

US   1970   98m   Technicolor
Universal/Krofft Enterprises

A dejected boy is led by his talking flute on a talking boat to Living Island, full of strange but friendly animals in fear of an incompetent witch.

Amalgam of a TV series using life-size puppets to project a mildly pleasing variation on *The Wizard of Oz*, without quite achieving the right blend of wit and charm.

w John Fenton Murray, Si Rose   d Hollingsworth Morse   ph Kenneth Peach   m Charles Fox   ad Alexander Golitzen

Jack Wild, Billie Hayes, Martha Raye, Mama Cass

The Pure Hell of St Trinian's*
GB 1960 94m bw
Hallmark/Tudor (Frank Launder, Sidney Gilliat)

After the girls burn down St Trinian's, a dubious headmaster offers to create a new school for them.

Bright comedy performances from some of the best of character actors add a gloss to familiar material.

w Frank Launder, Sidney Gilliat, Val Valentine d Frank Launder ph Gerald Gibbs m Malcolm Arnold ed Thelma Connell

Cecil Parker, Joyce Grenfell, George Cole, Thorley Walters, Irene Handl, Eric Barker, Dennis Price, Raymond Huntley, Julie Alexander

The Purple Mask
US 1955 82m Technicolor Cinemascope
U-I (Howard Christie)

In 1802 Paris the Royalist resistance to Napoleon is led by the mysterious Purple Mask, who also disguises himself as a foppish dandy.

Cheeky rewrite of *The Scarlet Pimpernel*, with plenty of gusto but not much style.

w Oscar Brodney d Bruce Humberstone ph Irving Glassberg m Joseph Gershenson

Tony Curtis, Dan O'Herlihy, Colleen Miller, Gene Barry, Angela Lansbury, George Dolenz, John Hoyt

'Sir Percy, one feels, would have personally conducted this lot to the guillotine.' – *MFB*

Putting Pants on Philip*
US 1927 20m bw silent
Hal Roach

A respectable man meets his randy Scottish nephew who wears nothing under his kilt.

Early star comedy, allegedly their first as a team but before their more recognizable characteristics had developed. Not at all bad in its way, though developing into one long chase.

w H. M. Walker d Clyde Bruckman

Laurel and Hardy, Sam Lufkin, Harvey Clark

Q

Queen of Hearts*
GB 1989 112m colour
Enterprise/TVS Films/Nelson
 Entertainment/Film Four International/
 Telso International (John Hardy)
L

A ten-year-old, part of a large and happy Italian family living in London, watches while his father risks everything by gambling.

Odd and ultimately unsatisfactory mix of fantasy and reality, contrasting Italian warmth and British cool to the detriment of both.

w Tony Grisoni   d Jon Amiel
ph Mike Southon   m Michael Convertino   pd Jim Clay
ed Peter Boyle

Vittorio Duse, Joseph Long, Anita Zagaria, Eileen Way, Vittorio Amandola, Roberto Scateni, Stefano Spagnoli, Alec Bregonzi

'Theirs was a time of love and violence!'

Quentin Durward*
GB 1955 101m Eastmancolor
 Cinemascope
MGM (Pandro S. Berman)
aka: *The Adventures of Quentin Durward*

An elderly English lord sends his nephew to woo a French lady on his behalf; but the boy falls in love with her himself.

Haphazardly constructed and produced, but quite enjoyable, period romp, with a bold black villain and several rousing set-pieces including a final set-to on bell ropes.

w Robert Ardrey   novel Sir Walter Scott   d Richard Thorpe
ph Christopher Challis
m Bronislau Kaper

Robert Taylor, Kay Kendall, Robert Morley, Alec Clunes, Marius Goring, Wilfrid Hyde White, Ernest Thesiger, Duncan Lamont, Harcourt Williams, Laya Raki, George Cole

'In making this film, MGM feel privileged to add something of permanent value to the cultural treasure house of mankind...'
'Ancient Rome is going to the dogs, Robert Taylor is going to the lions, and Peter Ustinov is going crazy!'

Quo Vadis**
US 1951 171m Technicolor
MGM (Sam Zimbalist)
V, L

A Roman commander under Nero falls in love with a Christian girl and jealous Poppea has them both thrown to the lions.

Spectacular but stagey and heavy-handed Hollywood version of a much-filmed colossus which shares much of its plot line with *The Sign of the Cross*. Three hours of solemn tedium with flashes of vigorous acting and a few set-pieces to take the eye; but the sermonizing does not take away the bad taste of the emphasis on physical brutality.

w John Lee Mahin, S. N. Behrman, Sonya Levien d Mervyn Le Roy ph Robert Surtees, William V. Skall m Miklos Rozsa ad Cedric Gibbons, Edward Carfagno, William Horning ed Ralph E. Winters

Robert Taylor, Deborah Kerr, *Peter Ustinov, Leo Genn, Patricia Laffan,* Finlay Currie, Abraham Sofaer, Marina Berti, Buddy Baer, Felix Aylmer, Nora Swinburne, Ralph Truman, Norman Wooland

AAN: best picture; Robert Surtees, William V. Skall; Miklos Rozsa; Peter Ustinov; Leo Genn; art direction; editing

R

Race for the Yankee Zephyr
New Zealand/Australia 1981
108m Eastmancolor Panavision

Adventurers discover an American aircraft wrecked in 1944, and argue over the loot without knowing that it contains a 50-million-dollar payroll.

Very moderate adventure story distinguished only by good locations.

w Everett de Roche *d* David Hemmings *ph* Vincent Monton *m* Brian May

Kan Wahl, Lesley Ann Warren, Donald Pleasence, George Peppard, Bruno Lawrence, Robert Bruce

Radio Flyer
US 1992 113m Technicolor
Columbia (Lauren Schuler-Donner)
V

Brothers build a flying machine to escape from their violent stepfather.

An earthbound mix of fantasy and reality.

w David Mickey Evans *d* Richard Donner

Lorraine Bracco, John Heard, Elijah Wood, Joseph Mazello, Adam Baldwin, Ben Johnson, Tom Hanks (uncredited)

Raiders of the Lost Ark**
US 1981 115m Metrocolor
Panavision
Paramount/Lucasfilm (Frank Marshall)
V, L

In the thirties, an American archaeologist and explorer beats the Nazis to a priceless artefact, the magical box containing fragments of the stones on which God wrote his laws.

Commercially very successful, this attempted wrap-up of the Saturday morning serials of two generations ago spends a great deal of money and expertise on frightening us rather than exciting us; in Dolby sound the experience is horrendous. Second time round, one can better enjoy the ingenious detail of the hero's exploits and ignore the insistence on unpleasantness; still, there are boring bits in between, and the story doesn't make a lot of sense.

w Lawrence Kasdan *d* Steven Spielberg *ph* Douglas Slocombe *m* John Williams *pd* Norman Reynolds

Harrison Ford, Karen Allen, Ronald Lacey, Paul Freeman, John Rhys-Davies, Denholm Elliott

'Both de trop and not enough.' – *Sight and Sound*

'Children may well enjoy its simple-mindedness, untroubled by the fact that it looks so shoddy and so uninventive.' – *Observer*

'Kinesthetically, the film gets to you, but there's no exhilaration, and no surge of feeling at the end.' – *Pauline Kael, New Yorker*

'An out of body experience, a movie

of glorious imagination and breakneck speed that grabs you in the first shot, hurtles you through a series of incredible adventures, and deposits you back in reality two hours later – breathless, dizzy, wrung-out, and with a silly grin on your face.' – *Roger Ebert*

† Tom Selleck was the first choice for the lead, but was tied up with his TV series *Magnum*.

AA: editing (Michael Kahn); visual effects
AAN: best picture; Steven Spielberg; Douglas Slocombe; John Williams

BFA: Norman Reynolds

'A film for adults to take their children, too!'

The Railway Children***
GB 1970 108m Technicolor
EMI (Robert Lynn)

Three Edwardian children and their mother move into Yorkshire when their father is imprisoned as a spy, and have adventures on the railway line while helping to prove his innocence.

Fresh and agreeable family film with many pleasing touches to compensate for its meandering plot.

wd Lionel Jeffries, *novel* E. Nesbit *ph* Arthur Ibbetson *m* Johnny Douglas

Dinah Sheridan, William Mervyn, Jenny Agutter, Bernard Cribbins, Iain Cuthbertson, Gary Warren, Sally Thomsett

'There are passages in Mr Jeffries' deliberately nostalgic film which may appeal more to sensitive parents than to their bloodthirsty offspring. But everybody, I hope, will enjoy the playing.' – *Dilys Powell*

Raising the Wind
GB 1961 91m colour
GHW/Anglo Amalgamated
V
US title: *Roommates*

Misadventures of students at a music academy.

A Carry On in all but name, from the same stable; good moments among the dross.

w Bruce Montgomery *d* Gerald Thomas

James Robertson Justice, Leslie Phillips, Kenneth Williams, Sidney James, Paul Massie, Liz Fraser, Eric Barker, Jennifer Jayne, Geoffrey Keen, Esma Cannon

Ratboy
US 1986 104m Technicolor
Malpaso/Warner

A half-rodent alien gets the anticipated rough treatment when he visits Earth.

Clint Eastwood's favourite co-star was given leave to make the film of her choice, but the choice is inexplicable in the wake of so many other *E.T.* imitations.

w Rob Thompson *d* Sondra Locke

Sondra Locke, Robert Townsend, Christopher Hewett, Larry Hankin

Reach for the Sky*
GB 1956 135m bw
Rank/Pinnacle (Daniel M. Angel)
V

Douglas Bader loses both legs in a 1931 air crash, learns to walk on artificial limbs and flies again in World War II.

Box-office exploitation of one man's personal heroism, adequately but not inspiringly put together with many stiff upper lips and much jocular humour.

wd Lewis Gilbert *book* Paul Brickhill *ph* Jack Asher *m* John Addison

Kenneth More, Muriel Pavlow, Lyndon Brook, Lee Patterson, Alexander Knox, Dorothy Alison, Sydney Tafler, Howard Marion Crawford

'It is least successful in what should be exciting action.' – *Dilys Powell*

Rebecca of Sunnybrook Farm
US 1938 80m bw
TCF (Raymond Griffith)

A child performer becomes a pawn in the fight to exploit her talents on radio.

Unrecognizable revamping of a famous story makes a very thin star vehicle.

w Karl Tunberg, Don Ettlinger *novel* Kate Douglas Wiggin and Charlotte Thompson *d* Allan Dwan *ph* Arthur Miller *m* Arthur Lange *songs* various

Shirley Temple, Randolph Scott, Jack Haley, Gloria Stuart, Phyllis Brooks, Helen Westley, Slim Summerville, Bill Robinson

'More fitting title would be *Rebecca of Radio City* . . . a weak story, indifferently directed and acted.' – *Variety*

The Red Balloon****
France 1955 34m Technicolor
Films Montsouris
V

A lonely boy finds a balloon which becomes his constant companion and finally lifts him to the skies.

Absorbing and quite perfectly timed fantasy, one of the great film shorts.

wd Albert Lamorisse *ph* Edmond Sechan *m* Maurice Le Roux *pd* Pascal Lamorisse

AA: best original screenplay

The Red Pony
US 1949 88m Technicolor
Republic (Lewis Milestone)

When his pet pony dies after an illness, a farmer's son loses faith in his father.

Sincere but rather obvious little fable which although capably made does not make inspiring film drama.

w John Steinbeck *d* Lewis Milestone *ph* Tony Gaudio *m* Aaron Copland *pd* Nicolai Remisoff

Myrna Loy, Robert Mitchum, Peter Miles, Louis Calhern, Shepperd Strudwick, Margaret Hamilton

Red River**
US 1948 133m bw
UA/Monterey (Howard Hawks)
V, L

How the Chisholm Trail was developed as a cattle drive.

Brawling Western, a bit serious and long drawn out but with splendid action sequences.

w Borden Chase, Charles Schnee *d* Howard Hawks *ph* Russell Harlan *m* Dimitri Tiomkin *ed* Christian Nyby

John Wayne, Montgomery Clift, Joanne Dru, Walter Brennan, Colleen Gray, John Ireland, Noah Beery Jnr, Harry Carey Jnr
AAN: original story (Borden Chase); editing

Red Sonja
US 1985 89m Metrocolor
MGM-UA/Thorn EMI (Christian Ferry)
V, L

In the times of sword and sorcery, Sonja avenges her sister's death and deposes an evil queen.

Absolute comic strip nonsense: even the monsters look mechanical.

w Clive Exton, George MacDonald Fraser stories Robert E. Howard d Richard Fleischer ph Giuseppe Rotunno m Ennio Morricone pd Danilo Donati ed Frank J. Urioste

Brigitte Nielsen, Arnold Schwarzenegger, Sandahl Bergman, Paul Smith, Ronald Lacey

The Reluctant Dragon**
US 1941 72m Technicolor
Walt Disney
V

A tour of the Disney Studios affords some glimpses of how cartoons are made.

Amiable pot-pourri of cartoon shorts (*Baby Weems*, *How to Ride a Horse* and the title story) linked by a studio tour of absorbing interest.

w various d Alfred Werker (live action), various

Robert Benchley, Frances Gifford, Nana Bryant

The Rescuers*
US 1977 77m Technicolor
Walt Disney (Ron Miller)
V, L

The Mouse Rescue Aid Society volunteer to bring back a girl lost in a swamp.

Feature-length cartoon which, while by no means as bad as some of Disney's very routine seventies product, still seems light years away from his classics of the thirties.

w Larry Clemmons, Ken Anderson stories Margery Sharp d Wolfgang Reitherman, John Lounsbery, Art Stevens m Artie Butler

voices of Bob Newhart, Eva Gabor, Geraldine Page, Joe Flynn, Jim Jordan, John McIntire

'The people who really need rescuing are the Disney animators and cameramen.' – *Time Out*
'It's no *Snow White* but there are long moments when its inventiveness and skill are entirely captivating. I have only this one lingering doubt: if you are going to put this amount of effort into a movie shouldn't you have more at the end than a snappy collection of 330,000 drawings and a bill for six million dollars?' – *Barry Took, Punch*
AAN: song 'Someone's Waiting for You' (m Sammy Fain, ly Carol Connors, Ayn Robbins)

The Rescuers Down Under**
US 1990 77m Technicolor
Warner/Walt Disney/Silver Screen Partners IV (Thomas Schumacher)
V, L

The mouse Rescue Aid Society goes to help a trapped eagle and a boy in Australia.

Slick, lively and enjoyable animated feature, an improvement on the original.

w Jim Cox, Karey Kirkpatrick, Byron Simpson, Joe Ranft d Hendel Butoy, Mike Gabriel m Bruce Broughton ad Maurice Hunt ed Michael Kelly, Mark Hester

voices of Bob Newhart, Eva Gabor, John Candy, Tristan Rogers, Adam Ryen, George C. Scott, Wayne

Robson, Douglas Seale, Frank Walker, Peter Firth, Bill Barty

'Comes on like an Indiana Jones movie which has been reconceived as animation and then proceeded to push back that medium's technical boundaries.' – *Sight and Sound*

Return from Witch Mountain
US 1978 93m Technicolor
Walt Disney (Ron Miller, Jerome Courtland)

A brother and sister from outer space come back to Earth for a vacation and are used by crooks for their own purposes.

Acceptable sequel to *Escape from Witch Mountain*, with improved special effects.

w Malcolm Marmorstein d John Hough ph Frank Phillips m Lalo Schifrin sp Eustace Lycett, Art Cruickshank, Danny Lee

Bette Davis, Christopher Lee, Ike Eisenmann, Kim Richards, Jack Soo

The Return of Monte Cristo*
US 1946 92m bw
Columbia/Edward Small-Grant Whytock
GB title: *Monte Cristo's Revenge*

The grandson of the original count is framed and sent to Devil's Island, but escapes.

Very tolerable action romp of its time, with a fair troupe of actors enjoying themselves.

w George Bruce, Alfred Neumann, Kurt Siodmak d Henry Levin ph Charles Lawton Jnr m Lucien Moraweck

Louis Hayward, Barbara Britton, George Macready, Una O'Connor, Henry Stephenson, Steve Geray, Ray Collins, Ludwig Donath, Ivan Triesault

Return of the Jedi*
US 1983 132m DeLuxe Panavision
TCF/Lucasfilm (Howard Kazanjian)
V, V(W), L

'Episode 6' of the *Star Wars* serial: our heroes combat Darth Vader and Jabba the Hutt.

More expensive fantasy for the world's children of all ages, especially the undemanding ones.

w Lawrence Kasdan, George Lucas d Richard Marquand ph Alan Hume m John Williams pd Norman Reynolds

Mark Hamill, Harrison Ford, Carrie Fisher, Billy Dee Williams, Anthony Daniels, Peter Mayhew, Kenny Baker

'I admire the exquisite skill and talent which have been poured into these films, while finding the concepts behind these gigantic video games in the sky mindlessly tedious.' – *Margaret Hinxman, Daily Mail*
'An impersonal and rather junky piece of moviemaking.' – *Pauline Kael, New Yorker*
'Only the effects are special.' – *Sight and Sound*
AAN: John Williams; art direction

The Return of the Musketeers
GB/France/Spain 1989 101m colour
Entertainment/Timoth Burrill Productions/Fildebroc-Cine 5/Iberoamericana (Pierre Spengler)
V

The daughter of Milady de Winter vows vengeance on the Musketeers who were responsible for her mother's execution.

A sequel to *The Four Musketeers*, it is a

lacklustre affair of four middle-aged failures attempting to redeem themselves.

w George MacDonald Fraser
novel *Vingt Ans Après* by Alexandre Dumas   d Richard Lester
ph Bernard Lutic   m Jean-Claude Petit   pd Gil Parrondo   ed John Victor Smith

Michael York, Oliver Reed, Frank Finlay, C. Thomas Howell, Kim Cattrall, Geraldine Chaplin, Roy Kinnear, Christopher Lee, Philippe Noiret, Richard Chamberlain, Eusebio Lazaro, Alan Howard, Jean-Pierre Cassel

Return to Oz
US   1985   110m   Technicolor
Walt Disney/Silver Screen Partners (Paul Maslansky)

Dorothy has traumas because of her Oz experiences, and suffers further nightmares under shock treatment.

A weird way to treat a children's classic, the result being a movie which appealed strongly to nobody except, possibly, the producer. The Disney people should have known better.

w Walter Murch, Gill Dennis
d Walter Murch   ph David Watkin   m David Shire

Fairuza Balk, Jean Marsh, Nicol Williamson, Piper Laurie, Matt Clark, Emma Ridley

'Astonishingly sombre, melancholy, and sadly unengaging.' – *Variety*
'Without musical numbers this narrative seems a perilously thin journey with no particular purpose.' – *Time Out*

Rhubarb
GB   1969   37m   Technicolor
ABPC/Avalon

Various village notables congregate on the golf course.

Virtually silent comedy (nobody says anything but 'rhubarb') which could have been very funny with better jokes. A TV remake in 1979 was however much worse.

wd Eric Sykes

Harry Secombe, Eric Sykes, Jimmy Edwards, Hattie Jacques, Gordon Rollins, Graham Stark, Kenneth Connor

The Riddle of the Sands*
GB   1978   102m   Eastmancolor Panavision
Rank/Worldmark (Drummond Challis)

In 1901 a British yachtsman in the North Sea hits upon a German trial invasion.

Rather too placid adaptation of a semi-classic adventure story in which too little happens to make a rousing action film; points of interest along the way, though.

w Tony Maylam, John Bailey
novel Erskine Childers   d Tony Maylam   ph Christopher Challis
ph Hazel Peiser   m Howard Blake

Michael York, Simon MacCorkindale, Jenny Agutter, Alan Badel, Jurgen Andersen

Ride the Wild Surf
US   1964   101m   Eastmancolor
Columbia/Jana (Jo and Art Napoleon)

Surf riders go to Hawaii and find romance.

Pleasant, overlong, open air fun and games.

w Jo and Art Napoleon   d Don Taylor   ph Joseph Biroc   m Stu Phillips

Fabian, Shelley Fabares, Tab Hunter, Barbara Eden

Ring of Bright Water*
GB 1969 107m Technicolor
Palomar/Brightwater (Joseph Strick)
V

A civil servant buys a pet otter and moves to a remote cottage in the western Highlands.

Disneyesque fable for animal lovers, from a bestselling book.

w Jack Couffer, Bill Travers
book Gavin Maxwell d Jack Couffer ph Wolfgang Suschitsky m Frank Cordell

Bill Travers, Virginia McKenna, Peter Jeffrey, Roddy McMillan, Jameson Clark

Rio Bravo**
US 1959 141m Technicolor
Warner/Armada (Howard Hawks)
V, L

A wandering cowboy and a drunken sheriff hold a town against outlaws.

Cheerfully overlong and slow-moving Western in which everybody, including the director, does his thing. All very watchable for those with time to spare, but more a series of revue sketches than an epic.

w Jules Furthman, Leigh Brackett
d Howard Hawks ph Russell Harlan m Dimitri Tiomkin

John Wayne, Dean Martin, Ricky Nelson, Angie Dickinson, Walter Brennan, Ward Bond, John Russell, Pedro Gonzalez Gonzalez, Claude Akins, Harry Carey Jnr, Bob Steele

'After we finished we found we could have done it a lot better . . . and that's why we went ahead and made *El Dorado*.' – Howard Hawks

† More or less remade in 1966 as *El Dorado* and in 1970 as *Rio Lobo*.

Rio Lobo*
US 1970 114m Technicolor
Cinema Center (Howard Hawks)
V, L

A Union colonel near the end of the Civil War recovers a gold shipment and exposes a traitor.

Rambling Western with traces of former glory, enjoyable at least for its sense of humour.

w Leigh Brackett, Burton Wohl
d Howard Hawks ph William Clothier m Jerry Goldsmith

John Wayne, Jorge Rivero, Jennifer O'Neill, *Jack Elam*, Victor French, Chris Mitchum, Mike Henry

THE 'ROAD' SERIES:
Road to Singapore*
US 1940 84m bw
Paramount (Harlan Thompson)

Two rich playboys swear off women until they quarrel over a Singapore maiden.

The first Hope-Crosby-Lamour 'road' picture is basically a light romantic comedy and quite forgettable; the series got zanier as it progressed.

w Don Hartman, Frank Butler
story Harry Hervey d Victor Schertzinger ph William C. Mellor m Victor Young

Bing Crosby, Bob Hope, Dorothy Lamour, Charles Coburn, Judith Barrett, Anthony Quinn, Jerry Colonna

'A deft blend of romance and comedy, songs and fisticuffs.' – *Picture Show*
'Two of the most congenially harmonized performances caught by

the camera in recent years.' – *Motion Picture Herald*

† The script was originally designed for Fred MacMurray and Jack Oakie, who weren't available; then for Burns and Allen, who turned it down.

Road to Zanzibar**
US 1941 92m bw
Paramount (Paul Jones)

The trio on safari in Africa, with *Hellzapoppin* gags breaking in and an anything-goes atmosphere.

w Frank Butler, Don Hartman
d Victor Schertzinger   ph Ted Tetzlaff   m Victor Young
songs Johnny Burke, Jimmy Van Heusen

Hope, Crosby, Lamour, Una Merkel, Eric Blore, Luis Alberni, Douglass Dumbrille

'The funniest thing I've seen on the screen in years. Years.' – *Otis Ferguson*

Road to Morocco**
US 1942 83m bw
Paramount (Paul Jones)

Hollywood Arab palaces, a captive princess, topical gags and talking camels.

w Frank Butler, Don Hartman
d David Butler   ph William C. Mellor   md Victor Young
songs Johnny Burke, Jimmy Van Heusen

Hope, Crosby, Lamour, Anthony Quinn, Dona Drake

'A bubbly spontaneous entertainment without a semblance of sanity.' – *Variety*
'It would be difficult to find a screen pantomime with better wartime credentials.' – *Kine Weekly*
'This is the screwiest picture I've ever been in.' – *Camel*
AAN: script

Road to Utopia**
US 1945 89m bw
Paramount (Paul Jones)
V, L

The Klondike gold rush, with all the previous gag styles in good order, capped by a cheeky epilogue and constant explanatory narration by Robert Benchley.

w Norman Panama, Melvin Frank
d Hal Walker   ph Lionel Lindon
m Leigh Harline   songs Johnny Burke, Jimmy Van Heusen

Hope, Crosby, Lamour, Douglass Dumbrille, Hillary Brooke, Jack La Rue
AAN: script

Road to Rio**
US 1947 100m bw
Paramount (Daniel Dare)

Guest stars are given their head, plot intrudes again in the shape of a hypnotized heiress, and the style is more constrained (but still funny).

w Edmund Beloin, Jack Rose
d Norman Z. McLeod   ph Ernest Laszlo   md Robert Emmett Dolan   songs Johnny Burke, Jimmy Van Heusen

Hope, Crosby, Lamour, Gale Sondergaard, Frank Faylen, the Wiere Brothers, the Andrews Sisters

'Enough laughs to pass the time easily and to remind you how completely, since sound came in, the American genius for movie comedy has disintegrated.' – *James Agee*
AAN: Robert Emmett Dolan

Road to Bali*

US 1952 91m Technicolor
Paramount (Harry Tugend)

In and around the South Seas, with colour making the sets obvious and the gags only tediously funny.

The team's zest was also flagging.

w Frank Butler, Hal Kanter, William Morrow d Hal Walker
ph George Barnes md Joseph J. Lilley songs Johnny Burke, Jimmy Van Heusen

Hope, Crosby, Lamour, Murvyn Vye, Peter Coe

Roar*

US 1981 102m colour Panavision
Noel Marshall/Banjiro Uemura

A research biologist lives in the African bush with assorted wild animals. He is expecting his family, but they arrive a day early when he is out . . .

A rather silly story takes in some of the most remarkable animal photography on record, and there is a sub-plot involving villainous game hunters.

wd Noel Marshall ph Jan de Bont m Dominic Frontière

Noel Marshall, Tippi Hedren, and family

† The Marshalls live with their 150 lions and other wild animals in a ranch near Los Angeles. During production the film, which eventually cost 17 million dollars, was halted by flood, fire, epidemic and injury.

Rob Roy the Highland Rogue

GB 1953 81m Technicolor
Walt Disney (Perce Pearce)

After the defeat of the clans in the 1715 rebellion, their leader escapes and after several adventures is granted a royal pardon.

A kind of Scottish Robin Hood, so stiffly acted and made that it might as well – or better – be a cartoon.

w Lawrence E. Watkin d Harold French ph Guy Green m Cedric Thorpe Davie

Richard Todd, Glynis Johns, James Robertson Justice, Michael Gough, Finlay Currie, Geoffrey Keen, Archie Duncan

Robin Hood**

US 1922 127m approx (24 fps)
  bw silent
Douglas Fairbanks

Robin Hood combats Prince John and the Sheriff of Nottingham.

An elaborate version of the legend which featured some of Hollywood's most celebrated sets and allowed the star to perform a selection of exhilarating stunts.

w Douglas Fairbanks d Allan Dwan ph Arthur Edeson
ad Wilfrid Buckland, Irvin J. Martin

Douglas Fairbanks, Wallace Beery, Alan Hale, Enid Bennett

'The high water mark of film production. It did not grow from the bankroll, it grew from the mind.' – R. E. Sherwood
'A story book picture, as gorgeous and glamorous a thing in innumerable scenes as the screen has yet shown . . . thrilling entertainment for the whole family group.' – National Board of Review

† See also *The Adventures of Robin Hood* and *The Story of Robin Hood and his Merrie Men*.

Robin Hood

US 1973 83m Technicolor
Walt Disney (Wolfgang Reitherman)
V, L

Alarmingly poor cartoon feature with all the characters 'played' by animals; songs especially dim and treatment quite lifeless.

w Larry Clemmons, Ken Anderson, others   d Wolfgang Reitherman

voices of Brian Bedford, Peter Ustinov, Terry-Thomas, Phil Harris, Andy Devine, Pat Buttram
AAN: song 'Love' (m George Bruns ly Floyd Huddleston)

Robin Hood

US 1990 104m colour
TCF/Working Title (Sarah Radclyffe, Tim Bevan)
V, L

Condemned for saving a poacher, a Saxon nobleman, Robert Hode, becomes the outlaw Robin Hood.

Dully facetious re-telling of a familiar tale.

w Mark Allen Smith, John McGrath   d John Irvin
ph Jason Lehel   m Geoffrey Burgon   pd Austen Spriggs
ed Peter Tanner

Patrick Bergin, Uma Thurman, Jurgen Prochnow, Edward Fox, Jeroen Krabbé, Owen Teale, David Morrissey, Alex North, Gabrielle Reidy

'The film increasingly comes to resemble a 1960s Hammer cheapie.'
– Sight and Sound

Robin Hood: Prince of Thieves*

US 1991 143m Technicolor
Warner/Morgan Creek (John Watson, Pen Densham, Richard B. Lewis)
V

Returning from the Crusades to discover that his father has been killed by the Sheriff of Nottingham, Robin of Locksley becomes an outlaw to get his revenge.

A glum version, with little sense of community among the outlaws and an odd mix of acting styles. But it found great favour with the public, becoming one of the most commercially successful films of the year.

w Pen Densham, John Watson
d Kevin Reynolds   ph Douglas Milsome   m John Blakeley
pd John Graysmark   ed Peter Boyle

Kevin Costner, Morgan Freeman, Mary Elizabeth Mastrantonio, Christian Slater, Alan Rickman, Sean Connery (uncredited), Geraldine McEwan, Michael McShane, Brian Blessed, Michael Wincott, Nick Brimble
AAN: song '(Everything I Do) I Do For You' (m Michael Kamen, ly Bryan Adams, Robert John Lange)

Robinson Crusoe and the Tiger

Mexico 1969 110m
   Eastmancolor
Avant/Avco Embassy

Simple but extremely handsome version of the famous story, with the addition of a tiger which Crusoe takes as a pet.

w Mario Marzac, Rene Cardona Jnr   novel Daniel Defoe   d Rene Cardona Jnr

Hugo Stieglitz, Ahui

Robinson Crusoeland

France/Italy 1950 98m bw
Sirius/Franco-London/Fortezza
V
aka: Atoll K; Escapade; Utopia

Stan and Ollie inherit an island in the

Pacific, but uranium is discovered on it.

Laurel and Hardy's last film is a dispiriting mess, and the less said about it the better.

w unknown   d Leo Joannon, John Berry   ph Armand Thirard, Louis Née   m Paul Misraki

Stan Laurel, Oliver Hardy, Suzy Delair

Rock-a-Doodle
GB 1990 74m Technicolor
Rank/Goldcrest/Sullivan Bluth (Don Bluth, Gary Goldman, John Pomeroy, Robert Enrietto)
V, L

A farmboy, transformed into a cat by a wicked owl, travels to the big city to persuade a rock-singing rooster to return home and make the sun shine again.

Excellent animation is rendered pointless by a poor and confusing narrative.

w David N. Weiss   story Don Bluth, David N. Weiss, John Pomeroy, T. J. Kuenster, David Steinberg, Gary Goldman   d Don Bluth
m Robert Folk, T. J. Kuenster
pd David Goetz   ed Bernard Caputo, Fiona Trayler, Lisa Dorney, Joe Gall

voices of Phil Harris, Glen Campbell, Eddie Deezen, Kathryn Holcomb, Toby Scott Ganger, Stan Ivar, Christian Hoff, Jason Marin, Christopher Plummer, Sandy Duncan

Rock around the Clock*
US 1956 74m bw
Columbia (Sam Katzman)

A band playing a new form of jive – rock 'n' roll – becomes a nationwide sensation.

A cheap second feature with guest artists, this cheerful little movie deserved at least a footnote in the histories because it spotlights the origins and the leading purveyors of rock 'n' roll. It also caused serious riots in several countries. A sequel in 1957, *Don't Knock the Rock*, was merely cheap.

w Robert E. Kent, James B. Gordon   d Fred F. Sears
ph Benjamin H. Kline

Bill Haley and the Comets, the Platters, Little Richard, Tony Martinez and his Band, Freddie Bell and the Bellboys, Johnny Johnson, Alan Freed, Lisa Gaye, Alix Talton

The Rocketeer
US 1991 108m Technicolor Panavision
Walt Disney/Silver Screen Partners IV (Lawrence Gordon, Charles Gordon, Lloyd Levin)
V, L

In 1938 a racing pilot finds a one-man rocket pack which he uses to foil a Nazi's attempt at world domination.

Tame attempt at a period adventure that never gets off the ground.

w Danny Bilson, Paul De Meo
graphic novel by Dave Stevens   d Joe Johnston   ph Hiro Narita
m James Horner   pd Jim Bissell
sp Jon G. Belyeu   ed Arthur Schmidt

Bill Campbell, Jennifer Connelly, Alan Arkin, Timothy Dalton, Paul Sorvino, Terry O'Quinn, Ed Lauter, James Handy

'This high-octane, high-flying, live-action comic strip has been machine-tooled into agreeable lightweight summer fare.' – *Variety*

'His whole life was a million-to-one shot!'
Rocky**
US 1976 119m Technicolor
UA/Chartoff-Winkler (Gene Kirkwood)
V, L

A slightly dimwitted Philadelphia boxer makes good.

Pleasantly old-fashioned comedy-drama with rather unattractive characters in the modern manner. Despite the freshness, on the whole *Marty* is still preferable.

w Sylvester Stallone d John G. Avildsen ph James Crabe m Bill Conti

Sylvester Stallone, Burgess Meredith, Talia Shire, Burt Young, Carl Weathers, Thayer David

AA: best picture; John G. Avildsen
AAN: Sylvester Stallone (as writer); song 'Gonna Fly Now' (m Bill Conti, ly Carol Connors, Ayn Robbins); Sylvester Stallone (as actor); Burgess Meredith; Talia Shire; Burt Young

Rocky II
US 1979 119m Technicolor
UA/Irwin Winkler, Robert Chartoff
V, L

After success comes failure; then Rocky marries his sweetheart and works for another big fight.

Over-inflated but under-nourished sequel with absolutely nothing new to offer.

wd Sylvester Stallone ph Bill Butler m Bill Conti

Sylvester Stallone, Talia Shire, Burt Young, Carl Weathers, Burgess Meredith

'A Fighter. A Lover. A Legend. The Greatest Challenge.'
Rocky III
US 1982 99m Technicolor
United Artists/Chartoff-Winkler (James D. Brubaker)
V, L

Rocky is challenged by a brutal slugger who beats him at the first match . . .

Unnecessary regurgitation of bits and pieces from the first two Rocky movies.

wd Sylvester Stallone ph Bill Butler m Bill Conti pd William J. Cassidy ed Don Zimmerman, Mark Warner

Sylvester Stallone, Talia Shire, Burt Young, Burgess Meredith, Carl Weathers, Tony Burton, Mr T, Hulk Hogan

'The time has surely come for Rocky Balboa to take the final count.' – *Tom Milne, MFB*
'The first Rocky was primitive in a relatively innocent way. This picture is primitive too, but it's also shrewd and empty and inept.' – *New Yorker*
AAN: original song 'Eye of the Tiger' by Jim Peterik and Frankie Sullivan III

Rocky IV
US 1985 91m Metrocolor
MGM/UA/Winkler-Chartoff
V, L

Rocky takes on a Russian champion.

Hilarious, hysterical, would-be allegorical, this is the pits; but it took a lot of money.

wd Sylvester Stallone ph Bill Butler m Vince DiCola, Bill Conti pd Bill Kenney ed Don Zimmerman, John W. Wheeler

Sylvester Stallone, Dolph Lundren,

Carl Weathers, Talia Shire, Burt Young, Brigitte Nielsen

'Ludicrous rubbish, but efficient with it.' – *Shaun Usher, Daily Mail*

'Where does a champion go when he takes off the gloves?'

Rocky V
US 1990 104m DeLuxe
UIP/United Artists/Star Partners III (Robert Chartoff, Irwin Winkler)
V, L

Rocky, suffering, unsurprisingly, from brain-damage, takes on a young protégé.

The series continues its steep, downward spiral into insipid nonsense.

w Sylvester Stallone d John G. Avildsen ph Steven Poster m Bill Conti pd William J. Cassidy ed John G. Avildsen, Michael N. Knue

Sylvester Stallone, Talia Shire, Burt Young, Sage Stallone, Burgess Meredith, Tommy Morrison, Richard Gant, Tony Burton

† Stallone's original ending had Rocky dying in his moment of final triumph.

Rogues of Sherwood Forest*
US 1950 80m Technicolor
Columbia (Fred M. Packard)

Robin Hood's son helps the barons to force the signing of Magna Carta.

Satisfactory action adventure.

w George Bruce d Gordon Douglas ph Charles Lawton Jnr m Heinz Roemheld, Arthur Morton

John Derek, Diana Lynn, George Macready, Alan Hale, Paul Cavanagh, Lowell Gilmore, Billy House

Romancing the Stone*
US 1984 106m DeLuxe Panavision
TCF/El Corazon (Michael Douglas)
V

A best-selling lady romance novelist gets more than she bargained for when she tries to find her kidnapped sister in Colombia.

Spoof adventure thriller which takes too long to get going and then finds it has nowhere to go. But commercial . . .

w Diane Thomas d Robert Zemeckis ph Dean Cundey m Alan Silvestri pd Lawrence G. Paull

Michael Douglas, Kathleen Turner, Danny DeVito, Zack Norman, Alfonso Arau

'The picture has a bravura opening and a jolly kind of movement, but it becomes too slambang.' – *Pauline Kael, New Yorker*

Romeo and Juliet*
GB 1968 152m Technicolor
Paramount/BHE/Verona/Dino de Laurentiis (Anthony Havelock-Allan, John Brabourne, Richard Goodwin)
V, L

The with-it version for modern youngsters.

Unfortunately the admirably rapid style does not suit the verse, and long before the much-deferred end the thing becomes just as tiresome as the other versions.

w Franco Brusati, Masolino D'Amico d Franco Zeffirelli ph Pasquale de Santis m Nino Rota

Leonard Whiting, Olivia Hussey, John McEnery, Michael York, Pat Heywood, Milo O'Shea, Paul Hardwick, Natasha

Parry, Antonio Pierfederici, Esmeralda Ruspoli, Bruce Robinson, Roberto Bisacco, Laurence Olivier as prologue speaker

'A large gold watch should be tossed to Zeffirelli for his part in reversing the movies' reputation for emasculating the classics.' – *Newsweek*

AA: Pasquale de Santis; costumes (Danilo Donati)
AAN: best picture; Franco Zeffirelli

Rooster Cogburn*
US 1975 108m Technicolor
 Panavision
Universal (Paul Nathan)
V, L

An elderly marshal after a gang of outlaws is helped by the Bible-thumping daughter of a priest.

Disappointing Western too obviously patterned after *True Grit* and *The African Queen*. Having had the idea for outrageous star casting, the producers obviously decided erroneously that the film would make itself.

w Martin Julien   d Stuart Millar
ph Harry Stradling Jnr   m Laurence Rosenthal

John Wayne, Katharine Hepburn, Anthony Zerbe, Richard Jordan, John McIntyre, Strother Martin

'Like one of those infuriating exhibition bouts in which two resilient old pros bob, weave and spar without ever landing any punches.' – *Michael Billington, Illustrated London News*

† 'Martin Julien' allegedly covers the writing talents of Hal Wallis, his wife Martha Hyer, and some friends.

Roxanne*
US 1987 107m DeLuxe
Columbia/Michael Rachmil, Daniel Melnick
V, L

An ugly man writes love letters for his friend ... but true love will find a way.

Zany modernization of Rostand's *Cyrano de Bergerac*, funny in spots but way overlong.

w Steve Martin   d Fred Schepisi
ph Ian Baker   m Bruce Smeaton   pd Jack DeGovia

Steve Martin, Daryl Hannah, Rick Rossovich, Shelley Duvall, John Kapelos, Fred Willard, Michael J. Pollard

Royal African Rifles
US 1954 75m Cinecolor
Allied Artists
GB title: *Storm over Africa*

In British East Africa in 1914, a lieutenant tracks down a consignment of stolen guns.

Mini-budgeted *Boy's Own Paper* heroics; quite enjoyable on its level.

w Dan Ullman   d Lesley Selander

Louis Hayward, Veronica Hurst, Michael Pate, Angela Greene, Steve Geray, Bruce Lester

Royal Flash
GB 1975 118m Technicolor
TCF/Two Roads (David V. Picker, Denis O'Dell)

A Victorian bully and braggart has various adventures in Europe and Ruritania.

A rather unsatisfactory romp which takes pot shots at every 19th-century person and object in the encyclopaedia, but is never as funny as it intends to be.

w George Macdonald Fraser
novel George Macdonald Fraser
d Richard Lester   ph Geoffrey Unsworth   m Ken Thorpe
pd Terence Marsh

Malcolm McDowell, Oliver Reed, Alan Bates, Florinda Bolkan, Britt Ekland, Lionel Jeffries, Tom Bell, Joss Ackland, Leon Greene, Richard Hurndall, Alastair Sim, Michael Hordern

Run Wild, Run Free*
GB 1969 98m Technicolor
Columbia/Irving Allen (John Danischewsky)
V

A mute boy living on Dartmoor gains self-confidence through the love of animals.

Rather vaguely developed family film with agreeable sequences.

w David Rook   novel The White Colt by David Rook   d Richard C. Sarafian   ph Wilkie Cooper
m David Whitaker

John Mills, Sylvia Syms, Mark Lester, Bernard Miles, Gordon Jackson, Fiona Fullerton

Safety Last***

US 1923 70m (24 fps) bw silent
Harold Lloyd
V

A small-town boy goes to the big city and to impress his girl friend enters a contest to climb a skyscraper.

Marvellous star comedy which set a new standard not only in sight gags but in the comedy-thrill stunts which became Lloyd's stock-in-trade.

w Harold Lloyd, Sam Taylor, Tim Whelan, Hal Roach *d* Sam Taylor, Fred Newmeyer *ph* Walter Lundin

Harold Lloyd, Mildred Davis, Noah Young

Sailor Beware

US 1952 103m bw
Paramount/Hal B. Wallis

Martin and Lewis in the navy.

Unlovable star antics.

w James Allardice, Martin Rackin *play* Kenyon Nicholson, Charles Robinson *d* Hal Walker *ph* Daniel L. Fapp *m* Joseph J. Lilley

Dean Martin, Jerry Lewis, Corinne Calvet, Marion Marshall, Robert Strauss, Leif Erickson

Saludos Amigos*

US 1943 43m Technicolor
Walt Disney

Donald Duck has various South American adventures with a parrot named Joe Carioca.

Basically a naïve implementation of the good neighbour policy, but with flashes of brilliant animation and some mingling of live-action with cartoon.

production supervisor Norman Ferguson

'Self-interested, belated ingratiation embarrasses me, and Disney's famous cuteness, however richly it may mirror national infantilism, is hard on my stomach.' – *James Agee*
AAN: music (Edward H. Plumb, Paul J. Smith, Charles Wolcott); title song (*m* Charles Wolcott, *ly* Ned Washington)

Sammy Going South*

GB 1963 128m Eastmancolor Cinemascope
Bryanston (Hal Mason)
US title: *A Boy Ten Feet Tall*

A 10-year-old boy is orphaned in Port Said and hitch-hikes to his aunt in Durban.

Disappointing family-fodder epic in which the mini-adventures follow each other too predictably.

w Denis Cannan *novel* W. H. Canaway *d* Alexander Mackendrick *ph* Erwin Hillier *m* Tristam Cary

Fergus McClelland, Edward G.

Robinson, Constance Cummings, Harry H. Corbett

Sandokan the Great

Italy/France/Spain 1963 114m Techniscope
Filmes/CCF/Ocean

The son of the Sultan of Borneo wages jungle war against the oppressive British.

A curious mixture of Tarzan and Robin Hood, this character appeared in several adventures before expiring; the first chapter is the best, or least worst.

w Fulvio Gicca, Umberto Lenzi
novel Emilio Salgari d Umberto Lenzi

Steve Reeves, Genevieve Grad, Rik Battaglia, Andrea Bosic

Sands of the Desert

GB 1960 92m Technicolor
Associated British
V

A diminutive travel agent goes out to investigate a desert holiday camp which has suffered from sabotage.

Limp star comedy with poor studio work and meandering script.

wd John Paddy Carstairs

Charlie Drake, Peter Arne, Sarah Branch, Raymond Huntley, Peter Illing, Harold Kasket

The Sandwich Man*

GB 1966 95m Eastmancolor
Rank/Titan (Peter Newbrook)

In the course of a walking day around London a sandwich man encounters many of his eccentric acquaintances.

Spurned when it was first released, this comedy variety show, mostly in mime, can now be seen to be of a kind popularized by TV, and may have been simply ahead of its time. It certainly seems funnier than it did.

w Michael Bentine, Robert Hartford-Davis d Robert Hartford-Davis
ph Peter Newbrook m Mike Vickers

Michael Bentine, Dora Bryan, Suzy Kendall, Norman Wisdom, Harry H. Corbett, Bernard Cribbins, Ian Hendry, Stanley Holloway, Alfie Bass, Diana Dors, Ron Moody, Wilfrid Hyde White, Donald Wolfit, Max Bacon, Fred Emney, Frank Finlay, Peter Jones, Michael Medwin, Ronnie Stevens, John Le Mesurier, Sidney Tafler, John Junkin, Warren Mitchell

Santa Claus

GB 1985 112m Rank colour Panavision
Alexander Salkind (Ilya Salkind, Pierre Spengler)
V, L

An old woodcutter is given immortality by the elves and turned into Santa Claus; in modern times, he goes to New York to rescue a discontented elf from the clutches of a demon toymaker.

Utterly charmless treatment of an extremely vague legend, with the two halves entirely failing to coalesce and the level of invention low throughout.

w David Newman d Jeannot Szwarc ph Arthur Ibbetson
m Henry Mancini pd Anthony Pratt ed Peter Hollywood

David Huddleston, Dudley Moore, John Lithgow, Judy Cornwell, Christian Fitzpatrick, Burgess Meredith

'For children of all ages, but it skews

Saps at Sea

US 1940 60m bw
Hal Roach
V, V(C)

Olly needs a rest after working in a horn factory, so he and Stan take a boating holiday but are kidnapped by a gangster.

Disappointing star comedy with gags too few and too long drawn out.

w Charles Rogers, Harry Langdon, Gil Pratt, Felix Adler   *d* Gordon Douglas   *ph* Art Lloyd   *m* Marvin Hatley

Stan Laurel, Oliver Hardy, James Finlayson, Dick Cramer, Ben Turpin

The Saracen Blade

US 1954 76m Technicolor
Columbia (Sam Katzman)

In the 13th century a young Italian crusader devotes himself to avenging the murder of his father.

Cut-price swashbuckler full of unintentional laughs and therefore quite watchable.

w DeVallon Scott, Worthing Yates *novel* Frank Yerby   *d* William Castle

Ricardo Montalban, Betta St John, Rick Jason, Carolyn Jones, Michael Ansara

'The Sound of Freedom.'
'Her story will move you. Her struggle will change you. Her spirit will inspire you.'

Sarafina!

South Africa 1992 116m Agfacolor
Warner/Ideal/Distant Horizon/Videovision/Ariane/VPI/BBC (Anant Singh, David M. Thompson)

A South African schoolgirl in Soweto realizes she has to fight for freedom, following the example of her history teacher and her mother – and learning from her own experiences when she is imprisoned and tortured.

An odd mix of musical and near-documentary realism that obstinately fails to comes to life on the screen.

w William Nicholson, Mbongeni Ngema   *musical* Mbongeni Ngema   *d* Darrell James Roodt *ph* Mark Vincente   *m* Stanley Myers   *ch* Michael Peters, Mbongeni Ngema   *ed* Peter Hollywood, Sarah Thomas

Leleti Khumalo, Whoopi Goldberg, Miriam Makeba, John Kani, Dumisani Diamini, Mbongeni Ngema, Sipho Kunene

'If one is prepared to forgive it its large measure of amateurishness and naivety, and is braced for the distress inherent in the subject matter, this can be cautiously recommended as a vivid testament to the unacceptable circumstances in which too many children grow up.' – *Angie Errigo, Empire*

Savage Islands

New Zealand 1983 94m colour
Paramount (Lloyd Phillips, Rob Whitehouse)

On the morning of his execution, a pirate recalls rescuing a beautiful Englishwoman from a rival brigand.

Standard adventure fare, given a slight novelty by being set in the era of steam warships.

w John Hughes, David Odell *story* Lloyd Phillips   *d* Ferdinand Fairfax   *ph* Tony Imi   *m* Trevor Jones   *pd* Maurice Cain   *ed* John Shirley

Tommy Lee Jones, Michael O'Keefe, Max Phipps, Jenny Seagrove, Bruce Allpress, Grant Tilley

Savage Sam*

US 1962 104m Technicolor
Walt Disney (Bill Anderson)

The youngest son of a homesteading family has a troublesome dog which redeems itself by tracking down Apaches.

Folksy boy-and-dog Western, good of its kind, with adequate suspense and scenery.

w Fred Gipson, William Tunberg d Norman Tokar ph Edward Colman m Oliver Wallace

Brian Keith, Tommy Kirk, Kevin Corcoran, Dewey Martin, Jeff York

'A cadet edition of the best of Ford.' – *MFB*

Scalawag

US/Italy 1973 93m Technicolor
Bryna/Inex-Oceania (Anne Douglas)

Mexico 1840: a one-legged pirate and a boy try to trace a hidden treasure.

Flagrant reworking of *Treasure Island*, heavily overdone by stars and rhubarbing extras alike.

w Albert Maltz, Sid Fleischman d Kirk Douglas ph Jack Cardiff m John Cameron

Kirk Douglas, Mark Lester, Neville Brand, David Stroud, Lesley-Anne Down, Phil Brown

Scaramouche**

US 1952 115m Technicolor
MGM (Carey Wilson)

A young man disguises himself as an actor to avenge the death of his friend at the hands of a wicked marquis.

Cheerful swashbuckler set in French revolutionary times, first filmed in the twenties with Ramon Novarro. MGM costume production at somewhere near its best.

w Ronald Millar, George Froeschel novel Rafael Sabatini d George Sidney ph Charles Rosher m Victor Young ad Cedric Gibbons, Hans Peters

Stewart Granger, Mel Ferrer, Eleanor Parker, Janet Leigh, Henry Wilcoxon, Nina Foch, Lewis Stone, Robert Coote, Richard Anderson

† The sword fight, at 6½ minutes, is credited with being the longest in cinema history.

The Scarlet Pimpernel***

GB 1934 98m bw
London Films (Alexander Korda)
L

In the early days of the French revolution, an apparently foppish Englishman leads a daring band in rescuing aristocrats from the guillotine.

First-class period adventure with a splendid and much imitated plot, strong characters, humour and a richly detailed historical background.

w Robert E. Sherwood, Sam Berman, Arthur Wimperis, Lajos Biro novel Baroness Orczy d Harold Young ph Harold Rosson m Arthur Benjamin

Leslie Howard, Merle Oberon, Raymond Massey, Nigel Bruce, Bramwell Fletcher, Anthony Bushell, Joan Gardner, Walter Rilla

'Excellent British import that will do business.' – *Variety*
'One of the most romantic and durable of all swashbucklers.' – *New Yorker*, 1976

'A triumph for the British film world.'
– *Sunday Times*

† Some scenes were directed by Alexander Korda, others by Rowland Brown.

†† The story was remade as *The Elusive Pimpernel* (qv) and in 1982 in a TV version starring Anthony Andrews. See also *The Return of the Scarlet Pimpernel*.

Scott of the Antarctic**
GB 1948 111m Technicolor
Ealing (Sidney Cole)
V

After long preparation, Captain Scott sets off on his ill-fated 1912 expedition to the South Pole.

The stiff-upper-lip saga par excellence; inevitable knowledge of the end makes it pretty downbeat, and the actors can only be sincere; but the snowscapes, most of them artificial, are fine.

w Ivor Montagu, Walter Meade, Mary Hayley Bell *d* Charles Frend *ph* Geoffrey Unsworth, Jack Cardiff, Osmond Borradaile *m* Ralph Vaughan Williams

John Mills, James Robertson Justice, Derek Bond, Harold Warrender, Reginald Beckwith, Kenneth More, James McKechnie, John Gregson

Scram!*
US 1932 20m bw
Hal Roach
V

Two vagrants are ordered out of town but by a series of misadventures are found drunk with the judge's wife.

Generally sprightly star comedy culminating in a marathon laughing session.

w H. M. Walker *d* Ray McCarey

Laurel and Hardy, Arthur Housman, Rychard Cramer, Vivien Oakland

Scrooge*
GB 1935 78m bw
Twickenham (Julius Hagen, John Brahm)

A miser reforms after ghosts haunt him on Christmas Eve.

Acceptable unambitious version with interesting performances.

w Seymour Hicks, H. Fowler Mear *novel* Charles Dickens *d* Henry Edwards *ph* Sidney Blythe, William Luff

Seymour Hicks, Donald Calthrop (Cratchit), Athene Seyler, Oscar Asche, Barbara Everest, Maurice Evans, C. V. France, Marie Ney

Scrooge***
GB 1951 86m bw
Renown (Brian Desmond Hurst)
V
US title: *A Christmas Carol*

By far the best available version of the classic parable; casting, art direction, pace and general handling are as good as can be.

w Noel Langley *d* Brian Desmond Hurst *ph* C. Pennington-Richards *m* Richard Addinsell

Alastair Sim, Mervyn Johns, Kathleen Harrison, Jack Warner, Michael Hordern, Hermione Baddeley, George Cole, Miles Malleson

Scrooge*
GB 1970 113m Technicolor Panavision
Cinema Center/Waterbury (Robert H. Solo)
V, L

Dim musical version, darkly coloured

and quite lost on the wide screen; but it has its macabre moments of trick photography.

w/m/ly Leslie Bricusse   d Ronald Neame   ph Oswald Morris   pd Terry Marsh

Albert Finney, Michael Medwin, Alec Guinness, Edith Evans, Kenneth More, David Collings, Laurence Naismith, Kay Walsh

† Richard Harris and Rex Harrison were both sought before Finney was signed.
AAN: song 'Thank You Very Much' (m/ly Leslie Bricusse)

Scrooged*
US   1988   101m   Technicolor
Paramount/Mirage (Richard Donner, Art Linson)
V, L

Updated version of Dickens's *A Christmas Carol*, centring on the president of a New York television company.

Energetic and sometimes genuinely scary seasonal entertainment for modern kids.

w Mitch Glazer, Michael O'Donoghue   d Richard Donner   ph Michael Chapman   m Danny Elfman   pd J. Michael Riva

Bill Murray, Karen Allen, John Forsythe, Robert Mitchum, John Housman, Lee Majors

'If you miss it, you will owe yourself an apology!'

The Sea Hawk***
US   1940   122m   bw
Warner (Hal B. Wallis, Henry Blanke)
V, L

Elizabeth I encourages one of her most able captains to acts of piracy against the Spanish.

Wobbly-plotted but stirring and exciting seafaring actioner, with splendid battle and duel scenes.

w Seton I. Miller, Howard Koch   d Michael Curtiz   ph Sol Polito   m Erich Wolfgang Korngold   ad Anton Grot

Errol Flynn, Flora Robson, Brenda Marshall, *Henry Daniell*, Claude Rains, Donald Crisp, Alan Hale, Una O'Connor, James Stephenson, Gilbert Roland, William Lundigan

'Endless episodes of court intrigue tend to diminish the effect of the epic sweep of the high seas dramatics.' – *Variety*
AAN: Erich Wolfgang Korngold; Anton Grot

The Secret Garden*
US   1949   92m   bw (Technicolor sequence)
MGM (Clarence Brown)
V

An orphan girl goes to stay with her moody uncle and brightens up the lives of those around her.

Subdued, richly produced, rather likeable Victorian fable with the same moral as *The Bluebird* and *The Wizard of Oz*: happiness is in your own back yard.

w Robert Ardrey   *novel* Frances Hodgson Burnett   d Fred M. Wilcox   ph Ray June   m Bronislau Kaper

Margaret O'Brien, Herbert Marshall, Gladys Cooper, Elsa Lanchester, Dean Stockwell, Brian Roper

'Uneven, but oddly and unexpectedly interesting.' – *Richard Mallett, Punch*
'Let's have more pictures in this kindly vein.' – *Picturegoer*

The Secret Garden**
US 1993 101m Technicolor
Warner/American Zoetrope (Fred Fuchs, Fred Roos, Tom Luddy)
V

A young, lonely, orphaned girl, sent to live with her aristocratic uncle, helps her invalid cousin back to life.

A charming version of the classic children's story, deftly-made, though its appeal may be too tame for today's audiences.

w Caroline Thompson
novel Frances Hodgson Burnett
d Agnieszka Holland

Maggie Smith, Kate Maberly, Heydon Prowse, Andrew Knott, Laura Crossley, John Lynch, Walter Sparrow, Irene Jacob

'Executed to near perfection in all artistic departments.' – *Variety*

The Secret of Nimh*
US 1982 82m Technicolor
Aurora/Don Bluth

Forced out of her cosy field, a widowed mouse seeks the help of Nicodemus, king of the rat pack.

Animated cartoon by Disney artists who rejected that company's declining standards and set up their own factory. Alas, though they have the skills, the narrative they have chosen needed refining.

w Don Bluth, John Pomeroy, Gary Foldman, Will Finn novel *Mrs Frisby and the Rats of Nimh* by Robert C. O'Brien d Don Bluth m Jerry Goldsmith

'Vintage techniques are proudly invoked, but the story desperately needs loving care.' – *Sight and Sound*

Sequoia
US 1934 73m bw
MGM

A girl living in the High Sierras defends wild animals from hunters.

Refreshingly unusual outdoor drama with good location photography.

w Ann Cunningham, Sam Arnstrong, Carey Wilson d Chester Franklin ph Chester Lyons

Jean Parker, Russell Hardie, Samuel S. Hinds, Paul Hurst

'It was unlikely that either Miss Parker or the deer would eat the puma, but I hung on hoping that the puma would eat the deer or Miss Parker.' – *James Agate*

Sgt Pepper's Lonely Hearts Club Band
US 1978 111m Technicolor Panavision
Universal/Robert Stigwood (Dee Anthony)
L

A family band finds a new sound despite the activities of villains.

Oddball hotch-potch of middle-aged comedy and youth nostalgia with an American small-town setting. Some moments please, but most of it simply doesn't gell.

w Henry Edwards d Michael Schultz ph Owen Roizman
m various (mostly the Beatles)
pd Brian Eatwell

Peter Frampton, Barry Gibb, Robin Gibb, Maurice Gibb, George Burns, Frankie Howerd, Donald Pleasence, Paul Nicholas, Sandy Farina, Alice Cooper, Steve Martin, Earth Wind and Fire

'Another of those films which serve as feature-length screen advertising for an album.' – *Variety*

Seven Faces of Dr Lao*
US 1964 100m Metrocolor
MGM/George Pal

An elderly Chinaman with a penchant for spectacular disguise solves the problems of a western desert town.

A pleasant idea and excellent production are submerged in a sloppily sentimental and verbose script.

w Charles Beaumont novel The Circus of Dr Lao by Charles G. Finney d George Pal ph Robert Bronner m Leigh Harline make-up William Tuttle

Tony Randall, Arthur O'Connell, John Ericson, Barbara Eden, Noah Beery Jnr, Lee Patrick, Minerva Urecal, John Qualen

The Seventh Voyage of Sinbad*
US 1958 89m Technicolor
Columbia/Morningside (Charles Schneer)
V, L

Sinbad seeks a roc's egg which will restore his fiancée from the midget size to which an evil magician has reduced her.

Lively fantasy with narrative drive and excellent effects.

w Kenneth Kolb d Nathan Juran ph Wilkie Cooper m Bernard Herrmann sp Ray Harryhausen

Kerwin Mathews, Kathryn Grant, Torin Thatcher, Richard Eyer, Alec Mango

The Shaggy DA
US 1976 92m Technicolor
Walt Disney (Ron Miller)

A magic ring enables a young lawyer to become a talking dog and thus expose corruption.

Rather feeble sequel to *The Shaggy Dog*, with overtones of Watergate.

w Don Tait d Robert Stevenson ph Frank Phillips m Buddy Baker sp Eustace Lycett, Art Cruickshank, Danne Lee

Dean Jones, Tim Conway, Suzanne Pleshette, Jo Anne Worley, Vic Tayback, Keenan Wynn, Dick Van Patten

The Shaggy Dog*
US 1959 101m bw
Walt Disney (Bill Walsh)

A small boy turns into a big shaggy dog and catches some crooks.

Simple-minded, overlong Disney comedy for kids and their indulgent parents; good laughs in the chase scenes.

w Bill Walsh, Lillie Hayward novel The Hound of Florence by Felix Salten d Charles Barton ph Edward Colman m Paul Sawtell

Fred MacMurray, Jean Hagen, Tommy Kirk, Cecil Kellaway, Annette Funicello, Tim Considine, Kevin Corcoran, Alexander Scourby

The Shakiest Gun in the West
US 1967 101m Techniscope
Universal (Edward J. Montagne)

A cowardly dentist becomes a Western hero.

Dreary farce, an unsubtle remake of *The Paleface*.

w Jim Fritzell, Everett Greenbaum d Alan Rafkin ph Andrew Jackson m Vic Mizzy

Don Knotts, Barbara Rhoades, Jackie Coogan, Don Barry

Shane***
US 1953 118m Technicolor
Paramount (George Stevens, Ivan Moffat)
V, L

A mysterious stranger helps a family of homesteaders.

Archetypal family Western, but much slower and statelier than most, as though to emphasize its own quality, which is evident anyway.

w A. B. Guthrie Jnr novel Jack Schaefer d George Stevens
ph Loyal Griggs m Victor Young

Alan Ladd, Jean Arthur, Van Heflin, *Jack Palance*, Brandon de Wilde, Ben Johnson, Edgar Buchanan, Emile Meyer, Elisha Cook Jnr, John Dierkes

'A kind of dramatic documentary of the pioneer days of the west.' – *MFB*
'Westerns are better when they're not too self-importantly self-conscious.' – *New Yorker, 1975*
'Stevens managed to infuse a new vitality, a new sense of realism into the time-worn story through the strength and freshness of his visuals.' – *Arthur Knight*

AA: Loyal Griggs
AAN: best picture; A. B. Guthrie Jnr; George Stevens; Jack Palance; Brandon de Wilde

Shark's Treasure*
US 1974 95m DeLuxe
UA/Symbol (Cornel Wilde)

Treasure hunters seek buried gold in the Caribbean where sharks abound.

Fairly thrilling action hokum.

wd Cornel Wilde ph Jack Atcheler, Al Giddings m Robert O. Ragland

Cornel Wilde, Yaphet Kotto, John Neilson, David Canary, Cliff Osmond

'Wilde maintains his reputation for making the most likeable bad movies around.' – *Tom Milne*

'Young and beautiful for 500 years – and wicked every one of them!'
She*
US 1935 89m bw
RKO (Merian C. Cooper)

Ancient papers lead a Cambridge professor and his friends to the lost city where dwells a queen who cannot die – until she falls in love.

The producers have the right spirit for this Victorian fantasy, but tried too hard to emulate the mood of their own *King Kong*, and it was a mistake to transfer the setting from Africa to the Arctic. One for connoisseurs, though.

w Ruth Rose, Dudley Nichols
novel H. Rider Haggard d Irving Pichel, Lansing G. Holden ph J. Roy Hunt m Max Steiner
ch Benjamin Zemach

Randolph Scott, Nigel Bruce, Helen Gahagan

'Beautiful production, but story dubious for discriminating adults.' – *Variety*
'To an unrepentant Haggard fan it does sometimes seem to catch the thrill as well as the childishness of his invention.' – *Graham Greene*
'A spectacle of magnificent proportions with the decadent effluvium of the tomb period.' – *Photoplay*
'The stagey décor of Kor is in the art deco style of Radio City Music Hall, and you keep expecting the Rockettes to turn up.' – *Pauline Kael, 70s*
AAN: Benjamin Zemach

She

GB 1965 105m Technicolor Hammerscope
ABP/Hammer (Michael Carreras, Aida Young)

Flat, uninventive and tedious remake which reverts to Africa but does nothing else right; it ignores the essential Cambridge prologue and ignores all suggestions of fantasy.

w David T. Chantler novel H. Rider Haggard d Robert Day ph Harry Waxman m James Bernard ad Robert Jones, Don Mingaye ed James Needs, Eric Boyd-Perkins

Peter Cushing, Ursula Andress, Christopher Lee, John Richardson, Bernard Cribbins, André Morell, Rosenda Monteros

The Sheriff of Fractured Jaw

GB 1958 103m Eastmancolor Cinemascope
TCF/Daniel M. Angel

A London gunsmith in the old west accidentally becomes a hero.

Tame, predictable comedy with a clear lack of invention.

w Arthur Dales d Raoul Walsh ph Otto Heller m Robert Farnon

Kenneth More, Jayne Mansfield, Robert Morley, Ronald Squire, David Horne, Henry Hull, Eynon Evans, Bruce Cabot, William Campbell

Sherlock Holmes and the Secret Weapon*

US 1942 68m bw
Universal (Howard Benedict)
V

Sherlock Holmes saves a stolen bombsight from Nazi agents.

Slightly stiff modernized Holmes story with amusing ingredients.

w Edward T. Lowe, W. Scott Darling, Edmund L. Hartmann, vaguely based on *The Dancing Men* by Sir Arthur Conan Doyle d Roy William Neill ph Les White m Frank Skinner

Basil Rathbone, Nigel Bruce, Lionel Atwill (as Moriarty), Dennis Hoey, Karen Verne, William Post Jnr, Mary Gordon

Sherlock Junior**

US 1924 45m (24 fps) bw silent
Metro/Buster Keaton (Joseph M. Schenck)
V

A film projectionist, unjustly accused of stealing a watch, has dreams of being a great detective.

Fast-moving, gag-filled comedy which ranks among its star's best.

w Clyde Bruckman, Jean Havez, Joseph Mitchell d/ed Buster Keaton ph Elgin Lessley, Byron Houck

Buster Keaton, Kathryn McGuire, Ward Crane, Joseph Keaton

Short Circuit*

US 1986 98m Metrocolor Panavision
Rank/PSO (David Foster, Lawrence Turman)
V, L

An electric shock transforms a military robot into a creature with a mind of its own.

Amusing, if predictable comedy that owes much to *E.T.*

w S. S. Wilson, Brent Maddock d John Badham ph Nick McLean m David Shire ad Dianne Wager ed Frank Morriss

Ally Sheedy, Steve Guttenberg, Fisher

Stevens, Austin Pendleton, G. W. Bailey, Brian McNamara, Tim Blaney

Short Circuit 2
US 1988 110m Technicolor
Columbia TriStar (David Foster, Lawrence Turman, Gary Foster)
V

At large in the big city, a robot with human sensibilities is fooled into helping jewel thieves.

Ineffectual sequel, lacking in laughs and bungling the action.

w S. S. Wilson, Brent Maddock
d Kenneth Johnson ph John McPherson m Charles Fox
pd Bill Brodie ed Conrad Buff

Fisher Stevens, Michael McKean, Cynthia Gibb, Jack Weston, Dee McCafferty, David Hemblen, Tim Blaney

The Siege of the Saxons
GB 1963 85m Technicolor
Columbia/Ameran (Jud Kinberg)

When King Arthur is ill, the Saxons plot his overthrow but are foiled by a handsome outlaw.

Comic strip adventure with action highlights borrowed from older and better films.

w John Kohn, Jud Kinberg
d Nathan Juran ph Wilkie Cooper, Jack Willis m Laurie Johnson

Ronald Lewis, Janette Scott, Ronald Howard, Mark Dignam, John Laurie, Richard Clarke, Jerome Willis

'Against his ruthless pagan lusts – the power of a woman's love!'
The Sign of the Pagan
US 1954 92m Technicolor Cinemascope
U-I (Albert J. Cohen)

Attila the Hun is defeated by the Romans.

Historic horse opera, rather cheaply done.

w Oscar Brodney, Barre Lyndon
d Douglas Sirk ph Russell Metty
m Frank Skinner, Hans Salter

Jeff Chandler, Jack Palance, Rita Gam, Ludmilla Tcherina, Jeff Morrow, George Dolenz, Eduard Franz, Alexander Scourby

Silent Movie*
US 1976 87m DeLuxe
TCF/Crossbow (Michael Hertzberg)
V, L

An alcoholic producer gets the idea that a silent movie would be a great novelty, and tries to get stars to take part.

Fairly lively spoof with the talents concerned in variable form. The shortage of laughter made it a hit in the seventies, but at no time does it approach the Keaton or Laurel and Hardy level.

w Mel Brooks, Ron Clark, Rudy de Luca, Barry Levinson d Mel Brooks ph Paul Lohmann
m John Morris

Mel Brooks, Marty Feldman, Dom De Luise, Bernardette Peters, Sid Caesar, Harold Gould, Fritz Feld, Harry Ritz, Henny Youngman guest stars Anne Bancroft, Paul Newman, Burt Reynolds, James Caan, Liza Minnelli, Marcel Marceau

† Marcel Marceau utters the only word in the movie, which is *'Non'*.

Sinbad and the Eye of the Tiger
GB 1977 113m Metrocolor
Columbia/Andor (Charles H. Schneer, Ray Harryhausen)
V, L

Sinbad frees a city from a wicked woman's spell.

Lumpish sequel to a sequel: even the animated monsters raise a yawn this time.

w Beverly Cross *d* Sam Wanamaker *ph* Ted Moore
m Roy Budd *sp* Ray Harryhausen

Patrick Wayne, Taryn Power, Jane Seymour, Margaret Whiting, Patrick Troughton

Sinbad the Sailor

US 1947 117m Technicolor
RKO (Stephen Ames)
L

Sinbad sets off on his eighth voyage to find the lost treasure of Alexander.

Well-staged but humourless Arabian Nights swashbuckler.

w John Twist *d* Richard Wallace *ph* George Barnes
m Roy Webb

Douglas Fairbanks Jnr, Walter Slezak, Maureen O'Hara, Anthony Quinn, George Tobias, Jane Greer, Mike Mazurki, Sheldon Leonard

Sing

US 1988 98m Technicolor
Columbia TriStar (Craig Zadan)

Students at a school faced with closure organise a singing and dancing competition.

Dim, cliché-ridden movie that offers little, even for its target audience of the young and undemanding.

w Dean Pitchford *d* Richard Baskin *ph* Peter Sova *m* Jay Gruska *pd* Carol Spier *ed* Bud Smith, Jere Huggins, Scott Smith

Lorraine Bracco, Peter Dobson, Jessica Steen, Louise Lasser, Goerge DiCenzo, Patti LaBelle, Susan Peretz

'Remarkably old-fashioned.' – *MFB*

Singin' in the Rain****

US 1952 102m Technicolor
MGM (Arthur Freed)
V, L

When talkies are invented, the reputation of one female star shrivels while another grows.

Brilliant comic musical, the best picture by far of Hollywood in transition, with the catchiest tunes, the liveliest choreography, the most engaging performances and the most hilarious jokes of any musical.

w Adolph Green, Betty Comden
d/ch Gene Kelly, Stanley Donen
ph Harold Rosson *md* Lennie Hayton *m* Nacio Herb Brown
ly Arthur Freed

Gene Kelly, Donald O'Connor, Debbie Reynolds, Millard Mitchell, Jean Hagen, Rita Moreno, Cyd Charisse, *Douglas Fowley*

'Perhaps the most enjoyable of all movie musicals.' – *New Yorker*, 1975
AAN: Lennie Hayton; Jean Hagen

Skateboard

US 1977 95m Technicolor
Universal

A small-time theatrical agent in trouble builds up a professional skateboard team.

Unsatisfactory exploitation item which devotes more time to its plot than to its sport.

w Richard A. Wolf, George Gage
d George Gage

Allen Garfield, Kathleen Lloyd, Leif Garrett, Richard Van Der Wyk

'Pray they never have to rescue YOU...!'
Ski Patrol
US 1989 92m DeLuxe
Entertainment/Epic/Sarlui/Diamant/Paul Maslansky (Phillip B. Goldfine, Donald L. West)
V, L

A developer attempts to sabotage the safety record of a ski resort.

Broad farce in the style of the *Police Academy* series and no funnier.

w Steven Long Mitchell, Craig W. Van Sickle d Richard Correll ph John Stephens m Bruce Miller pd Fred Weiler ed Scott Wallace

Roger Rose, Yvette Nipar, T. K. Carter, Leslie Jordan, Paul Feig, Sean Gregory Sullivan, Tess, George Lopez, Ray Walston

'A love story about two people who hate each other!'
Sleeper**
US 1973 88m DeLuxe
UA/Jack Rollins, Charles Joffe (Jack Grossberg)
V, L

A health food store owner is deep frozen after an operation and wakes two hundred years in the future.

Predictable star vehicle with an agreeable string of bright gags.

w *Woody Allen, Marshall Brickman* d Woody Allen ph David M. Walsh m Woody Allen pd Dale Hennesy

Woody Allen, Diane Keaton, John Beck, Mary Gregory

'Verbal and visual gags rain down like hailstones.' – *Michael Billington, Illustrated London News*

The Sleeping Beauty*
US 1959 75m Technirama 70
Walt Disney (Ken Peterson)
V

Rather stodgy, unwisely Cinemascoped feature cartoon of the old legend; very fashionable and detailed, but somehow lifeless.

d Clyde Geronimi md George Bruns pd Don da Gradi, Ken Anderson

voices of Mary Costa, Bill Shirley, Eleanor Audley, Verna Felton, Barbara Jo Allen, Barbara Luddy

AAN: George Bruns

'You'll forget every love story you ever saw – or sang to!'
The Slipper and the Rose*
GB 1976 146m Technicolor Panavision
Paradine Co-Productions (David Frost, Stuart Lyons)
V

The story of Cinderella.

The elements are charming, but the treatment is fussy yet uninventive and the film is immensely overlong and lacking in magic and wit. Alas, not the renaissance of the family film that was hoped for.

w Bryan Forbes, Robert and Richard Sherman d Bryan Forbes ph Tony Imi songs Robert and Richard Sherman pd Ray Simm

Richard Chamberlain, Gemma Craven, Kenneth More, Michael Hordern, Edith Evans, Annette Crosbie, Margaret Lockwood, *Christopher Gable*, Julian Orchard, Lally Bowers, John Turner

'The tunes, I'm afraid, go in one ear and out the other; and, as Dr Johnson said of *Paradise Lost*, no man

wished it a minute longer.' – *Michael Billington, Illustrated London News*
AAN: music; song 'He Danced with Me'

Slipstream

GB 1989 102m Eastmancolor
Entertainment/Entertainment Film
   Productions (Gary Kurtz)
V, L

In a post-holocaust future, an android learns human feelings while being hunted by a policeman and woman.

Futuristic chase movie, a little lacking in imagination.

w Tony Kayden *story* Bill Bauer *d* Steven M. Listberger *ph* Frank Tidy *m* Elmer Bernstein *pd* Andrew McAlpine *ed* Terry Rawlings

Mark Hamill, Bob Peck, Bill Paxton, Kitty Aldridge, Eleanor David, Ben Kingsley, F. Murray Abraham, Robbie Coltrane

Smiley*

GB 1956 97m Technicolor
Cinemascope
TCF/London Films (Anthony Kimmins)

An adventurous Australian boy has various adventures and finally gets the bicycle he wants.

An open-air 'William'-type story for children, quite nicely made and generally refreshing. *Smiley Gets a Gun* was a less effective sequel.

w Moore Raymond, Anthony Kimmins *novel* Moore Raymond *d* Anthony Kimmins *ph* Ted Scaife, Russ Wood *m* William Alwyn

Colin Petersen, Ralph Richardson, Chips Rafferty, John McCallum

Smiley Gets a Gun

Australia 1958 90m
   Technicolor Cinemascope
Canberra Films

Smiley is promised a rifle if he can keep out of trouble.

Unexceptional sequel.

w Anthony Kimmins, Rex Rienits
d Anthony Kimmins

Keith Calvert, Bruce Archer, Sybil Thorndike, Chips Rafferty

Smokey and the Bandit*

US 1977 97m Technicolor
Universal/Rastar (Robert L. Levy)
V

A Georgia bootlegger on a mission picks up a girl in distress and is chased by her irate sheriff fiancé.

Frantic chase comedy full of car crashes and low lines: a surprise box-office smash.

w James Lee Barrett, Charles Shyer, Alan Mandel *d* Hal Needham *ph* Bobby Byrne *m* Bill Justis, Jerry Reed, Art Feller

Burt Reynolds, Jackie Gleason, Sally Field, Jerry Reed, Mike Henry, Pat McCormick, Paul Williams

Smokey and the Bandit II

US 1980 101m Technicolor
Universal/Rastar/Mort Engelberg
GB title: *Smokey and the Bandit Ride Again*

A trucker is hired to take a pregnant elephant to the Republican convention.

More mindless chasing and crashing, with even less wit than before and rather more wholesale destruction.

w Jerry Belson, Brock Yates *d* Hal Needham *ph* Michael Butler *md* Snuff Garrett

Burt Reynolds, Jackie Gleason, Sally Field, Jerry Reed, Dom DeLuise, Paul Williams

Smoky

US 1946 87m Technicolor
TCF (Robert Bassler)

An especially independent horse virtually runs the ranch on which he lives.

Family saga of the great outdoors, well enough assembled.

w Dwight Cummings, Lillie Hayward, Dorothy Yost *novel* Will James d Louis King ph Charles Clarke md Emil Newman m David Raksin

Fred MacMurray, Anne Baxter, Burl Ives, Bruce Cabot, Esther Dale

† The story was also made by Fox in 1933 with Victor Jory, and in 1966 with Fess Parker.

Snow White and the Seven Dwarfs****

US 1937 82m Technicolor
Walt Disney

Disney's first feature cartoon, a mammoth enterprise which no one in the business thought would work. The romantic leads were wishy-washy but the splendid songs and the marvellous comic and villainous characters turned the film into a worldwide box-office bombshell which is almost as fresh today as when it was made.

w Ted Sears, Otto Englander, Earl Hurd, Dorothy Ann Blank, Richard Creedon, Dick Richard, Merrill de Maris, Webb Smith, from the fairy tale by the brothers Grimm *supervising director* David Hand m Frank Churchill, Leigh Harline, Paul Smith *songs* Larry Morey, Frank Churchill

voices of Adriana Caselotti, Harry Stockwell, Lucille La Verne, Billy Gilbert

'The first full-length animated feature, the turning point in Disney's career, a milestone in film history, and a great film.' – *Leonard Maltin*
'Sustained fantasy, the animated cartoon grown up.' – *Otis Ferguson*

AA: Special Award to Walt Disney for 'a significant screen innovation'. He was given one Oscar and seven miniature statuettes.
AAN: Frank Churchill, Leigh Harline, Paul Smith

Snow White and the Three Stooges*

US 1961 107m DeLuxe Cinemascope
(TCF) Chanford (Charles Wick)
GB title: *Snow White and the Three Clowns*

The old story retold as a vehicle for a champion skater and three veteran clowns.

Surprisingly tolerable as a holiday attraction, once you get over the shock.

w Noel Langley, Elwood Ullman d Walter Lang ph Leon Shamroy m Lyn Murray ad Jack Martin Smith, Maurice Ransford

Carol Heiss, Moe Howard, Larry Fine, Joe de Rita, Edson Stroll, Patricia Medina, Guy Rolfe, Buddy Baer, Edgar Barrier

Snowball Express

US 1972 99m Technicolor
Walt Disney (Ron Miller)

An insurance accountant inherits a dilapidated skiing hotel in the Colorado Rockies.

Uninspired family comedy with slapstick on the snow slopes.

w Don Tait, Jim Parker, Arnold Margolin novel *Château Bon Vivant* by Frankie and John O'Rear d Norman Tokar ph Frank Phillips m Robert F. Brunner

Dean Jones, Nancy Olson, Henry Morgan, Keenan Wynn, Mary Wickes, Johnny Whittaker

'As wholesome and bland as that old American favourite the peanut butter and jelly sandwich.' – *MFB*

'Only once in 3000 years – anything like it!'

Solomon and Sheba
US 1959 142m Super Technirama 70
UA/Edward Small (Ted Richmond)

When David names his younger son as heir, his older son plots revenge.

Dullish biblical spectacle, alternating between pretentiousness and cowboys and Indians.

w Anthony Veiller, Paul Dudley, George Bruce d King Vidor ph Frederick A. Young m Mario Nascimbene ad Richard Day, Alfred Sweeney

Yul Brynner, Gina Lollobrigida, George Sanders, Marisa Pavan, David Farrar, John Crawford, Laurence Naismith, Alejandro Rey, Harry Andrews

'Penance is due.' – *Hollis Alpert*
'Watch out it doesn't put you to sleep.' – *New York Times*

Some Like It Hot***
US 1959 122m bw
UA/Mirisch (Billy Wilder)
V, L

Two unemployed musicians accidentally witness the St Valentine's Day Massacre and flee to Miami disguised as girl musicians.

Overstretched but sporadically very funny comedy which constantly flogs its central idea to death and then recovers with a smart line or situation. It has in any case become a milestone of film comedy.

w Billy Wilder, I. A. L. Diamond d Billy Wilder ph Charles Lang Jnr m Adolph Deutsch ad Ted Howarth

Jack Lemmon, Tony Curtis, Marilyn Monroe, Joe E. Brown, George Raft, Pat O'Brien, Nehemiah Persoff, George E. Stone, Joan Shawlee

'A comedy set in the Prohibition era, with transvestism, impotence, role confusion, and borderline inversion – and all hilariously innocent, though always on the brink of really disastrous *double-entendre*.' – *Pauline Kael*
'Most of the time Billy Wilder's new piece – a farce blacker than is common on the American screen – whistles along at a smart, murderous pace.' – *Dilys Powell*
'Hectic slapstick, smartass movie pardies, sexist stereotyping, crass one-liners, and bad taste galore.' – *Time Out, 1984*
AAN: script; Billy Wilder (as director); Charles Lang Jnr; Jack Lemmon; art direction

Something Wicked This Way Comes*
US 1983 95m Technicolor
Walt Disney/Bryna (Peter Vincent Douglas)

A sinister carnival with a power over time and age visits a small town in Illinois.

A curious departure for the Disney studio is this grim fairy tale from a novel which was probably intractable. In the cinema, this is the sort of film very lucky to find an audience despite its good qualities.

w Ray Bradbury novel Ray Bradbury d Jack Clayton
ph Stephen H. Burum m James Horner pd Richard MacDonald

Jason Robards, Jonathan Pryce, Diane Ladd, Pam Grier, Royal Dano, Vidal Peterson, Shawn Carson

Son of Ali Baba
US 1952 75m Technicolor
U-I (Leonard Goldstein)

A cadet of the military academy outwits a wicked caliph.

Routine Arabian Nights hokum.

w Gerald Drayson Adams d Kurt Neumann ph Maury Gertsman m Joseph Gershenson

Tony Curtis, Piper Laurie, Susan Cabot, Victor Jory

Son of Captain Blood
Italy/Spain 1962 95m Eastmancolor Dyaliscope
CCM/BP/Harry Joe Brown

Captain Blood's son routs his father's enemies.

Lively swashbuckler with the original star's son rather unhappily cast.

w Mario Caiano d Tullio Demichelli

Sean Flynn, Ann Todd, José Nieto, John Kitzmiller

Son of Fury*
US 1942 102m bw
TCF (William Perlberg)

An 18th-century Englishman is deprived of his inheritance, flees to a South Sea island but comes back seeking restitution.

Elaborate costumer which suffers from loss of suspense during the central idyll. Much to enjoy along the way.

w Philip Dunne novel Benjamin Blake by Edison Marshall d John Cromwell ph Arthur Miller
m Alfred Newman

Tyrone Power, Gene Tierney, George Sanders, Frances Farmer, Roddy McDowall, John Carradine, Elsa Lanchester, *Dudley Digges*, Harry Davenport, Halliwell Hobbes

† Remade as *Treasure of the Golden Condor* (qv).

Son of Godzilla
Japan 1967 86m (dubbed) colour
Toho Company (Tomoyuki Tanaka)

Intrepid scientists, experimenting with the weather on a remote island, battle against back projections of spiders and a giant mantis as a motherless son is born to Godzilla.

Standard monster hokum, with actors in rubber suits trampling on model buildings.

w Shinichi Sekizawa, Kazue Shiba
d Jun Fukuda ph Kazuo Yamada m Masaru Sato
ad Takeo Kita ed Ryohei Fujii

Tadeo Takashima, Bibari Maeda, Akira Kubo, Akihiko Hirata, Kenji Sahara, Yoshio Tsuchiya

Son of Kong*
US 1933 69m bw
RKO (Merian C. Cooper)

After Kong has wrecked New York, producer Carl Denham flees from his creditors and finds more monsters on the old island.

Hasty sequel to the splendid *King Kong*; the results were so tame and unconvincing that the film was sold as a comedy, but it does have a few lively moments after four reels of padding.

w Ruth Rose d Ernest B. Schoedsack ph Eddie Linden, Vernon Walker, J. O. Taylor m Max Steiner sp Willis O'Brien

Robert Armstrong, Helen Mack, Frank Reicher, John Marston, Victor Wong

'The sequel to and wash-up of the *King Kong* theme, consisting of salvaged remnants from the original production ... the punch is no longer there.' – *Variety*

Son of Lassie
US 1945 100m Technicolor
MGM (Samuel Marx)

A dog follows its young master to the war and helps settle the hash of a few Nazis.

Silly dog story, the first sequel to *Lassie Come Home;* far too slow to start with, then packed with serial-like action.

w Jeanne Bartlett d S. Sylvan Simon ph Charles Schoenbaum m Herbert Stothart

Peter Lawford, Donald Crisp, June Lockhart, Nigel Bruce, Leon Ames, Nils Asther

'Good old sentimental hokum.' – *Variety*

Son of Monte Cristo*
US 1940 102m bw
(UA) Edward Small

The masked avenger who quashes a dictatorship in 1865 Lichtenstein is none other than the son of Edmond Dantes.

Cheerful swashbuckler of the second class.

w George Bruce d Rowland V. Lee ph George Robinson m Edward Ward ad John DuCasse Schulze

Louis Hayward, Joan Bennett, George Sanders, Florence Bates, Lionel Royce, Montagu Love, Clayton Moore, Ralph Byrd
AAN: art direction

Son of Paleface*
US 1952 95m Technicolor
(Paramount) Bob Hope (Robert L. Welch)

A tenderfoot and a government agent compete for the attentions of a lady bandit.

Gagged-up sequel to *The Paleface;* much of the humour now seems self-conscious and dated in the *Road* tradition which it apes, but there are still moments of delight.

w Frank Tashlin, Joseph Quillan, Robert L. Welch d Frank Tashlin ph Harry J. Wild m Lyn Murray

Bob Hope, Roy Rogers, Jane Russell, Trigger, Douglass Dumbrille, Harry Von Zell, Bill Williams, Lloyd Corrigan
AAN: song 'Am I in Love' (m/ly Jack Brooks)

Son of Robin Hood
GB 1958 77m Eastmancolor
Cinemascope
TCF/Argo (George Sherman)

Robin's daughter joins with the Regent's brother to overthrow the Black Duke.

Empty-headed romp, more or less in the accepted tradition.

w George George, George Slavin d George Sherman ph Arthur Grant m Leighton Lucas

David Hedison, June Laverick, David Farrar, Marius Goring, Philip Friend,

Delphi Lawrence, George Coulouris, George Woodbridge

Son of Sinbad*
US 1955 88m Technicolor Superscope
RKO (Robert Sparks)

Sinbad and Omar Khayyam are imprisoned by the Caliph but escape with the secret of green fire.

Arabian Nights burlesque, mainly quite bright, with the forty thieves played by harem girls.

w Aubrey Wisberg, Jack Pollexfen d Ted Tetzlaff ph William Snyder m Victor Young

Dale Robertson, Vincent Price, Sally Forrest, Lili St Cyr, Mari Blanchard, Leon Askin, Jay Novello

Song of the South*
US 1946 94m Technicolor
Walt Disney (Perce Pearce)
V

On a long-ago southern plantation, small boys listen to the Brer Rabbit stories from an elderly black servant.

Too much Uncle Remus and not enough Brer Rabbit, we fear, but children liked it. The cartoons were actually very good.

w Dalton Raymond d Harve Foster ph Gregg Toland m Daniele Amfitheatrof, Paul J. Smith, Charles Wolcott cartoon credits various

Ruth Warrick, Bobby Driscoll, James Baskett, Luana Patten, Lucile Watson, Hattie McDaniel

'The ratio of live to cartoon action is approximately two to one, and that is the ratio of the film's mediocrity to its charm.' – Bosley Crowther

AA: song 'Zip-a-Dee-Do-Dah' (m Allie Wrubel, ly Ray Gilbert); James Baskett (special award)
AAN: Daniele Amfitheatrof, Paul J. Smith, Charles Wolcott

Sons of the Desert****
US 1934 68m bw
Hal Roach
V, L
GB title: *Fraternally Yours*

Stan and Ollie want to go to a Chicago convention, but kid their wives that they are going on a cruise for health reasons.

Archetypal Laurel and Hardy comedy, unsurpassed for gags, pacing and sympathetic characterization.

w Frank Craven, Byron Morgan d William A. Seiter ph Kenneth Peach

Stan Laurel, Oliver Hardy, Charlie Chase, Mae Busch, Dorothy Christie

The Sound of Music***
US 1965 172m DeLuxe Todd-AO
TCF/Argyle (Robert Wise)
V, V(W), L

In 1938 Austria, a trainee nun becomes governess to the Trapp family, falls in love with the widower father, and helps them all escape from the Nazis.

Slightly muted, very handsome version of an enjoyably old-fashioned stage musical with splendid tunes.

w Ernest Lehman book Howard Lindsay, Russel Crouse d Robert Wise ph Ted McCord md Irwin Kostal pd Boris Leven m/ ly Richard Rodgers, Oscar Hammerstein II

Julie Andrews, Christopher Plummer, Richard Haydn, Eleanor Parker, *Peggy Wood*, Anna Lee, Marni Nixon

'The success of a movie like *The Sound of Music* makes it even more difficult for anyone to try to do anything worth doing, anything relevant to the modern world, anything inventive or expressive.' – *Pauline Kael, New Yorker*

'This last, most remunerative and least inspired, let alone sophisticated, of the Rodgers and Hammerstein collaborations is square and solid sugar. Calorie-counters, diabetics and grown-ups from eight to eighty had best beware.' – *Judith Crist*

'. . . sufficient warning to those allergic to singing nuns and sweetly innocent children.' – *John Gillett*

AA: best picture; Robert Wise; Irwin Kostal
AAN: Ted McCord; Julie Andrews; Peggy Wood

A Southern Yankee*

US 1948 90m bw
MGM (Paul Jones)
GB title: My Hero

During the Civil War a southern bellboy masquerades as a spy and finds himself behind enemy lines.

A rather feeble reworking of Buster Keaton's *The General*, with some excellent gags supervised by the master himself.

w Harry Tugend   d Edward Sedgwick   ph Ray June   m David Snell

Red Skelton, Brian Donlevy, Arlene Dahl, George Coulouris, Lloyd Gough, John Ireland, Minor Watson, Charles Dingle

Space Raiders

US 1983 82m colour
Millennium (Roger Corman)

A space mercenary promises to help return a 10-year-old stowaway to his home planet.

Low-budget *Star Wars* rip-off for juvenile audiences, incorporating footage from *Battle beyond the Stars*.

wd Howard R. Cohen   ph Alec Hirschfeld

Vince Edwards, David Mendenhall, Patsy Pease, Thom Christopher, Dick Miller

Spaceballs

US 1987 96m Metrocolor
MGM/UA (Mel Brooks, Ezra Swerdlow)
V

A ruthless race is out to steal the air supply from the planet Druidia.

Flabby spoof of *Star Wars*, without any funny ideas.

w Mel Brooks, Thomas Meehan, Ronny Graham   d Mel Brooks   ph Nick McLean   m John Morris   pd Terence Marsh   ed Conrad Buff IV

Mel Brooks, John Candy, Rick Moranis, Bill Pullman, Daphne Zuniga, Dom DeLuise, John Hurt

'At its worst, it displays a colossal ego at work and humour better left to home movies.' – *Daily Variety*

Spaced Invaders

US 1989 100m CFI
Medusa/Smart Egg Pictures (Luigi Cingolani)
V, L

A spaceship load of inept Martians mistakenly try to conquer the Earth.

Inane spoof of the current cycle of science fiction films.

w Patrick Read Johnson, Scott Alexander   d Patrick Read Johnson   ph James L. Carter   m David Russo   pd Tony

Tremblay   ed Seth Gaven, Daniel Bross

Douglas Barr, Royal Dano, Ariana Richards, J. J. Anderson, Gregg Berger, Fred Applegate, Patrika Darbo

The Spaceman and King Arthur
GB 1979 93m Technicolor
Walt Disney
US title: *Unidentified Flying Oddball*

An astronaut and his robot accidentally land themselves back at the court of King Arthur.

Mindless but occasionally funny rewrite of Mark Twain's *A Connecticut Yankee*.

w Don Tait   d Russ Mayberry

Dennis Dugan, Jim Dale, Ron Moody, Kenneth More, John Le Mesurier, Rodney Bewes, Robert Beatty

Spartacus**
US 1960 196m Super Technirama 70
U-I/Bryna (Edward Lewis)
V, V(W), L

The slaves of ancient Rome revolt and are quashed.

Long, well-made, downbeat epic with deeper than usual characterization and several bravura sequences.

w Dalton Trumbo   novel Howard Fast   d Stanley Kubrick   ph Russell Metty   m Alex North   pd Alexander Golitzen   ed Robert Lawrence

Kirk Douglas, Laurence Olivier, Charles Laughton, Tony Curtis, Jean Simmons, Peter Ustinov, John Gavin, Nina Foch, Herbert Lom, John Ireland, John Dall, Charles McGraw, Woody Strode

'Everything is depicted with a lack of imagination that is truly Marxian.' – *Anne Grayson*

'A lot of first-rate professionals have pooled their abilities to make a first-rate circus.' – *Stanley Kauffmann*

'One comes away feeling rather revolted and not at all ennobled.' – *Alan Dent, Illustrated London News*

AA: Russell Metty; Peter Ustinov; art direction
AAN: Alex North; editing

Spartacus the Gladiator
Italy 1953 103m bw
Consorzio Spartacus

Action-oriented remake of a familiar story.

w Jean Ferry, Mario Bori   d Riccardo Freda   ph Gabor Pigany   m Renzo Rossellini

Massimo Girotti, Ludmilla Tcherina, Maria Canala

Speedy**
US 1928 90m approx bw silent
Paramount (Harold Lloyd)

A young man saves his girl's grandfather's trolley car business.

One of its star's most stylish comedies, and his last silent film, with a trolley car ride for climax.

w John Grey, Lex Neal, Howard Emmett Rogers, Jay Howe   d Ted Wilde   ph Harold Lloyd, Ann Christy, Bert Woodruff, Brooks Benedict, Babe Ruth
AAN: Ted Wilde

Spies Like Us
US 1985 109m Technicolor
Warner (Brian Grazer, George Folsey Jnr)
V, L

Bumbling bureaucrats are mistakenly chosen for a spy mission.

Inept attempts at humour fall flat throughout this dreary venture, which is as though Hope and Crosby had set out on the road to Morocco without a script.

w Dan Aykroyd, Lowell Ganz, Babaloo Mandel d John Landis ph Robert Paynter m Elmer Bernstein pd Peter Murton ed Malcolm Campbell

Chevy Chase, Dan Aykroyd, Steve Forrest, Donna Dixon, Bruce Davison, William Prince, Bernie Casey

'She was the woman of his dreams. She had large dark eyes, a beautiful smile, and a great pair of fins.'
Splash!*
US 1984 110m Technicolor
Touchstone/Buena Vista (Brian Grazer)
V, L

A New York wholesaler on holiday off Cape Cod falls in love with a mermaid.

A kind of updated and mildly sexed-up *Miranda:* occasionally funny but far too long.

w Lowell Ganz, Babaloo Mandel, Bruce Jay Friedman, Brian Grazer d Ron Howard ph Don Peterman m Lee Holdridge

Tom Hanks, Daryl Hannah, Eugene Levy, John Candy, Dody Goodman, Shecky Greene, Richard B. Shull, Howard Morris

'A typically Disney subject trying to be grown up.' – *Kim Newman, MFB*
'The picture is frequently on the verge of being more wonderful than it is ... more lyrical, a little wilder.' – *Pauline Kael, New Yorker*
AAN: screenplay

The Spy Who Loved Me
GB 1977 125m Eastmancolor
Panavision
UA/Eon (Albert R. Broccoli)
V, L

James Bond and a glamorous Russian spy combine forces to track down and eliminate a megalomaniac shipping magnate with an undersea missile base.

Witless spy extravaganza in muddy colour, with the usual tired chases and pussyfoot violence but no new gimmicks except a seven-foot villain with steel teeth.

w Christopher Wood, Richard Maibaum novel Ian Fleming d Lewis Gilbert ph Claude Renoir m Marvin Hamlisch pd Ken Adam

Roger Moore, Barbara Bach, Curt Jurgens, Richard Kiel, Caroline Munro, Walter Gotell, Bernard Lee, Lois Maxwell, George Baker, Desmond Llewellyn, Edward De Souza, Sydney Tafler

'The film, bearing no relation to its nominal source, seems to do nothing more than anthologize its forerunners.' – *Tim Pulleine, MFB*
AAN: Marvin Hamlisch; song 'Nobody Does It Better' (m Marvin Hamlisch, ly Carole Bayer Sager)

'The human adventure is just beginning!'
Star Trek: The Motion Picture
US 1979 132m Metrocolor
Panavision
Paramount (Gene Roddenberry)
V, V(W), L

In the 23rd century, Admiral Kirk resumes command of the *Enterprise* to combat an alien force.

And a surprisingly boring one. Vast sets and big-screen solemnity hardly make this more enjoyable than some of the TV episodes which got more tricks and philosophical fun into one-third of the length.

w Harold Livingstone, Alan Dean Foster d Robert Wise ph Richard H. Kline, Richard Yuricich m Jerry Goldsmith pd Harold Michelson ed Todd Ramsey

William Shatner, Leonard Nimoy, DeForest Kelley, Stephen Collins, Persis Khambatta
AAN: Jerry Goldsmith; visual effects (Douglas Trumbull, John Dykstra and others); art direction

'At the end of the universe lies the beginning of vengeance!'
Star Trek: The Wrath of Khan
US 1982 114m Movielab
  Panavision
Paramount (Harve Bennett)
V, V(W), L

The crew of the starship *Enterprise* counter the wiles of an evil genius on a distant planet.

Comic strip capers a long way from the controlled intelligence of some episodes of the TV series; but more entertaining than the first movie.

w Jack B. Sowards d Nicholas Meyer ph Gayne Rescher m James Horner pd Joseph R. Jennings

William Shatner, Leonard Nimoy, Ricardo Montalban, DeForest Kelley, Ike Eisenmann

'A pitiful snack for the eyes with some unappetizing crumbs left over for the mind to chew on.' – *Philip Strick, MFB*

Star Trek III: The Search for Spock
US 1984 105m Metrocolor
  Panavision
Paramount/Cinema Group Venture (Harve Bennett)
V, V(W), L

Admiral Kirk discovers that Spock is not dead but has been reborn as a Vulcan child . . .

Very silly, empty and unamusing follow-up.

w Harve Bennett d Leonard Nimoy ph Charles Correll m James Horner

William Shatner, DeForest Kelley, James Doohan, Walter Koenig, Michelle Nichols, Robert Hooks, Leonard Nimoy

Star Trek IV: The Voyage Home*
US 1986 119m Technicolor
  Panavision
Paramount/Harve Bennett
V, V(W), L
GB title: *The Voyage Home: Star Trek IV*

The *Enterprise* crew is called home to face trial for mutiny: they find a very alien world.

The best of the series: it isn't saying much, but at least there are shreds of wit in the script.

w Harve Bennett, Steve Meerson, Peter Krikes, Nicholas Meyer d Leonard Nimoy ph Don Peterman m Leonard Rosenman pd Jack T. Collis ed Peter E. Berger

William Shatner, Leonard Nimoy, DeForest Kelley, James Doohan, George Takei, Walter Koenig, Jane Wyatt, Catherine Hicks
AAN: Don Peterman; Leonard Rosenman

Star Trek V: The Final Frontier

US 1989 107m Technicolor Panavision
UIP/Paramount (Harve Bennett)
V, V(W), L

Captain Kirk goes in search of a legendary planet, said to be inhabited by God.

Mystic moments, tamely rendered, that indicate it is long after the time when the series should have been laid to rest.

w David Loughery *story* William Shatner, Harve Bennett, David Loughery *d* William Shatner *ph* Andrew Laszlo *m* Jerry Goldsmith *pd* Herman Zimmerman *ed* Peter Berger

William Shatner, Leonard Nimoy, DeForest Kelley, James Doohan, Walter Koenig, Nichelle Nichols, George Takei, David Warner, Laurence Luckinbill

'The battle for peace has begun.'

Star Trek VI: The Undiscovered Country**

US 1991 110m Technicolor
UIP/Paramount (Ralph Winter, Steven-Charles Jaffe)
V, L

Mr Spock attempts to solve the murder of a Klingon peace delegate after Captain Kirk and Dr McCoy are convicted of the crime.

The last voyage of the original crew of the Starship *Enterprise* turns out to be their finest hour and fifty minutes.

w Nicholas Meyer, Denny Martin Flynn *story* Leonard Nimoy, Lawrence Konner, Mark Rosenthal *d* Nicholas Meyer *ph* Hiro Narita *m* Cliff Eidelman *pd* Herman Zimmerman *sp* Industrial Light and Magic *ed* Ronald Roose, William Hoy

William Shatner, Leonard Nimoy, DeForest Kelley, James Doohan, Walter Koenig, George Takei, Christian Slater, Kim Cattrall, Mark Lenard, Christopher Plummer, David Warner

'A lumbering and self-indulgent picture, dragged down at every turn by the weight of twenty-five years of illogical mediocrity, as if the series' notional science-fiction aspects pre-empted the need for characters, stories or a universe that made any dramatic sense.' – *Kim Newman, Sight and Sound*

'There are no signs of waning energy here, not even in an *Enterprise* crew that looks ever more ready for intergalactic rocking chairs.' – *Janet Maslin, New York Times*

Star Wars***

US 1977 121m Technicolor Panavision
TCF/Lucasfilm (Gary Kurtz)
V, V(W), L

A rebel princess in a distant galaxy escapes, and with the help of her robots and a young farmer overcomes the threatening forces of evil.

Flash Gordon rides again, but with timing so impeccably right that the movie became a phenomenon and one of the top grossers of all time. In view of the hullaballoo, some disappointment may be felt with the actual experience of watching it ... but it's certainly good harmless fun, put together with style and imagination.

wd George Lucas *ph* Gilbert Taylor *m* John Williams *pd* John Barry *sp* many and various *ed* Paul Hirsch, Marcia Lucas, Richard Chew

Mark Hamill, Harrison Ford, Carrie Fisher, Peter Cushing, Alec Guinness, Anthony Daniels (See Threepio), Kenny Baker (Artoo Detoo), Dave Prowse (Darth Vader)

'A great work of popular art, fully deserving the riches it has reaped.' – *Time*
'Acting in this movie I felt like a raisin in a giant fruit salad. And I didn't even know who the coconuts or the canteloups were.' – *Mark Hamill*
'He intended his film, Lucas confesses, for a generation growing up without fairy tales. His target audience was fourteen years and younger ... It was a celebration, a social affair, a collective dream, and people came again and again, dragging their friends and families with them.' – *Les Keyser, Hollywood in the Seventies*
'The loudness, the smash and grab editing and the relentless pacing drive every idea from your head, and even if you've been entertained you may feel cheated of some dimension – a sense of wonder, perhaps.' – *New Yorker, 1982*
'Heartless fireworks ignited by a permanently retarded director with too much clout and cash.' – *Time Out, 1984*

AA: John Williams; John Barry; editing; costumes (John Mollo); visual effects (John Stears, John Dykstra and others); sound
AAN: best picture; script; direction; Alec Guinness

Start the Revolution without Me*
US 1969 90m Technicolor
Warner/Norbud (Norman Lear)

Two sets of twins get mixed up at the court of Louis XVI.

Historical spoof of the kind subsequently made familiar by Mel Brooks; the script might have suited Abbott and Costello better than these two actors.

w Fred Freeman, Lawrence J. Cohen   d Bud Yorkin   ph Jean Tournier   m John Addison

Donald Sutherland, Gene Wilder, Hugh Griffith, Jack McGowran, Billie Whitelaw, Victor Spinetti, Ewa Aulin

State Fair**
US 1933 98m bw
Fox (Winfield Sheehan)

Dad wants his prize pig to win at the fair, but the younger members of his family have romance in mind.

Archetypal family film, much remade but never quite so pleasantly performed.

w Paul Green, Sonya Levien
novel Phil Stong   d Henry King
ph Hal Mohr   md Louis de Francesco

Will Rogers, Janet Gaynor, Lew Ayres, Sally Eilers, Norman Foster, Louise Dresser, Frank Craven, Victor Jory, Hobart Cavanaugh

'A pungent, good-humoured motion picture.' – *Pare Lorentz*
'Vigour, freshness and sympathy abound in its admittedly idealized fantasy treatment of small-town life.' – *Charles Higham, 1972*
AAN: best picture; script

State Fair**
US 1945 100m Technicolor
TCF (William Perlberg)
V, L
TV title: *It Happened One Summer*

Musical remake with an amiable cast and a rousing score.
w/ly Oscar Hammerstein II   d Walter Lang   ph Leon Shamroy
md Alfred Newman   m Richard Rodgers

Charles Winninger, Jeanne Crain, Dana Andrews, Vivian Blaine, Dick Haymes, Fay Bainter, Frank McHugh, Percy Kilbride, Donald Meek

'Surely the sort of theme that clamours for movie treatment. But no, say Twentieth Century Fox: let's make the fair look like a night club. Let's look around for stars of pristine nonentity. Let's screw the camera down to the studio floor. The result, "an epic that sings to the skies . . . with glorious, glamorous new songs".' – *Richard Winnington*
'Comes pretty close to being another *Oklahoma*.' – *Motion Picture Herald*

AA: song 'It Might As Well Be Spring'
AAN: Alfred Newman

State Fair
US 1962 118m DeLuxe Cinemascope
TCF (Charles Brackett)

Dullsville modernized version, condescending towards the rurals and peopled by unattractive youngsters.

w Richard Breen   d José Ferrer
ph William C. Mellor   md Alfred Newman

Pat Boone, Alice Faye, Tom Ewell, Pamela Tiffin, Ann-Margret, Bobby Darin, Wally Cox

Stay Tuned
US 1992 87m Technicolor
Warner/Morgan Creek (James G. Robinson)

A couple are trapped in a cable television system run by the Devil.

An unsuccessful send-up of obsessive television viewing, mainly because it picks targets, such as *Wayne's World*, that are beyond parody.

w Tom S. Parker, Jim Jennewein
d Peter Hyams   ph Peter Hyams
m Bruce Broughton   pd Philip Harrison   sp Rhythm and Hues Inc.   ed Peter E. Berger

John Ritter, Pam Dawber, Jeffrey Jones, David Thom, Heather McComb, Bob Dishy

'High class trash . . . redeemed by a manic script, good special effects and production values.' – *Sheila Johnston, Independent*
'A picture with nothing for everybody.' – *Variety*

'It's five years later for Tony Manero. The fever still burns!'
Staying Alive
US 1983 96m Metrocolor
Paramount/Robert Stigwood/Cinema Group Venture (Sylvester Stallone)
V, L

Tony Manero becomes a Broadway dancer.

Fragile sequel to *Saturday Night Fever*, with some of its frenetic quality but none of its impact.

w Sylvester Stallone, Norman Wexler   d Sylvester Stallone
ph Nick McLean   m Johnny Mandel, Robin Garb, others
pd Robert Boyle

John Travolta, Cynthia Rhodes, Finola Hughes, Steve Inwood, Julie Bovasso

'By turns exhilarating and absurd.' – *Nick Roddick, MFB*
'Stallone doesn't bother much with character, scenes or dialogue. He just puts the newly muscle-plated Travolta in front of the camera, covers him with what looks like oil slick, and goes for the whambams.' – *Pauline Kael, New Yorker*

Steamboat Bill Jnr*
US 1928 71m (24 fps) bw
silent
UA/Buster Keaton/Joseph Schenck

A student takes over his father's old Mississippi steamboat, and wins the daughter of his rival.

Rather flat comedy redeemed by a magnificent cyclone climax.

w Carl Harbaugh, Buster Keaton
d Charles Riesner   ph J. Devereaux Jennings, Bert Haines

Buster Keaton, Ernest Torrence, Marion Byron

Steptoe and Son
GB 1972 98m Technicolor
EMI/Associated London Films (Aida Young)
V

Harold gets married, mislays his wife but thinks he is a father.

Strained attempt to transfer the TV rag-and-bone comedy (which in the US became *Sanford and Son*) to the big screen. Not the same thing at all.

w Ray Galton, Alan Simpson
d Cliff Owen   ph John Wilcox
m Roy Budd, Jack Fishman

Wilfrid Brambell, Harry H. Corbett, Carolyn Seymour, Arthur Howard, Victor Maddern

† *Steptoe and Son Ride Again*, which followed in 1973, was even more crude and out of character.

Stories from a Flying Trunk
GB 1979 88m Technicolor
EMI/Sands (John Brabourne, Richard Goodwin)

Three Hans Andersen stories are performed by stop frame animation and by ballet dancers dressed as vegetables.

Lugubrious attempt to repeat the success of *Tales of Beatrix Potter*; moments to make one smile, but on the whole a depressing experience.

wd Christine Edzard   ph Robin Browne, Brian West
m Gioacchino Rossini

Murray Melvin, Ann Firbank, Johanna Sonnex, Tasneem Maqsood

The Story of Robin Hood and his Merrie Men
GB 1952 84m Technicolor
Walt Disney (Perce Pearce)
L

When Prince John starts a ruthless taxation campaign, Robert Fitzooth turns outlaw.

Fairly competent but quite forgettable version of the legend, softened for children.

w Laurence E. Watkin   d Ken Annakin   ph Guy Green
m Clifton Parker

Richard Todd, Joan Rice, James Hayter, Hubert Gregg, James Robertson Justice, Martita Hunt, Peter Finch

Strike Up the Band*
US 1940 120m bw
MGM (Arthur Freed)

A high-school band takes part in a nationwide radio contest.

Rather tiresomely high-spirited musical with the stars at the top of their young form.

w Fred Finklehoffe, John Monks Jnr   d/ch Busby Berkeley
ph Ray June   m Roger Edens
ly Arthur Freed

Judy Garland, Mickey Rooney, Paul Whiteman and his Orchestra, June Preisser, William Tracy, Larry Nunn
AAN: Georgie Stoll, Roger Edens;

song 'Our Love Affair' (m/ly Roger Edens, Georgie Stoll)

The Strongest Man in the World
US 1976 92m Technicolor
Walt Disney (Bill Anderson)

An accident in a science lab gives a student superhuman strength.

Formula comedy for older children.

w Joseph L. McEveety, Herman Groves d Vincent McEveety
ph Andrew Jackson m Robert F. Brunner

Kurt Russell, Joe Flynn, Eve Arden, Cesar Romero, Phil Silvers, Dick Van Patten, Harold Gould, William Schallert, James Gregory, Roy Roberts, Fritz Feld, Raymond Bailey, Eddie Quillan, Burt Mustin

Summer Holiday*
GB 1962 109m Technicolor Cinemascope
ABP/Ivy (Kenneth Harper)
V

Four young London Transport mechanics borrow a double-decker bus for a continental holiday.

Pacy, location-filmed youth musical with plenty of general appeal.

w Peter Myers, Ronnie Cass d Peter Yates ph John Wilcox
md Stanley Black

Cliff Richard, Lauri Peters, Melvyn Hayes, Una Stubbs, Teddy Green, Ron Moody, Lionel Murton, David Kossoff

Summer Magic*
US 1963 104m Technicolor
Walt Disney (Ron Miller)

Children help their widowed mother in 1912 Boston.

Amiable remake of *Mother Carey's Chickens*, irreproachably presented.

w Sally Benson d James Neilson
ph William Snyder m Buddy Baker songs the Sherman Brothers

Hayley Mills, Burl Ives, Dorothy McGuire, Darren McGavin, Deborah Walley, Una Merkel, Eddie Hodges, Michael J. Pollard

Super Mario Brothers
US 1993 104m Technicolor
Entertainment/Lightmotive/Allied/Cinergi (Jake Eberts, Roland Joffé)
V

The Mario brothers, two plumbers, rescue a princess from a universe in another dimension, where reptilean humanoids, descended from dinosaurs, plan to rule both worlds.

An attempt to transfer a best-selling Nintendo video game to the screen; it doesn't work.

w Parker Bennett, Terry Runt, Ed Solomon story based on characters and concept created by Shigeru Miyamoto, Takashi Tezuka d Rocky Morton, Annabel Jankel ph Dean Semler m Alan Silvestri
pd David L. Snyder sp Christopher Francis Woods, Patrick Tatopoulos ed Caroline Ross

Bob Hoskins, John Leguizamo, Dennis Hopper, Samantha Mathis, Fisher Stevens, Richard Edson, Rona Shaw, Dana Kaminski, Lance Henriksen

'One and a half square miles of plywood went into the making of *Super Mario Brothers*, and that was just for the performances.' – *Sight and Sound*

Superdad
US 1974 95m Technicolor
Walt Disney

A lawyer is determined to rule the life of his teenage daughter.

Bumbling farce with frenzied and unattractive characters.

w Joseph L. McEveety d Vincent McEveety

Bob Crane, Barbara Rush, Kurt Russell, Joe Flynn, Kathleen Cody

Supergirl*
GB 1984 124m colour Panavision
Cantharus/Ilya Salkind (Pierre Spengler, Timothy Burrill)
V

A Krypton power source falls into the hands of a power-hungry witch, and Supergirl is sent to retrieve it.

Playful comic strip spectacular which entertains in *Wizard of Oz* style for most of its way but was savaged by the critics.

w David Odell d Jeannot Szwarc ph Alan Hume m Jerry Goldsmith pd Richard MacDonald

Helen Slater, Faye Dunaway, Peter O'Toole, Mia Farrow, Brenda Vaccaro, Peter Cook, Simon Ward, Marc McClure, Hart Bochner, David Healy

'You'll believe a man can fly!'
Superman
US/GB 1978 142m colour Panavision
Warner/Alexander Salkind (Pierre Spengler)
V, L

A baby saved from the planet Krypton when it explodes grows up as a newspaperman and uses his tremendous powers to fight evil and support the American way.

Long, lugubrious and only patchily entertaining version of the famous comic strip, with far too many irrelevant preliminaries and a misguided sense of its own importance.

w Mario Puzo, David Newman, Robert Benton, Leslie Newman d Richard Donner ph Geoffrey Unsworth m John Williams pd John Barry sp various ed Stuart Baird

Christopher Reeve, Marlon Brando, Margot Kidder, Jackie Cooper, Glenn Ford, Phyllis Thaxter, Trevor Howard, Gene Hackman, Ned Beatty, Susannah York, Valerie Perrine

'Though one of the two or three most expensive movies made to date, it's cheesy-looking, and the plotting is so hit or miss that the story never seems to get started; the special effects are far from wizardly and the editing often seems hurried and jerky just at the crucial points.' – *New Yorker*

'It gives the impression of having been made in panic – in fear that style or too much imagination might endanger its approach to the literal-minded.' – *Pauline Kael, New Yorker*

'The epitome of supersell.'
– *Les Keyser, Hollywood in the Seventies*

† Reprehensible records were set by Brando getting three million dollars for a ten-minute performance (and then suing for a share of the gross); and by the incredible 7½-minute credit roll at the end.

†† Tiny roles were played by Noel Neill, who was Lois Lane in the TV series, and by Kirk Alyn, who was Superman in two serials.
AAN: John Williams; editing; sound; visual effects

Superman 2

US 1980 127m Technicolor Panavision
Warner/Alexander Salkind (Pierre Spengler)
V, L

Three renegade Kryptonians threaten Earth with a space bomb.

Half the first episode was devoted to a creaky and unnecessary setting up of plot and characters. This sequel is all the better for diving straight into action, but a classic it isn't, even of the comic strip kind.

w Mario Puzo, David Newman, Leslie Newman d Richard Lester
ph Geoffrey Unsworth, Robert Paynter m Ken Thorne

Christopher Reeve, Gene Hackman, Ned Beatty, Jackie Cooper, Sarah Douglas, Margot Kidder, Valerie Perrine, Susannah York, Terence Stamp, Jack O'Halloran, E. G. Marshall

Superman 3

GB 1983 125m colour Panavision
Dovemead/Cantharus (Pierre Spengler)
L

Synthetic Kryptonite warps Superman's character, but his conscience is reawakened by a plea from a small boy.

Sometimes humorous but overwritten and overacted variation on a tired theme. The special effects are the thing, but there's too much padding in between.

w David Newman, Leslie Newman d Richard Lester ph Robert Paynter m Ken Thorne pd Peter Murton

Christopher Reeve, Richard Pryor, Jackie Cooper, Marc McClure, Annette O'Toole, Annie Ross, Pamela Stephenson, Robert Vaughn, Margot Kidder

Superman 4: The Quest for Peace

GB 1987 89m colour JDC widescreen
Cannon
V, L

Superman determines that the world shall lay down its nuclear arms.

Stolid dialogue and poor technicalities are evident throughout what will surely be the last of the series.

w Lawrence Konner, Mark Rosenthal, Christopher Reeve
d Sidney J. Furie

Christopher Reeve, Gene Hackman, Jackie Cooper, Marc McClure, Sam Wanamaker, Mariel Hemingway, Margot Kidder

Susannah of the Mounties*

US 1939 78m bw
TCF (Kenneth MacGowan)

A little girl who is the only survivor of a wagon train massacre is looked after by the Canadian Mounties.

Adequate star action romance, Shirley's last real success.

w Robert Ellis, Helen Logan
d William A. Seiter ph Arthur Miller md Louis Silvers

Shirley Temple, Randolph Scott, Margaret Lockwood, J. Farrell MacDonald, Maurice Moscovitch, Moroni Olsen, Victor Jory

'Strictly for the juvenile trade ... illogical situations make it no more than a moderate fairy tale.' – Variety

Swallows and Amazons

GB 1974 92m Eastmancolor
EMI/Theatre Projects (Richard Pilbrow)

In the twenties four children have adventures in the Lake District.

Mild family film, great to look at but lacking in real excitement or style.

w David Wood novel Arthur Ransome d Claude Whatham ph Denis Lewiston m Wilfred Josephs

Virginia McKenna, Ronald Fraser, Simon West, Sophie Neville, Zanna Hamilton, Stephen Grenville

Swashbuckler*
US 1976 101m Technicolor Panavision
Universal/Elliott Kastner (Jennings Lang)
L
GB title: *The Scarlet Buccaneer*

Rival pirates help a wronged lady.

Uninspired reworking of some old Errol Flynn ideas; the idea was pleasant, but the old style is sadly lacking.

w Jeffrey Bloom d James Goldstone ph Philip Lathrop m John Addison pd John Lloyd

Robert Shaw, James Earl Jones, Peter Boyle, Geneviève Bujold, Beau Bridges, Geoffrey Holder

'This tacky pastepot job can't make up its mind whether it's serious, tongue-in-cheek, satirical, slapstick, burlesque, parody or travesty; but be assured it is all of the above.' – *Variety*
'The talented cast is left to play living statues, immobilized by dumb dialogue and awkward action.' – *Judith Crist*

The Swiss Family Robinson
US 1940 93m bw
(RKO) Gene Towne, Graham Baker

A shipwrecked family builds a new home on a desert island.

Pleasing low-budgeter.

w Gene Towne, Graham Baker, Walter Ferris novel Johann Wyss d Edward Ludwig ph Nicholas Musuraca

Thomas Mitchell, Edna Best, Freddie Bartholomew, Tim Holt, Terry Kilburn

'In outlook, dialogue and manner it is frankly old-fashioned.' – *MFB*

The Swiss Family Robinson*
GB 1960 126m Technicolor Panavision
Walt Disney (Bill Anderson, Basil Keys)

Quite pleasing comedy adventure from the children's classic.

w Lowell S. Hawley d Ken Annakin ph Harry Waxman m William Alwyn

John Mills, Dorothy McGuire, James MacArthur, Tommy Kirk, Kevin Corcoran, Janet Munro, Sessue Hayakawa, Cecil Parker

Swiss Miss*
US 1938 73m bw
(MGM) Hal Roach
V, V(C)

Two mousetrap salesmen in Switzerland run into trouble with a cook, a gorilla and two opera singers.

Operetta style vehicle which constrains its stars, since their material is somewhat below vintage anyway. Not painful to watch, but disappointing.

w James Parrott, Felix Adler, Charles Nelson d John G. Blystone ph Norbert Brodine

Stan Laurel, Oliver Hardy, Walter Woolf King, Della Lind, Eric Blore

'Story, production, acting and direction suggest a revival of early sound filmusicals presented with stage technique.' – *Variety*

The Sword and the Rose
GB 1952 91m Technicolor
Walt Disney (Perce Pearce)

The romantic problems of young Mary Tudor.

Unhistorical charade not quite in the usual Disney vein, and not very good.

w Laurence E. Watkin *novel When Knighthood Was in Flower* by Charles Major d Ken Annakin
ph Geoffrey Unsworth m Clifton Parker

Richard Todd, Glynis Johns, James Robertson Justice, Michael Gough, Jane Barrett, Peter Copley, Rosalie Crutchley, Jean Mercure, D. A. Clarke-Smith

The Sword and the Sorcerer
US 1982 99m DeLuxe
Sorcerer Productions/Group One/Brandon Chase
V, L

A tyrant wins an idyllic kingdom with the help of an evil sorcerer; young Prince Talon gets it back.

Medieval magic and violence, laid on with a shovel; hopefully the last attempt to start an ill-fated cycle.

w Tom Karnowski, Albert Pyun, John Stuckmeyer d Albert Pyun
ph Joseph Mangine m David Whitaker

Lee Horsley, Kathleen Beller, Simon MacCorkindale, George Maharis, Richard Lynch

The Sword in the Stone**
US 1963 80m Technicolor
Walt Disney (Ken Peterson)
V, L

In the Dark Ages, a young forest boy named Wart becomes King Arthur.

Feature cartoon with goodish sequences but disappointingly showing a flatness and economy of draughtsmanship.

w Bill Peet *novel The Once and Future King* by T. H. White
d Wolfgang Reitherman m George Bruns songs The Sherman Brothers
AAN: George Bruns

Sword of Ali Baba
US 1965 81m Technicolor
Universal

Ali Baba is forced from the royal court to become a king of thieves.

Cut-rate programme filler utilizing great chunks of *Ali Baba and the Forty Thieves* (twenty-one years older), with one actor, Frank Puglia, playing the same role in both films.

w Edmund Hartmann, Oscar Brodney d Virgil Vogel

Peter Mann, Jocelyn Lane, Peter Whitney, Gavin McLeod

Sword of Monte Cristo
US 1951 80m Supercinecolor
Edward L. Alperson

Virtuous rebels and a villainous minister all seek the fabulous treasure of Monte Cristo.

Rubbishy sequel apparently shot in somebody's back garden by people only recently acquainted with film techniques.

wd Maurice Geraghty

George Montgomery, Paula Corday, Berry Kroeger, Robert Warwick, William Conrad

Sword of Sherwood Forest

GB 1960 80m Technicolor Megascope
Columbia/Hammer/Yeoman (Richard Greene, Sidney Cole)
V

Robin Hood reveals the villainy of the Sheriff of Nottingham and the Earl of Newark.

This big-screen version of a popular TV series makes a rather feeble addition to the legend, but the actors try hard.

w Alan Hackney   d Terence Fisher   ph Ken Hodges   m Alan Hoddinott

Richard Greene, Peter Cushing, Richard Pasco, Niall MacGinnis, Jack Gwyllim, Sarah Branch, Nigel Green

Sword of the Valiant

GB 1984 101m Fujicolor JDC Wide Screen
Cannon (Michael Kagan, Philip M. Breen)

In the mythical middle ages, squire Gawain takes on a challenge from the magical Green Knight.

An unsatisfactory mixture of realism, fantasy and deadly seriousness. Spoofing might have worked better.

w Stephen Weeks, Philip M. Breen, Howard C. Pen   d Stephen Weeks   ph Freddie Young, Peter Hurst   m Ron Geesin   pd Maurice Fowler, Derek Nice   ed Richard Marden, Barry Peters

Miles O'Keeffe, Sean Connery, Trevor Howard, Leigh Lawson, Cyrielle Claire, Peter Cushing, Ronald Lacey, Lila Kedrova, John Rhys Davies, Douglas Wilmer, Wilfred Brambell

T

'His love challenged the flames of revolution!'
A Tale of Two Cities**
US 1935 121m bw
MGM (David O. Selznick)
V, L

A British lawyer sacrifices himself to save another man from the guillotine.

Richly detailed version of the classic melodrama, with production values counting more than the acting.

w W. P. Lipscomb, S. N. Behrman *novel* Charles Dickens   d Jack Conway   ph Oliver T. Marsh   m Herbert Stothart   ed Conrad A. Nervig

Ronald Colman, Elizabeth Allan, Basil Rathbone, Edna May Oliver, Blanche Yurka, Reginald Owen, Henry B. Walthall, Donald Woods, Walter Catlett, H. B. Warner, Claude Gillingwater, Fritz Leiber

'A screen classic . . . technically it is about as flawless as possible . . . it has been made with respectful and loving care.' – *Variety*
'A prodigiously stirring production . . . for more than two hours it crowds the screen with beauty and excitement.' – *New York Times*

† Originally prepared at Warners' for Leslie Howard.
AAN: best picture; editing

A Tale of Two Cities*
GB 1958 117m bw
Rank (Betty E. Box)
V

Modest but still costly remake with good moments but a rather slow pace.

w T. E. B. Clarke   d Ralph Thomas   ph Ernest Steward   m Richard Addinsell

Dirk Bogarde, Dorothy Tutin, Christopher Lee, Athene Seyler, Rosalie Crutchley, Ernest Clark, Stephen Murray, Paul Guers, Donald Pleasence, Ian Bannen, Cecil Parker, Alfie Bass

'Serviceable rather than imaginative.' – *MFB*

Tales of Beatrix Potter**
GB 1971 90m Technicolor
EMI (Richard Goodwin)
US title: *Peter Rabbit and the Tales of Beatrix Potter*

Children's stories danced by the Royal Ballet in animal masks.

A charming entertainment for those who can appreciate it, though hardly the most direct way to tell these stories.

w Richard Goodwin, Christine Edward   d Reginald Mills   ph Austin Dempster   m John Lanchbery   ch Frederick Ashton   masks Rotislav Doboujinsky   pd Christine Edward

'In the war between the sexes, there always comes a time to surrender unconditionally!'

The Taming of the Shrew*

US 1967 122m Technicolor Panavision

Columbia/Royal/FAI (Richard McWhorter)

V, L

Petruchio violently tames his shrewish wife.

Busy version of one of Shakespeare's more proletarian comedies; the words in this case take second place to violent action and rioting colour.

w Suso Cecchi d'Amico, Paul Dehn, Franco Zeffirelli   d Franco Zeffirelli   ph Oswald Morris, Luciano Trasatti   m Nino Rota

Richard Burton, Elizabeth Taylor, Michael York, Michael Hordern, Cyril Cusack, Alfred Lynch, Natasha Pyne, Alan Webb, Victor Spinetti

'As entertainment *Kiss Me Kate* is infinitely better but then Cole Porter was a real artist and Burton is a culture vulture.' – *Wilfrid Sheed*

'The old warhorse of a comedy has been spanked into uproarious life.' – *Hollis Alpert*

Tarzan

The talkie *Tarzans* began with Johnny Weissmuller and tailed off from there. (See *Filmgoer's Companion* for the silents.) The 1932 version more or less followed the original Edgar Rice Burroughs novel, and all the MGM entries had a special vivid quality about them, but subsequently the productions, usually produced under the aegis of Sol Lesser, tailed off towards the standard of the TV series of the sixties starring Ron Ely.

1929: TARZAN THE TIGER (qv)
1932: TARZAN THE APE MAN** (MGM: Weissmuller with Maureen O'Sullivan: *d* W. S. Van Dyke: 99m). Publicity line: 'Mothered by an ape – he knew the law of the jungle – to seize what he wanted!'
1933: TARZAN THE FEARLESS (qv)
1934: TARZAN AND HIS MATE*** (MGM: Weissmuller with Maureen O'Sullivan: *d* Cedric Gibbons: 105m). 'Certainly one of the funniest things you'll ever see.' – *Otis Ferguson*
1935: THE NEW ADVENTURES OF TARZAN (qv)
1936: TARZAN ESCAPES** (MGM: Weissmuller with Maureen O'Sullivan: *d* Richard Thorpe: 95m)
1938: TARZAN'S REVENGE (Sol Lesser: Glenn Morris: *d* D. Ross Lederman: 70m); TARZAN AND THE GREEN GODDESS (Principal: Herman Brix (Bruce Bennett): *d* Edward Kull: 72m: largely a re-edit of NEW ADVENTURES)
1939: TARZAN FINDS A SON (MGM: Weissmuller with O'Sullivan: *d* Richard Thorpe: 90m)
1941: TARZAN'S SECRET TREASURE (MGM: Weissmuller with O'Sullivan: *d* Richard Thorpe: 81m)
1942: TARZAN'S NEW YORK ADVENTURE (MGM: Weissmuller with O'Sullivan: *d* Richard Thorpe: 71m)
1943: TARZAN TRIUMPHS (RKO: Weissmuller: *d* William Thiele: 78m); TARZAN'S DESERT MYSTERY (RKO: Weissmuller: *d* William Thiele: 70m)
1945: TARZAN AND THE AMAZONS (RKO: Weissmuller: *d* Kurt Neumann: 76m)
1946: TARZAN AND THE LEOPARD WOMAN (RKO: Weissmuller: *d* Kurt Neumann: 72m)
1947: TARZAN AND THE HUNTRESS (RKO: Weissmuller: *d* Kurt Neumann: 72m)
1948: TARZAN AND THE MERMAIDS (RKO: *d* Robert Florey: Weissmuller: 68m)

1949: TARZAN'S MAGIC FOUNTAIN
(RKO: Lex Barker: *d* Lee Sholem:
73m)
1950: TARZAN AND THE SLAVE
GIRL (RKO: Lex Barker: *d* Lee Sholem:
74m)
1951: TARZAN'S PERIL (RKO: Lex
Barker: *d* Byron Haskin: 79m)
1952: TARZAN'S SAVAGE FURY
(RKO: Lex Barker: *d* Cy Endfield:
80m)
1953: TARZAN AND THE SHE-DEVIL
(aka: *Tarzan Meets the Vampire*) (RKO:
Lex Barker: *d* Kurt Neumann: 76m)
1955: TARZAN'S HIDDEN JUNGLE
(RKO: Gordon Scott: *d* Harold
Schuster: 73m)
1957: TARZAN AND THE LOST
SAFARI (colour) (Solar: Gordon
Scott: *d* Bruce Humberstone: 84m)
1958: TARZAN'S FIGHT FOR LIFE
(colour) (MGM: Gordon Scott:
d Bruce Humberstone: 86m)
1959: TARZAN'S GREATEST
ADVENTURE (colour) (Solar:
Gordon Scott: *d* John Guillermin:
90m)
1959: TARZAN THE APE MAN
(colour: remake of the original story)
(MGM: Denny Miller: *d* Joseph
Newman: 82m)
1960: TARZAN THE MAGNIFICENT
(colour) (Paramount: Gordon Scott:
d Robert Day: 88m)
1962: TARZAN GOES TO INDIA
(colour) (MGM: Jock Mahoney:
d John Guillermin: 86m)
1963: TARZAN'S THREE
CHALLENGES (colour) (MGM: Jock
Mahoney: *d* Robert Day: 92m)
1966: TARZAN AND THE VALLEY OF
GOLD (colour) (NatGen: Mike Henry:
d Robert Day: 90m)
1967: TARZAN AND THE GREAT
RIVER (colour) (Paramount: Mike
Henry: *d* Robert Day: 88m)
1968: TARZAN AND THE JUNGLE
BOY (colour) (Paramount: Mike
Henry: *d* Robert Day: 90m)

1981: TARZAN THE APE MAN
(colour)
1983: GREYSTOKE (L) (MGM: Miles
O'Keefe: *d* John Derek; 112m). A
debased version with the emphasis on
the undressed Jane played by Bo
Derek. Publicity line: 'The most
exciting pair in the jungle!'
1984: GREYSTOKE: THE LEGEND OF
TARZAN, LORD OF THE APES (qv). A
pretentious retelling of the original
story.

Teen Agent

US 1991 88m Technicolor
Warner (Craig Zadan, Neil Meron)
V
aka: *If Looks Could Kill*

A student is mistaken for a CIA
undercover agent and assigned to
guard a top European politician.

Tired teenage copy of the James Bond
formula of gags and gadgetry.

w Darren Star story Fred
Dekker *d* William Dear
ph Doug Milsome *m* David
Foster *pd* Guy J. Comtois
ed John F. Link, Mark Stevens

Richard Grieco, Linda Hunt, Roger
Rees, Robin Bartlett, Gabrielle
Anwar, Geraldine James, Roger
Daltrey

Teen Wolf

US 1985 91m United Color Lab
 Color
Entertainment/Atlantic (Mark Levinson,
 Scott Rosenfelt)
V

An ineffective college basketball
player finds he is a hereditary
werewolf, and in his altered form
becomes a star.

Bewilderingly silly teenage variation

on a famous legend, good-natured but totally empty.

w Joseph Loeb III, Matthew Weisman d Rod Daniel ph Tim Suhrstedt m Miles Goodman ed Lois Freeman-Fox

Michael J. Fox, James Hampton, Scott Paulin, Susan Ursitti

Teen Wolf Too
US 1987 94m colour
Entertainment/Atlantic (Kent Bateman)
V, L

A college student with a talent for boxing makes the most of the fact that he is a werewolf.

Drear comedy sequel that attempts to reprise the original with a leaden touch.

w R. Timothy Kring story Joseph Loeb III, Matthew Weisman d Christopher Leitch ph Jules Brenner m Mark Goldenberg ad Peg McClellan ed Steven Polivka, Kim Secrist, Harvey Rosenstock, Raja Gosnell

Jason Bateman, Kim Darby, John Astin, Paul Sand, James Hampton, Mark Holton, Estee Chandler

'Mean. Green. And on the screen'
Teenage Mutant Ninja Turtles*
US 1990 93m Technicolor
Virgin/Golden Harvest/Limelight (Kim Dawson, Simon Fields, David Chan)
V

Pizza-loving, sewer-dwelling turtles and their rat guru, mutated into half-human creatures by radioactivity, battle against a gang of teenage martial arts experts led by an evil Japanese ninja.

Comic-book mayhem brought to the screen in the frenetic style of rock videos, it took more money at the box-office than any other independent film has ever done.

w Todd W. Langen, Bobby Herbeck, from comic-book characters created by Kevin Eastman and Peter Laird d Steve Barron ph John Fenner m John Du Prez pd Roy Forge Smith sp creatures designed by Jim Henson's Creature Shop ed William Gordean, Sally Menke, James Symons

Judith Hoag, Elias Koteas, Josh Pais, Michelan Sisti, Leif Tilden, David Forman, James Sato

Teenage Mutant Ninja Turtles II: The Secret of the Ooze
US 1991 87m colour
TCF/Golden Harvest (Thomas K. Gray, Kim Dawson, David Chan)
V

The four mutant ninja turtles go into battle against their arch-enemy Shredder and his two new monsters, a mutant dog and tortoise.

A tame sequel, seemingly aimed at the young audience that watches the anodyne animated TV cartoon versions of the four sewer-dwelling heroes.

w Todd W. Langen d Michael Pressman ph Shelly Johnson m John Du Prez pd Ray Forge Smith ed John Wright, Steve Mirkovich

Paige Turco, David Warner, Michelan Sisti, Leif Tilden, Kenn Troum, Mark Caso, Kevin Clash, Ernie Reyes Jnr, François Chau

'If watching the first Turtles film was like chewing a good pizza, watching *II* is more like munching on the cardboard packaging, but – as fast food goes – even that can taste good enough in parts.' —David Lusted, Sight and Sound

'What a story it tells! What majesty it encompasses! What loves it unveils! What drama it unfolds!'

The Ten Commandments*

US 1956 219m Technicolor Vistavision
Paramount/Cecil B. de Mille (Henry Wilcoxon)
V, V(W), L

The life of Moses and his leading of the Israelites to the Promised Land.

Popular but incredibly stilted and verbose bible-in-pictures spectacle. A very long haul along a monotonous route, with the director at his pedestrian worst.

w Aeneas Mackenzie, Jesse L. Lasky Jnr, Jack Gariss, Frederic M. Frank d Cecil B. de Mille ph Loyal Griggs m Elmer Bernstein ad Hal Pereira, Walter H. Tyler, Albert Nozaki ed Anne Bauchens

Charlton Heston, Yul Brynner, Edward G. Robinson, Anne Baxter, Nina Foch, Yvonne de Carlo, John Derek, H. B. Warner, Henry Wilcoxon, Judith Anderson, John Carradine, Douglass Dumbrille, Cedric Hardwicke, Martha Scott, Vincent Price, Debra Paget

'De Mille not only moulds religion into a set pattern of Hollywood conventions; he has also become an expert at making entertainment out of it.' – Gordon Gow, Films and Filming
'The result of all these stupendous efforts? Something roughly comparable to an eight-foot chorus girl – pretty well put together, but much too big and much too flashy. . . . What de Mille has really done is to throw sex and sand into the moviegoers' eyes for almost twice as long as anyone else has ever dared to.' – *Time*

AA: special effects (John Fulton)
AAN: best picture; Loyal Griggs; art direction; editing; sound; costumes (Edith Head and others)

Teenage Mutant Ninja Turtles III

US 1992 96m Technicolor TCF/GoldenHarvest/Clearwater (Thomas K. Gray, Kim Dawson, David Chan)
V

The turtles travel back to seventeenth century Japan to rescue their friend.

The least of the adventures, a tired and aimless movie lacking in fun.

wd Stuart Gillard ph David Gurfinkel

Elias Koteas, Paige Turco, Stuart Wilson, Sab Shimono, Vivian Wu, Mark Caso, Matt Hill, Jim Raposa, David Fraser, James Murray, Henry Hayashi

That Darn Cat!*

US 1965 116m Technicolor
Walt Disney (Bill Walsh, Ron Miller)

A troublesome cat inadvertently helps to trail bank robbers.

Overlong but generally pleasing small-town comedy with well-paced sequences and a fascinating feline hero.

w The Gordons, Bill Walsh novel *Undercover Cat* by The Gordons d Robert Stevenson ph Edward Colman m Bob Brunner

Hayley Mills, Dean Jones, Dorothy Provine, Roddy McDowall, Neville Brand, Elsa Lanchester, William Demarest, Frank Gorshin, Grayson Hall, Ed Wynn

That's Dancin'!**
US 1985 105m Metrocolor
MGM-UA/David Niven Jnr, Jack Haley Jnr
V, L

Selections from the golden age of the movie musical, featuring the likes of Fred Astaire, Gene Kelly, Eleanor Powell, Busby Berkeley.

Fascinating compilation which made little impact at the box-office.
narrators Gene Kelly, Sammy Davis Jnr, Mikhail Baryshnikov, Liza Minnelli, Ray Bolger

'Boy! do we need it now!'

That's Entertainment**
US 1974 137m Metrocolor
70mm (blown up)/scope
MGM (Daniel Melnick, Jack Haley Jnr)
V, L

Fred Astaire, Gene Kelly, Elizabeth Taylor, James Stewart, Bing Crosby, Liza Minnelli, Donald O'Connor, Debbie Reynolds, Mickey Rooney and Frank Sinatra introduce highlights from MGM's musical past.

A slapdash compilation which was generally very big at the box-office and obviously has fascinating sequences, though the narration is sloppily sentimental and the later wide-screen sequences let down the rest.

wd Jack Haley Jnr   *ph* various
m various

Principal stars as above plus Judy Garland, Esther Williams, Eleanor Powell, Clark Gable, Ray Bolger

'While many ponder the future of MGM, none can deny that it has one hell of a past.' – *Variety*
'It is particularly gratifying to get the key sequences from certain movies without having to sit through a fatuous storyline.' – *Michael Billington, Illustrated London News*

'No other film in town offers such a harvest of undiluted joy.' – *Sunday Express*

That's Entertainment Part Two**
US 1976 133m Metrocolor
70mm (blown up)/scope
MGM (Saul Chaplin, Daniel Melnick)
V, L

More of the above, introduced by Fred Astaire and Gene Kelly, with comedy and drama sequences as well as musical.

d Gene Kelly   *titles* Saul Bass
ph various

Principal stars as above plus Jeanette MacDonald, Nelson Eddy, the Marx Brothers, Laurel and Hardy, Jack Buchanan, Judy Garland, Ann Miller, Mickey Rooney, Oscar Levant, Louis Armstrong, etc

That's My Wife*
US 1929 20m bw silent
Hal Roach

Stan dresses up as Ollie's wife to impress his rich uncle.

Lesser-known star comedy which well sustains its basic joke and includes some splendidly timed farce in a restaurant.

w Leo McCarey, H. M. Walker
d Lloyd French

Laurel and Hardy, Vivien Oakland, William Courtright

Their First Mistake**
US 1932 20m bw
Hal Roach
V

Ollie decides to improve his marriage by adopting a baby, only to find that his wife has left him.

Sublimely silly but endearing star comedy with brilliant passages of imbecilic conversation followed by well-timed farce.

w H. M. Walker d George Marshall (who also plays a bit)

Laurel and Hardy, Mae Busch

Their Purple Moment
US 1928 20m bw silent
Hal Roach

Stan and Ollie go out on the town, only to discover that Stan's wife has replaced his money with grocery coupons.

Minor star comedy with efficient but predictable restaurant scenes ending in a pie fight.

w H. M. Walker d James Parrott

Laurel and Hardy, Anita Garvin, Kay Deslys

Them Thar Hills**
US 1934 20m bw
Hal Roach

Stan and Ollie go camping, drink from a well full of moonshine whisky, and get drunk with another camper's wife.

Consistently funny star comedy culminating in a tit-for-tat routine which was reprised in *Tit for Tat* the following year.

w Stan Laurel, H. M. Walker d Charles Rogers

Laurel and Hardy, Charlie Hall, Mae Busch, Billy Gilbert

There's No Business like Show Business**
US 1954 117m DeLuxe
  Cinemascope
TCF (Sol C. Siegel)
V, L

The life and times of a family of vaudevillians.

Mainly entertaining events and marvellous tunes make up this very Cinemascoped musical, in which the screen is usually filled with six people side by side.

w Phoebe and Henry Ephron d Walter Lang ph Leon Shamroy m Lionel Newman, Alfred Newman m/ly Irving Berlin ad John DeCuir, Lyle Wheeler

Ethel Merman, Dan Dailey, Marilyn Monroe, Donald O'Connor, Johnny Ray, Mitzi Gaynor, Hugh O'Brian, Frank McHugh
AAN: original story (Lamar Trotti); Lionel Newman, Alfred Newman

They Shall Have Music
US 1939 105m bw
Samuel Goldwyn
GB title: *Melody of Youth*

Jascha Heifetz conducts a charity concert to help a music school for slum children.

Formula family film given the best possible production.

w *John Howard Lawson, Irmgard Von Cube* d Archie Mayo ph Gregg Toland md Alfred Newman

Joel McCrea, Jascha Heifetz, Andrea Leeds, Gene Reynolds, Walter Brennan, Porter Hall, Terry Kilburn, Diana Lynn (Dolly Loehr)

'A natural for the musically minded ... elemental and surefire audience appeal.' – *Variety*
AAN: Alfred Newman

Thicker than Water
US 1935 20m bw
Hal Roach
V

Ollie spends his savings on a grandfather clock which is promptly destroyed by a passing truck.

Well made but slightly tiresome star comedy, the last short ever made featuring Stan and Ollie.

w Stan Laurel   d James W. Horne

Laurel and Hardy, Daphne Pollard, James Finlayson

The Thief of Baghdad****
GB 1940 109m Technicolor
London Films (Alexander Korda)
L

A boy thief helps a deposed king thwart an evil usurper.

Marvellous blend of magic, action and music, the only film to catch on celluloid the overpowering atmosphere of the Arabian Nights.

w *Miles Malleson, Lajos Biro*
d *Michael Powell, Ludwig Berger, Tim Whelan* ph *Georges Périnal, Osmond Borradaile* m *Miklos Rozsa*
ad *Vincent Korda* sp *Lawrence Butler*

Conrad Veidt, Sabu; John Justin, June Duprez, Morton Selten, Miles Malleson, *Rex Ingram*, Mary Morris

ABU (Sabu): 'I'm Abu the thief, son of Abu the thief, grandson of Abu the thief, most unfortunate of ten sons with a hunger that yearns day and night . . .'

AGED KING (Morton Selten): 'This is the Land of Legend, where everything is possible when seen through the eyes of youth.'

'The true stuff of fairy tale.' – *Basil Wright*
'Both spectacular and highly inventive.' – *NFT, 1969*
'Magical, highly entertaining, and now revalued by Hollywood moguls Lucas and Coppola.' – *Time Out, 1980*

AA: Georges Périnal; Vincent Korda
AAN: Miklos Rozsa

The Thief of Baghdad
Italy/France 1960 100m
Eastmancolor Cinemascope
Titanus/Lux

A very moderate remake in the form of an action star vehicle.

w *Augusto Frassinetti, Filippo Sanjust, Bruno Vailati* d Arthur Lubin

Steve Reeves, Georgia Moll, Arturo Dominici

Third Man on the Mountain
GB 1959 103m Technicolor
Walt Disney (Bill Anderson)

In 1865 a Swiss dishwasher dreams of conquering the local mountain, and befriends a distinguished mountaineer.

Handsomely photographed boys' adventure story.

w Eleanore Griffin novel *Banner in the Sky* by James Ramsay Ullman
d Ken Annakin ph Harry Waxman, *George Tairraz* m William Alwyn

James MacArthur, Michael Rennie, Janet Munro, James Donald, Herbert Lom, Laurence Naismith, Walter Fitzgerald, Nora Swinburne

Thirty Years of Fun**
US 1962 85m bw
Robert Youngson Productions

A compilation of silent comedy, including Chaplin's *The Floorwalker, Easy Street, The Pawnshop* and *The Rink*; Keaton's *The Balloonatic* and *Daydreams*; Langdon's *Smile Please*; and Laurel and Hardy's first meeting in *Lucky Dog*.

Not the most hilarious of the compilations, but historically important, with the usual high quality prints which Youngson alone seemed able to provide.

wd Robert Youngson   *film quality control* Paul Guffanti

Those Calloways
US 1964 131m Technicolor
Walt Disney (Winston Hibler)

Adventures of a marsh trapper and his family who live near a Maine village and try to protect wild geese from hunters.

Predictable family saga with pleasant backgrounds.

w Louis Pelletier   *novel* Swift Water by Paul Annixter   *d* Norman Tokar   *ph* Edward Colman   *m* Max Steiner

Brian Keith, Vera Miles, Brandon de Wilde, Walter Brennan, Ed Wynn, Linda Evans, Philip Abbott, John Larkin, John Qualen

Those Daring Young Men in Their Jaunty Jalopies
US/Italy/France 1969 125m Technicolor Panavision
Paramount/Dino de Laurentiis/Marianne (Ken Annakin, Basil Keys)
V
GB title: Monte Carlo or Bust

Accidents befall various competitors in the Monte Carlo Rally.

Rough-edged imitation of *The Great Race* and *Those Magnificent Men in Their Flying Machines*, much feebler than either but with the waste of a big budget well in evidence.

w Jack Davies, Ken Annakin   *d* Ken Annakin   *ph* Gabor Pogany   *m* Ron Goodwin

Peter Cook, Dudley Moore, Tony Curtis, Bourvil, Walter Chiari, Terry-Thomas, Gert Frobe, Susan Hampshire, Jack Hawkins, Eric Sykes

Those Magnificent Men in Their Flying Machines, or How I Flew from London to Paris in 25 hours and 11 Minutes**
GB 1965 133m Technicolor Todd-AO
TCF (Stan Marguilies, Jack Davies)
V, L

In 1910, a newspaper owner sponsors a London to Paris air race.

Long-winded, generally agreeable knockabout comedy with plenty to look at but far too few jokes to sustain it.

w Jack Davies, Ken Annakin   *d* Ken Annakin   *ph* Christopher Challis   *m* Ron Goodwin   *pd* Tom Morahan

Sarah Miles, Stuart Whitman, Robert Morley, Eric Sykes, Terry-Thomas, James Fox, Alberto Sordi, Gert Frobe, Jean-Pierre Cassel, Karl Michael Vogler, Irina Demich, Benny Hill, Flora Robson, Sam Wanamaker, Red Skelton, Fred Emney, Cicely Courtneidge, Gordon Jackson, John Le Mesurier, Tony Hancock, William Rushton

'There is many a likely gag, but none that survives the second or third reprise. It could have been a good bit funnier by being shorter: the winning time is 25 hours 11 minutes, and by observing some kind of neo-Aristotelian unity the film seems to last exactly as long.' – *John Simon*
AAN: script

A Thousand and One Nights*
US 1945 92m Technicolor
Columbia (Samuel Bischoff)

Aladdin seeks his princess.

Amusing take-off on the Arabian Nights, with good jokes and music.

w Wilfrid H. Pettitt, Richard English, Jack Henley   d Alfred E. Green   ad Stephen Goosson, Rudolph Sternad

Cornel Wilde, Phil Silvers, Evelyn Keyes, Adele Jergens, Dusty Anderson, Dennis Hoey
AAN: art direction

Three Amigos
US 1986 105m Technicolor
Orion (Lorne Michaels, George Folsey Jr)
V

Three wimpish cowboy stars find themselves hired to defend a desert town from a bandit.

Weak take-off of *The Magnificent Seven*, with performances that grate.

w Steve Martin, Lorne Michaels, Randy Newman   d John Landis   ph Ronald W. Browne   m Elmer Bernstein   pd Richard Sawyer   ed Malcolm Campbell

Chevy Chase, Steve Martin, Martin Short, Patrice Martinez, Alfonso Arau

The Three Caballeros***
US 1945 70m Technicolor
Walt Disney (Norman Ferguson)

A programme of shorts about South America, linked by Donald Duck as a tourist.

Rapid-fire mélange of fragments supporting the good neighbour policy, following the shorter *Saludos Amigos* of 1943. The kaleidoscopic sequences and the combination of live action with cartoon remain of absorbing interest.

w various   d various   m Edward Plumb, Paul J. Smith, Charles Wolcott

† Stories include Pablo the Penguin, Little Gauchito, a Mexican sequence and some adventures with Joe Carioca
AAN: Edward Plumb, Paul J. Smith, Charles Wolcott

The 300 Spartans*
US 1962 114m DeLuxe Cinemascope
TCF (Rudolph Maté, George St George)

Sparta leads the ancient Greek states against Persia's attack at Thermopylae.

Quite a lively epic with some dignity.

w George St George   d Rudolph Maté   ph Geoffrey Unsworth   m Manos Hadjikakis

Richard Egan, Ralph Richardson, David Farrar, Diane Baker, Barry Coe, Donald Houston, Kieron Moore, John Crawford, Robert Brown

The Three Lives of Thomasina
GB 1963 97m Technicolor
Walt Disney
L

In a Scottish village in 1912, a vet finds that his methods are no match for a local girl who treats animals by giving them love.

Syrupy film for children: the animals are the main interest and one of them narrates . . .

w Robert Westerby
novel *Thomasina* by Paul Gallico
d Don Chaffey   ph Paul Beeson   m Paul Smith

Susan Hampshire, Patrick McGoohan, Karen Dotrice, Vincent Winter, Laurence Naismith, Finlay Currie, Wilfrid Brambell

'They changed her diapers – she changed their lives!'

Three Men and a Baby

US 1987 102m DeLuxe
Touchstone/Silver Screen III (Ted Field, Robert W. Cort)
V, L

Three swinging bachelors find a baby on their doorstep.

Slight comedy, given some momentum by a heroin-dealing subplot, which proved surprisingly successful with audiences thanks to energetic playing.

w James Orr, Jim Cruickshank *d* Leonard Nimoy *ph* Adam Greenberg *m* Marvin Hamlisch *pd* Peter Larkin

Tom Selleck, Steve Guttenberg, Ted Danson, Nancy Travis

† Remake of the more thoughtful and elegant *Trois Hommes et un Couffin* of 1985, whose director Coline Serreau was to have directed the US version but backed out.

Three Men and a Little Lady

US 1990 100m
Touchstone/Jean François LePetit-Interscope Communications (Ted Field, Robert W. Cort)
V, L

Three bachelors prevent the mother of the child they 'adopted' marrying an Englishman.

Dire sequel to *Three Men and a Baby*, notably silly in its depiction of England as a backward rural country inhabited entirely by eccentrics.

w Charlie Peters *story* Sara Parriott, Josann McGibbon *d* Emilio Ardolino *ph* Adam Greenberg *m* James Newton Howard *pd* Stuart Wurtzel *ad* David M. Haber *ed* Michael A. Stevenson

Tom Selleck, Steve Guttenberg, Ted Danson, Nancy Travis, Robin Weisman, Christopher Cazenove, Sheila Hancock, Fiona Shaw

'Thinking people will be hard-pressed to find a single interesting moment in this relentlessly predictable fantasy.' – *Variety*

Three Men in a Boat

GB 1956 94m Eastmancolor
Cinemascope
Romulus (Jack Clayton)

In the 1890s, misadventures befall three men holidaying on the Thames.

Flabby burlesque of a celebrated comic novel whose style is never even approached.

w Hubert Gregg, Vernon Harris *novel* Jerome K. Jerome *d* Ken Annakin *ph* Eric Cross *m* John Addison *ad* John Howell

David Tomlinson, Jimmy Edwards, Laurence Harvey, Shirley Eaton, Robertson Hare, Jill Ireland, Lisa Gastoni, Martita Hunt, A. E. Matthews, Ernest Thesiger, Adrienne Corri

† A previous version in 1933 starred William Austin, Edmond Breon and Billy Milton; directed by Graham Cutts for ATP.

The Three Musketeers***

US 1948 125m Technicolor
MGM (Pandro S. Berman)
V

High-spirited version of the famous story, with duels and fights presented like musical numbers.

Its vigour and inventiveness is a pleasure to behold.

w Robert Ardrey *d* George Sidney *ph* Robert Planck *m* Herbert Stothart

Gene Kelly, Lana Turner, June Allyson, Frank Morgan, Van Heflin, Angela Lansbury, Vincent Price, Keenan Wynn, John Sutton, Gig Young, Robert Coote, Reginald Owen, Ian Keith, Patricia Medina

'A heavy, rough-housing mess. As Lady de Winter, Lana Turner sounds like a drive-in waitress exchanging quips with hotrodders, and as Richelieu, Vincent Price might be an especially crooked used car dealer. Angela Lansbury wears the crown of France as though she had won it at a county fair.' – *New Yorker, 1980*
AAN: Robert Planck

The Three Musketeers (The Queen's Diamonds)**
Panama 1973 107m Technicolor
Film Trust (Alex Salkind)

Jokey version with realistic blood; despite very lively highlights it wastes most of its high production cost by not giving its plot a chance; but money was saved by issuing the second half separately as *The Four Musketeers* (*The Revenge of Milady*). The latter section was less attractive.

w George MacDonald Fraser
d Richard Lester   ph David Watkin
m Michel Legrand   pd Brian Eatwell

Michael York, Oliver Reed, Richard Chamberlain, Frank Finlay, Raquel Welch, Geraldine Chaplin, Spike Milligan, Faye Dunaway, Charlton Heston, Christopher Lee, Jean-Pierre Cassel

'It's one dragged-out forced laugh. No sweep, no romance, no convincing chivalric tradition to mock.' – *Stanley Kauffmann*

3 Ninjas*
US 1992 84m Technicolor
Buena Vista/Touchstone/Global Venture Hollywood (Martha Chang)

The sons of an FBI agent, taught martial arts by their grandfather, defeat an evil arms dealer.

Amiable martial arts caper that should please the pre-teens.

w Edward Emanuel   story Kenny Kim   d John Turtletaub
ph Richard Michalak   m Rick Marvin   pd Kirk Petruccelli
ed David Rennie

Victor Wong, Michael Treanor, Max Elliott Slade, Chad Power, Rand Kingsley, Alan McRae, Margarita Franco, Toru Tanaka

'The gracefully choreographed spectacle of three little boys fighting hordes of evil adult ninjas is a surefire juve crowd-pleaser.' – *Variety*

The Three Worlds of Gulliver
US/Spain 1959 100m Technicolor
Columbia/Morningside (Charles Schneer)
V, L

Gulliver's adventures in Lilliput and Brobdingnag.

Flat treatment of marvellous material, with all the excitement squeezed out of it and not even much pizazz in the trick photography.

w Arthur Ross, Jack Sher   d Jack Sher   ph Wilkie Cooper
m Bernard Herrmann   sp Ray Harryhausen

Kerwin Mathews, Basil Sydney, Mary Ellis, Jo Morrow, June Thorburn, Grégoire Aslan, Charles Lloyd Pack, Martin Benson

Thunderball**
GB 1965 132m Technicolor Panavision
UA/Eon/Kevin McClory
V, V(W), L

James Bond goes underwater.

Commercially the most successful Bond, but certainly not the best despite a plethora of action sequences.

w Richard Maibaum, John Hopkins novel Ian Fleming
d Terence Young ph Ted Moore
m John Barry

Sean Connery, Adolfo Celi, Claudine Auger, Luciana Paluzzi, Rik Van Nutter, Bernard Lee, Lois Maxwell, Martine Beswick

'The screenplay stands on tiptoe at the outermost edge of the suggestive and gazes yearningly down into the obscene.' – *John Simon*

AA: special visual effects (John Stears)

Thunderbird Six
GB 1968 90m Techniscope
UA/AP/Century 21 (Gerry and Sylvia Anderson)

International Rescue combats the Black Phantom.

Bright, suspenseful puppetoon based on the TV series.

w Gerry and Sylvia Anderson
d David Lane ph Harry Oakes
m Barry Gray ad Bob Bell

'Holds some charm for adults, or at least for those who enjoy playing with miniature trains.' – *MFB*

Thunderhead, Son of Flicka*
US 1945 78m Technicolor
TCF (Robert Bassler)

More where *My Friend Flicka* came from.

Unexceptional family film with excellent outdoor photography.

w Dwight Cummins, Dorothy Yost
novel Mary O'Hara d Louis King
ph Charles Clarke m Cyril Mockridge

Roddy McDowall, Preston Foster, Rita Johnson, James Bell, Carleton Young

Tiger Bay**
GB 1959 105m bw
Rank/Wintle-Parkyn (John Hawkesworth)
V

A Polish seaman in Cardiff kills his faithless girl friend and kidnaps a child who proves more than a match for him.

Generally very proficient police chase melodrama with strong characterizations: a considerable box-office success of its time.

w John Hawkesworth, Shelley Smith d J. Lee-Thompson ph Eric Cross m Laurie Johnson

Hayley Mills, John Mills, Horst Buchholz, Megs Jenkins, Anthony Dawson, Yvonne Mitchell

A Tiger Walks*
US 1963 91m Technicolor
Walt Disney (Ron Miller)

In a small Western town, a tiger escapes from the circus.

A splendid animal and a happy ending help to make this a pretty good film for children.

w Lowell S. Hawley novel Ian Niall d Norman Tokar
ph William Snyder m Buddy Baker

Sabu, Brian Keith, Vera Miles, Pamela Franklin, Kevin Corcoran, Edward Andrews, Una Merkel, Frank McHugh

'The Disney message runs true to form — grown-ups should practise what they preach and children are right about animals.' – *MFB*

Time Bandits*
GB 1981 113m Technicolor
HandMade Films (Terry Gilliam)
V

A schoolboy is taken through time by a group of demonic dwarfs.

Curious tall tale in which schoolboy fantasy alternates with violence and black comedy. In general, much less funny than it intended to be, but with some hilarious moments.

w Michael Palin, Terry Gilliam d Terry Gilliam ph Peter Biziou m Mike Moran pd Millie Burns

John Cleese (as Robin Hood), Sean Connery (as Agamemnon), Ian Holm (as Napoleon), Ralph Richardson (as God), David Warner (as Satan), Shelley Duvall, Katherine Helmond, Michael Palin, Peter Vaughan, David Rappaport

The Time Machine*
US 1960 103m Metrocolor
MGM/Galaxy (George Pal)
V, L

A Victorian scientist builds a machine which after some trial and error transports him into the year 802701.

Surprisingly careful recreation of a period, and an undeniably charming machine, go for little when the future, including the villainous Morlocks, is so dull.

w David Duncan novel H. G. Wells d George Pal ph Paul C. Vogel m Russell Garcia ad George W. Davis, William Ferrari

Rod Taylor, Yvette Mimieux, Alan Young, Sebastian Cabot, Tom Helmore, Whit Bissell, Doris Lloyd

AA: special effects (Gene Warren, Tim Baar)

The Titfield Thunderbolt***
GB 1952 84m Technicolor
Ealing (Michael Truman)
V

When a branch railway line is threatened with closure, the villagers take it over as a private concern.

Undervalued on its release in the wake of other Ealing comedies, this now seems among the best of them as well as an immaculate colour production showing the England that is no more; the script has pace, the whole thing is brightly polished and the action works up to a fine climactic frenzy.

w T. E. B. Clarke d Charles Crichton ph Douglas Slocombe m Georges Auric

Stanley Holloway, George Relph, John Gregson, Godfrey Tearle, *Edie Martin,* Naunton Wayne, Gabrielle Brune, Hugh Griffith, Sidney James, Jack McGowran, Ewan Roberts, Reginald Beckwith

Toby Tyler*
US 1959 96m Technicolor
Walt Disney (Bill Walsh)

In 1910, a young orphan runs away to join a travelling circus in the midwest, and with the help of a chimp becomes a famous star.

Acceptable, predictable family fare.

w Bill Walsh, Lillie Hayward novel James Otis Kaler d Charles Barton ph William Snyder m Buddy Baker

Kevin Corcoran, Henry Calvin, Gene Sheldon, Bob Sweeney, James Drury

Tom Brown's Schooldays*
US 1940 86m bw
(RKO) The Play's the Thing (Gene Towne, Graham Baker)

Tom Brown finds life at Rugby brutal, but helps to become a civilizing influence.

Pretty lively Hollywood version of a rather unattractive semi-classic.

w Walter Ferris, Frank Cavell novel Thomas Hughes d Robert Stevenson ph Nicholas Musuraca m Anthony Collins

Jimmy Lydon, Cedric Hardwicke, Billy Halop, Freddie Bartholomew, Gale Storm, Josephine Hutchinson

Tom Brown's Schooldays
GB 1951 96m bw
Talisman (George Minter)

Unexciting remake featuring one surprisingly strong performance.

w Noel Langley d Gordon Parry ph C. Pennington-Richards m Richard Addinsell

Robert Newton, John Howard Davies, Diana Wynyard, Francis de Wolff, Kathleen Byron, Hermione Baddeley, James Hayter, Rachel Gurney, Amy Veness, Max Bygraves, Michael Hordern, John Charlesworth, John Forrest

'An odd mixture of the brutal and the solemnly improving.' – *Richard Mallett, Punch*

Tom Sawyer
US 1973 103m DeLuxe Panavision
UA/Readers Digest (Arthur P. Jacobs)

Reverential, rather tediously over-produced version for family audiences of the seventies, with brief songs and real Mississippi locations.

w/m/ly Richard and Robert Sherman d Don Taylor ph Frank Stanley md John Williams pd Philip Jefferies

Johnnie Whitaker, Celeste Holm, Warren Oates, Jeff East, Jodie Foster

† There had been a version with Jackie Coogan in 1930. Selznick's *The Adventures of Tom Sawyer* followed in 1937. In 1939 Billy Cook was Tom Sawyer, Detective, with Donald O'Connor as Huckleberry Finn.
AAN: Richard and Robert Sherman; John Williams

Tom Thumb*
GB 1958 98m Eastmancolor
MGM/Galaxy (George Pal)

A tiny forest boy outwits a couple of thieves.

Slight musical built round the legend of a two-inch boy; good trickwork and songs make it a delightful film for children.

w Ladislas Fodor d George Pal ph Georges Périnal m Douglas Gamley, Kenneth V. Jones sp Tom Howard

Russ Tamblyn, Jessie Matthews, Peter Sellers, Terry-Thomas, Alan Young, June Thorburn, Bernard Miles, Ian Wallace

† Donald O'Connor badly wanted the role, but it went to the MGM contractee.

AA: special effects

Tommy the Toreador
GB 1959 86m Technicolor
Fanfare/AB
V

A seaman takes the place of a bullfighter framed for smuggling.

Acceptable star comedy of its time.

w Nicholas Phipps, Sid Colin, Talbot Rothwell d John Paddy Carstairs

Tommy Steele, Sid James, Janet Munro, Pepe Nieto, Noel Purcell, Kenneth Williams, Eric Sykes

Tonka
US 1958 97m Technicolor
Walt Disney

A Sioux Indian tames a magnificent white horse, and after many adventures is reunited with him at Little Big Horn.

Unremarkable and overlong adventure story.

w Lewis R. Foster, Lillie Hayward novel *Comanche* by David Appel d Lewis R. Foster ph Loyal Griggs

Sal Mineo, Phil Carey, Jerome Courtland, Rafael Campos, H. M. Wynant

Top Hat****
US 1935 100m bw
RKO (Pandro S. Berman)
V

The path of true love is roughened by mistaken identities.

Marvellous Astaire-Rogers musical, with a more or less realistic London supplanted by a totally artificial Venice, and show stopping numbers in a style which is no more, separated by amusing plot complications lightly handled by a team of deft *farceurs*.

w Dwight Taylor, Allan Scott d Mark Sandrich ph David Abel, Vernon Walker m/ly Irving Berlin ch Hermes Pan ad Van Nest Polglase, Carroll Clark

Fred Astaire, Ginger Rogers, Edward Everett Horton, Helen Broderick, Eric Blore, Erik Rhodes

'The theatres will hold their own world series with this one. It can't miss.' – *Variety*

'In 25 years *Top Hat* has lost nothing of its gaiety and charm.' – *Dilys Powell, 1960*

AAN: best picture; song 'Cheek to Cheek'; Hermes Pan; art direction

Towed in a Hole***
US 1932 20m bw
Hal Roach

Two would-be fishermen wreck the boat they have just bought.

Brilliant star farce, filled with wonderfully lunatic dialogues and freshly conceived slapstick.

w Stan Laurel d George Marshall

Laurel and Hardy

'Laughter Is A State of Mind.'

Toys
US 1992 121m CFI colour
TCF (Mark Johnson, Barry Levinson)

An uptight army officer inherits a toy factory and switches production from cuddly toys to increasingly aggressive ones.

Visually splendid but otherwise totally incoherent movie.

w Valerie Curtin, Barry Levinson d Barry Levinson ph Adam Greenberg m Hans Zimmer, Trevor Horn pd Ferdinando Scarfiotti ed Stu Linder

Robin Williams, Michael Gambon, Joan Cusack, Robin Wright, LL Cool J, Donald O'Connor, Jack Warden

'Only a filmmaker with Barry Levinson's clout would have been so

indulged to create such a sprawling, seemingly unsupervised mess ... It will be hard to top as the season's major clunker.' – *Variety*
'A disaster ... It is quite unlike anything Levinson has done before, and it is sincerely to be hoped that he never does anything like it again.' – *Derek Malcolm, Guardian*
AAN: Ferdinando Scarfiotti; Albert Wolsky (costume design)

Traffic*
France/Italy 1970 96m Eastmancolor
Corona/Gibe/Selenia (Robert Dorfman)

The designer of a camping car has various little accidents on the way from the works to a show.

Rambling comedy with understated jokes and an almost invisible star.

w Jacques Tati, Jacques Legrange d Jacques Tati (with Bert Haanstra) ph Edouard Van Den Enden, Marcel Weiss m Charles Dumont

Jacques Tati

The Tramp*
US 1915 20m approx (24 fps)
bw silent
Mutual

A tramp saves a girl from crooks, is wounded and cared for by her, deliriously happy – until her lover arrives.

Fairly funny star comedy, the first with sentimental touches and the origin of the into-the-sunset fade-out.

wd Charles Chaplin ph Rollie Totheroh

Charles Chaplin, Edna Purviance, Bud Jamison, Leo White, Lloyd Bacon

Tramp Tramp Tramp*
US 1926 65m approx (24 fps)
bw silent
Harry Langdon

Harry enters a cross-country walking contest in order to impress his girl.

Well-staged peripatetic comedy, the star's first feature.

w Frank Capra, Tim Whelan, Hal Conklin, Gerald Duffy, Murray Roth, J. Frank Holliday d Harry Edwards

Harry Langdon, Joan Crawford, Alec B. Francis

Treasure Island**
US 1934 105m bw
MGM (Hunt Stromberg)

An old pirate map leads to a long sea voyage, a mutiny, and buried treasure.

Nicely mounted Hollywood version of a classic adventure story, a little slow in development but meticulously produced.

w John Lee Mahin novel Robert Louis Stevenson d Victor Fleming ph Ray June, Clyde de Vinna, Harold Rosson m Herbert Stothart

Wallace Beery, Jackie Cooper, Lewis Stone, *Lionel Barrymore*, Otto Kruger, Douglass Dumbrille, Nigel Bruce, Chic Sale

'While much of it entrances, the whole is somewhat tiring.' – *Variety*
'The first three-quarters is so lively and well established in its mood as to make the whole quite worth going to.' – *Otis Ferguson*

Treasure Island*
GB 1950 96m Technicolor
RKO/Walt Disney (Perce Pearce)
L

Cheerful Disney remake, poor on detail but transfixed by a swaggeringly overplayed and unforgettable leading performance.

w Lawrence Edward Watkin
d Byron Haskin ph F. A. Young m Clifton Parker
pd Thomas Morahan ed Alan Jaggs

Robert Newton, Bobby Driscoll, Walter Fitzgerald, Basil Sydney, Denis O'Dea, Geoffrey Wilkinson, Ralph Truman

'Serviceable rather than imaginative.' – *Lindsay Anderson*
'The result is an absolutely super party, but not "the world's greatest adventure story". Walt Disney may have, as Synopsis suggests, "much in common with Stevenson". But not this; shiver my timbers, not *Treasure Island*.' – *C. A. Lejeune*.
'The Long John Silver of Robert Newton . . . is the finest I ever saw . . . as succulent as peach-fed ham, as sweet as a spoonful of sugar held high over the porridge plate, as darkly oily as a car sump, as tricky as an ageing jockey.' – *Paul Holt*

Treasure Island
GB/France/Germany/Spain 1971
95m colour
Massfilms/FDL/CCC/Eguiluz (Harry Alan Towers)

Spiritless and characterless international remake with poor acting, production and dubbing.

w Wolf Mankowitz, O. W. Jeeves (Welles) d John Hough
ph Cicilio Paniagua m Natal Massara

Orson Welles, Kim Burfield, Lionel Stander, Walter Slezak, Rik Battaglia

'Sail the high seas. Battle the pirates. Live the adventure.'

Treasure Island
US 1990 132m colour
Warner/Agamemnon/British Lion (Fraser C. Heston)
V, L

Faithful to the original, but a version lacking in panache, and plodding when it should be exciting.

wd Fraser C. Heston novel Robert Louis Stevenson ph Robert Steadman m Paddy Maloney
pd Tony Woollard ed Eric Boyd-Perkins, Bill Parnell, Gregory Gontz

Charlton Heston, Christian Bale, Oliver Reed, Christopher Lee, Richard Johnson, Julian Glover, Clive Wood, John Benfield, Isla Blair

The Treasure of Lost Canyon
US 1952 82m Technicolor
U-I (Leonard Goldstein)

A small boy robbed of his inheritance finds it with the help of a country doctor who turns out to be his uncle.

Modest juvenile adventure, rather boringly narrated.

w Brainerd Duffield, Emerson Crocker
story Robert Louis Stevenson
d Ted Tetzlaff ph Russell Metty
m Joseph Gershenson

William Powell, Julia Adams, Charles Drake, Rosemary de Camp, Henry Hull, Tommy Ivo

Treasure of Matecumbe
US 1976 116m Technicolor
Walt Disney (Bill Anderson)

Two boys seek buried gold in the Florida keys.

Cheerful adventure tale with a few nods to *Treasure Island*; all very competent in the Disney fashion.

w Don Tait *d* Vincent McEveety *ph* Frank Phillips *m* Buddy Baker

Robert Foxworth, Joan Hackett, Peter Ustinov, Vic Morrow, Jane Wyatt, Johnny Duran, Billy Attmore

Tron*

US 1982 96m Technicolor Super Panavision 70mm
Walt Disney/Lisberger-Kushner

A computer games designer gets his revenge on an enemy by fighting things out in the computer world he has created.

Complicated science fantasy chiefly interesting for its computerized blend of live action and animation, which isn't always successful.

wd Steven Lisberger *ph* Bruce Logan *m* Michael Femer *associate producer (animation)* Harrison Ellenshaw *pd* Dean Edward Mitzner

Bruce Boxleitner, Jeff Bridges, David Warner, Barnard Hughes

'Loaded with the expected visual delights, but falls way short of the mark in story and viewer involvement.' – *Variety*
AAN: costume design; sound

Troop Beverly Hills

US 1989 106m Metrocolor
Columbia TriStar/Weintraub Entertainment/Fries Entertainment (Ava Ostern Fries, Martin Mickelson, Peter MacGregor-Scott)
V, L

A wealthy mother transforms her daughter's disintegrating Girl Scout troop by giving them badges in shopping and other consumer activities.

A broad and far from sparkling comedy which emphasises that it is best to be born rich.

w Pamela Norris, Margaret Grieco Oberman *story* Ava Ostern Fries *d* Jeff Kanew *ph* Donald E. Thorin *m* Randy Edelman, Lou Hemsey *pd* Robert F. Boyle *ed* Mark Melnick

Shelley Long, Craig T. Nelson, Betty Thomas, Mary Gross, Stephanie Beacham, David Gautreaux, Karen Kopins, Dinah Lacey, Shelley Morrison

Trouble in Store*

GB 1953 85m bw
GFD/Two Cities (Maurice Cowan)
V

A stock assistant causes chaos in a department store.

First, simplest and best of the Wisdom farces.

w John Paddy Carstairs, Maurice Cowan, Ted Willis *d* John Paddy Carstairs *ph* Ernest Steward *m* Mischa Spoliansky

Norman Wisdom, Jerry Desmonde, Margaret Rutherford, Moira Lister, Derek Bond, Lana Morris, Megs Jenkins, Joan Sims

Turner & Hooch

US 1989 99m Metrocolor
Warner/Touchstone/Silver Screen Partners IV (Raymond Wagner)
V, L

In order to solve a murder, a cop teams up with the only witness, a large dog.

The cycle of police buddy-buddy movies reaches its nadir in this strenuously unfunny release.

w Dennis Shryack, Michael Blodgett, Daniel Petrie Jr, Jim Cash, Jack

Epps Jr   d Roger Spottiswoode
ph Adam Greenberg   m Charles
Gross   pd John DeCuir Jnr
ed Paul Seydor, Mark Conte, Kenneth
Morrisey, Lois Freeman-Fox

Tom Hanks, Mare Winningham, Craig
T. Nelson, Reginald VelJohnson,
Scott Paulin, J. C. Quinn, John
McIntire

Twenty Thousand Leagues under the Sea**
US   1954   122m   Technicolor
   Cinemascope
Walt Disney

Victorian scientists at sea are wrecked and captured by the mysterious captain of a futuristic submarine.

Pretty full-blooded adaptation of a famous yarn, with strong performances and convincing art and trick work.

w Earl Felton   novel Jules Verne
d Richard Fleischer   ph Franz Planer,
Franz Lehy, Ralph Hammeras, Till
Gabbani   m Paul Smith   ad John
Meehan   ed Elmo Williams

Kirk Douglas, James Mason, Paul Lukas, Peter Lorre, Robert J. Wilke, Carlton Young, Ted de Corsia

AA: art direction; special effects
AAN: editing

Twice Two
US   1933   20m   bw
Hal Roach
V, V(C)

Stan and Ollie have each married the other's twin sister . . .

Strained and laboured trick comedy in which neither the double exposures nor the gags quite come off.

w Stan Laurel   d James Parrott

Laurel and Hardy

Twins*
US   1988   107m   DeLuxe
UIP/Universal (Ivan Reitman)
V, L

A 36-year-old man, bred in a genetic experiment as the perfect man, discovers that he has a less-than-perfect twin brother.

Amusing, if sometimes ponderous, comedy with the joke depending on the physical disparity of its two protagonists.

w William Davies, William Osborne, Timothy Harris, Herschel
Weingrod   d Ivan Reitman
ph Andrzej Bartkowiak
m Georges Delerue, Randy
Edelman   pd James D. Bissel
ed Sheldon Kahn, Donn Cambern

Arnold Schwarzenegger, Danny DeVito, Kelly Preston, Chloe Webb, Bonnie Bartlett, Marshall Bell, Trey Wilson, David Caruso, Hugh O'Brien

Twist around the Clock
US   1961   83m   bw
Columbia/Sam Katzman

An astute manager discovers a small-town dance called the twist and promotes it nationally.

Rock around the Clock revisited, with an even lower budget and fewer shreds of talent.

w James B. Gordon   d Oscar
Rudolph   ph Gordon Avil
md Fred Karger

Chubby Checker, the Marcels, Dion, John Cronin, Mary Mitchell

Two Tars****
US   1928   20m   bw   silent
Hal Roach
V

Two sailors in an old banger cause a

traffic jam and a consequent
escalation of violence.

Marvellous elaboration of a tit-for-tat situation, with the stars already at their technical best.

w Leo McCarey, H. M. Walker
d James Parrott

Laurel and Hardy, Edgar Kennedy, Charley Rogers

U

The Ugly Dachshund*
US 1965 93m Technicolor
Walt Disney (Winston Hibler)

A dachshund bitch fosters among its puppies an orphan Great Dane.

Cheerful, fast-moving animal farce.

w Albert Aley   novel G. B. Stern
d Norman Tokar   ph Edward Colman   m George Bruns

Dean Jones, Suzanne Pleshette, Charles Ruggles, Kelly Thordsen, Parley Baer, Mako, Charles Lane

'Actually filmed along the route he travelled 3000 years ago!'

Ulysses*
Italy 1954 103m Technicolor
Lux Film/Ponti-de Laurentiis (Fernando Cinquini)

Ulysses and his crew sail under the curse of Cassandra, and encounter Circe, the sirens and the cyclops.

Peripatetic adventure yarn not too far after Homer; narrative style uncertain but highlights good.

w Franco Brusati, Mario Camerini, Ennio de Concini, Hugh Gray, Ben Hecht, Ivo Perelli, Irwin Shaw
poem The Odyssey by Homer   d Mario Camerini   ph Harold Rosson
m Alessandro Cicognini

Kirk Douglas, Silvana Mangano, Anthony Quinn, Rosanna Podesta

Unaccustomed as We Are
US 1929 20m bw silent
Hal Roach
V(C)

Ollie takes a friend home to dinner, but his wife walks out, leaving him to get into all kinds of trouble.

The team's first sound comedy, rather hesitant in its use of the new medium. The story was later reworked as the last half hour of *Blockheads*.

w Leo McCarey and H. M. Walker
d Lewis R. Foster

Laurel and Hardy, Edgar Kennedy, Mae Busch, Thelma Todd

Up in Arms**
US 1944 106m Technicolor
Samuel Goldwyn

A hypochondriac joins the army.

Loose, generally pleasant introductory vehicle for Danny Kaye.

w Don Hartman, Robert Pirosh, Allen Boretz   d Elliott Nugent   ph Ray Rennahan   md Ray Heindorf, Louis Forbes

Danny Kaye, Dinah Shore, Constance Dowling, Dana Andrews, Louis Calhern, Lyle Talbot

'Not since Greta Garbo made her bow has there been anything so terrific as the inimitable Danny, one of the most exhilarating and spontaneous

personalities in film history.' – *New York Daily Mirror*
AAN: song 'Now I Know' (*m* Harold Arlen, *ly* Ted Koehler); Ray Heindorf, Louis Forbes

Up the Front
GB 1972 89m Technicolor
EMI/Associated London Films (Ned Sherrin)
V

A footman is hypnotized into enlisting in World War I and has an enemy 'plan' tattooed on his buttocks.

Threadbare end-of-the-pier romp.

w Sid Colin, Eddie Braben   *d* Bob Kellett   *ph* Tony Spratling
m Patrick Greenwell   *ad* Seamus Flannery

Frankie Howerd, Bill Fraser, Zsa Zsa Gabor, Stanley Holloway, Hermione Baddeley, Robert Coote, Lance Percival, Dora Bryan

Used Cars*
US 1980 111m Metrocolor
Columbia (Bob Gale)

For the love of his boss's daughter, a fast-talking car salesman saves a used-car lot from being taken over by a mean-spirited rival.

Vigorous broad comedy, amusing enough if you're feeling indulgent.

w Robert Zemeckis, Bob Gale
d Robert Zemeckis   *ph* Donald M. Morgan   *m* Patrick Williams
pd Peter M. Jamison   *ed* Michael Kahn

Kurt Russell, Gerrit Graham, Frank McRae, Deborah Harmon, Jack Russell

'A classic screwball fantasy – a neglected modern comedy that's like a more restless and visually high-spirited version of the W. C. Fields pictures.' – *Pauline Kael, New Yorker*

V

The Valley of Gwangi
US 1968 95m Technicolor
Warner/Morningside (Charles H. Schneer)

Cowboys and scientists discover prehistoric monsters in a 'forbidden' Mexican Valley.

Tedious adventure yarn enhanced by good special effects.

w William E. Best d James O'Connelly ph Erwin Hillier m Jerome Moross sp Ray Harryhausen

Richard Carlson, Laurence Naismith, James Franciscus, Gila Golan, Freda Jackson

Vice Versa*
GB 1947 111m bw
Rank/Two Cities (Peter Ustinov, George H. Brown)

A magic stone enables an unhappy Victorian boy to change places with his pompous father.

Funny moments can't disguise the fact that this overlong comedy is a bit of a fizzle, its talented creator not being a film-maker. A pity, as British films have so rarely entered the realms of fancy.

wd Peter Ustinov novel F. Anstey

Roger Livesey, Kay Walsh, Anthony Newley, *James Robertson Justice*, David Hutcheson, Petula Clark, Joan Young

'A repository of English oddities.' – *John Russell Taylor*

Vice Versa
US 1988 98m colour
Columbia (Dick Clement, Ian La Frenais)
V, L

A father and his 11-year-old son find their minds transplanted into the other's body by a magic skull.

One of the last and certainly the least of the mid-1980s cycle of role swapping movies.

w Dick Clement, Ian La Frenais d Brian Gilbert ph King Baggott m David Shire pd Jim Schoppe ed David Garfield

Judge Reinhold, Fred Savage, Corinne Bohrer, Swoosie Kurtz, David Profal, Jane Kaczmerek, Gloria Gifford

A View to a Kill
GB 1985 121m Metrocolor Panavision
MGM-UA/Albert R. Broccoli
V, L

James Bond tangles with a ruthless international industrialist.

A tedious Bond adventure in which even the expensive highlights are unmemorable.

w Richard Maibaum, Michael G. Wilson d John Glen ph Alan Hume m John Barry pd Peter Lamont ed Peter Davies

Roger Moore, Christopher Walken, Grace Jones, Tanya Roberts, Patrick MacNee, David Yip, Fiona Fullerton

The Viking Queen
GB 1967 91m Technicolor
Warner/Hammer (John Temple-Smith)

During the first century AD, the queen of the Iceni tries to keep peace with the occupying Romans but has trouble with hot-headed Druids.

Stuff and nonsense from the Dark Ages; light should not have been shed upon it.

w Clarke Reynolds story John Temple-Smith d Don Chaffey ph Stephen Dade m Gary Hughes pd George Provis ed James Needs, Peter Boita

Don Murray, Carita, Donald Houston, Andrew Keir, Patrick Troughton, Adrienne Corri, Niall MacGinnis, Wilfrid Lawson, Nicola Pagett

The Vikings***
US 1958 116m Technirama
UA/KD Productions (Jerry Bresler)

Two Viking half-brothers quarrel over the throne of Northumbria.

Slightly unpleasant and brutal but extremely well-staged and good-looking epic in which you can almost feel the harsh climate. Fine colour, strong performances, natural settings, vivid action, and all production values as they should be.

w Calder Willingham novel The Viking by Edison Marshall
d Richard Fleischer ph Jack Cardiff m Mario Nascimbene

sp credit titles United Productions of America narrator Orson Welles

Kirk Douglas, Tony Curtis, Ernest Borgnine, Janet Leigh, Alexander Knox, Frank Thring, James Donald, Maxine Audley, Eileen Way

Viva Las Vegas
US 1964 85m Metrocolor
Panavision
MGM (Jack Cummins, George Sidney)
L
GB title: Love in Las Vegas

A sports car racer has fun in the gambling city.

Tolerable star musical.

w Sally Benson d George Sidney ph Joseph Biroc md George Stoll

Elvis Presley, Ann-Margret, Cesare Danova, William Demarest, Nicky Blair, Jack Carter

Voyage to the Bottom of the Sea*
US 1961 105m DeLuxe
Cinemascope
TCF/Windsor (Irwin Allen)
V

USN Admiral Nelson takes scientists in his futuristic atomic submarine to explode a belt of radiation.

Childish but sometimes entertaining science fiction which spawned a long-running TV series.

w Irwin Allen, Charles Bennett d Irwin Allen ph Winton Hoch, John Lamb m Paul Sawtell, Bert Shefter ad J. M. Smith, Herman A. Blumenthal

Walter Pidgeon, Robert Sterling, Joan Fontaine, Peter Lorre, Barbara Eden, Michael Ansara, Henry Daniell, Regis Toomey, Frankie Avalon

W

War Games*
US 1983 113m Metrocolor
MGM-UA/Sherwood (Leonard Goldberg, Harold Schneider)
V, L

A teenager unwittingly taps his home computer into the Pentagon and pretends to be Russia on the point of launching missiles.

Mildly intriguing science fantasy which becomes uncomfortable and finally boring because of the excess of jargon and flashing lights.

w Lawrence Lasker, Walter F. Parkes d John Badham
ph William A. Fraker m Arthur B. Rubenstein pd Angelo P. Graham

Matthew Broderick, Dabney Coleman, John Wood, Ally Sheedy, Barry Corbin, Kent Williams

'All the film's adventure and suspense is inevitably at odds with its ostensible sentiments . . . [but] the result has a kind of seamless efficiency.' – *Steve Jenkins, MFB*
AAN: screenplay; cinematography

The War of the Worlds*
US 1953 85m Technicolor
Paramount/George Pal
L

Terrifying aliens invade Earth via the American midwest.

Spectacular battle scenes are the mainstay of this violent fantasy, which goes to pieces once the cardboard characters open their mouths.

w Barre Lyndon novel H. G. Wells d Byron Haskin
ph George Barnes m Leith Stevens ad Hal Pereira, Albert Nozaki ed Everett Douglas

Gene Barry, Ann Robinson, Les Tremayne, Bob Cornthwaite, Sandra Giglio

AA: special effects
AAN: editing

Warlords of Atlantis
GB 1978 96m Technicolor
EMI/John Dark, Kevin Connor

Victorian sea scientists discover a lost land under the Mediterranean.

Predictable compote of monsters and unwearable costumes, without a trace of wit in the script. For infants only.

w Brian Hayles d Kevin Connor ph Alan Hume m Mike Vickers pd Elliot Scott

Doug McClure, Peter Gilmore, Shane Rimmer, Lea Brodie, Michael Gothard

The Watcher in the Woods
US 1980/82 100m or 83m Technicolor
Walt Disney (Tom Leetch)
L

The teenage daughter of an American composer has strange and apparently supernatural experiences in the British countryside.

Unsatisfactory attempt by the Disney people to aim at a wider audience than is expected of them. The mixture of cuteness, menace and the supernatural simply doesn't gel, and the film was much re-edited between its two appearances.

w Brian Clemens, Harry Spaulding, Rosemary Anne Sisson
novel Florence Engel Randall
d John Hough (and Vincent McEveety) ph Alan Hume
m Stanley Myers

Bette Davis, Carroll Baker, David McCallum, Lynn-Holly Johnson, Kyle Richards, Ian Bannen, Richard Pasco

The Water Babies
GB/Poland 1978 92m colour
Ariadne/Studio Miniatur Filmowych (Peter Shaw)

An 1850 chimney sweep evades his pursuers by jumping into a pool, where he becomes involved in an underwater adventure.

The live action bookends are strangely subdued, the animated middle totally characterless and seeming to bear little relation to the rest. A considerable disappointment.

w Michael Robson novel Charles Kingsley d Lionel Jeffries
ph Ted Scaife m Phil Coulter

James Mason, Billie Whitelaw, Bernard Cribbins, Joan Greenwood, David Tomlinson, Tommy Pender

'The men, the battle, the glory the world will remember forever!'

Waterloo*
Italy/USSR 1970 132m Technicolor Panavision
Columbia/DDL/Mosfilm (Dino de Laurentiis)
V

Historical events leading up to the 1815 battle.

The battle forms the last hour of this historical charade, and looks both exciting and splendid, though confusion is not avoided. The rest is a mixed blessing.

w H. A. L. Craig, Sergei Bondarchuk
d Sergei Bondarchuk ph Armando Nannuzzi m Nino Rota pd Mario Garbuglia

Rod Steiger, Christopher Plummer, Orson Welles, Jack Hawkins, Virginia McKenna, Dan O'Herlihy, Rupert Davies, Ian Ogilvy, Michael Wilding

Watership Down
GB 1978 92m Technicolor
Nepenthe (Martin Rosen)
V

A colony of rabbits seek a new home following a vision of the destruction of their warren.

A brilliantly written if somewhat pretentious parable becomes a rather flatly made cartoon in which it is difficult to distinguish one rabbit from another; the whole thing becomes a bit doomladen for family audiences, while adults will presumably prefer to re-read the novel.

wd Martin Rosen novel Richard Adams animation director Tony Guy m Angela Morley
voices John Hurt, Richard Briers, Ralph Richardson, Zero Mostel, Roy

Kinnear, Denholm Elliott, John Bennett, Simon Cadell

Way Out West****
US 1937 66m bw
Hal Roach (Stan Laurel)
V, V(C), L

Laurel and Hardy come to Brushwood Gulch to deliver the deed to a gold mine.

Seven reels of perfect joy, with the comedians at their very best in brilliantly-timed routines, plus two song numbers as a bonus.

w Jack Jevne, Charles Rogers, James Parrott, Felix Adler d James Horne ph Art Lloyd, Walter Lundin m Marvin Hatley

Stan Laurel, Oliver Hardy, James Finlayson, Sharon Lynne, Rosina Lawrence

'Thin returns indicated ... for added feature on duallers.' – *Variety*
'Not only one of their most perfect films, it ranks with the best screen comedy anywhere.' – *David Robinson, 1962*
'The film is leisurely in the best sense; you adjust to a different rhythm and come out feeling relaxed as if you'd had a vacation.' – *New Yorker, 1980*
AAN: Marvin Hatley

'You'll laugh. You'll cry. You'll hurl.'
Wayne's World
US 1992 95m Technicolor
UIP/Paramount (Lorne Michaels)
V

A ramshackle cable TV show, put together by two girl- and rock-obsessed teenagers, is given big-time exposure by a sleazy TV executive.

Tedious teen comedy, based on characters developed for the *Saturday Night Live* TV show, which long outstays its welcome. It was, though, one of 1992's surprise hits, ranking sixth at the US box-office and doing well in Europe.

w Mike Myers, Bonnie Turner, Terry Turner d Penelope Spheeris ph Theo Van de Sande m J. Peter Robinson pd Gregg Fonseca ed Malcolm Campbell

Mike Myers, Dana Carvey, Rob Lowe, Tia Carrere, Brian Doyle-Murray, Lara Flynn Boyle, Michael DeLuise, Dan Bell

'Aggressively pitched at a young white male audience, feature is unlikely to appeal to mainstream moviegoers ... Even for fans of the TV comics, the laugh-to-running-time ratio is extremely low.' – *Variety*

Wayne's World 2*
US 1993 94m DeLuxe
UIP/Paramount (Lorne Michaels)

In a dream, Wayne is told to organise Waynestock, the ultimate rock concert.

The mixture much the same as the first, but funnier.

w Mike Myers, Bonnie Turner, Terry Turner d Stephen Surjik

Mike Myers, Dana Carvey, Christopher Walken, Tia Carrere, Kim Basinger

Wee Willie Winkie**
US 1937 99m bw
TCF (Gene Markey)

A small girl becomes the mascot of a British regiment in India.

Vaguely based on a Kipling tale, this was the most expensive Temple vehicle and a first-rate family action picture with sentimental asides.

w Ernest Pascal, Julien Josephson story Rudyard Kipling d John Ford ph Arthur Miller m Alfred

Newman *ad* William S. Darling, David Hall

Shirley Temple, Victor McLaglen, C. Aubrey Smith, June Lang, Michael Whalen, Cesar Romero, Constance Collier, Gavin Muir

'Will add another clean-up to her cycle, but those knees are losing their contour ... a pretentiously produced melodrama which launches the leading feminine box office star into a distinctly new phase of her career and story material.' – *Variety*
AAN: art direction

West Side Story***

US 1961 155m Technicolor
 Panavision 70
(UA) Mirisch/Seven Arts (Robert Wise)
V, L

The Romeo and Juliet story in a New York dockland setting.

The essentially theatrical conception of this entertainment is nullified by determinedly realistic settings which make much of it seem rather silly, but production values are fine and the song numbers electrifying.

w Ernest Lehman   *play* Arthur Laurents, after William Shakespeare   *d* Robert Wise, Jerome Robbins   *ph* Daniel L. Fapp
m Leonard Bernstein   *ly* Stephen Sondheim   *pd* Boris Leven

Natalie Wood (sung by Marni Nixon), Richard Beymer (sung by Jimmy Bryant), Russ Tamblyn, *Rita Moreno*, George Chakiris

AA: best picture; Robert Wise, Jerome Robbins; Daniel L. Fapp; Rita Moreno; George Chakiris; Saul Chaplin; musical direction (Saul Chaplin, Johnny Green, Sid Ramin, Irwin Kostal); art direction; sound; costume design

AAN: Ernest Lehman

Westward Ho the Wagons

US 1956 85m Technicolor
 Cinemascope
Walt Disney (Bill Walsh)

A wagon train defends itself against Indians.

Slow and simple-minded family Western.

w Tom Blackburn   *d* William Beaudine   *ph* Charles Boyle
m Paul Smith

Fess Parker, Kathleen Crowley, Jeff York, David Stollery, Sebastian Cabot, George Reeves

What a Crazy World

GB 1963 88m bw
Capricorn/AB Pathe (Michael Carreras)

A working-class London boy sets out to be a rock-and-roller.

Unsurprising star musical, quite lively of its kind.

w Alan Klein   *play* Alan Klein
d Michael Carreras

Joe Brown, Susan Maughan, Marty Wilde, Harry H. Corbett, Avis Bunnage

What's Up, Doc?**

US 1972 94m Technicolor
Warner/Saticoy (Peter Bogdanovich)
V, L

In San Francisco, an absent-minded young musicologist is troubled by the attentions of a dotty girl who gets him involved with crooks and a series of accidents.

Madcap comedy, a pastiche of several thirties originals. Spectacular slapstick and willing players are somewhat let down by exhausted patches and a tame final reel.

w Buck Henry, David Newman, Robert Benton *d* Peter Bogdanovich *ph* Laszlo Kovacs *m* Artie Butler *pd* Polly Pratt

Barbra Streisand, Ryan O'Neal, Kenneth Mars, Austin Pendleton, Madeleine Kahn, Mabel Albertson, Sorrell Booke

'A comedy made by a man who has seen a lot of movies, knows all the mechanics, and has absolutely no sense of humour. Seeing it is like shaking hands with a joker holding a joy buzzer: the effect is both presumptuous and unpleasant.' – *Jay Cocks*
'It's all rather like a 19th-century imitation of Elizabethan blank verse drama.' – *Stanley Kauffmann*
'It freely borrows from the best screen comedy down the ages but has no discernible style of its own.' – *Michael Billington, Illustrated London News*

What's Up, Tiger Lily?*
US 1966 80m Eastmancolor Tohoscope
Benedict/Toho (Woody Allen)
V

A Japanese agent searches for the world's greatest egg salad recipe.

Woody Allen and his American cast re-dub a Japanese spy film to create an off-beat comedy that is amusing in fits and starts.

w Kazuo Yamada, Woody Allen and others *d* Senkichi Taniguchi *m* Jack Lewis, The Lovin' Spoonful *ed* Richard Krown

Tatsua Mihashi, Mie Hama, Akiko Wakabayashi, Tadeo Nakamuru, Susumu Kurobe, Woody Allen, Frank Buxton, Len Maxwell, Louise Lasser, Mickey Rose

'The jokes get rather desperate, but there are enough wildly sophomoric ones to keep this pop stunt fairly amusing until about midway.' – *Pauline Kael, New Yorker*

When Comedy Was King***
US 1959 84m bw
Robert Youngson Productions

Valuable compilation of silent comedy sequences, with the high print quality and poor commentary to be expected from this source. Extracts include Buster Keaton in *Cops*, Laurel and Hardy in *Big Business*, and a Fatty Arbuckle comedy.

ed Robert Youngson

When Dinosaurs Ruled the Earth
GB 1969 100m (96m US) Technicolor
Warner/Hammer (Aida Young)
L

In prehistoric times, a girl is swept out to sea by a cyclone and adopted by a dinosaur.

Sequel to *One Million Years BC*, all very silly but tolerably well done.

wd Val Guest, from a treatment by J. G. Ballard *ph* Dick Bush *m* Mario Nascimbene *ad* John Blezard *sp* Jim Danforth *ed* Peter Curran

Victoria Vetri, Patrick Allen, Robin Hawdon, Patrick Holt, Imogen Hassall

'I'm very proud that my first screen credit was for what is, without doubt, the worst film ever made.' – *J. G. Ballard*
AAN: special visual effects (Jim Danforth, Roger Dicken)

When I Grow Up*
US 1951 90m bw
Horizon (S. P. Eagle)

A boy about to run away changes his mind after reading his grandfather's diaries.

Pleasant, sentimental family film with an unusual approach.

wd Michael Kanin *ph* Ernest Laszlo *m* Jerome Moross

Bobby Driscoll, Robert Preston, Charley Grapewin, Martha Scott, Ralph Dumke

When the Whales Came
GB 1989 100m Fujicolor
Fox/Golden Swan/Central Television (Simon Channing Williams)
V, L

In 1914, fishermen on one of the Scilly Isles are persuaded by a recluse and a boy to save a beached whale, an act which brings them luck.

Ecologically sound, dramatically dull story, not helped by its insistently soft focus photography.

w Michael Morpurgo *novel Why the Whales Came* by Michael Morpurgo *d* Clive Rees *ph* Robert Paynter *m* Christopher Gunning *pd* Bruce Grimes *ed* Andrew Boulton

Helen Mirren, Paul Scofield, David Suchet, Barbara Jefford, David Threlfall, Barbara Ewing, John Hallan, Jeremy Kemp, Max Rennie, Helen Pearce

When Worlds Collide
US 1951 82m Technicolor
Paramount (George Pal)
L

Another planet is found to be rushing inevitably towards Earth, but before the collision a few people escape in a space ship.

Stolid science fiction with a spectacular but not marvellous climax following seventy minutes of inept talk.

w Sidney Boehm *novel* Philip Wylie, Edwin Balmer *d* Rudolph Maté *ph* John Seitz, W. Howard Greene *m* Leith Stevens

Richard Derr, Barbara Rush, Larry Keating, Peter Hanson, John Hoyt

AA: special effects
AAN: John Seitz, W. Howard Greene

Where Do We Go from Here?*
US 1945 77m Technicolor
TCF (William Perlberg)

A writer stumbles on a genie who takes him through periods of American history, including a voyage with Christopher Columbus.

Well-staged and rather funny charade with at least one memorable song.

w Morrie Ryskind *d* Gregory Ratoff *ph* Leon Shamroy *songs* Kurt Weill, Ira Gershwin *m* David Raksin

Fred MacMurray, June Haver, Joan Leslie, Gene Sheldon, Anthony Quinn, Carlos Ramirez, Fortunio Bonanova, Alan Mowbray, Herman Bing, Otto Preminger

'Nine parts heavy facetiousness to one part very good fun.' – *James Agee*

Where No Vultures Fly*
GB 1951 107m Technicolor
Ealing (Leslie Norman)
US title: *Ivory Hunter*

Adventures of an East African game warden.

Pleasantly improving family film, nicely shot on location; a sequel, *West of Zanzibar*, was less impressive.

w W. P. Lipscomb, Ralph Smart,

Leslie Norman d Harry Watt
ph Geoffrey Unsworth m Alan Rawsthorne

Anthony Steele, Dinah Sheridan, Harold Warrender, Meredith Edwards

'These expeditionary films are really journalistic jobs. You get sent out to a country by the studio, stay as long as you can without getting fired, and a story generally crops up.' – *Harry Watt*

'No one will wonder why it was chosen for this year's royal film show. It is not sordid, as so many new films are; it has a theme that almost everyone will find appealing; and the corner of the Empire where it is set is fresh, beautiful and exciting to look at.' – *Daily Telegraph*

'If you laugh yourself sick at this picture – sue Bob Hope!'

Where There's Life
US 1947 75m bw
Paramount (Paul Jones)

A timid New Yorker turns out to be heir to the throne of a Ruritanian country, and is harassed by spies of both sides.

Mild star comedy with slow patches.

w Allen Boretz, Melville Shavelson d Sidney Lanfield
ph Charles Lang Jnr m Irwin Talbot

Bob Hope, Signe Hasso, William Bendix, George Coulouris

Where's Charley?*
GB 1952 97m Technicolor
Warner

An Oxford undergraduate impersonates the rich aunt of his best friend.

Slow and rather stately musical version of the famous farce *Charley's Aunt*, unsatisfactorily shot on a mixture of poor sets and sunlit Oxford locations; worth cherishing for the ebullient performance of its over-age star.

w John Monks Jnr play Brandon Thomas (via stage musical)
book George Abbott d David Butler ph Erwin Hillier
ch Michael Kidd m Frank Loesser

Ray Bolger, Robert Shackleton, Mary Germaine, Allyn McLerie, Margaretta Scott, Horace Cooper

Whisky Galore****
GB 1948 82m bw
Ealing (Monja Danischewsky)
V
US title: *Tight Little Island*

During World War II, a ship full of whisky is wrecked on a small Hebridean island, and the local customs and excise man has his hands full.

Marvellously detailed, fast-moving, well-played and attractively photographed comedy which firmly established the richest Ealing vein.

w *Compton Mackenzie*, Angus Macphail novel Compton Mackenzie d *Alexander Mackendrick* ph Gerald Gibbs
m Ernest Irving

Basil Radford, Joan Greenwood, Jean Cadell, Gordon Jackson, James Robertson Justice, Wylie Watson, John Gregson, Morland Graham, Duncan Macrae, Catherine Lacey, Bruce Seton, Henry Mollinson, Compton Mackenzie, A. E. Matthews

'Brilliantly witty and fantastic, but wholly plausible.' – *Sunday Chronicle*

Whistle Down the Wind*
GB 1961 99m bw
Rank/Allied Film Makers/Beaver (Richard Attenborough)

Three north country children think a murderer on the run is Jesus Christ.

Charming allegorical study of childhood innocence, extremely well made, amusing, and avoiding sentimentality.

w Keith Waterhouse, Willis Hall *novel* Mary Hayley Bell *d* Bryan Forbes *ph* Arthur Ibbetson *m* Malcolm Arnold

Hayley Mills, Bernard Lee, Alan Bates, Norman Bird, Elsie Wagstaff, Alan Barnes

White Fang
US 1990 109m Eastmancolor
Warner/Hybrid/Disney/Silver Screen Partners IV (Marykay Powell)
V, L

A youth, who goes to the Klondike to take over his dead father's gold-mining claim, befriends a dog that is half-wolf.

Tame, youth-oriented version, far closer to *Lassie* than to Jack London's original.

w Jeanne Rosenberg, Nick Thiel, David Fallon *novel* Jack London *d* Randal Kleiser *ph* Tony Pierce-Roberts *m* Basil Poledouris *pd* Michael Bolton *ed* Lisa Day

Klaus Maria Brandauer, Ethan Hawke, Seymour Cassel, Susan Hogan, James Remar, Bill Moseley, Clint B. Youngreen

Who Framed Roger Rabbit**
US 1988 103m Rank Color/Metrocolor/DeLuxe
Warner/Touchstone/Amblin (Robert Watts, Frank Marshall)
V, L

Cartoon characters become involved in Dashiel Hammett-style whodunnit.

Criticisms of thin plotting are irrelevant: the seamless integration of animation and live-action enchanted audiences.

w Jeffrey Price, Peter S. Seaman *book* Who Censored Roger Rabbit? by Gary K. Wold *d* Robert Zemeckis *ph* Dean Cundey *m* Alan Silvestri *pd* Elliot Scott *animation* Richard Williams *ed* Arthur Schmidt

Bob Hoskins, Christopher Lloyd, Joanna Cassidy, Stubby Kaye *voices* Charles Fleischer, Kathleen Turner, Amy Irving, Lou Hirsch, Mel Blanc

'A deplorable development in the possibilities of animation – and a melancholy waste of the gifts of one of our most gifted actors.' – *Dilys Powell*

AA: Arthur Schmidt; visual effects
AAN: Dean Cundey; art direction

Who's Minding the Store?*
US 1963 90m Technicolor
Paramount/York/Jerry Lewis (Paul Jones)

An accident-prone young man gets a job in a department store.

Better-than-average star comedy, slapstick being allowed precedence over sentimentality.

w Frank Tashlin, Harry Tugend *d* Frank Tashlin *ph* W. Wallace Kelley *m* Joseph J. Lilley

Jerry Lewis, Jill St John, Agnes Moorehead, John McGiver, Ray Walston, Nancy Kulp

The Wildcats of St Trinian's
GB 1980 91m Technicolor
Wildcat (E. M. Smedley-Aston)

The awful schoolgirls get unionized,

and kidnap an Arab's daughter to gain attention.

Crude and belated tailpiece to a series which was never very satisfactory. (See *The Belles of . . .*, *Blue Murder at . . .*, *The Pure Hell of . . .*, *The Great St Trinian's Train Robbery*.)

wd Frank Launder ph Ernest Steward m James Kenelm Clarke

Sheila Hancock, Michael Hordern, Joe Melia, Thorley Walters, Rodney Bewes, Maureen Lipman, Ambrosine Philpotts

Willow*

US 1988 126m colour
UIP/MGM (Nigel Wooll)
V

In a time of magic, two heroes set out to bring a baby to safety and fulfil a prophecy that will overthrow an evil empire.

Spectacular jaunt around familiar material, plundered from mythology, fairy-tales and old movies, that relies on special effects to maintain interest.

w Bob Dolman story George Lucas d Ron Howard ph Adrian Biddle m James Horner pd Allan Cameron sp John Richardson ed Daniel Hanley, Michael Hill

Val Kilmer, Joanne Whalley, Warwick Davies, Jean Marsh, Patricia Hayes, Billy Barty, Pat Roach, Gavan O'Herlihy, David Steinberg

'It's doubtful if any action-adventure director has a strong enough style to give this script a tone and a shape, and Ron Howard, who's got the job, is lost.' – *Pauline Kael, New Yorker*

Willy Wonka and the Chocolate Factory*

US 1971 100m Technicolor
David Wolper
V, L

A boy wins a tour of the local chocolate factory and finds himself in the power of a magician.

Semi-satiric Grimms Fairy Tale pastiche which looks good but never seems quite happy with itself.

w Roald Dahl novel Roald Dahl d Mel Stuart ph Arthur Ibbetson songs Leslie Bricusse, Anthony Newley md Walter Scharf ad Harper Goff

Gene Wilder, Jack Albertson, Peter Ostrum, Roy Kinnear, Aubrey Woods
AAN: Walter Scharf

Wind

US 1992 125m Technicolor
Filmlink International/American Zoetrope (Mata Yamamoto, Tom Luddy)

A young sailor, who loses the America's Cup to the Australians, persuades a designer to create a new yacht to win back the title.

Uninteresting and water-logged drama.

w Rudy Wurlitzer, Mac Gudgeon story Jeff Benjamin, Roger Vaughan, Kimball Livingston d Carroll Ballard ph John Toll m Basil Poledouris pd Laurence Eastwood ed Michael Chandler

Matthew Modine, Jennifer Grey, Stellan Skarsgard, Rebecca Miller, Ned Vaughn, Cliff Robertson, Jack Thompson

'Despite the sometimes striking images of expert crews guiding their beautiful boats through challenging waters, predictable story trajectory and bland human element will keep this physically ambitious picture in a b.o. stall.' – *Variety*

Windbag the Sailor
GB 1936 85m bw
Gainsborough (Edward Black)

An incompetent seaman is washed away on an old ketch and lands on a South Sea isle.

Rather uninventive star comedy with inevitable pleasing moments.

w Marriott Edgar, Stafford Dickens, Will Hay   d William Beaudine
ph Jack Cox   md Louis Levy

Will Hay, Moore Marriott, Graham Moffatt, Norma Varden

The Winslow Boy***
GB 1948 117m bw
British Lion/London Films (Anatole de Grunwald)
V

A naval cadet is expelled for stealing a postal order; his father spends all he has on proving his innocence.

Highly enjoyable middle-class British entertainment based on an actual case; performances and period settings are alike excellent, though the film is a trifle overlong.

w Terence Rattigan, Anatole de Grunwald   play Terence Rattigan
d Anthony Asquith   ph Frederick Young   m William Alwyn

Robert Donat, Cedric Hardwicke, Margaret Leighton, Frank Lawton, Jack Watling, Basil Radford, Kathleen Harrison, Francis L. Sullivan, Marie Lohr, Neil North, Wilfrid Hyde White, Ernest Thesiger

'Only a clod could see this film without excitement, laughter and some slight moisture about the eyes.' – *Daily Telegraph*

The Witches**
US 1990 91m Eastmancolor
Warner/Lorimar (Mark Shivas)
V

A small boy, who has been turned into a mouse, schemes with his granny to thwart witches' plans to poison all the children in Britain.

Superior entertainment, intended for children, but as likely to be enjoyed by adults.

w Allan Scott   novel Roald Dahl
d Nicolas Roeg   ph Harvey Harrison   m Stanley Myers
pd Voytek, Andrew Sanders
ed Tony Lawson

Anjelica Huston, Mai Zetterling, Jasen Fisher, Rowan Atkinson, Bill Patterson, Brenda Blethyn, Charlie Potter, Anne Lambton, Jane Horrocks

'A controlled and suitably dark piece of filmmaking.' – *Variety*

The Wiz*
US 1978 134m Technicolor
Universal/Motown (Robert Cohen)
V

A black version of *The Wizard of Oz*, set in New York.

Glossy version of the Broadway musical hit; it offers some rewards, but on the whole the first is the best.

w Joel Schumacher   play Charlie Smalls (m/ly)   book William Brown   d Sidney Lumet
ph Oswald Morris   md Quincy Jones   m Quincy Jones   pd Tony Walton   songs Charlie Smalls

Diana Ross, Michael Jackson, Nipsey Russell, Ted Ross, Lena Horne, Richard Pryor, Mabel King, Theresa Merritt
AAN: Oswald Morris; Quincy Jones

The Wizard

US 1989 97m DeLuxe
UIP/Universal (David Chisholm, Ken Topolsky)

A young boy runs away with his almost-mute even younger brother in order to compete in a video-game championship.

Uninteresting pre-teen road movie, which has no other purpose than to sell video games.

w David Chisholm   d Todd Holland   ph Robert Yeoman   m J. Peter Robinson   pd Michael Mayer   ed Tom Finan

Fred Savage, Luke Edwards, Christian Slater, Beau Bridges, Vincent Leahr, Wendy Phillips, Dea McAllister, Sam McMurray, Will Seltzer

The Wizard of Oz

US 1925 70m bw silent
Larry Semon
V

On her 18th birthday a girl abandoned as a small baby at a Kansas farm discovers that she is the Queen of Oz and, after deposing its dictator, lives there happily ever after.

The emphasis is on farmyard slapstick comedy, mainly executed with a heavy hand, which makes it hard to appreciate why Semon was once almost as popular as Chaplin and Keaton, but it has its moments — particularly a chase sequence in wooden boxes.

w L. Frank Baum Jnr, Leon Lee, Larry Semon   novel L. Frank Baum   d Larry Semon   ph H. F. Koenenkamp, Frank Good, Leonard Smith   ad Robert Stevens   ed Sam Zimbalist

Larry Semon (as the Scarecrow), Oliver N. Hardy (as the Tin Woodsman), Dorothy Dwan, Mary Carr, Virginia Pearson, Bryant Washburn, Josef Swickard, Otto Lederer, Charles Murray

† The film is available on video with a musical accompaniment.

The Wizard of Oz**

US 1939 102m Technicolor
MGM (Mervyn Le Roy)
V, L

Unhappy Dorothy runs away from home, has adventures in a fantasy land, but finally decides that happiness was in her own back yard all the time.

Classic fairy tale given vigorous straightforward treatment, made memorable by performances, art direction and hummable tunes.

w Noel Langley, Florence Ryerson, Edgar Allan Wolfe   book Frank L. Baum   d Victor Fleming   ph Harold Rosson   songs E. Y. Harburg, Harold Arlen   md Herbert Stothart   ad Cedric Gibbons, William A. Horning

Judy Garland, Frank Morgan, Ray Bolger, Jack Haley, Bert Lahr, Margaret Hamilton, Billie Burke, Charley Grapewin, Clara Blandick

SCARECROW (Ray Bolger):
'I could while away the hours
Conversin' with the flowers
Consultin' with the rain.
And perhaps I'd deserve you
And be even worthy erv you
If I only had a brain . . .'

COWARDLY LION (Bert Lahr):
'Oh, it's sad to be admittin'
I'm as vicious as a kitten
Widout de vim and voive;
I could show off my prowess
Be a lion, not a mowess
If I only had de noive.'

GLINDA, the good witch (Billie

Burke): 'Close your eyes and tap your heels together three times. And think to yourself, there's no place like home.'
DOROTHY (Judy Garland): 'If I ever go looking for my heart's desire again, I won't look any further than my own back yard, because if it isn't there, I never really lost it to begin with.'
DOROTHY, LION, SCARECROW, TIN MAN:
'We're off to see the Wizard
The wonderful Wizard of Oz.
We hear he is a whiz of a wiz
If ever a wiz there was.
If ever a wever a wiz there was
The Wizard of Oz is one because
Because of the wonderful things he does . . .'

'There's an audience for it wherever there's a projection machine and a screen.' – *Variety*
'I don't see why children shouldn't like it, but for adults there isn't very much except Bert Lahr.' – *Richard Mallett, Punch*
'As for the light touch of fantasy, it weighs like a pound of fruitcake soaking wet.' – *Otis Ferguson*

† Ray Bolger was originally cast as the tin man but swapped roles with Buddy Ebsen who was to have been the scarecrow. Ebsen then got sick from the metal paint and was replaced by Jack Haley. Edna May Oliver was originally cast as the wicked witch. For Dorothy MGM wanted Shirley Temple, but Twentieth Century Fox wouldn't loan her.

†† The sepia scenes at beginning and end were directed by King Vidor.

AA: song 'Over the Rainbow'; Herbert Stothart
AAN: best picture; art direction

The Wolves of Willoughby Chase
GB 1988 93m colour
Entertainment/Subatomnic/Zenith (Mark Forstater)
V

Two girls discover that their wicked governess is attempting to steal the family estate.

Lively children's film with relishable villains.

w William M. Akers novel Joan Aiken d Stuart Orme ph Paul Beeson m Colin Towns pd Christopher Hobbs ed Martin Walsh

Stephanie Beacham, Mel Smith, Geraldine James, Richard O'Brien, Emily Hudson, Aleks Darowska, Jane Horrocks, Eleanor David, Jonathan Coy

Wombling Free
GB 1977 96m Eastmancolor
Rank/Ian Shand
V

The furry creatures who live under Wimbledon Common at last make contact with humans.

Disastrous attempt to film a popular TV series for children. The series came in five-minute chunks; this elephantine transcription leaves several talents high and dry.

wd Lionel Jeffries, from characters created by Elizabeth Beresford ph Alan Hume m Mike Batt

David Tomlinson, Frances de la Tour, Bonnie Langford, Bernard Spear

'A fiasco. If you really must take your kids, it would be less of a pain to go shopping at the same time.' – *Derek Malcolm, Guardian*

Won Ton Ton, the Dog Who Saved Hollywood

US 1976 92m colour
Paramount/David V. Picker, Arnold Schulman, Michael Winner

In twenties Hollywood, a lost Alsatian dog becomes a movie star but later suffers some ups and downs before being reunited with his mistress.

Scatty, unlikeable comedy with too frantic a pace, apparently in desperation at the dearth of funny lines and situations. The sixty 'guest stars' barely get a look in; the director seems to think (erroneously) that their appearance makes some kind of point even though they have nothing to do. Altogether, an embarrassment.

w Arnold Schulman, Cy Howard d Michael Winner ph Richard H. Kline m Neal Hefti

Madeleine Kahn, Art Carney, Bruce Dern, Ron Leibman; and Dennis Morgan, William Demarest, Virginia Mayo, Rory Calhoun, Henry Wilcoxon, Ricardo Montalban, Jackie Coogan, Johnny Weissmuller, Aldo Ray, Ethel Merman, Joan Blondell, Yvonne de Carlo, Andy Devine, Broderick Crawford, Richard Arlen, Jack La Rue, Dorothy Lamour, Phil Silvers, Gloria de Haven, Stepin Fetchit, Rudy Vallee, George Jessel, Ann Miller, Janet Blair, the Ritz Brothers, Victor Mature, Fernando Lamas, Cyd Charisse, Huntz Hall, Edgar Bergen, Peter Lawford, Regis Toomey, Alice Faye, Milton Berle, John Carradine, Walter Pidgeon, etc

'The film tries to conceal its deficiencies in comic ideas and comic skill by doing everything at the pace of a clockwork toy with a too-tight spring.' – *Dave Robinson, Times*

Wonder Man**

US 1945 97m Technicolor
Samuel Goldwyn

A mild-mannered student is persuaded by the ghost of his dead twin to avenge his murder.

Smooth, successful mixture of *Topper*, a night-club musical, a gangster drama and the star's own brand of fooling; this is possibly his best vehicle after *The Court Jester*.

w Don Hartman, Melville Shavelson, Philip Rapp story Arthur Sheekman d Bruce Humberstone ph Victor Milner, William Snyder md Louis Forbes, Ray Heindorf sp John Fulton

Danny Kaye, Vera-Ellen, Virginia Mayo, Steve Cochran, S. Z. Sakall, Allen Jenkins, Ed Brophy, Donald Woods, Otto Kruger, Richard Lane, Natalie Schaefer
AAN: Louis Forbes, Ray Heindorf; song 'So in Love' (m David Rose, ly Leo Robin)

Wonderful Life*

GB 1964 113m Techniscope
EMI/Elstree Distributors/Ivy (Kenneth Harper)

Four entertainers on a luxury liner are hired by a film crew in Africa.

Slight but zestful youth musical with highly illogical detail; the highlight is a ten-minute spoof history of the movies.

w Peter Myers, Ronald Cass d Sidney J. Furie ph Ken Higgins pd Stanley Dorfman

Cliff Richard, Walter Slezak, Susan Hampshire, Melvyn Hayes, Richard O'Sullivan, Una Stubbs, Derek Bond, Gerald Harper, the Shadows

The Wonderful World of the Brothers Grimm*
US 1962 134m Technicolor Cinerama
MGM/Cinerama/George Pal

An account of the lives of the German fairy tale writers is supplemented by three of their stories, *The Dancing Princess*, *The Cobbler and the Elves* and *The Singing Bone*.

Saccharine, heavy-handed pantomime with insufficient comedy, menace or spectacle.

w David P. Harmon, Charles Beaumont, William Roberts
d Henry Levin, George Pal ph Paul C. Vogel m Leigh Harline
songs Bob Merrill ad George W. Davis, Edward Carfagno

Laurence Harvey, Karl Boehm, Claire Bloom, Barbara Eden, Walter Slezak, Oscar Homolka, *Martita Hunt*, Russ Tamblyn, Yvette Mimieux, *Jim Backus*, Beulah Bondi, Terry-Thomas, Buddy Hackett, Otto Kruger
AAN: Paul C. Vogel; Leigh Harline

The Wonders of Aladdin
Italy 1961 92m Technicolor Cinemascope
Embassy/Lux

With the help of a genie, Aladdin defeats a usurper and wins the princess's hand.

Flat and disappointing pantomime with virtually no charm.

w Luther Davis d Henry Levin, Mario Bava ph Tonino Delli Colli m Angelo Lavagnino

Donald O'Connor, Vittorio de Sica, Aldo Fabrizi, Michèle Mercier

The World's Greatest Athlete
US 1973 92m Technicolor
Walt Disney (Bill Walsh)

An American sports coach on an African holiday finds a young Tarzan with amazing powers.

Simple-minded comedy with lame tomfoolery and trickwork.

w Gerald Gardiner, Dee Caruso
d Robert Scheerer ph Frank Phillips m Marvin Hamlisch

Tim Conway, Jan-Michael Vincent, John Amos, Roscoe Lee Browne

Wrong Again
US 1929 20m bw silent
Hal Roach

A horse instead of a painting is delivered to a rich man's house.

Pleasing but not very inventive star comedy.

w Lewis R. Foster, Leo McCarey, H. M. Walker d Leo McCarey

Laurel and Hardy, Del Henderson

The Wrong Arm of the Law*
GB 1962 94m bw
Romulus/Robert Verlaise (Aubrey Baring, E. M. Smedley Aston)

London gangsters plan retaliation against Australian interlopers, and offer Scotland Yard a temporary truce.

Forgettable but pretty funny crook comedy in the British vein, with pacy script and excellent comedy timing.

w Ray Galton, Alan Simpson, John Antrobus screenplay Len Heath, John Warren d Cliff Owen
ph Ernest Steward m Richard Rodney Bennett

Peter Sellers, Lionel Jeffries, Bernard Cribbins, Davy Kaye, Nanette Newman, Bill Kerr, John Le Mesurier

X

Xanadu
US 1980 93m Technicolor
Universal/Lawrence Gordon
V, L

The muse Terpsichore comes to Earth and becomes involved in the opening of a roller-derby disco.

Misguided attempt at a clean nostalgic musical, apparently conceived in a nightmare after somebody saw *Down to Earth* on the late show.

w Richard Christian Danus, Marc Reid Rubel *d* Robert Greenwald *ph* Victor J. Kemper *m* Barry de Vorzon *songs* Jeff Lynne, John Farrar *pd* John W. Corso

Olivia Newton-John, Gene Kelly, Michael Beck

'Truly a stupendously bad film whose only salvage is the music.' – *Variety*
'A forties musical submerged by contemporary tat.' – *Guardian*
'Mushy and limp, so insubstantial it evaporates before our eyes.' – *Roger Ebert*

† Gene Kelly uses the same character name, Danny McGuire, as he did in *Cover Girl*.

Y

'They tamed a tropic wilderness!'
The Yearling**
US 1946 134m Technicolor
MGM (Sidney Franklin)
L

The son of an old-time country farmer is attached to a stray deer.

Excellent family film for four-handkerchief patrons.

w Paul Osborn   novel Marjorie Kinnan Rawlings   d Clarence Brown   ph Charles Rosher, Leonard Smith   m Herbert Stothart   ad Cedric Gibbons, Paul Groesse   ed Harold Kress

Gregory Peck, Jane Wyman, Claude Jarman Jnr, Chill Wills, Clem Bevans, Margaret Wycherly, Henry Travers, Forrest Tucker

AA: Claude Jarman Jnr (Special Award as outstanding child actor); Charles Rosher, Leonard Smith (and Arthur Arling); art direction
AAN: best picture; Clarence Brown; Gregory Peck; Jane Wyman; editing

Yellow Submarine*
GB 1968 87m DeLuxe
King Features/Apple (Al Brodax)

The happy kingdom of Pepperland is attacked by the Blue Meanies.

Way-out cartoon fantasia influenced by Beatlemania and the swinging sixties; hard to watch for non-addicts.

w Lee Minoff, Al Brodax, Jack Mendelsohn, Erich Segal   d George Duning   m John Lennon, Paul McCartney

'The film is fun, and an animated feature that holds the interest of adults of all ages (I don't think there are children of any age left) is not to be sneezed at.' – *John Simon*

'A picture filled with swashbucklers, privateers, public floggings, saucy tarts, looney lords, beggars, queens, and even a very jolly Roger!'
Yellowbeard
US 1983 96m DeLuxe
Orion/Seagoat (Carter de Haven Jnr)
V, L

Farcical adventures of a 17th-century pirate captain.

A spoofy saga in deliberately bad taste, this ragbag of old gags and new unpleasantness sank rapidly to the bottom of the box-office barrel.

w Graham Chapman, Peter Cook, Bernard McKenna   d Mel Damski   ph Gerry Fisher   m John Morris   pd Joseph R. Jennings

Graham Chapman, Peter Boyle, Cheech and Chong, Peter Cook, Marty Feldman, Michael Hordern, Eric Idle, Madeline Kahn, James Mason, John Cleese, Kenneth Mars, Spike Milligan, Susannah York, Beryl Reid, Ferdy Mayne, Peter Bull

'The atrocious script and haphazard

direction elicit generally embarrassing performances from all concerned.' – *Kim Newman, MFB*

You Only Live Twice**

GB 1967 117m Technicolor Panavision
UA/Eon (Harry Saltzman, Albert R. Broccoli)
V, V(W), L

James Bond goes to Japan.

The Bond saga at its most expensive and expansive, full of local colour and in-jokes, with an enormously impressive set for the climactic action.

w Roald Dahl   *novel* Ian Fleming   *d* Lewis Gilbert
ph Freddie Young, Bob Huke
m John Barry   *pd* Ken Adam

Sean Connery, Tetsuro Tamba, Akiko Wakabayashi, Mie Hama, Karin Dor, Bernard Lee, Lois Maxwell, Desmond Llewellyn, *Charles Gray, Donald Pleasence*

Young Einstein

Australia 1988 91m colour
Warner/Serious Productions (Yahoo Serious, Warwick Ross, David Roach)
V, L

Einstein discovers the theory of relativity, falls in love with Marie Curie, and then invents the surfboard, the electric guitar and rock 'n' roll.

A smash-hit in its native land, it is a ramshackle, slapstick comedy that, relatively speaking, does not travel well.

w Yahoo Serious, David Roach
d Yahoo Serious   *ph* Jeff Darling   *m* William Motzing, Martin Armiger, Tommy Tycho
ad Steve Marr, Laurie Faen, Colin Gibson, Ron Highfield   *ed* Yahoo Serious

Yahoo Serious, Odile Le Clezio, John Howard, Peewee Wilson, Su Cruikshank

'A film which manages to be innocuous and appalling at the same time.' – *MFB*

Young Giants

US 1983 97m DeLuxe Panavision
Entertainment Enterprises (Tom Moyer, Megan Moyer)

A San Diego priest helps a boys' home by re-organizing a football team so that an old priest can die happy.

Shades of *Going My Way*, but somewhat ineptly done, with a guest appearance from Pele as *deus ex machina*.

w Tom Moyer, Terrill Tannen, Mike Lammers   *d* Terrill Tannen
ph Raoul Lomas   *m* Rick Patterson   *ad* Daniel R. Webster
ed Denine Rowan, Marion W. Cronin, Daniel Gross

Peter Fox, John Huston, Lisa Wills, F. William Parker, Severn Darden

'At least it has the courage of its throwback convictions.' – *Kim Newman, MFB*

The Young Ones*

GB 1961 108m Technicolor Cinemascope
ABP (Kenneth Harper)
V
US title: *Wonderful to be Young*

The son of a tycoon starts a youth club and puts on a musical to raise funds.

A shopworn idea is the springboard for a brave try in a field where Britain was presumed to have failed; despite the enthusiasm with which it was greeted at the time, it has dated badly.

w Peter Myers, Ronald Cass
d Sidney J. Furie   ph Douglas Slocombe   m Stanley Black

Cliff Richard, Robert Morley, Carole Grey, Richard O'Sullivan, Melvyn Hayes, Gerald Harper, Robertson Hare

Young Sherlock Holmes

US 1985 109m Technicolor
Paramount/Amblin (Mark Johnson)
V, L
GB title: *Young Sherlock Holmes and the Pyramid of Fear*

Holmes and Watson meet as teenage students, and trace some mysterious murders to an eastern cult.

More expensive gimmickry with acres of tedium in between the technical highlights. Nothing for Holmes buffs.

w Chris Columbus   d Barry Levinson   ph Stephen Goldblatt   m Bruce Broughton   pd Norman Reynolds   ed Stu Linder

Nicholas Rowe, Alan Cox, Sophie Ward, Anthony Higgins, Freddie Jones, Nigel Stock

'Another Steven Spielberg version of those lamps made from driftwood and coffee tables from redwood burl. It's not art but they all serve their purpose and sell by millions.' – *Variety* (This one was a box-office disappointment.)

AAN: visual effects

Young Winston**

GB 1972 157m Eastmancolor
Panavision
Columbia/Open Road/Hugh French (Carl Foreman)
V

The adventurous life of Winston Churchill up to his becoming an MP.

Generally engaging if lumpy film which switches too frequently from action to family drama to politics to character study and is not helped by irritating directorial tricks.

w Carl Foreman   book *My Early Life* by Winston Churchill   d Richard Attenborough   ph Gerry Turpin   m Alfred Ralston   pd Don Ashton, Geoffrey Drake

Simon Ward, Robert Shaw, Anne Bancroft, Jack Hawkins, Ian Holm, *Anthony Hopkins*, John Mills, Patrick Magee, Edward Woodward

AAN: Carl Foreman

You're Darn Tootin'***

US 1929 20m bw silent
Hal Roach

Two musicians get into trouble at work, in their digs and in the street.

Star comedy which though early in their teaming shows Stan and Ollie at their best in a salt shaker routine and in a surreal pants-ripping contest.

w H. M. Walker   d Edgar Kennedy

Laurel and Hardy, Agnes Steele

You're in the Army Now**

US 1941 79m bw
Warner (Ben Stoloff)

Two incompetent vacuum cleaner salesmen accidentally join the army.

An excellent vehicle for two star comedians who have often suffered from poor material, with a silent-comedy-style climax involving a house on wheels.

w Paul Gerard Smith, George Beatty   d Lewis Seiler   ph James Van Trees   m Howard Jackson

Jimmy Durante, Phil Silvers, Donald MacBride, Jane Wyman, Regis Toomey

Zotz!

US 1962 87m bw
Columbia/William Castle

A professor finds a rare coin with occult powers.

Footling farce patterned after *The Absent-Minded Professor*. Poor, to say the least.

w Ray Russell novel Walter Karig d William Castle
ph Gordon Avil m Bernard Green

Tom Poston, Fred Clark, Jim Backus, Cecil Kellaway, Margaret Dumont

Zulu*

GB 1964 135m Technirama
Paramount/Diamond (Stanley Baker, Cyril Endfield)
V, L

In 1879 British soldiers stand fast against the Zulus at Rorke's Drift.

Standard period heroics, well presented and acted.

w John Prebble, Cy Endfield d Cy Endfield ph Stephen Dade
m John Barry

Stanley Baker, Jack Hawkins, *Michael Caine*, Ulla Jacobsson, James Booth, Nigel Green, Ivor Emmanuel, Paul Daneman

Zulu Dawn

US/Netherlands 1979 117m Technicolor Panavision
Samarkand/Zulu Dawn NV (Barrie Saint Clair)

In 1878, 1,300 British troops are massacred at Isandlwhana.

Confusing historical action adventure, very similar to *Zulu* but failing in its cross-cut attempt to show both sides.

w Cy Endfield, Anthony Storey
d Douglas Hickox ph Ousama Rawi m Elmer Bernstein
pd John Rosewarne

Burt Lancaster, Denholm Elliott, Peter O'Toole, John Mills, Simon Ward, Nigel Davenport, Michael Jayston, Ronald Lacey, Freddie Jones, Christopher Cazenove, Ronald Pickup, Anna Calder-Marshall

Halliwell's Filmgoer's Companion
10th Edition

Edited by John Walker

Halliwell's Filmgoer's Companion is unique as the only complete encyclopedia of movie people from cinema's silent monochrome beginnings to the colourful, wide-screen present. Packed with biographical profiles of actors, directors, producers, writers, cinematographers, film editors and other key personnel, definitions of technical terms, notes on the studios, movements and national film industries, the *Companion* is the one indispensable guide for anyone with an interest in films, from the dedicated film buff and movie star fan to the late-night TV film addict.

All existing entries are fully up-dated and over 1,000 new entries added for the 10th Edition.

'The *Companion* is everything people say it is. It is indispensable; it is a bargain at the price; it is one of the most fascinating books you ever saw' – Benny Green, *Spectator*

ISBN 0 586 09174 2